Reaching the Other

The journal of an American who stayed to witness Vietnam's postwar transition

Earl S. Martin

Almost without exception, American books on Vietnam have been about cold-war politics or the inferno of combat. Here at last is a book that engages directly and intimately the essential character of the Vietnamese people.

Earl Martin is a man of rare virtue.

Twelve years ago, this young Mennonite from the tranquil farms of central Pennsylvania *chose* to go to war-wracked Vietnam—not to fight, indeed, not even to take sides. He went to help people in need: orphans, the maimed, those made homeless. His principal effort was "to plow up swords": the millions of undetonated bombs, shells, and grenades strewn in the soil, threatening mutilation or death at every step, at every stroke of the hoe.

Earl Martin lived, not in sybaritic Saigon, but in a thirty-dollar-a-month house in Quang Ngai; he traveled not by helicopter but on foot and by bicycle; he learned to speak Vietnamese fluently and he spoke to people everywhere: in the fields, in their homes, in hospitals, churches, jails. More importantly, Earl Martin *listened* to Vietnamese everywhere, and when the Americans left and the South's army was routed, he stayed put. Although his good works were known to both sides, Martin's role was so unlikely that he was thought by many to be a Viet Cong sympathizer, and by others to be a CIA agent.

As control by the Thieu government collapsed and the Viet Cong and North Vietnamese took over, Martin was an eyewitness to the apprehension, chaos, and astounding calm that ensued. His wife took their children to Saigon—only temporarily

(continued on back flap)

The author with his wife, Pat, and children Minh Douglas and Lara Mai outside their Quang Ngai home. *Photo by John Spragens, Jr.*

REACHING THE OTHER SIDE

REACHING

THE OTHER SIDE

THE JOURNAL OF AN AMERICAN WHO STAYED TO WITNESS VIETNAM'S POSTWAR TRANSITION

Earl S. Martin

CROWN PUBLISHERS, INC., NEW YORK

Inquiries should be addressed to Crown Publishers, Inc.,
One Park Avenue,
New York, N.Y. 10016

Printed in the United States of America
Published simultaneously in Canada by
General Publishing Company Limited

Library of Congress Cataloging in Publication Data
Martin, Earl S.
Reaching the other side.
1. Vietnam—History—1975-   2. Martin,
Earl S.   I. Title.
DS559.912.M37   1978   959.704   78-131
ISBN 0-517-53315-4

BOOK DESIGN: *Shari de Miskey*

Photos by author unless otherwise indicated.

TO LARA MAI, MINH AND HANS
AND THE CHILDREN OF THEIR GENERATION,
VIETNAMESE AND AMERICAN, WHOSE
FRIENDSHIP WILL BE UNSCARRED BY WAR.

ACKNOWLEDGMENTS

If writing a book is for a man the nearest experience to giving birth, I am much indebted to the many persons who have given special prenatal and midwiving assistance. My gratitude goes to friends at Mennonite Central Committee, who gave the initial encouragement and assistance; to David Marr and John Spragens, Jr., whose detailed criticisms of the manuscript and unfailing optimism prevented miscarriage at crucial points; to Sig Moglen at Crown for his skill and sensitivity; and to Doug Hostetter, without whose spiritual and material support we would have been unable to continue.

Whatever there may be of beauty or hope in these pages springs in greatest measure from our Vietnamese friends, who have shown what it means to "bloom within the furnace."

As with other offspring, this story really has two parents. Pat has not only given the manuscript much needed love and care, but has made its shared writing a time of joy and new life.

"Pilgrims Still"
Tet 1978

TUESDAY NIGHT, 25 MARCH 1975. Rifle shots? So close to the house? But all the troops left town last night. I bolted up in bed. Was I just dreaming? Enough light filtered through the louvres on the front wall for me to be able to see through my mosquito net to the bed on the other side of the room. Hiro was sitting up too.

"Did you hear that!"

"Sounded like shooting to me, but—hey, do you suppose—?" I tore the net aside and jumped to the floor. "Hiro, you don't suppose—?" Forgetting even to grab a shirt, I ran to pull back the pipe that bolted shut the small trapdoor that led to the second-story porch. Shoving the door open I crawled out into the night air. Hiro was right behind. A motorcycle engine broke the silence. Then voices. We slithered up to the front edge of the porch, making sure to stay within the shadow of the mimosa tree that blocked the flickering fluorescent streetlight a quarter block away. Propping ourselves on our elbows, we looked down to the street below.

"Hiro, look at that, would you! *Hiro, this is it!*"

Guerrillas. Three guerrillas, casually standing on the street in front of our house. Right here in the heart of town. The motorcycle did a U-turn up the street and came back. It stopped in front of our gate. One guerrilla shouted to his comrades, then swung his AK-47 over his back and jumped on the motorcycle behind the driver. They sped downtown.

The other two stayed put. They stood halfway between our house and the neighbor's. They gave no indication of leaving. They looked up the street, then down. Then at our house. Were they looking for us? But they couldn't possibly know our house from all the others around us. These guys had lived in the boondocks all their lives. They couldn't possibly find us. But suppose a neighbor reported us? What would a guerrilla do face-to-face with an American? A Japanese?

"The sign, Kien, the sign!" Hiro's shouted whisper came from behind me. He was already snaking his body—bare except for a pair of shorts—

1

backward toward the trapdoor in the wall. He disappeared into the bedroom with me at his heels, maneuvering noiselessly through the small door.

Now remember, at the first sound of gunfire, hang the sign on your gate or front door. The instructions rang in my mind as clear as if I had heard them just yesterday. Yesterday! Could it have been just yesterday that they told me about the sign! How could the world be turned upside down within one day!

"Yeah, the sign—where did I put the thing last night?" I was trying to collect my thoughts as I pulled on my black peasant shirt.

"You put it on the kitchen table, didn't you?" Hiro too was grabbing some clothes.

I raced down the stairs, gripping the concrete banister to support me in case I slipped in the darkness. Thank God for the sign! But how would they react to it? What guarantee was there that these particular guerrillas on the street in front of our house would understand the sign? Or believe it? It was a chance you had to take.

I felt my way through the maze of sandbags outside the darkroom door at the bottom of the stairs. That was our makeshift bunker. Just in case—. Stumbling past the bicycles in the hall, I moved through the shuttered bedroom toward the kitchen. Enough moonlight filtered through the louvered shutters to illuminate the sign on the table where I had placed it just hours before. I snatched the wire fastened to the top of the sign and felt for the back door. Sliding open the two metal bolts, I slowly pushed the door open and cautiously stepped out into the night.

Here at the back of the house, all was tranquil. The not-quite-full moon in the southwest silhouetted the tall coconut palm down the street toward the CIA house. I started out the corridor between the house and the neighbor's concrete wall. I suddenly could not remember why I, the only American in the house, had been "volunteered" the evening before to hang the sign on the gate. But now was not the time for deliberation. Keeping within the shadow of the wall, I made my way toward the front of the house. I paused to listen for any unusual activity on the street. Voices. As I came to the edge of the wall, I saw a small group of people in front of the neighbor's house. In the center of the group a young guerrilla talked with animation. His partner was standing at the edge of the group, his AK-47 by his side. Neither was looking in my direction.

I seized the opportunity.

Following the shadows, I darted across the patio in front of the house and crouched behind the high concrete gatepost. I lifted the board in my hands to check it again. It would be impossible for the guerrillas to misread the bold white paint on the sign:

"357"

I hung the sign over the fence and then hurried back into the house.

A WEEK EARLIER . . .

TUESDAY EVENING, 18 MARCH. Naked under the Asian stars, I shivered delightfully as the chilly water splashed down over my body. How many more baths by this open well? Or was this the last? The Americans (sometimes I almost forgot I was one too) said it was time to get out of town. No hard data—just vague references to captured documents and scattered guerrilla activity here and there.

Was the water colder tonight or was I just more keyed up than usual? At any rate, it felt great. My body loved the vigorous, soapy rub.

It was not just the Americans either. The whole town was tense. There was no doubt about it. "What, you're still here! Don't you know everybody's leaving town?" We must have heard that a dozen times today.

Actually, most people were not leaving. "We just don't have the means, even if we wanted to leave. We don't have the money for a plane ticket." Others said, "We couldn't support ourselves anywhere else besides here. This is home."

I peeked around the corner of the landlord's house to make sure that none of his children would inadvertently intrude upon my nocturnal bath. But no problem. The courtyard was empty except for the banana trees standing at quiet attention like sentries. A week-old moon hung by its points in the western sky. Several small lanterns threw carpets of warm yellow light outside windows and doors of the houses beyond the garden fence. From the pagoda, a gong's clear tone reverberated over the neighborhood like the concentric waves in the well when my bucket hit the water's black surface.

How could we possibly leave this place? And yet, how could we stay?

The first serious alarm had been sounded on Monday afternoon by David Harr, an American "consulate" official. (Actually Harr and his cohorts did not perform normal consular functions, such as providing passports and birth certificates for overseas Americans. "Consulate representative" was merely the most recent title for official Americans who performed advisory and intelligence functions but who now sought to bypass the 1973 Paris Agreement's prohibition against American military advisors.) When I had chanced upon Harr outside the Provincial Hospital, his square jaw seemed even more tense than usual. "Earl, I'm glad to see you. I don't want to alarm you, but I just want to make sure we know where you're going to be the next couple days—just in case things start heating up fast."

When I pressed him for details, Harr had insisted, "No, there's nothing to worry about—nothing more than usual for Quang Ngai, that is."

Quang Ngai Province, with its province seat, popularly called Quang Ngai City, never had been the most tranquil region of Vietnam. Situated 500 miles north of Saigon along the South China Sea, Quang Ngai was less richly endowed by nature than the more fertile rice-growing deltas of the Red River in the North and the Mekong in the South. The western mass of the province, dominated by the Truong Son Range, or the Indochinese Cordilleras, was sparsely populated by groups of Hre tribal people who practiced some sedentary, some slash and burn, agriculture. Even the five- to fifteen-mile-wide strip of littoral flatland east of the mountains was barely productive enough to provide for the approximately 500 thousand ethnic Vietnamese who lived in the province. Perhaps it was the rigors of subsistence that had created the leathery will of the Quang Ngai people. They had gained a national reputation for being stubbornly loyal to a friend but equally stubborn in their resistance against an unkind nature or unkind overlord. Resistance against French colonialism was so complete that the Viet Minh revolutionaries—precursors of the National Liberation Front—were able to declare Quang Ngai a "free zone," that is, devoid of any French strongholds. Even counterrevolutionary Quang Ngai people spoke with a certain pride of the long list of revolutionaries that their province had produced, most prominent of whom was Pham Van Dong, premier of North Vietnam. During the American intervention some of Vietnam's bloodiest battlefields were in Quang Ngai Province. It was the scene of the war's most notorious massacre of My Lai. The American computerized "hamlet evaluation system," which ranked South Vietnam's forty-four provinces from "most secure" to "least secure," usually placed Quang Ngai near the bottom.

But while David Harr had tried to appear casual Monday afternoon, Tuesday morning had found him knocking on our door with an urgent message. "I came to tell you that we think you should plan to leave town as soon as possible," he said after sitting down in our living room/office. "We still have nothing specific to report. There is no evidence of major NVA troop movements"—American officials habitually credited the North Vietnamese Army rather than southern guerrilla forces with the capability of launching offensives—"but the threat to Quang Ngai is considerable since the forces of resistance are decreased."

He explained that many of the Saigon Government troops had been repositioned 40 miles to the north to defend Tam Ky because commanders feared an imminent attack on that town. In fact, by this date the revolutionary forces had mounted an awesomely successful offensive in the highlands. The mountain provinces of Phuoc Long and Ban Me Thuot had been overrun, and Pleiku and Kontum provinces had been abandoned by the Saigon forces in what President Thieu insisted was a strategic retreat to consolidate his forces. But that move had spawned rumors around town that Quang Ngai too would be abandoned by Saigon if the guerrillas staged a serious threat to the town. Harr dismissed that rumor out of hand.

"They'll not abandon Quang Ngai. This province is rich in resources. It's

4

Quang Ngai. A land of rice, bamboo and majestic skies . . .

. . . skies that were known to rain fire and steel.

along the seacoast, along Highway One. Saigon hasn't lost control of any province along Highway One. Besides, this is a Vietnamese province, not a *montagnard* province." He was apparently suggesting that the Saigon command considered the mountain provinces more dispensable because they were populated primarily by darker skinned tribal people, often the objects of discrimination from the ethnic Vietnamese.

"There's liable to be a big fight for Quang Ngai," Harr surmised. "There could be heavy bombing of the town if the V.C. occupy it. We are beginning to evacuate our people today. We'll be flying some of our Vietnamese employees up to Danang. I think you should prepare to go as soon as possible."

A month before, at a quarterly conference of our Mennonite Central Committee personnel in Saigon, we had discussed the eventuality of increased fighting throughout the country and what our response might be. My wife, Pat, and I, along with other Mennonite personnel, had expressed our readiness to stay with our work regardless of which side was in control if a peaceful transition of power seemed likely. We personally had assured our Saigon office that should we decide to leave Quang Ngai, we would try to anticipate the right moment far enough in advance so that we could leave quietly by the commercial Vietnamese airlines or by Vietnamese bus, rather than be "evacuated" by U.S. Government aircraft. But by this time in mid-March, frightened businessmen and scalpers in Quang Ngai had bought up all the tickets so there was a two-week backlog of passengers on the waiting list for Air Vietnam. Besides, there was no guarantee that even the scheduled planes would fly. That left only one option in our scenario.

"We'll probably go by road—if we go," I had informed the "consulate representative."

Tuesday evening before my shower at the well, I had ridden our bicycle around town to get a sense of the moment. Town was quiet but edgy. There was no lack of people, but the mood was different. Most shops were still open, but their metal folding doors, usually wide open, were now partially closed. The usual cacophony of static and barely discernible music blaring from the loudspeakers at the square was periodically interrupted by a recorded message from the province chief assuring the townsfolk that all was well and that "the forces of the Republic of Vietnam are strong and capable of dealing with any threats of the Communists." That the province chief issued the message at all, however, belied the image of normalcy that he tried to convey.

The pajama-clad young women who sold *che* were spooning their thick, sweet drinks of tapioca and white beans into glasses on low tables along the post office street as usual, but the normal exuberant conversation and laughter of the patrons was gone. Two broad-shouldered military police with revolvers by their sides and polished black helmets emblazoned with large white letters "QC"—the Vietnamese equivalent for "MP"—were talking in anxious undertones as they nursed their *che* at a table next to mine.

6

On my way home I heard the loudspeakers announce a ten o'clock curfew, one hour earlier than usual. Light streamed from doors that were drawn even closer together now. The rays from one shop etched a silhouette around a young man and woman looking intently into each other's eyes. Their world of love seemed uncharacteristically exempt from the growing turbulence of the evening. As I passed a small café I heard recorded strains of Trinh Cong Son's much-loved folk song, "I Shall Go Visiting." I sang the Vietnamese words to myself as I pedaled.

> *When my land has peace*
> *I shall go and never stop*
> *To Saigon, to the center,*
> *To Hanoi, to the south,*
> *I shall go in celebration*
> *And I hope I will forget*
> *The story of this war.*
>
> *When my land has peace*
> *I shall go visiting.*
> *I shall go visiting*
> *Villages turned into prairies.*
> *Go visiting*
> *The forests destroyed by fire;*
> *When my people are no longer killing each other*
> *Everyone will go out on the street*
> *To cry out with smiles. . . .*

Pulling into our short alley, I parked the bicycle in the courtyard in front of our house. There was only one other house in this cul-de-sac at the end of our alley, the house of the Chau family. Over the previous year a close relationship had grown between the Chaus and ourselves. The younger ones of their ten children had become like brothers and sisters to our own two children. Mr. Chau was a history teacher in the local public high school. He had earned a master's degree from the University of Saigon through self-study and correspondence. His peers regularly sought his advice, but he seemed always a modest man—riding a bicycle about town, stripping to T-shirt and shorts to work in his vegetable and flower garden and squatting by the well every week to wash his clothes. His children and his students saw him as a strict disciplinarian, but he was gracious and unpretentious with his adult friends. Mr. Chau was a devout Buddhist but rarely attended the local pagoda because he thought the religious organization was too ritualized to be meaningful. As a daily listener to Voice of America and British Broadcasting Corporation newscasts, he regularly quizzed me on the vagaries of American politics. Tonight as I parked my bicycle I noticed Mr. Chau standing alone on his porch.

7

"Anh Kien"—it was my Vietnamese name—"I really don't know what to do. The town is getting more tense all the time. And from the radio it sounds as though your Congress is not going to vote the additional military aid for Vietnam. They do not understand that this will damage the credibility of the United States immensely. If the Communists should take over Vietnam—" Mr. Chau's voice snagged with emotion.

Mr. Chau was a Nationalist. Although he had officially dissociated himself from the Nationalist Party in 1963 after the death of President Ngo Dinh Diem, he still retained his strong sentiments. Like others of the Nationalist Party, he felt that a Communist government would be anathema for Vietnam. In conversations with me he frequently criticized the American involvement in Vietnam, primarily because he felt that the particular methods of U.S. intervention were ineffective in preventing the success of the Communist side. For that same reason, he was also a bitter opponent of President Thieu, whom he regarded as nothing but a corrupt yes-man for the Americans, incapable of inspiring support for the anti-Communist struggle. We had learned that Mr. Chau was the only teacher in his high school who had mustered enough courage to resist the immense pressure to join the "Democracy Party" which President Thieu had crafted to coerce allegiance from South Vietnam's 250,000 civil servants. For acts of independence such as this, Mr. Chau had earned the mistrust of many Saigon Government officials.

Now this fifty-eight-year-old man was close to tears. "Frankly, Kien, the Communists don't like me very much, but this side hates me." Mr. Chau, about to lose composure, turned and hurried into his house.

Somewhere off in the distance I heard two explosions—likely a nervous sentry firing an M-79 grenade launcher at a suspicious noise in a dark field.

WEDNESDAY, 19 MARCH. By seven-thirty Wednesday morning David Harr, the "consulate" man, was again at the door. "I hope you've come to a decision about leaving today," Harr began as we invited him into our house.

"We're considering leaving today or tomorrow—by road," I told him. "We'll perhaps take a bus south—or north to Danang—depending on which route is open."

Harr shook his head. "Well, I guess that's up to you to decide, but you know the services of Air America are at your disposal."

We thanked him and reiterated our hope to travel by civilian bus. We did not explain to him that we had always attempted to avoid using Air America. It was one of those identity problems.

Throughout the war it was always the tendency of United States advisors and "consulate" personnel to view us in the "volags"—voluntary agencies—

8

as part of "the American team." We were hardly comfortable with that view. Some of us "volag" people were conscientious objectors to all war. Beyond that, on a more pragmatic level, we had come to believe that American involvement in Vietnam had been far more destructive than helpful.

The Mennonite Central Committee had focused especially on rendering assistance to civilian refugees from the war. In 1966 when the MCC assigned Pat and me—we were unmarried at the time—to Quang Ngai Province for our first three-year term, we quickly learned that the majority of the refugees had lost their homes and were driven off their land as a result of American military operations.

In early 1974 when we returned to Quang Ngai—now married and parents of a two-year-old daughter and newborn son—the MCC commissioned us to investigate the problem of unexploded munitions that lay dormant in the fields of the refugee farmers who were beginning to trickle back to their countryside homes after the 1973 Paris Cease-fire Agreement. After a year's research and groundwork, we discovered that a horrific constellation of undetonated ordnance lay sprinkled throughout the fallow fields and thickets, ready to plague returning farmers. On the United States side alone, the tonnage of munitions used in the war was staggering. Estimates said that 250 million American bombs and artillery shells had been used in the war. That was five times the number of people who lived in all of Vietnam, north and south. And of that amount a certain percentage—ordnance experts estimated from 2 to 10 percent—failed to explode as designed. It was believed that more than 2 million artillery shells alone did not detonate upon impact. In addition there were likely some millions more grenades, rockets, mines, mortar shells and booby traps lying untriggered in the fields and forests of Vietnam.

After extensive study of the unexploded litter in Quang Ngai Province, we settled on one category of the total problem: the small M-79 grenades that saturated the fields surrounding former American outposts. American sentries had attempted to defend the perimeters of their outposts by firing profuse quantities of these egg-shaped grenades from launchers, which looked like fat, stubby shotguns, up to a range of 400 yards. Because of faulty detonation mechanisms many of these grenades failed to explode on impact as intended. But months or years after they were fired, these duds were exploding in the face of farmers when struck by a hoe or plowshare. The hidden M-79 rounds, more than any other type of ordnance, were causing severe casualties among farmers as they reinitiated cultivation in their fallow fields around the outposts. While the steel pellets of these grenades—later models used perforated steel wire—were devastating to human flesh and body organs, by trial and error certain farmers had learned that these grenades would not pierce even the quarter-inch shield over the Rototiller-type plow, which was pulled behind small tractors. The driver of the tractor would get the scare of his life when his plow struck an M-79

The very soil that gives the Vietnamese life . . .

grenade, but ordinarily he survived the ordeal. The main problem was that there was a shortage of such tractors in Quang Ngai and other poor provinces. Furthermore, the few existing tractor owners were less than enthusiastic about plowing up such fields. So MCC decided we should purchase our own tractor and make it available to farmers with grenade-ridden fields. In a new kind of way it would be a contest between swords and plowshares. We dubbed the project "Plowing Up Swords."

Throughout all our years in Vietnam we felt it desirable—indeed essential—to establish an identity separate from the American Government. It was a matter of principle. It was also, we felt, a matter of expedience. Our work took us to remote villages in the countryside where the American Government presence was not always welcome. Being opposed to carrying weapons of any sort, we had early decided that our best protection was to establish a reputation conspicuously different from the official American presence. Wearing a pair of rubber-tire sandals instead of army boots, riding a bicycle or a scooter instead of a Scout pickup or military jeep, developing an ability to speak directly with the farmers instead of working through an interpreter—we counted these to be among our strongest defenses. In the town of Quang Ngai we lived in a small, unguarded house on the edge of

10

. . . has been sprinkled with hidden seeds of death. Combing through high grasses here reveals "live" M-79 grenade rounds.

The joys of the future harvest await the faithful tiller . . .

. . . unless his hoe first strikes a "gauva bomblet," mine or shell.

town and we did our shopping at the town market rather than at the American commissary. We also avoided using Air America, which was the CIA-funded air service available only to officials and people with "connections."

In general, we felt an acceptance and appreciation from our Vietnamese acquaintances in Quang Ngai, which encouraged us immensely. But the identity problem was never fully conquered. We were reminded of the dilemma whenever we biked down a new street and mere toddlers, on spotting our "high noses" and "round eyes," would peel forth in glee, "American! American!" making us feel about as covered as the emperor in his new clothes!

Wednesday morning after David Harr left our house, Pat and I concurred that it would be important to confer with friends, Vietnamese and Americans, at the Rehabilitation Center at the Quang Ngai Provincial Hospital. We had come to respect deeply the perspectives of many of the staff there. The Rehab Center was sponsored by the American Friends Service Committee (AFSC) to provide artificial limbs and rehabilitation for paraplegics and other victims of the war. Of all the projects of the thirty-odd American private organizations in Vietnam, perhaps none were of finer conception and execution than this Quaker-sponsored rehabilitation and prosthetics center. While most of the private organizations claimed to be politically neutral, few had done as well as AFSC in actually serving the civilians on all sides of the war. The amputees who were fitted with prostheses at the Quaker center came both from areas controlled by the Saigon Government and from those on "the other side" under the Provisional Revolutionary Government (PRG). Furthermore, the Quakers had established programs, as had the Mennonites, to send medical assistance to North Vietnam and PRG areas in the South. Many of the Vietnamese staff of the Quang Ngai Rehab Center were amputees themselves and several had previously lived on "the other side."

As I walked into the center, Chi Mai, the receptionist, waved me over to her desk. As I sat down, Chi Mai quickly glanced around to make certain no one was within earshot. "Well, Anh Kien, it's looking better all the time! I think the town will 'go' without much of a fight. Your family is planning to stay in Quang Ngai, I trust. There won't be any problem." Chi Mai was euphoric.

"But, Chi Mai, everyone says there's apt to be heavy bombing, and we wonder about the wisdom of keeping our children here through all that," I said.

"Well, at least one of you should stay. Americans like you and Pat should be here to take pictures and report to the world on what happens." Then, with a slight nod of her head toward the mountains, the other side, she continued, "They would welcome your staying. They know who you are!" Chi Mai's throaty undertone lent a certain power to her provocative statements. Her unflinching eyes dramatized a streak of pert irreverence in her.

"But look, Chi Mai, isn't there always a chance that *they* will be unable to distinguish us from agents of the American Government?" Chi Mai's answer was spoken with nonchalance, but it hit like a bombshell. "Matter of fact, in just the last week or so I've been getting reports that most of the high-school teachers in town are convinced that you and Pat are CIA agents."

That was hardly comforting. Not only did we morally consider ourselves to be in diametrical opposition to the clandestine operations of the CIA and its Phoenix-type assassination programs to wipe out political suspects, but on pragmatic grounds alone the suspicion made it seem infeasible for us to remain in Quang Ngai if the PRG forces should occupy the city. If a Communist provincial authority decided we were linked to the CIA, we might be staying in this town longer than we bargained for, and not in a social service capacity either!

This was not, of course, the first time that volunteers of our sort were suspected of being underground agents for the United States Government. In spite of our style of living and our work, there was no way to avoid that suspicion totally. In fact, to many of our Vietnamese neighbors, it must have seemed entirely logical that the United States Government would use a family such as ours, living as close to Vietnamese neighbors and refugee farmers as we did. What better intelligence agents could there have been! And it was likely that just that line of reasoning was being followed by the high-school teachers in Quang Ngai.

Even so, the teachers would probably not harm us. But if the PRG guerrillas should take control of Quang Ngai city and follow a similar logic, what then? Or, if the PRG should question the high-school teachers in an attempt to find out just who we really were, would our lives be in jeopardy?

"But you needn't worry," Chi Mai concluded, "the high school teachers have no way of knowing the truth about you. The PRG intelligence is reliable. They know that you have no connections with any government; they will trust you. They would want you to stay."

Chi Mai made it all sound so easy. But how could Pat and I be sure that Chi Mai had any basis for the claims she was making about the PRG?

It had been more than a year since the Quakers had introduced Chi Mai to Pat and me. Since that time we had had many serious conversations with her and a deep trust had developed between her and us. We had learned that Chi Mai had a long revolutionary history herself. Her father had fought with Viet Minh against the French colonialists in Central Vietnam for many years, and the same kind of revolutionary zeal fired Chi Mai's imagination. Among our acquaintances in Quang Ngai, she had always been the most outspoken supporter of the PRG and, by the same token, the most opposed to United States Government involvement in Vietnam.

In addition to her family roots, Chi Mai had a very personal reason for feeling unkindly toward American military intervention in Vietnam. Where

13

once there were two strong legs, Chi Mai now had only stumps with artificial limbs. As a sixteen-year-old girl, she had worked as a communications courier for the guerrillas in the mountains. She had eventually been given the responsibility of training other women to become effective revolutionaries. Her work had required her to travel extensively north and south along the Truong Son, the main range of mountains in Central Vietnam. During one of her missions in 1970, Chi Mai stepped on an American land mine that had been set as an ambush along a mountain trail. After the explosion she had remained conscious long enough to remember seeing her left leg blown to a bloody pulp. When she awoke, she was in an American helicopter, flying toward Chu Lai, the headquarters of the U.S. Americal Division. The American military doctors amputated Chi Mai's left leg above the knee. Several days later they decided to amputate the right leg also, this one below the knee. Chi Mai had never forgiven the doctors for this final cut. She was still persuaded, five years later, that her right leg had sustained merely superficial wounds and would have healed quickly. She believed that the second amputation was a deliberate attempt to remove her once and for all from service as a guerrilla.

So there was no doubt in our minds that Chi Mai had once had connections with "the other side." But that was five years before. The pertinent question for us was whether, at this point in March 1975, Chi Mai had any basis for predicting that the PRG would respond favorably to our staying in Quang Ngai city.

Throughout our four and one half years in Quang Ngai—and especially when we returned in early 1974—Pat and I had nurtured the idealistic hope that we could cultivate friendships with people on all sides of the war. We had developed relationships with some officials of the Saigon Government administration in Quang Ngai and had on occasion discussed our projects with them. Our primary contacts and sources of direction, however, came directly from the Vietnamese farmers who lived in the refugee camps. We felt the farmers were fully supportive of the Plowing Up Swords program. But there was still that one group of Vietnamese we had never knowingly met: the Viet Cong.

The longer we lived in Quang Ngai the more imperative it became for us to establish communication with the Viet Cong, or the Provisional Revolutionary Government as they called themselves. For one, as Mennonites we had been taught from childhood to believe that Jesus' Sermon on the Mount was not merely a lofty-sounding exercise in forensics but the most sensible outline available for workable human ethics. Although time and experience had altered some of our childhood religious beliefs, we were still fascinated by the simple profundity of the mandate to "love your enemy" and "live at peace with one another."

Then, too, the Mennonite Central Committee was clear in its statement that our service should be rendered to all persons in need, regardless of race, creed, or political persuasion. That meant we should be offering our services to persons living on both sides of the war.

Furthermore, the Paris Cease-fire Agreement signed in early 1973 made it clear that there were two governments—Saigon *and* the PRG—in South Vietnam. Since the United States had recognized the reality of the PRG by signing the Paris Accords, it would follow that Americans should relate equally with both governments in South Vietnam. To date our bureaucratic dealings had been exclusively with the Saigon regime. We believed that if a social welfare program was to be truly nonpartisan, authorities from both those governments should be consulted.

Then, too, there were pragmatic reasons. If we were to be plowing up fields throughout the countryside, we felt it imperative to receive at least tacit approval from the PRG. The fields we had projected for plowing were considered to be under Saigon Government control during the daytime, but at night the PRG guerrillas had free run of much of the area. If any parties should mistakenly believe that the Plowing Up Swords project was part of the American Government's psychological warfare program to "win hearts and minds"—the WHAM program—they could create much trouble for our project and our people. One large mine placed in the middle of a field slated for plowing would mean the end of the tractor and possibly the driver as well. (It was equally essential not to upset any Saigon Government officials, because they, too, were capable of making life difficult. A Red Cross tractor had been blown up by a mine in a province north of us, and Red Cross officials believed it was caused by Saigon Government officials in one village who were upset with the Red Cross program of plowing up local village land for refugees from another area.)

Finally—there was no denying it—we were simply curious. *Ben kia*— "the other side." The term cropped up constantly in conversations with farmers and students, market-goers and carpenters. We had heard and read much about "the other side." Indeed, we had met many persons whose sympathies seemed to lie with the guerrillas, although living in the Saigon zone as we did, even the most revolutionary persons had to be guarded in the way they spoke, especially to an American. And, given the underground nature of the war, we had very likely encountered, unaware, active agents of "the other side" during their routine duties in Quang Ngai city or during our trips into the countryside. And we had met official representatives from the Provisional Revolutionary Government and from the Democratic Republic of [North] Vietnam during two stopovers in Paris. But still we had never met Vietnamese revolutionaries on their own turf, where they could respond naturally and be in full control of the situation.

So our urge to meet "the other side" sprang from many sources: our theological roots, MCC's principles of no political discrimination, the dictates of the Paris Accords, pragmatic considerations for our own safety, and sheer unrepressible curiosity. It would be unthinkable not to establish direct

15

communication with "the other side."

But how? Geographically, the two warring sides in Quang Ngai were sometimes literally within a stone's throw of one another. Yet it was far easier for us to establish direct communication with our parents 10,000 miles away than with the guerrillas a few kilometers away.

Such a message would have to go underground. But to find a courier in whom we could have absolute trust and, even more important, one who could trust us totally would not be an easy task. After months of trust building, the link was finally forged by a young refugee who had worked with us in planning the Plowing Up Swords project. He agreed that it was crucial for the safety of the program to communicate with "the Front." He divulged that he had an uncle with close ties to the PRG who would carry a letter from us.

Our letter to "the people and authorities of the Provisional Revolutionary Government of Quang Ngai" explained our purpose for living in Quang Ngai, our plowing project and the goals of MCC. Finally we said that we would welcome an opportunity to have discussions with a representative of the PRG at a place and time of their choosing.

Somehow—we never learned his method—the uncle delivered the letter to middle-level guerrilla officials. He assured us the letter would go "to the top of the province" and that we would likely receive a reply within a short time. That had been in November 1974.

By the following January, when we had still heard nothing from the PRG we decided to try to communicate through another personal acquaintance: Chi Mai. After we explained our rationale for wanting to make contact with the PRG, Chi Mai assured us she would try "to talk to friends" about us.

That proved more fruitful. At least apparently so. In early March Chi Mai had invited our family to share an evening meal with her "for some special reason." That night after the rice bowls were set aside, Chi Mai straightened herself up on her legs and walked to a tall closet in a dark corner of her room. After reaching deep into the closet she returned and sat on the bench beside us. She adjusted the wick on the lantern to give more light.

"These are for you," she said, handing us two small metal cases six inches long. Undoing a clasp at one end, Pat opened one of the cases into a lovely paper fan, painted in bright blues, yellows and oranges with a large sampan and towering rocks, a scene similar to photos we had seen of the Ha Long Bay in North Vietnam. A printed inscription at the top of the fan read: *Hoa Binh Hoa Hop Dan Toc.*—"Peace and National Concord!" That clearly identified this innocuous-looking gift. It was the slogan of the Provisional Revolutionary Government. This fan had been smuggled across the lines!

"This is for you too," Chi Mai continued, handing us a tiny roll of paper, no larger than half a lollipop stick. The thin paper unrolled to postcard size. The message was written by hand, with a ball-point pen. There was no seal affixed. It looked much like a note a fifth-grade schoolboy would pass across the aisle to his girl friend. It began: *"Than gui cac ban . . ."*

Dear friends,

Representing the People's Revolutionary Committee of Quang Ngai and ourselves personally, we send best wishes. We hope that your family and close friends are enjoying good health.

In the concrete situation facing our country, our people are still continuing to fight for a foundation of true peace, national independence, people's democracy and national unification. There is no question but that the innermost aspiration of our people will be achieved. Our people will welcome a visit from you, our friends, in a most fraternal spirit.

And now, if there are any needs you may have of us, we will give them our highest priority. We are sending you two fans as gifts.

Finally, we wish you good health.

March 4   Warm regards,
                                    (signed) Le Quang Vinh

Chi Mai beamed silently, trying to appear matter-of-fact about the note. She knew, however, that for us this little shred of crumpled paper represented the dramatic breakthrough we had been searching for for months. *Contact!* Communication between us and those mysterious guerrillas somewhere "out there." Mixed with the delight of the moment was a more sobering realization of the risk involved in sending and receiving a note like this. Such notes, when discovered by Saigon police, had resulted in most unmerciful treatment for their carriers or recipients. On returning home that night we would slip the note into a hidden crack in our bedroom wardrobe.

But, while risky, receiving the message reassured us tremendously. Now at least "the other side" knew about us. And this was certainly not a hostile response. Now if we should happen to be captured by guerrillas in some remote village, someone in the PRG structure would have already heard about us in advance. Further, if this note reflected their feelings about our work in Quang Ngai, they certainly would not hinder any plowing projects we might initiate. And—incredibly—they said they welcomed a visit from us!

But as we ruminated over the note in the following days we found ourselves asking just how significant was this note anyway? It was not even typed, and surely there were typewriters in PRG zones. The note had no seal, and any Vietnamese letter or document with authority would be stamped with an official seal. Besides, the signature was most unimpressive. The writer did not even claim a title. No "second secretary" or "deputy chairman" or anything. Merely "Le Quang Vinh." A most ordinary name. There were probably a dozen Le Quang Vinhs in Quang Ngai Province.

Certainly Chi Mai had given us the impression that this was an important message, but Chi Mai had been living in the Saigon-controlled zones for

Chi Mai longed to be back in the hills with the guerrillas, but an exploding mine had taken both her legs.

nearly five years. She was possibly no longer in direct liaison with "the other side." At this point Chi Mai, whose loyalties obviously lay with the revolutionaries, was likely looking for ways to "contribute to the cause." But perhaps her only active contacts were a few persons just marginally involved with the PRG. Perhaps this "Le Quang Vinh"—if that was his real name at all!—was merely some hamlet guerrilla with no authority.

At any rate, now with the threat of heavy fighting and bombing hanging ominously over Quang Ngai, we could not afford to equivocate. Whether the note was significant or not, the critical question could not be delayed: Was it wise for our family to risk staying in Quang Ngai?

Wednesday afternoon David Harr was back, increasing the pressure on us to leave. "We have a chopper on the pad. I hope you can be packed up and ready to go by five-thirty. We'll be holding a place for you."

"Are the Quakers leaving this afternoon?" Pat asked, referring to the four foreign personnel who were working with the Rehab Center.

"They're planning to leave in the morning on a C-47 we have coming in."

Pat informed Harr that we would not take the afternoon helicopter, but possibly we too would leave on the morning flight.

Wednesday evening before dinner our closest friend, Em Trinh, returned to our house. This young country woman had lived in our home for more than a year, and with the growing nervousness in town, Trinh had decided to visit her older sister in the district town of Duc Pho, twenty miles south of Quang Ngai city. Now she was returning with an optimistic report.

"Things are so quiet in the countryside. No one there can figure out why people here in town are so nervous. Down in Duc Pho people are going about their business as usual. But as soon as I got back here to Quang Ngai, I could sense a different mood. Here everyone is so—what's the word they're all using?—oh yes, *disoriented*. Quang Ngai is so disoriented!" Trinh also reported that the National Highway One south of Duc Pho had been closed to traffic. We asked Trinh her opinion of whether we should remain in Quang Ngai. Initially she gave a customary noncommittal response. "Anything's fine, whatever you decide," she said. But after we had talked at length, it became obvious that she thought a major military battle might be waged over Quang Ngai city, and, consequently, it would be unwise for the children to stay.

We had come to hold a great deal of respect for Trinh's counsel. On first meeting Trinh more than a year before, we had wondered if we would ever develop a close relationship with her. She had seemed an extraordinarily bashful country girl. She was short in stature even for a Vietnamese woman and instead of the fair complexion coveted by the upper classes, Trinh's skin was a deep bronze color, testifying to long hours of work in the fields. But in the year that Trinh lived and worked in our home, she had virtually become a member of the family. Our children clearly considered Trinh an older sister. Pat and I considered her a helper, a teacher, a friend. Many of our evenings during the year had been spent talking about her experiences and seeking her counsel on our Plowing Up Swords project. Perhaps no other person had taught us so much of the reality of the war for the rice farmers of Vietnam.

Trinh's family was itself a microcosm of the war. Her father had died of smallpox when she was six. Her mother was killed in 1968.

"I was out in the field irrigating the rice when it happened," Trinh had confided to us one evening after we had lived together long enough for her to trust us. "Then, just like that, the jets were there, swooping down over the hamlet. I ran and hid by the paddy dike. A little safer there. The explosions were—well, the ground just bounced up and down. I looked up and saw black smoke all over the hamlet. It was the fire bomb. Napalm, you call it. The jets circled over again and then went away. I ran home as fast as I could. When I got to the hamlet I saw our house. Burning! Scared, I was so scared. Some of the villagers were trying to go toward our house, but the flames were too hot. Sister came running up, yelling, 'Where's Mama? Where's Mama?' Then we all knew: Mama was in the burning house. There was nothing we could do."

Just before the death of her mother, Trinh and her older sister had been preparing to leave home to go into the hills to do seamstress work for "the Front." They would have sewed hats and uniforms for the guerrillas. But after the loss of their mother, the older sister decided they should stay home to take care of the younger children. Eventually the children had to leave their hamlet and move into a refugee camp close to Duc Pho district headquarters. There Trinh's older sister mothered a daughter after she had married a first lieutenant in the ARVN, the Army of the Republic of Vietnam, the Saigon forces. "No, I don't like the ARVN, but Anh Minh is a nice man," her sister had told Trinh to explain the marriage. But her next younger brother left the camp and went to the hills to join the guerrillas. By informal word of mouth Trinh learned that in the ensuing several years her brother had been injured twice in ambushes with ARVN soldiers. In 1974 he had been sent up the Ho Chi Minh trail to North Vietnam for recuperation.

Another younger brother had been arrested by American soldiers when he was thirteen and was held in the Quang Ngai Correctional Center—the province jail—for two years. A younger sister was wounded seriously in the hip when an NLF mortar, intended for the nearby ARVN district head-quarters, fell into their refugee camp.

Trinh also had an uncle who had gone to North Vietnam in 1954 with two teen-age children, but her aunt stayed in the south with the younger children, some of whom fought with the Saigon Government forces. The family had occasional clandestine communications with their relatives in North Vietnam, but they carried Saigon Government identification cards and spent nearly all their time in Saigon-controlled zones.

It had often struck Pat and me as ironic that Trinh, whose mother was killed by Americans and who herself had been arrested for several days by Americans, should now be living with us as an integral part of the family. As might be expected, Trinh had strong feelings about the war, but unlike Chi Mai and some of our other friends, Trinh never seemed to be "making a point" when she related her stories. Discussions of political theory interested her little. For her the war was not a question of ideology or political rationale. War for Trinh was the day-to-day reality she had witnessed in her home village.

Trinh related one night the story of a young Saigon Government soldier, an acquaintance of hers, who was guarding her hamlet during a particular time when the Saigon forces controlled that region. To defend his encampment, the soldier set a land mine one evening before going to sleep. Just as the first glow of dawn warmed the sky on the following morning, the squad of soldiers was awakened by an exploding mine. The young soldier ran to the site of his mine where he found the mangled body of his dying brother, whom he had not seen since his brother had joined the NLF guerrilla forces three years before.

War for Trinh was hearing the helicopters buzzing over her hamlet late one summer evening, during a period when the hamlet was under partial NLF control. The Americans were making a surprise visit to the hamlet. Trinh with her older brothers and sisters huddled together in a deep hole dug as a bunker underneath their bed. Trinh and her older sister had re-membered to pull on dirty blouses quickly and to rub charcoal on their lovely bronze skin to make themselves appear unattractive in case the soldiers barged into their house. What would the soldiers do? Lanterns all over the hamlet were snuffed out and all the houses were noiseless. No one dared to make a sound that might attract the attention of the soldiers. Wait. The helicopters were silent. What were the soldiers doing? Wait—in silence. Then, off in the distance, a muffled throbbing of the earth. What was it? The low throbbing picked up intensity. Now it became clearer. Yes, it was—the boots. The throb came closer and clearer. Now it paused, now started again. The boots. Louder and louder. Now the boots were close to Trinh's house. Would they stop? Louder. Now very distinct. Still throbbing. Now—now, moving on. Still moving. Softer. The boots. Still throbbing. Quieter—farther—farther—Gone.

Trinh's eye-widening stories cropped up daily, triggered by casual references in our conversations with her. But despite all that Trinh had experienced in her nineteen years she seemed strangely unimpaired by it all. So puzzlingly free of bitterness. In fact, she constantly injected a spirit of lightness and joy into our household. She would endlessly tease the Chau children, her quick smile revealing sparkling white teeth. Our children quickly came to think of her as "older sister" and would count on "Chi Trinh" to accompany us on any trip we made as a family. Pat had frequently commented that Trinh, more than any other person, had made our sojourn in Vietnam meaningful.

How could Trinh be so pleasant when her life had seen so much tragedy? Some would have called her attitude fate. It appeared to parallel closely the response of some people of religious faith who can say in the face of the harshest adversity, "God's will be done." But somehow Trinh's attitude seemed less otherworldly than that. For Trinh it was as though her very genes and chromosomes were paired to understand that hardship—excruciating hardship—and joy are inextricably woven together into the thread of life-death. To suffer hardship and then to grieve—and sometimes even to be angry—is human. To suffer hardship and then to be bitter is to choke the very breath of one's soul.

Wednesday night when we tucked our children into bed, one-year-old Minh Douglas seemed totally oblivious of the swirl of activity and anxiety around him. Lara Mai, three, only understood that in the morning we would probably be going to Saigon in an airplane, a trip that she had made numerous times before.

The howitzers at the fire bases outside town were more busy than usual. We could hear the shells whistle over town as the cannons at the airport fired toward the southeast. Over the past year the children had learned to sleep in spite of the guns. Minh was born with the sounds of war around him and was still too young to question them. Lara had come to understand that cannons "hurt people," and she felt more secure at bedtime when we closed the shutters at the windows. A year earlier when we first arrived in

Quang Ngai, loud artillery or gunfire would frequently wake her. Often in the evenings before she crawled in under her mosquito net, she would turn toward the window and utter what must have been her first bedtime prayer: "No shoot—no shoot—!"

Pat and I quickly packed up our most valued possessions—our writings, the journals we had kept for our children, our file on unexploded munitions and several changes of clothes for ourselves and the children. Then we too retired to wrest a few hours' sleep from the night.

Through the night I was aware that the ARVN kept their cannons busy. I would hear the howitzer at the airport bark. The drowsy eyes of my mind would trace the shell's trajectory as it whined its long, low arc over town. And then that dull "haa-rum" of the exploding missile. And then another— and another "Haa-rum. Haa-rum." The cruel lullaby of war. I wondered to myself, as I had so often before, what person might have happened to be at the spot of that last haa-rum? What person now huddled where the next haa-rum would explode? Was there any common humanity between that person in the remote countryside of Quang Ngai and a man in a nation's capital on the opposite side of the globe who had authorized those shells to be sent to this country?

My sleep came and went. Finally it went completely. I looked at the clock. Quarter past four. Now that I was fully awake, the disturbing questions of the night became less philosophic. If we did not get our children out of town soon, it might be they who would be huddling at the spot of a bursting shell. From this perspective it made little difference where the shell came from or who had authorized it to be sent to Vietnam. How could we possibly justify keeping our children here through the impending battle?

THURSDAY, 20 MARCH.   The soft light of dawn was beginning to filter through the louvres high in the walls, giving the faintest suggestion of outline to the footlocker and bags scattered over the floor. The mosquito net canopy over our double bed gave a feeling of security, of privacy. Even though the flimsy muslin would keep out neither sight nor sound—we were gratified for those times that it managed to keep the ravenous mosquitoes at bay—it did offer the illusion of being protected from the harsh "outside world."

During the next hour within that muslin pavilion Pat and I again struggled with the options we had discussed so many times before. To stay or to leave? How many people all over town under thousands of mosquito nets were battling with their own questions of what to do and where to go in the event of heavy fighting? We tried to weigh the factors. The possibility of carpet bombing, the lack of an adequate bunker, the question of credibility with our Vietnamese friends if we should leave and later return, the possibility of implementing the plowing project if we stayed, the inexplicable urge within us to face the uncertainty with our Vietnamese friends, and the sheer inquisitiveness we felt to witness history unfold before us.

It all boiled down to two stark alternatives: stay, and affirm our commitment to our Vietnamese friends. Leave, and affirm our commitment to the safety and wholeness of the two persons whose lives were most linked with our own: our children.

How could we deny either of those instincts? There was that part of each of us which said "go." That part which said "stay." And therein was our only resolution: part of us would go; part, stay.

We tried to speculate on how long our separation could last. We decided that I would attempt to keep all options open, perhaps even to follow Pat and the children to Saigon after a day or two if staying seem inadvisable. On the other hand, if I should stay through a battle for Quang Ngai and a possible change of government, we recognized our separation could be a long one.

By 8:30 Thursday morning David Harr was again knocking at our door. Pat let him in.

"How are things?" he inquired.

"Well, people seem pretty tense in town," Pat replied.

"Yeah, but there's no need for alarm. It's a little puzzling why everyone is so worked up," Harr rejoined. "There seems to be no evidence of any major military activity in the province."

Pat could not help feeling irritated by the statement. It was Harr and the "consulate" representatives who had done much to create the sense of urgency about leaving, and now that she had reluctantly prepared herself to go, Harr sounded nonchalant. She answered Harr, "Yes, Earl thinks too there's nothing to be alarmed about, so he's planning to stay."

"Well—er—no, we still think it is important that you all leave town as soon as possible. Here, I have a letter from the vice-consul in Danang," Harr said quickly.

Just then I walked into the room and Pat showed me the letter. Although we had never met the vice-consul in Danang, she was writing specifically to Pat and me. She wrote that their representatives had given us warnings on three or four occasions to leave Quang Ngai. Once again this morning they were offering us a flight to Danang and Saigon on their planes. If we did not accept the morning's flight, they could not guarantee any flights in the future. The note ended strongly, urging us to leave immediately.

"Your wife says you're planning to stay?" Harr asked.

"We're talking about that possibility, yes," I said.

"Well, as far as we're concerned, we think it would be wise for all Americans to leave Quang Ngai as soon as possible. The flight leaves about noon today. We would like you to be at the OSA house by eleven."

The OSA house! That was one house in Quang Ngai we had always conspicuously avoided. OSA—the Office of Special Assistant to the Ambassador—was the latest euphemism for American intelligence operations in Vietnam. The common assumption in town was that OSA meant CIA. But I contained my astonishment and told David Harr that we would meet him there.

We completed final packing and after a difficult farewell to Trinh, Pat and the children piled onto our Lambretta scooter together with a few bags and we headed out for the CIA house. The streets of town pulsed with a faster, higher-strung tempo this morning. Here and there large blue camions, normally used to transport produce from city to city, were being loaded with the possessions and families of wealthy townsfolk. They were packing up to be ready to make a break for it as soon as the road to Danang opened up. Even if Quang Ngai was overrun, certainly Danang, South Vietnam's second largest city and the headquarters of the Saigon Government's Military Region I, was impregnable. It was primarily the wealthy who were trying to leave town. Not only would they have more to lose in the event of a PRG take-over, but it was only they who would have the resources to buy food in Danang, which was already plagued with skyrocketing food prices because of the influx of nearly 500,000 refugees.

Turning onto Phan Boi Chau Street, the main east-west street in Quang Ngai, we could see the CIA house several blocks away. The squarish three-story house was one of the tallest buildings in town. It was whitewashed. Its roof bristled with radio antennae. Surrounding the building stood a high cinder-block wall topped with coils of barbed wire, intended, presumably, to keep people out rather than in.

Even before we could ring a bell, the high metal gate swung open. The Vietnamese guard who had been peering out a square peephole had apparently been trained to open automatically to any white-skinned person. Just as soon as we passed through, the gate clanged shut again, closing out the stares of curious children on the street. As we were unloading ourselves from the scooter, David Harr appeared at the door.

"It'll still be a little while before we head out to the airport, so why don't you come in and sit down." Harr showed us to an office room off to the side of the living room, then left.

In five minutes Harr returned, accompanied by one of the tallest Americans I had seen in Vietnam. The high heels of his cowboy boots added even more to his height. Harr announced that the man had a few instructions before the group would go to the airport. First the OSA man read down the list of names on the airplane manifest. Last name on the list was "Mr. Martin."

"I won't be leaving on the plane," I said.

"Not going? You might not have another chance," the man responded.

"He won't be going along," Harr reiterated.

"Okay, now I think you should understand. It could be a pretty hairy scene at the airport. We don't anticipate any trouble, but if there is a storm of Vietnamese trying to get on the plane, we must be prepared. When you get to the airport, I want you all to be at the head of the line. As soon as the plane stops on the runway, I want you to board immediately, taking the seats in the very front of the plane." On our way outside, the OSA man told me it would not be permissible for me to drive my scooter to the airport since the guards at the airport might not let me pass. I could join them in their Bronco station wagon, but Pat and I agreed that it would be preferable to say good-bye here, rather than for me to have to ride back into town in the OSA car after the plane left.

"Okay, climb in," came the order. Pat and I embraced as best we could with children and bags in hand. They climbed into the back seat of the Bronco. Lara Mai looked up at Pat on the seat beside her and simply asked, "Daddy not go too?"

"No, Daddy's not coming just yet," Pat managed.

Minh Douglas just relaxed in his mother's lap with his head pillowed on her breast. Occasionally a smile would break out on both sides of the pacifier he was sucking. He was obviously anticipating the upcoming airplane ride.

It seemed a cruel irony that Pat and the children should have to be leaving this way. It was a long fall from grace for us who had come to believe that our purposes in Vietnam were diametrically opposed to those of the CIA. Now to see the three persons most lovely to me sitting in that CIA Bronco seemed the ultimate compromise. And yet these "agents" were offering their assistance to rescue my children from what might be a bombing holocaust in Quang Ngai city. Perhaps it was my need of them that angered me most.

The Bronco slammed into reverse and the large steel gate swung open. Suddenly everyone was gone. I was alone in the CIA compound, except for the gatekeeper who was looking at me.

"I'm leaving too," I said as I stared absently through the open gate.

I was not home more than half an hour when I heard the sound of airplane engines. Trinh and I ran out into the courtyard and watched as the C-47 transport slowly lifted into view above the bamboo trees. Its engines groaned and labored as the silver plane circled around—around—a third time around, until the craft gained sufficient altitude to head east toward the sea and lose itself in a white cloud. Trinh and I could hardly look each other in the eye. Mr. Chau's son stood with us in the courtyard, murmuring something about a helicopter the day before that rose twenty feet off the ground and then smacked down again because the load was too heavy. Trinh walked quietly into the house. I walked out into Mr. Chau's garden to collect my emotions. As I sat down on some concrete blocks under the squash arbor, trying to pull myself together, I felt a stinging on my bare feet. Instinctively I leaned down to brush away the nettlesome fire ants. At that moment it struck me that I had had an encounter with these red ants in Quang Ngai exactly nine years before.

After several months of language study in Saigon in early 1966, I had gone with a colleague for my first visit to Quang Ngai to look for a house. As we stood in the high grass behind the house we had eventually moved into, a collection of Quang Ngai's ubiquitous children had assembled outside a wire fence to size up the two new Americans who were moving into their neighborhood. Suddenly my feet blazed with fire. Not knowing the source of my grief I danced up and down, slapping at my stinging feet. Ants! All over my sandaled feet. I had just stepped into what must have been the command headquarters of Quang Ngai's First Division of Red Fire Devils!

The children outside the fence doubled with laughter. "*Kien can! Kien can! Kien can!*" they peeled. Being new in the country, I was not familiar with this vocabulary, but it did not necessitate much explaining. After I extricated myself from the anthill, I walked over to the fence where the still laughing children clacked their teeth when I asked them to tell me the meaning of *can*. By then nobody needed to explain what *kiens* were. In succeeding days, as I rode my bike through the neighborhood, I would frequently hear children call out, "There goes the fellow who got bitten by the *kiens*." Within a week or two, the children were calling me "Anh Kien," which translated "Brother Ant!" The name stuck. Sophisticated Vietnamese would tell me it was not an elegant name, but the unpretentious Quang Ngai folks and the children loved the name. At any rate, it was better than forever being called "Mr. American." Now, nine years later, I wondered if these same fiery devils stinging my feet were trying to tell me that my time in Quang Ngai had come full circle.

History seemed to be coming full circle for the Vietnamese people as well. In the tension of this moment it was difficult to maintain perspective on the historical development that led to the present. But Vietnam's past was replete with periods when their country, situated as it was on fertile rice-growing land at the crossroads of the Pacific and Indian oceans, had been subjugated by foreign powers. The Chinese to the north had annexed Vietnam as a province for most of the first millennium A.D. In the thirteenth century the Mongols attempted unsuccessfully to invade Vietnam. In the latter half of the nineteenth century the French colonized the country. During World War II the Japanese replaced the French for several years only to have the French return after the war. It was never the lot—indeed hardly the intent—of the Vietnamese to vanquish the foreign powers that occupied their nation. Rather, the Vietnamese resistance fighters in each case operated in the role of the "fire ants," stinging ferociously and persistently until the intruder deemed it in his best interest to withdraw his foot from the anthill.

The Americans had tried a new tack. They would create a new image of the invader. It was the "Communist" North Vietnam that was invading the "free" South, according to the schema of propagandists in Washington and

Saigon. The American purpose was to "defend freedom" in the South against the North's "outside aggression" (*ngoai xam*)—the same term is used for "outside" and "foreign" in Vietnamese. The image was never quite convincing. For one thing, during the initial phases of the war most of the revolution's personnel were actually from the South. Even in more recent years, after many local guerrillas had been killed, the southern component of "the Front" in many provinces was not insignificant. Furthermore, few Vietnamese—South or North—were able to pin the label "outside" on Ho Chi Minh, the revolution's prime mover. Although Ho was recognized by all to be a Communist, there was also widespread consensus that his paramount goal was that of self-determination for the Vietnamese people. By nearly all counts—appearance, culture, language and technology—the Americans had to bear the label "outside." That was a heavy legacy for the Saigon Government. In many people's eyes it made the Saigon Government look weak, even illegitimate. Finally, the American war tactics had been just too destructive of lives, property and culture to be regarded as defending the people's freedom or anything else precious to the Vietnamese.

Saigon and Washington strategists had hoped that the withdrawal of the American troops in 1973 would reverse the prevailing image of the Saigon Government as the exclusive creation of the Americans. But with the continuation of Nguyen Van Thieu as president in Saigon, the image had changed little. Moreover, the reality had also not changed much. The United States was still sending in massive quantities of military supplies and providing more than 80 percent of Saigon's national budget.

Along with the war of bullets had been the years of vicious propaganda that each side used to malign the other. Liberation Radio could hardly utter the word American without automatically attaching the tag "imperialist" or "invader." Saigon Radio constantly referred to the other side as "Communist aggressors" or often the "bloodthirsty Viet Cong." The Saigon Information Service posted billboards on every block with anti-Communist slogans or with graphic color paintings depicting the enemy as a poisonous snake or a blood-guzzling vampire. At the end of our block on Tran Hung Dao Street stood a full-color billboard painting with a burning thatch house in the background and a grotesque animal-like beast crowing over the fallen body of a peasant woman with a sword plunged through her back and a crying baby on the ground beside her in the foreground. The bold red-lettered caption read: "Viet Cong Atrocity."

Now all the attrition of the merciless war and its propaganda was taking its toll of fear among the people. Quang Ngai townsfolk seemed to be responding in different ways to the mounting tension. Some people were determined to get out of town at any cost. "There's no way I can live with the Communists," was the rationale some people gave. Others indicated they would try to leave town but only to escape the impending battle, which might be long and bloody.

Other people seemed to calculate that their best odds lay in staying in

Quang Ngai, in preparing themselves for whatever developed. "Even if I knew the Communists would take over Quang Ngai and I had the opportunity to leave, I would stay here," was the response of a number of people. "If I would run somewhere else I would be apt to starve there. Eventually the Communists would probably take over that area as well, and there might even be heavier fighting in that place. Who can know? We might as well stay with our homes in Quang Ngai."

When I talked with Mr. Chau Thursday evening, he seemed to be coming to that conclusion. He was more philosophic about the situation than he had been the night before. "The Communists don't like me much," he reiterated with a sigh, "but what choice have I got? Go to Danang? Danang is crawling with refugees. I hear a mere loaf of bread costs three hundred piasters in Danang. If we went to Danang we would be apt to starve. I guess I'll just stay here"—he paused a bit, then added stoically—"and be ready to die." Mr. Chau was much more in control of himself than he had been the previous evening. He continued without difficulty, "Besides, perhaps the bloodletting will not be as great if there is no strong resistance put up by our side. If the Communists don't have to worry about the Saigon forces or the Americans coming back in force, likely fewer people will be killed."

There was another class of people who seemed quietly eager for "the other side" to take control. It was nearly impossible to reckon accurately the size of this group, because these people were being most silent and inconspicuous during these days, just as they had been throughout the long

28

The foe became beast in the ruthless psychological war. A Saigon Government billboard version of a "Viet Cong Atrocity."

years of the war. Any open expression of sympathy for "the Front" could bring serious repercussions. It was better to remain silent until the right moment came.

For that reason I never had held much respect for the various "opinion polls" American agencies carried out in Vietnam. In an attempt to find out what the Vietnamese people were *really* thinking, American agencies had on occasion sponsored "confidential surveys" in which they tried to discern whether people were "pro-government," "neutral," or "anti-government."

It was our experience in Vietnam that one rarely learned the true feelings of another person by directly asking his or her opinion about a matter. Instead, there had to be a subtle and protracted process of listening, catching nuances and inflection, watching the person's eyes, observing what the person did *not* say, as well as what was said, and paying much attention to silences. Conversations were experiences of *mutual* testing and the establishing of confidences. They were as attentive to our communication as we to theirs. In the ultimate analysis, of course, it was a matter of trust. And trust was as much a function of a person's learning our true feelings as it was our learning his or hers.

Thursday evening I suggested to Em Trinh that we spend the night at the Quaker house uptown. Before they left, the Quakers had offered us their house, since it was a two-story masonry building and would be somewhat more effective in warding off any possible incoming mortars or shells than the thin tile roof of our small house. Furthermore, Trinh would welcome the companionship of the several Vietnamese members of the Rehab Center staff who would also be staying at the Quaker house.

When we arrived, Anh My, the center's medical technician, was reporting to the group that earlier in the day he had taken his wife and two children to the seacoast town seven miles to the east and put them on a boat sailing to an off-shore island for refuge from whatever would happen in Quang Ngai city. "Phu Tho was crawling like ants," Anh My told us. "Everybody was scrambling to get on boats to sail to the island. Fortunately, Chi Ba and the children were able to get on a boat that wasn't too crowded. I was afraid some of the boats would sink; they were so overloaded."

Anh My and I slept upstairs that night so that Trinh, Chi Mai and her two friends who also had artificial limbs would have easier access to the photography darkroom on the first floor, which we had decided was the most protected room in the house and would serve as our bunker in case the town was shelled during the night. Quang Ngai had reached a pitch of apprehension not seen since the Tet Offensive seven years before. Now, like then, one went to bed at night wondering what the morning would bring. Or whether the morning would come at all.

FRIDAY, 21 MARCH. Friday morning, after an uneventful night, I got up early, breakfasted quickly and jumped on the Lambretta to head toward the district of Nghia Hanh, which lay seven miles south of Quang Ngai city. Pat and I had long felt a special tie to Nghia Hanh because earlier our primary work with refugees had taken place in that district. In 1966 I had actually lived for six months in the district town of Nghia Hanh, which went by the same name. To me the district was reminiscent in size and disposition of the farming township where I grew up in the Pennsylvania Dutch region of southeastern Pennsylvania. The district town lay in a plain contiguous with the vast rice-growing area of eastern Quang Ngai Province. Five kilometers south of the district headquarters the mountains rose abruptly out of the plain.

This morning the Nghia Hanh plain was still covered with an uneven shroud of misty fog. The scooter seemed to glide frictionlessly over the road, carrying me through alternating patches of fog and clear areas where I could see the arching bamboos and subtly undulating rice.

I breathed deeply. The cool moist air charged my body and spirit with new confidence and optimism.

"Freedom!" I shouted aloud into the morning's nothingness. "Freedom!" I shouted again as I sped on. It was the air. It was different here. That oppressive atmosphere of the city polluted with fear and rumor was gone. Here in the domain of the farmers, the peasant folk of Vietnam, I felt free and fearless again.

In the last kilometer before arriving in the village of Nghia Hanh the fog lifted completely. The mountains seemed close and green this morning.

We peasants are like a banana-tree with many leaves.
The strong leaves protect the weak ones.
FOLK SAYING

Some things are unbreakable, even in war. *Photo, Doug Hostetter*

Farmers were harvesting in the golden paddies just off the road. With short sickles they stooped to cut enough stalks to make a small bundle that could be held with both hands. Then they walked over to a large basket with a woven bamboo screen rising high above the basket on three sides. Each harvester in turn would hold his or her sheaf at the stubble, raise it high, and slap it down on a bamboo grating above the basket. After all the grains were shaken into the basket the harvester deposited the straw in a pile to be carried home for fodder.

31

I could see the thatch roofs of Phu Binh refugee camp lying on the north edge of Nghia Hanh village. Of all the refugee camps we had worked in, Phu Binh had always had a special attraction for Pat and me. We knew personally many of the refugees here from the day they were forced off their farms and into the camp in June 1967. This morning I wanted to visit our very close friend and counselor, Anh Duong. He was near our age, but we had always called Duong *anh*, the familiar Vietnamese honorific meaning "older brother." *Chi* means "older sister," so we called his wife Chi Duong.

Anh Duong's home in the camp consisted of one small section of a long row house made of mud and thatch. Each refugee family had its own room, approximately eight by fifteen feet, with a lean-to kitchen attached in back. I walked to Anh Duong's room and stooped down to look into his door. It had taken me a long time to adapt to the Vietnamese custom of entering a house without knocking.

"Anh Kien, it's good to see you. Here, sit down," Duong called, pointing to a bench beside the small table that together with two bamboo beds nearly filled their whole room. "How are Chi Kien and the children?"

I explained how Pat and the children had left the day before, but that I was staying on for a day or so to see how the situation developed.

"Then there *is* something going on, eh?" Anh Duong asked eagerly. "We can't figure it out. Several people from the camp here have come back from a visit to Quang Ngai city and they say everything there is in an uproar. Some people are packing their bags and taking off to Danang or Ly Son island or wherever they can go. Here—well, we just can't figure out what's happening. Here in the countryside it's never been quieter!"

It was the message I heard from all the farmers I talked with that morning, but when I rode back to Quang Ngai city I was again struck with the change in atmosphere from the countryside. People were tense, talking anxiously in threes and fours along the streets. The post office was jammed with people trying to cable relatives to make plans.

Friday afternoon suddenly brought relief in the tension of the week. The road to the north had been reopened. People could again drive to Danang with no trouble. Just twenty-four hours earlier people spoke with envy of the ARVN major who had been able to "buy" a Chinook helicopter flight to Danang for his family by paying a million-and-a-half-piaster bribe. Now one could take a civilian bus to Danang for a few hundred piasters, and many people were deciding they would now stay in Quang Ngai.

The city in the last several days had become like a pressure cooker with all its escape valves blocked. Now that the "valve" to Danang had opened, some of the people immediately rushed to leave, but the general reaction was that the boiling point of the town—lowered over the previous days— had now stabilized somewhat. People appeared more expansive and confident. The price of gold in the past days had plummeted to less than half its normal level as fleeing merchants were desperately trying to exchange a tael or two for expendable currency. Now with the panic reduced, gold shot back up to its previous price.

People in town who had been most apprehensive over the past days now attempted to convince themselves that nothing would change. The crisis would soon blow over and all would return to normal. Now, as many times before, I sensed among people a remarkable mental resistance to contemplating any shift in the historical inertia to which they had become accustomed. It was as difficult to speak frankly with people in town about the possibility of a PRG take-over as to speak to a patient on a hospital bed about the fact that he might soon die. I had noticed this denial tendency especially in several ARVN officer acquaintances of ours.

Major Loc, for example, had been an acquaintance since 1967, when he happened to study in an English class I taught at the Quang Ngai Protestant Church. At that time he had been a captain, sedulous and disciplined in his study. Native to Quang Ngai Province, Major Loc's family possessed considerable landholdings, likely a prime reason for his firm anti-Communist sentiments. When we met Major Loc again in 1974 he was working as a representative to the Two-Party Joint Military Commission in Chu Lai, which was set up as a result of the 1973 Paris Cease-fire Agreement and was theoretically designed to monitor the cease-fire. In actuality his job entailed cataloging "Viet Cong cease-fire violations" and arguing that ARVN violations really were not violations at all.

In January 1975 when the PRG for the first time seized control of a complete province, Phuoc Long, Major Loc had come to visit us. He was refusing to grant significance to the event.

"There's nothing to worry about," he told us. "Phuoc Long is just a small, insignificant province. Besides, we didn't do much to defend it."

When I suggested that some people felt that if Phuoc Long could not be held other provinces might be taken as well, Major Loc refused to allow himself to believe the direction of history was changing.

"We will never lose. We can't lose," he said with assumed confidence. "We can lose all of Quang Ngai Province except Quang Ngai city or all of South Vietnam except for Saigon. And then things will get better again. Someone will come in to bail us out. Like the patient who looks like he is about to die until they pump that serum into his veins, then he springs back to life! That's the way it will be with us."

Major Loc had spent time in training in the United States, but I had sometimes wondered if that training had not seriously handicapped him in facing reality in Vietnam. In an attempt to improve the quality of the ARVN corps, the United States invited many officers to spend a year in training at an American military base. During that year the officers were able to travel and were quick to pick up impressive aspects of the American way of life, a fact that seemed to make them particularly unsuited for combating guerrilla warfare. For example, more than any specialized military training he received, Major Loc had been especially impressed by his visit to Disneyland in California. Back in Quang Ngai in early 1975 at a time when the ARVN troops were experiencing setbacks in the province and the refugees in the camp were desperately short of food, Major Loc was pushing his solution to the problem.

"I've made a proposal to the province chief," he had told us. "You see, the real problem is morale. We need to encourage the people. Give them something to be happy about. Then they'll be willing to stand up and fight the Communists. So I've submitted a proposal to the province chief that we construct an amusement park south of town around the hill that's now used as an ammo dump. We would have a small zoo and we could build a miniature railroad around the hill. Children from town could take rides on it. They'd love it! Kind of like a miniature Quang Ngai Disneyland!"

While the tension of town had lessened somewhat, I still felt apprehensive about remaining in Quang Ngai without any solid indication of how the PRG would respond to my presence. It seemed more imperative than ever that somehow I communicate directly with "the other side." Friday night at the Quaker house I determined to broach the issue with Chi Mai. Even though the extent of Chi Mai's communication with the PRG still seemed a bit dubious to me, at this point she appeared to be the only possible channel for contacting the revolutionary authorities at all. Chi Mai was sympathetic with my concern.

"Yes, I suppose it would be good for you to talk with them, to find out exactly how they feel about your work here. But there's no question about it, they would want you to stay. I'll see if I can learn anything more specific for you."

As on the night before, we all listened to both VOA and BBC, the American and British newscasts. The international news was devoted almost entirely to Vietnam. The radio reported that several more district towns had been overrun that day and that fighting around Hue was becoming more intense. As on the evening before, Anh My ran to bring the wall map of Vietnam from the central bedroom. With quick strokes of his pencil he excitedly circled the provinces and districts that had been taken by the PRG as the radio announced them. By the time the broadcast was completed, he had circled nearly all of the Central Highland region and some lowland districts as well.

Like an instant editorialist, Chi Mai would comment on the newcasts as soon as they were completed. She would attempt to sound dispassionate and analytical, and yet it was impossible for her to disguise her enthusiasm for the mounting successes of the Liberation Army. One could sense Chi Mai vicariously participating in the revolutionary struggle herself. Only her legs kept her from being in the hills at this moment.

Chi Bon, a prosthetist from the Rehab Center, was also spending Friday night at the Quaker house. Generally taciturn and unfailingly pleasant, this young country woman was taller and appeared stronger than many Vietnamese men. Chi Bon biked long distances and led a vigorous life in spite of her one disability, a leg amputated below the knee. She had related the story on a previous occasion when she visited Pat and me in our home. In 1969 she and several friends from her village were harvesting rice in a field along National Highway One. An American convoy passed along the highway. For some reason—it was never clear to me—the troops on the truck opened fire. A bullet ripped through Chi Bon's leg. Although Bon soon lost consciousness, a woman with her felt that she had not been wounded seriously. The Americans flew Bon in a helicopter to Chu Lai where they amputated her leg. Chi Bon, like Chi Mai in her case, suspected the doctors of having been too eager to amputate.

Tonight Chi Bon and I happened to be sitting somewhat apart from the other four persons in the room. As the others continued their discussion of the day's events and the evening's newscasts, Chi Bon opened a small purse she was holding. I watched her zip open one of the inside pockets of the purse and pull out a small photograph, barely larger than a commemorative postage stamp.

"I thought maybe you would like to see this," she said with a quiet pride. The photo Chi Bon handed me showed a single youth, dressed in a military uniform rather different from the ARVN uniform I was used to seeing in Quang Ngai.

"It's my brother, Em Sau. He was a *bo doi.*" *Bo doi.* That was one of those terms rarely used in Saigon Government circles. Literally, *bo doi* merely meant infantry, but it was used exclusively to refer to troops on "the other side," the revolutionary soldiers. On close scrutiny I could see Em Sau was wearing a sidearm. He was pictured standing confidently in a small clearing among thick undergrowth.

"He was killed seven months ago at Mo Duc in an ARVN ambush. Several other *bo doi* were killed at the same time. The ARVN just let their bodies lie for two days. My father who was living in a refugee camp on the Saigon side learned that Em Sau was killed, but he didn't dare go to claim the body for fear the ARVN would suspect and harass him as being *than cong*, a 'Commie lover.' Finally my father went to the ARVN and told them he happened to know that this boy was from his native village. The boy's parents were dead, he told the ARVN. Would they give him permission to bury the boy in behalf of his dead parents? After he received permission, my father went to the spot of the ambush and gathered up the body of Em Sau. He carried my brother's body back toward the countryside, to the 'native village' in the liberated zone. Several guerrillas met him and they helped him bury Em Sau in the native village. Then Father returned to the refugee camp in the Saigon zone."

Previously I had met few people who dared be so forthright as to talk with sympathy about family members fighting with "the Front." It would have been cause for arrest or harassment had police known her story. But now that it looked as if the military/political tables were beginning to turn, Chi Bon apparently felt free to divulge her experience.

"Are there other brothers and sisters?" I asked.

"Yes, two older sisters. Chi Hai was killed two months before Em Sau, when the ARVN set up a remote outpost in the Thi Pho area and made the people in the village build small houses on all sides to give more protection to the outpost. The guerrillas came one night and the ARVN fired M-79 grenades from the outpost. One exploded near her house. Chi Hai and her two-year-old daughter were killed. Chi Hai was four months pregnant."

Bon paused just for a moment as if to think who came next in her family. "Then Chi Ba—Chi Ba went somewhere," she said simply, with a slight sideways turn of her head. Her euphemism was clear: Her second sister was now "somewhere" with the guerrillas.

"I come next, and then Em Nam," the young woman continued. "Em Nam, he was killed too. The same way as Em Sau—in an ambush some time ago."

At the end of her story, I found myself unable to speak. Chi Bon sat composed and quiet. In the midst of this week when many people were depressed and panic-stricken, Chi Bon seemed absolutely calm and intrepid. If history was shifting, Chi Bon showed no signs of disquietude at the prospect.

After a minute of silence, Chi Bon matter-of-factly added, "Someday my folks want to get out of the refugee camp and move back to our native hamlet in Thi Pho. I'm going to go with them. I'll be able to help them a great deal in spite of my leg. And you know, Anh Kien, that time may not be far off. Liberation could come any day!"

SATURDAY, 22 MARCH. Saturday afternoon we were surprised by the sudden appearance of a colleague, Yoshihiro Ichikawa. "Hiro" had lived with us in Quang Ngai for several months before his recent home leave to Sapporo, Japan. Most of his six years with the Mennonite Central Committee in Vietnam he had spent in the province immediately north of Quang Ngai. With a full black beard and a mane of hair long enough to be pulled back into a ponytail, Hiro sometimes gave a first impression of being a mysterious ascetic in a society where only old men have beards and only wispy ones at that. But Hiro quickly surprised people with an easy laugh that always seemed to linger just below the surface, ready to erupt and punctuate any conversation.

And to converse is what Hiro enjoyed most. He had always been hesitant to push social service projects, partly because he felt those programs were frequently unjustified intrusions of foreign influence into Vietnamese affairs

Hiro. "I didn't want to miss anything, so I jumped on the first plane toward Quang Ngai!"

and partly because he preferred to spend his time conversing with village sages or visitors from the neighborhood. Because of his phenomenal grasp of the local idiom, Vietnamese were frequently astonished when they learned he was a foreigner.

Hiro relished controversy and adventure, but it had never occurred to me that Hiro, who had been in Saigon since his home leave, would try to join me in Quang Ngai. Now, there he stood in our doorway, dressed in the black baggy pants and shirt of a country farmer, casually asking "how's it going?" as if it were the most normal of times. Then he broke out in his hearty staccato laugh. "I heard things were beginning to happen in Quang Ngai and I didn't want to miss out on any of it. When I heard you were staying in Quang Ngai, Kien, I jumped on the first plane available. I actually had a ticket to fly to Chu Lai tomorrow, but I switched to today's flight to Danang. They say the planes coming into Saigon are crowded, but flying north I had nearly the whole plane to myself. What royal service! I'm lucky I took today's flight because tomorrow I might not have made it."

Hiro's presence infused me with new enthusiasm for staying in Quang Ngai. "How did you manage to get from Danang to here?" I asked.

"Bus. Perhaps the last bus into town. I wanted to stop off to spend the night in Tam Ky with my friends there, but the driver said if I stopped, I might not make it to Quang Ngai at all. He kept saying that this might be the last bus into Quang Ngai." Hiro was already stripping off his shirt as he talked. Then he turned to his box and started to loosen the carrying scarf around it. Hiro's box contained nearly everything he owned in Vietnam and he carried it wherever he traveled.

"I brought you some money," he announced. "We got your cable in Saigon saying you needed cash."

Hiro reported that Pat and the children had arrived safely in Saigon. As he discussed his trip north it became obvious that Hiro was prepared to stay in Quang Ngai "through everything."

Tired from the bus trip, Hiro lay down for a siesta. Within a few minutes a stranger appeared at the door.

"Hello, I'm Charles Courrier, from the consulate. I'm relatively new in town. I don't believe we have met before." I invited him to sit down in our small dining room so we wouldn't disturb Hiro's nap. "Yes, I've heard you've been in Quang Ngai for a few weeks," I said.

"I came to inform you that we have a helicopter here this afternoon and we would be very happy to provide transportation for you to go to Danang. Let me explain the situation as we see it."

In the next fifteen minutes or so Charles Courrier calmly and deliberately laid out his reason why "it would seem an act of prudence" for me to leave Quang Ngai. I listened with occasional questions and few comments. As his cohorts had done on previous days, Courrier reiterated that there was no evidence of any major "enemy troop movements," but they expected the town might well be hit with sapper attacks. They would try to sabotage the electric power company and perhaps a few military targets in town, he predicted. I asked him what he felt would be the response of the Saigon side if "the other side" should occupy the city. Would there be heavy bombing?

"It's impossible to predict for certain," Courrier answered. "There's a limited amount of air power available right now. So it is very possible they will decide to reserve the air force for cities they consider more important than Quang Ngai."

Courrier's appraisal could not have been more reassuring to me. If indeed there would be no bombing in Quang Ngai, there was little incentive for me to leave.

"I should also tell you," Courrier concluded, "tomorrow is Sunday. We do not plan to bring a chopper into Quang Ngai tomorrow. Tomorrow there will be no flight. But we do plan to return to Quang Ngai on Monday, if there are no unforeseen developments. I should also tell you that we are leaving a Vietnamese radio operator at our compound across from the hospital. If there is anything you want to communicate to us, feel free to use that radio."

"Thank you, but I don't anticipate that I will need to be in communication with anyone in Danang. And about the chopper, thank you for that too, but I hope we can stay in Quang Ngai. Our work is here and our friends are here. Our relationships with people here are built on many months and years of trust. That is important to us. We fear that if we should leave now and then come back in a few days or weeks, we may jeopardize some of the trust that has developed with our friends."

"That is something only you can know," Courrier responded. "I can appreciate your situation. To some extent the same is true of us and our Vietnamese acquaintances. All I can say is that from our perspective it may be advisable for your own safety that you leave. But that decision is really up to you. I should also say that if heavy fighting suddenly breaks out in Quang Ngai and there is shelling of the city, it may not be possible at that point for us to bring in a chopper to get you out."

"By all means, I not only understand that point, but I would like it to be clear that I would never want anyone to risk his life for me. In fact, I would like you to promise that no one will ever undertake any kind of rescue operation for me. That would be most unwelcome indeed."

"Then you won't be going with us this afternoon. I wish you well, Mr. Martin," he said as he stood to leave. And then reaching into his shirt pocket he said, "By the way, here is my card. Look me up sometime when you get a chance. I would be very eager—well, to talk more about what you are doing—sometime when things are more relaxed."

"I hope we will be able to do that sometime," I said as he walked out.

All the visits from the "consulate" representatives during these days dramatized one fundamental characteristic of United States involvement in Vietnam: The Americans, at will, could up and leave. For all the American Government talk about "our national honor" and "commitment to our allies" at stake in our involvement in Vietnam, the fact remained: At the point of its choosing, the United States could walk out. That fact had significantly affected the quality of American involvement. It went a long way in explaining the freedom that the United States felt to ravish the countryside with its bombs and shells, leaving an enormous wake of death traps in the form of unexploded munitions. It also influenced the American readiness to tear people out of their native homes and crowd them into refugee camps. Long-term effects of the war could be largely ignored because we would not have to live with the disaster we had helped create. Official American involvement was limited and conditional.

For the American humanitarian, this conditional commitment was often less obvious, but for that reason it was possibly more insidious. Generally, he was not aware of the cultural or social damage his programs of charitable largesse were creating. He could be more easily beguiled by motives of unalloyed altruism. It was he who often spoke in the lofty terms of having come to *serve* the Vietnamese people, to *identify* with them. Certainly not all his efforts were in vain. But the fact that he too could walk off the scene at the point of his choosing precluded him from truly identifying with these people who were destined to live with the consequences of the war for the rest of their lives.

That was, of course, one reason Pat and I wanted to stay in Vietnam: to "prove" to ourselves and our Vietnamese acquaintances that we were a different kind of American, that the motive for our presence was somehow purer, more honorable. But the fact remained that we too could leave if we so chose. And while we may have frequently rejected opportunities to leave, we had never ultimately revoked our prerogative to do so. After all, we still held foreign passports.

A Buddhist monk had once told us: "If you really want to understand my people, to identify with them, don't worry about your foreign looks or your cultural background. What you must do is revoke your American citizenship and take Vietnamese citizenship. Then you will understand." As Charles Courrier walked out the door Saturday afternoon, I thought again of the monk's words.

About 70,000 people lived in Quang Ngai city and its environs, but since houses were close and since several crowded refugee camps were included in that census, Quang Ngai actually seemed like a small town. Inevitably, I would meet acquaintances when I was downtown. Saturday afternoon was no exception. As I pedaled west on Phan Boi Chau Street, Mr. Thien, a primary-school teacher, flagged me down. His face was drawn anxiously. Unlike his normal habit, today his eyes met mine squarely as he talked.

"Kien, *troi oi*, you're still here! You haven't left yet! Then maybe things aren't too bad after all. But don't you see? Everyone's getting panicked again. It's just like Thursday. Lots of people are trying to leave again this afternoon, but there's a report that the roads have been cut again. What do you think I should do? What can you tell me, Kien? Oh, I'm so glad to see you. What should I do?"

Within a short time we were surrounded with perhaps ten persons who just happened to be walking past the spot and stopped to listen in on whatever news or direction they could pick up. They were all quiet. The Air America helicopter hammered overhead. That was the last flight out for the day. Perhaps forever. How could one know?

I felt the close presence of the people around me, but I could not look at them lest they would feel self-conscious and think they should leave. And I wanted them to stay. I wanted to be surrounded by people. Let the helicopters go. Let the tanks and trucks go. Let the walls of concrete crumble and the defenses of steel melt to the ground. Just let there be people. Weak, indefensible, vulnerable, loving people. Men and women and children and babies with no protection but soft, warm skin.

The threatening prospect of fire raining from the skies and the earth exploding around one's feet seemed too much to withstand. Why? Why did these people around me now have to bear the spiritual agony of not knowing what the night might bring? For madmen like myself who chose to be here, when I could have been on that chopper that just went overhead, it was different. I was a foreigner who for some strange, uncomprehensible motives chose to be in Quang Ngai city at this time, under these circumstances. But these men, these men *lived* here. Their homes were here. Their families were here. Their work, their fields, their shops, their fathers and mothers and the graves of their grandfathers and great-grandmothers, the spirits of their ancestors were here. Why were these men now being wrung through the presses of rolling armies and the impetuous wringers of history?

"I don't know, Mr. Thien. I don't know what you should do. I really don't know what I should do, so I can hardly know what would be best for you. I don't know what will happen in Quang Ngai. There are predictions there will be sapper attacks at some point on the city, but how can anyone know that for sure? For myself, I have no plans to leave Quang Ngai. I want to stay here."

"Stay. Yes, stay." Thien nodded his head slowly. His eyes were facing mine but they seemed to be focused somewhere far behind me. "Yes, it is best to stay. Where could one go anyway? Even if one could get to Danang. Yes, it's best to stay." He turned to grip the handlebars of his bicycle. Upon leaving, Thien turned, "Kien, we will meet again."

I pedaled slowly back to our home on Tran Hung Dao.

As Em Trinh, Hiro and I prepared to go to the Quaker house for the night, I noticed Mr. Chau standing in the courtyard in front of his house. I walked across the courtyard and greeted him.

"Come, let's sit on our porch for a minute," the teacher invited. "What do you make of the situation, Kien?" In spite of the fact that the tension in town was mounting again, Mr. Chau seemed calmer this evening.

"It's hard to figure out what is happening," I said. "The American consulate man this afternoon predicted there would be sapper attacks on the town tonight, but they've been predicting that all week. Certainly the town is more tense again this evening, but I really can't figure out what caused it."

Mr. Chau seemed little interested in the details, even though he had been polite enough to ask my assessment. Leaning forward on his stool, he said, "Kien, I've decided to stay. I'm going to send the rest of my children to Danang if the road opens again—there's no reason why they should go through all this. But as for me—I'm staying." The calmness in Mr. Chau's voice only dramatized the decision of this man whose political loyalties and former association with the Nationalist Party had placed him in a life and death antagonism against the Viet Cong over previous years.

"It's clear what is going to happen, Kien. The ARVN don't have a shred of morale left. The generals in Saigon are worried only about their own skins, and the Americans have lost heart. They are not going to help us. But that is all past. Now there is only one way things can go." Mr. Chau paused, but just for a moment. Then he picked up again with the same steady voice.

"And when they come into town, I will be here. I will be here in my house. I have something to say to them. I am staying to tell them one message: 'Spare the blood of our brothers and sisters.' I will stay to tell them that message. And then I will be ready to die."

Saturday night when we arrived at the Quaker house, Chi Mai proposed that we spend the night at her house, which was adjacent to the open-air market above the hospital. That house, Chi Mai said, had a more substantial bunker.

It was already dark when we were greeted at the door by a handsome man of perhaps sixty-five years. Chi Mai, who stayed in one room in the back of his house, had asked him previously if he would mind a few "foreign guests" spending the night in his house.

Sleep came fitfully. The thought of a possible sapper attack on the town that night floated in and out of my consciousness, and the quiet of the night was intermittently broken as the howitzers at the airport base boomed forth with their "friendly fire," as the American advisors had always been wont to call it. Above that, however, my mind was churning over a message that Chi Mai had just communicated to me before Hiro and I retired. I had again asked Chi Mai if there might be any way for me to communicate with "the Front" about our presence in Quang Ngai. Her casual reply caught me completely off guard.

"If all works out, tomorrow you will be able to travel up to the liberated zone to meet them. We'll talk more about it tomorrow morning."

"What! Are you sure about this, Chi Mai!" I stammered.

"I can't say any more right now. I'll let you know the details in the morning. Good night now."

SUNDAY, 23 MARCH. For years Pat and I had entertained the goal of being able to communicate directly with people on "the other side," but now that I was faced with the actual prospect I was suddenly besieged with second thoughts. Would it be safe? For me? For them? For our Vietnamese friends in town after I returned? Were Chi Mai's apparent connections with the guerrillas reliable? Sunday morning, before Hiro and I left the house, I pressed Chi Mai for more details.

"Are you absolutely sure about this, Chi Mai? Are you sure they know who I am?"

"Yes, they know who you are, all right. Unfortunately, we made the arrangements for the visit before Hiro arrived, so they are expecting only you." Chi Mai seemed to delight in revealing her information bit by bit.

"But then, well, do you really think I should go?"

"Only if you want to go, Anh Kien."

"Well—yes, of course, I think it would be important to talk with them. Don't you think so, Chi Mai?"

Chi Mai nodded. "You would be able to confer with them directly about how they viewed your staying in Quang Ngai."

"But where is this meeting supposed to take place?" I asked, eager for all the details possible.

"We'll discuss the details later. Why don't we get together at twelve-thirty? Let's meet at my house, the one over by the open market. That would be safer. We'll meet there and lay plans for you to go up to meet the other side." *Up* to meet them! Up, in local parlance, always meant west, toward the hills. My mind quickly painted the rendezvous scene: I would head west past the airport to the fringes of Saigon-controlled territory to a predetermined bamboo thicket where I would meet a few hamlet guerrillas!

With the morning to occupy, Hiro and I pedaled downtown to the post office to dispatch another cable to Saigon. In language that would be decipherable only to Pat, we informed them of the plans. It would be reassuring to Pat to know we were making contact.

On leaving the post office Hiro and I suddenly remembered it was Sunday. We biked to the Quang Ngai Protestant Church just around the corner from the post office. Only about half the normal number of believers were assembled for worship this morning. I was surprised to see Pastor Ngoc in the pulpit because I had learned that he had driven his family to Danang several days earlier, and I expected he might stay in Danang himself to wait until the Quang Ngai situation became clearer. But apparently he felt responsible to return to minister to "the flock" in Quang Ngai. Since we were late in arriving, Pastor Ngoc was already preaching when we took seats toward the back of the church. A large star made of bamboo frame covered with translucent red, blue, green and yellow paper hung above us in the peak of the roof, exactly where it had been placed for the Christmas celebration three months before. Faded and dusty red crepe paper twisted its way from the top point of the star to each of the four corners of the church building. The normal stirring of children walking in and out and of mothers attending to babies was absent this morning. The fifty or so assembled Christians were silent. Many had their heads slightly bowed. I could not tell if they were listening to Pastor Ngoc or engrossed in their own thoughts and prayers.

The Vietnam Evangelical Church, as the main body of Protestants in Vietnam was called, had tried to establish an image of being apolitical and totally uninvolved in political matters. And indeed, for the most part, the Protestants did not participate in open demonstrations either in support of or in opposition to the Saigon Government. In fact, however, it was impossible for anyone including ourselves to be apolitical in a milieu so politicized as Vietnam, and the political preferences of most Protestants were hardly on the side of the PRG. Many individual Protestants had been hurt deeply by the war. They lost homes and sons and fathers in battle. Yet for the church as a whole, the war years were a time of growth and expansion. During the war the number of American missionary personnel was higher than at any period since the inception of the church in 1911. It was also a time of tremendous expansion in social service institutions for the church, because there were numerous American agencies that funneled monies through the Vietnam Evangelical Church for schools, hospitals, orphanages and refugee programs. Many of the church buildings constructed during the war had been financed by American churches or U.S. military chaplains.

There were several instances of Protestant pastors staying to serve their churches in areas that had been taken over by the National Liberation Front, and there were some clandestine reports of Christians who were living in NLF-controlled areas, but the consensus among Protestants seemed to be that a Communist government would be inimical to the interests of the church.

This morning Pastor Ngoc's face was more drawn than usual as he spoke. Though he was voicing affirmations of the tranquility the Christian can experience in the face of crisis, the tone of his voice and the lines on his face seemed to be changing his statements into questions.

"We fear for all that is happening around us, but we must remember that we still have the Lord," the pastor said in closing. No one could answer the question that remained on everyone's mind, however. What did the Lord have in store for the Christians in the coming days and years?

Hiro and I rode home for lunch. Here and there along the street we saw families packing belongings into vehicles, although at the time the roads both north and south were closed. While we were eating I discussed with Hiro and Em Trinh the proposed visit to "the other side." They were both in full support of the venture. Hiro had repeatedly maintained that truly impartial service to victims of the war should be taking us to areas under PRG control as well as those under Saigon administration. And both Hiro and Em Trinh were also eager to receive clarification of the PRG's response to our presence in Quang Ngai.

At 12:30 I was knocking softly on the back door of the house, surrounded by betel-nut trees near the open-air market west of the hospital. The door opened slowly revealing the smiling face of Chi Mai. "Anh Kien, come in."

Chi Mai closed the door behind me and motioned with her metal cane for me to sit on the bamboo bed which dominated the tiny room. Sitting at the opposite end of the bed was a young woman I had not met before. A nondescript patterned gray blouse and the glossy black rayon pants common to all Vietnamese women only emphasized her unadorned charm.

"Sister, this is Anh Kien." Chi Mai introduced me so parenthetically that I was left to assume that this woman had heard about me before. I was not, however, to be told the woman's name. Chi Mai smiled again and then, leaning over a table to pull herself up and balance on her feet, she made a move to leave.

"Just excuse us for a minute, Kien. I must discuss a few matters with this sister." Chi Mai and the young woman walked into another room toward the front of the house.

Five minutes later the young woman appeared again at the door of the room. "Chi Mai would like you to come now." I walked into the darkened house and sat down at a small table in front of the ancestral altar where Chi Mai was waiting. A small lantern burned on the altar.

Chi Mai leaned toward me and spoke in hushed tones. "This is the plan. This sister will be your guide to go meet the Liberation Front. After we finish discussing plans here, this sister will leave town by herself. You will wait a half hour before you go so there will be no chance of police associating the two of you. Then you will meet again, west of the airport. Your rendezvous point will be in that small village to the north of the first intersection past the International Crossroads—"

"Wait, wait, I'm lost already," I interrupted nervously. Suddenly the venture seemed fraught with many possible snafus. I could imagine the whole trip aborting simply because I was unable to locate this woman at the appointed rendezvous spot. "I'm afraid I'm not even sure which intersection is called the International Crossroads," I said.

"Well, the International Crossroads is the first intersection west of the Tu Thuan market," the young woman explained patiently. I knew that all the roads in that area were small dirt paths and it struck me as ironic that an intersection of these roads should have the grandiose title of International Crossroads, but the present was no time to discuss the etymology of road names.

"Yes, I think I know which road you are referring to," I replied.

"Then you must continue to the next intersection and go north a bit into the village where we will meet," the young woman explained. "It will be no problem for you to find, I am sure. After International Crossroads you go over a small rise in the road, and just as you begin to come down on the other side this road cuts off to the right. Follow that path back into the small village and I will meet you there."

Still concerned that we might miss each other, I decided to suggest an alternative meeting point.

"Is there any chance you know of an older woman living in that region who has a son in Con Son prison? His name is Pham Quang Tu. I have visited her house several times with a student friend, who is her nephew."

"Pham Quang Tu on the Prison Island! Yes, I know his mother. Yes, yes, that's exactly where we are to meet. You go to her house and I will meet you there!" the young woman replied.

"Excellent!" Chi Mai beamed approvingly. "Now remember, there'll be no talking between you and the sister at the rendezvous point. No communicating of any kind! You notice that she is now wearing a gray blouse. When you get to the house of Pham Quang Tu's mother, you should probably visit with the mother for a short time. While you are in the house, keep on the watch for this sister. She will walk past the house slowly with a hoe over her shoulder. At that point she will be wearing a navy blue blouse. Just remain sitting in the house for a minute, then after this sister has had a chance to walk some distance, you should excuse yourself and nonchalantly get up and follow her. But remember, always keep considerable distance between yourself and this sister. No one—no one is to be able to make any association between you and her."

Chi Mai paused, her eyes revealing her delight with the intrigue. I could feel my pulse quickening.

"All right. Are you clear about the plan?" Chi Mai looked at both the young woman and me. I reiterated the scenario, step by step, to make sure I was certain of all the details.

"That's excellent!" Chi Mai affirmed. "Now, Kien, what vehicle are you riding?"

"The Lambretta scooter."

"That's too big and noisy. It'll be too conspicuous. It'd be better for you to use your bicycle, don't you agree, Chi Kha?" It was the first time I heard the name of this young woman who was to be my guide. I think Chi Mai intended not to tell me her name. If our trip across into "liberated territory" should be sabotaged by the police and I were to be arrested, the less I knew about my guide the better.

Chi Kha nodded.

I rode the Lambretta back to our MCC house to pick up the bike. Hiro and Trinh, surprised to see me back, listened eagerly to the plan for the trip. Hiro's eyes revealed the same excitement I was feeling. He obviously would have been happy to accompany me had it not been that "the Front" was expecting only one visitor.

"I expect I'll be back by evening at the latest," I said. "On the other hand, if I'm not—well, don't worry about me. Just assume I've stayed on the other side for some reason."

"Anh Kien, go in peace." Hiro grabbed my shoulder affectionately. "Go in peace."

I pedaled vigorously toward Chi Mai's house. My adrenal glands seemed particularly active and I was glad for the opportunity to burn up some nervous energy. Just before arriving at Chi Mai's house, my bike kicked with a blowout of the back tire. I quickly dropped the bike off at a nearby "patch-it" stall while I checked in with Chi Mai again.

"The sister's gone on ahead," Chi Mai announced. "All's clear for you. Go in peace."

Back on the main street I picked up the bicycle with the newly patched tire and started pedaling west, past the Quaker house, the CIA house, the USAID warehouse and out Peace Avenue toward the airport. As usual the road was dominated by enormous American-supplied "deuce and a half" military trucks emitting geysers of black diesel exhaust and churning up billows of dust, harbinger of the eight-month season of rainless summer. The trucks were loaded with unpainted wooden crates with rope handles: artillery shells for the howitzers at the ARVN base west of town. Preparing for a big fight.

I had gone not more than half a mile when I heard a loud explosion above the clangor of a passing truck. Another blowout on my rear tire. An omen? I quickly flushed the thought from my mind. Then I noticed another "patch-it" shop directly across the street. I took the coincidence as ample antidote to my ill fortune. But I couldn't afford to wait for the repair job. "Could you fix it up? It'll take a new tire and maybe a new tube. I'll be back for it some time later," I told the boy in the shop.

Back on the street I flagged down a xe om, one of the omnipresent 50 cc Hondas that roamed the streets looking for passengers with a few piasters.

The small Japanese cycles had been imported by the shiploads, under an American-financed Commodity Import Program, to be sold at greatly subsidized prices in order to give many families their own stake in the benefits of capitalism and the American presence.

"Where can I take you?" the sun-darkened driver asked.

"Out to the airport?"

"Sure thing, jump on."

"Fifty piasters?" It was always safest to bargain *before* the ride.

"How about a hundred?"

"Seventy."

"Fair enough, let's go." The cycle groaned off to a slow start. Bad compression. But we soon picked up momentum. "To the airport, you say? You don't expect any planes in today certainly?" The driver seemed eager to talk.

"Actually, I want to go out beyond the airport to visit a small village out there. I'll pay whatever it takes to get there."

"Oh, never mind that, I was just curious. I haven't seen any planes come in for the last day or two."

"No, I'm actually going out a bit beyond the Tu Thuan market. Mind taking me that far?"

"No problem."

The airstrip was vacant. There had not been a commercial plane into this strip for more than two months, and even military air traffic had been considerably reduced. Today there was not a plane on the whole premises except for the crashed DC-3 that had been rusting at the east end of the airstrip for several years. Even in the ARVN military camp across the road from the airstrip a lone helmeted guard at the gate was the only sign of life I detected. Of course, since it was just after two o'clock, everyone could still have been taking an afternoon siesta. Or perhaps much of this outfit had been pulled north to defend Tam Ky in recent days. Just beyond the gate of the camp, a roll of concertina wire was pulled in from both sides of the road, closing off all but a small lane in the middle.

After we passed the concertina wire, the macadam led into a packed earth road. Beyond this point nearly all the traffic was on foot or bicycle. For a stretch, the landscape was flat and barren. A deserted ARVN shooting range and training field lay on the left. We soon reached the place where the road detoured, first to the right and then the left, to circle around a compound with an archway at the entrance painted with the words *Nha Vinh Biet*. This "House of Eternal Separation" was the military morgue, one of the most-used facilities in Quang Ngai. On the porch of the main building I could see a few coffins draped in flags of the Saigon Government, yellow with three red stripes.

Soon we were driving through Tu Thuan village. Here all the houses were mud and thatch except for the primary school, the police station and the local headquarters of the ARVN's "Popular Forces." The road was virtually peopleless at this hour. Ahead of us I spotted a group of young ARVN troops along the right-hand shoulder of the road, Popular Forces militia men from the local outpost. This was still an area of firm ARVN control—during the daytime, at least—but I was eager that my presence attract as little attention as possible. I turned the back of my head toward the soldiers as we passed.

"Still farther?" the driver inquired.

"Yes, it's straight up this road."

We shortly came to an unobtrusive intersection. The narrow dirt roads leading off from ours were shaded with arching bamboos.

"Is this, perhaps, what they call the International Crossroads?" I inquired of the driver.

The driver gave out a short laugh. "I couldn't really tell you. I don't get up this way very often."

"I think I want to be going just a bit farther. Up over that rise in the road. Hope I'm not being too much bother for you."

"Oh, not at all." By this time the driver seemed to be curbing his natural curiosity. If we were heading toward suspicious territory, he perhaps preferred to remain uninformed. If subsequently interrogated, he could conveniently plead ignorance.

I decided that when we arrived at the next intersection I would jump off the cycle and cover the rest of the distance on foot. The fewer people who knew the rendezvous point the better. Besides, there was no point in creating difficulty for the driver.

"I'll jump off at the path up there," I told the driver as I pulled the wallet from my pocket. I wanted to have the money ready so I would not need to waste time along this road.

The driver brought the cycle to a stop in the middle of the road and turned, "Sure you don't want me to take you farther?"

"No, this is just fine." I jumped off and pressed a 200-piaster bill into his hand. "Thank you very much."

I walked briskly down the path lined with bamboos. Glancing back toward the road, I could see the driver still sitting on his cycle with a curious smile across his face. I soon rounded a curve in the path, which cut the main road from sight. I breathed more easily knowing that on the path ahead I would likely encounter no more soldiers, just local farmers. All was working well.

I walked quickly. Why so excited, I asked myself. Had I not been to this village twice before with Em Tu to visit his aunt? I had been quite relaxed those times. Tu had told me the ARVN rarely ventured up to this village, but then the guerrillas rarely visited it either, except at night. People in this village knew me and all would be well, I tried to persuade myself. Yet I was not able to shake off the edge of nervousness I felt. Suddenly I was startled by a piercing cry from behind.

"*Ong My, Ong My, di dau do!*" the shout was loud and insistent. I spun around to see two ARVN soldiers running down the path behind me. The leading soldier was waving his arms.

"*Toi vao day*, just in here," I quickly shouted back.

"*Ong My*, where are you going?" the soldier yelled again. Then I noticed in his right hand he gripped a pistol. He was still waving his arms.

Try to act as calm as possible, I reasoned to myself. "This village, this village just up ahead. I'm going to visit this village." I turned to continue walking, hoping he would be persuaded by my seeming confidence in the situation.

"Stop! There's Viet Cong up there!" Now he was only ten paces behind me. Then I heard a metallic click.

That stopped me cold. I turned around again and faced the soldier behind me. His thumb was still bent over the cocked hammer of his pistol.

"No, I know this village. I've been here before. There's nothing in this village to worry about." I forced myself to speak as calmly as possible.

The soldier scowled, "That village is dangerous."

"I know this village. I've been here several times before. I've visited people in this village. There's no problem." His pistol arm relaxed for a moment. I turned slightly to signal my intention of proceeding down the path. The soldier turned toward his partner who was just catching up.

"This American is heading into that village. It's dangerous in there," he said to the other soldier. His tone of voice was still angry, but he seemed more confused than before.

I seized onto his uncertainty. "I know this village. I know it," I reiterated as I slowly started to walk down the path. After a few steps, I turned and repeated, "I know it."

I continued toward the village. Behind me I could hear the soldiers murmuring to each other. When I glanced back, the soldiers were slowly walking back toward the main road.

What luck! I complained to myself as they disappeared from sight behind the bamboos. I had successfully eluded arrest by the soldiers. Yet it was a disquieting victory. The soldiers had retreated, but they were still upset. I had won the duel, but I had not won their trust. I feared I might not have seen the last of those soldiers. They could report my presence to the police and cause trouble for me later. Hopefully, I would be able to make my contact with the representative from "the Front" and hurry back to town before anyone became too suspicious.

Now the path was winding between simple houses of mud and thatch. A small barefoot girl came toward me with a lilting gait created by the two bobbing water buckets suspended from her shoulder pole. Well ahead of me I could see a boy sitting cross-legged on a rock with a bamboo stick propped against his shoulder. His tan cows were grazing beyond him. I felt strong and confident again. Yes, it was the people. Among the defenseless, vulnerable farmers I was at peace again.

I cut down a small path leading toward the aunt's house. It was perhaps four months since I had visited her. I felt in my shoulder bag for the bananas I had remembered to bring as a gift for Em Tu's aunt. Turning in the aunt's lane, I saw several young women talking by the squash arbor beyond the aunt's house. There, standing among them, was Chi Kha! In a navy blue blouse!

Reminding myself to remain casual, I stepped up to the open door of the aunt's house. No one was in the room. Not knowing where to go, I stepped inside the door. A child appeared from a side room. I had seen this child on former visits.

"Grandma is not home this afternoon," she said in a high voice, then disappeared into the other room. I sat on the edge of a bench near the door. Across the tamped earth courtyard a neighbor farmer emerged through the thatch that hung low over the cattle pen behind his house. He was one of the half dozen men who had joined the anniversary celebration of the death day of the aunt's husband the first time I had visited here with Em Tu nearly six months before.

"Well, if it's not Anh Kien!" he called midway across the courtyard. "The aunt isn't home just now. Why don't you come visit me for a little while?"

"Fine. It's good to see you again. You're not out in the fields this afternoon?" I asked.

"No, there's nothing pressing in the fields just now."

As I crossed the courtyard I glanced again toward Chi Kha. She was holding a conical hat, seemingly oblivious of my presence. A hoe leaned against the arbor.

I followed the neighbor under the thatch roof and into his house. We sat on the edge of a bed of black polished wood. As with most Vietnamese beds, it was covered only with a thin reed sleeping mat. The lanky farmer slipped off his sandals and swung his feet up onto the bed. Leaning toward an adjacent table, he lifted the lid from a large hollowed-out coconut shell, which served as a warmer for his teapot.

"Well, Kien, what do you make of the situation? I visited the city the other day and in talking to people there I got the impression that the soldiers are pretty frightened. What do you think?"

As he talked, he performed the tea ritual so common in Vietnamese homes that it seemed almost automatic. He lifted two small overturned cups from a tin tray in the center of the table and set them upright on the edge of the table. He poured a small amount of tea into the cup nearest me. Setting the teapot on the table, he lifted the cup, swished the tea in circles for a second and then poured it into his cup. After rinsing his cup in like manner, he threw this tea on the ground underneath the bed. Again he lifted the pot and poured both cups nearly full—first, the cup near me, then his.

The farmer continued talking, not waiting for my answer. "I don't have a radio, but they say Thieu has abandoned Pleiku and Kontum over to the other side. Appears to me the other side is pretty strong right now."

During recent days I had heard many civil servants and shopkeepers in Quang Ngai city say exactly these same words, but few of them would have spoken these words so casually, so cheerfully, while pouring tea for a friend. Setting the pot back on the table, he turned to me with a polite nod of his head, "Anh Kien, please—"

I nodded an acknowledgment but followed custom by disregarding the first invitation to drink. "Perhaps the other side is about to become this side," I ventured.

The farmer squinted for just an instant and then with a note of understanding chuckled, "Oh, do you think so!"

A small boy appeared at the door and addressed the farmer. "They want this man to come back to Grandma's house."

"You have to go," the farmer said warmly. "Do come to see me again." I gathered up my shoulder bag and was ready to stand.

"Oh, tea!" he said with a nod. We picked up our cups and drank in silence.

I followed the young boy back into the aunt's house, but still the aunt was not home. I thought about the bananas but decided to keep them. I might return later in the afternoon and I could give them to the aunt in person. Again I sat on the bench in the aunt's house, uncertain what should be happening. I did not have to wait long.

Momentarily, Chi Kha walked slowly across the courtyard with the hoe over her shoulder. Then she disappeared from view. I waited for a minute or two, trying to appear composed by engaging in small talk with the aunt's grandchildren. After a time I stood and told them that since the aunt was not at home, I would be leaving. Perhaps I would stop back later.

In the courtyard I looked toward the arbor, but the two remaining women had gone out to work in a garden. No one was paying attention to me. I walked out the lane and up the path toward the spot where I had earlier seen the small boy tending cows. I could not see Chi Kha, but I assumed she had gone down the hill beyond the cows. From the crest of the hill I spotted her 100 meters ahead, crossing over a small bridge. I also immediately noticed Hill 10, about a half mile to the southwest. Hill 10 was the last ARVN outpost on the western flank of Quang Ngai. Right now I preferred keeping as much distance between ARVN outposts and myself as possible, but it appeared that the trail Chi Kha chose was leading toward, not away from, Hill 10. Strange direction, indeed, to be looking for guerrillas!

Chi Kha ambled easily, hoe swaying back and forth on her shoulder. I had to slow my own pace so as not to shorten the distance between us. When I reached the bottom of the small hill, Hill 10 was momentarily blocked from view by an intervening row of trees.

Open country, this. No buildings, no vehicles. Just a few farmers working in the open fields ahead. This was border country. Between the lines. But the bucolic scene around me was far too tranquil to be the "no-man's-land" of a "conventional" war. Indeed, this guerrilla war never had lines per se. In general, the cities and district towns had been controlled by the Saigon Government, the mountains and deep countryside by the PRG. Between these zones were vast expanses of countryside that both sides claimed. Or more accurately, which neither side firmly controlled. The Vietnamese farmers had coined their own word for these middle areas: *xoi dau*. A mixture of *xoi*—glutinous rice—and *dau*—mung beans—when cooked together comprised a favorite Vietnamese breakfast. Hence in *xoi dau* areas both ARVN patrols and NLF ambushes would occasionally occur.

The farmers living in these "rice-bean" areas were caught between the hammer and anvil of the war. The preponderance of unexploded munitions lay in *xoi dau* fields. In the evenings American or ARVN cannons would lob "harassment and interdiction" shells—H&I fire—into these areas to strike targets, not where they had spotted enemy troops, but where they speculated their foe *might* be. The presence of H&I fire kept farmers sleeping in, or close to, foxholes dug under their beds. During the day, farmers here could be subject to the raids of Saigon Government police looking for "Viet Cong suspects." On the other hand, these farmers were expected to contribute a percentage of their rice harvest to the guerrillas in tax each year.

The path took a turn and once again Hill 10 loomed into view, this time even closer than before. I could see the profile of several ARVN troops walking near their command post. An unsettling sight. I could only hope that none of them would be scrutinizing the countryside for unusual activity at that moment. I found myself dropping my head and shoulders as I walked to more closely resemble the profile of the farmers in the fields. Whether this was a wise path to be taking or not, I had little choice but to follow the woman with the hoe.

The fields around us were lush with newly transplanted rice seedlings. Scattered here and there throughout the paddies, farmers worked singly or in couples, irrigating, spraying and weeding. In an attempt to demystify my presence I would make a point of greeting the farmers close to the path. Several expressed concern that I had lost my way and seemed confused when I managed to reply with assumed nonchalance that I was "just taking a walk."

But most farmers seemed more intrigued than concerned. Occasionally I could hear one call to another in undertone and the two would glance furtively in my direction and then whisper excitedly for a minute. One lanky farmer bending down among the flooded rice stalks straightened up when he saw me approach.

I took the initiative. "You're weeding your rice paddy, eh?"

"Uh, yes, and where might you be going, if I may ask?" The barefoot gentleman was obviously fascinated with this unusual diversion in his day.

"Me? I'm just out for a walk."

"Just out for a walk! Out in *that* direction?" His eyes flashed eagerly. "I see. That ought to be an interesting walk!"

When he spoke he looked up the path, which by now was virtually vacant except for a blue-bloused young woman with a hoe over her shoulder in the distance. He glanced back at me, then up the path toward Chi Kha again. I waited.

The farmer's smile and slight nod indicated that he might have discovered our secret. "Hope you have a nice walk," he said simply. I knew by his voice that our secret would be kept in confidence. It was the way communication often took place among the farmers.

In the following minutes bamboo trees along the path intermittently hid Hill 10 from my view—or, more pertinently, hid me from the view of Hill 10. Now it seemed possible that any of the bamboo thickets could serve as sufficient cover for a few local guerrillas, but Chi Kha kept walking steadily.

After we had walked what I figured was well over a mile, my estimation of this venture began to shift. This was not a quick trip to meet a hamlet guerrilla or two. It now appeared we were heading right into the heart of what the American soldiers used to call "V.C. Country"! For the first time I was becoming convinced that Chi Mai did indeed have liaison with people of some standing in the ranks of "the Front." Perhaps the note from the alleged "Le Quang Vinh" was authentic after all.

For the next fifteen minutes we did not encounter another person. And yet the fields around us were cultivated. Here a stand of corn. There a patch of beans or manioc. An area, I presumed, where the field work was done under the cover of night. During the American occupation I knew much of this area was a "free strike zone." During daylight hours small Cessna "spotter planes" had circled over these areas constantly, ready to call in a jet strike on anyone or anything that moved. The few farmers who tried to stick it out with their fields had to chart their existence around the tricks of surviving the "flying machines." If they needed to move in the daytime above ground, they had to wear large conical hats camouflaged with the foliage of the surrounding terrain: leafy branches in the planting season or rice straw during harvest time. On first sight or sound of a plane they squatted low in the field, hoping their hats would render them invisible to the scrutinizing eyes circling above. They built their camouflaged shelters under arching bamboos or entirely underground. Cooking had to be done underground, since even a trace of smoke was enough to attract phosphorous rockets or "500-pounders" from above. The farmers piped the smoke for some distance underground in hopes that the only casualty from a bomb on target would be a craterized smoke hole. Eventually, it just became too dangerous and the surviving farmers moved one way or the other: into the refugee camps that ringed Quang Ngai city or to the hills to join the guerrillas.

Now that the American military was gone, there were relatively few spotter planes in the air and the Saigon Air Force did not bomb as profusely as the Americans had. On occasion ARVN howitzers still shelled the area we were now traversing, but at this point my greater preoccupation was with the prospect of imminently encountering a Viet Cong guerrilla. Had the communications been clear? Were they expecting me? Or would some nervous and unsuspecting guerrilla be shocked at the sight of an American walking into his territory? Acquaintances back in Quang Ngai, trying to discourage us from visiting farmers in the hinterlands, used to say, "Surely, if the Communists knew who you were, they might not trouble you. But the trouble with the Viet Cong is that they shoot first and ask questions later." Such comments did little to discourage our travels, but still there always was the possibility of some mistake.

After walking for more than half an hour, I noticed that Chi Kha, who had always been at least a hundred meters ahead of me, had stopped in the path, waiting for me to catch up. She was standing silently on the bank of a river.

"Very lovely. What river is this, sister?" I welcomed the chance to re-establish communication with Chi Kha after all the intervening suspense.

"It's the Song Tra." She was smiling and relaxed.

"The Song Tra! The same river that flows by Quang Ngai city. Then I've swum in this river many times, downstream."

But Chi Kha was ready to continue her mission. "All right, shall we move on?"

Now within talking distance, but speaking little, we again wound our way through fields of manioc and waist-high corn. In some places bean tendrils spiraled up the stalks of corn. Here and there a jackfruit tree or a cluster of arching bamboos created spots of shade. The sky was clear and the mountains to the west were spring green in the full afternoon sun.

Then, as subtly and mysteriously as the emergence of a new character in a dream, I sensed a presence behind me. I saw nothing. I could remember hearing nothing. But instinctively I turned my head to look. To my shock, I was staring straight into the muzzle of a B-40 rocket!

This is it! The other side!

The awesome rocket launcher bobbed on the shoulder of a young guerrilla loping stealthily just ten feet behind me. A second guerrilla, also in black shirt and shorts and a green floppy hat like the first, came trotting behind. This one gripped an AK-47, the automatic rifle of "the Front."

Chi Kha, ten paces ahead, had not noticed our impressive new sojourners. For a moment I felt like I was a foreign envoy barging into a mysterious, secluded kingdom. I felt an urgency to present my "credentials" with dispatch, to communicate my amicable intentions before these fellows jumped to any hasty conclusions about me.

"*Chao anh*," I greeted the guerrilla behind me as casually as possible, without breaking stride. His response bypassed me.

"Chi Kha, where are you taking this man?"

Fantastic! The guerrilla knew my guide by name! That was comforting. Chi Kha glanced back for a moment to identify the source of the question and then, without losing a step, answered succinctly with a euphemism I'd never heard in the Saigon zones, "I'm on mission."

"Yes, of course you're on mission. But where are you taking him?" The young guerrilla found it difficult to curb his curiosity.

"I'm on mission," Chi Kha reiterated with a note of finality.

I decided to try to exploit the youth's unrequited inquisitiveness with a bit of direct diplomacy on my part. "This countryside of yours is just lovely; so peaceful," I offered with a slight turn of my head.

The reply again was not addressed to me. "Hey, this fellow speaks our language!" And then to me, "Say, where are you going, anyway?"

I would have to follow Chi Kha's cue of assumed vagueness. Besides, I still *didn't* really know where we were going. "Oh, just taking a walk, visiting the countryside." Our quartet continued single file up the narrow path between cornstalks on the left and high grass on the right. The two new-comers chatted between themselves. My mind groped for other conversational topics. "By the way, that's a B-40 rocket you're carrying there, isn't it?"

"This. No, this is a B-41; it's newer and bigger than a B-40. More powerful too!" Small comfort.

For a minute the trail wound through high grasses on both sides and then led into a wide open space by a river. There by the low bank of the river sat a group of fifteen guerrillas, resting in the grass. So these were the *bo doi*, the revolutionary soldiers. They looked young, late teens and early twenties. There were no black outfits here; they all wore uniforms, lighter green and baggier than uniforms I was used to seeing in Quang Ngai city. Their outfits carried no insignia of any kind, no obvious way to identify rank. All wore the strapped rubber sandals cut from discarded tires similar to those worn by many Quang Ngai farmers. Most of these *bo doi* were hatless.

On spotting Chi Kha and me approaching, several men jumped to their feet. One older man, different from the others only in that he was wearing a green brimmed helmet, stepped out from behind the group and walked toward Chi Kha. His squinted eyes had a glint of mystery, but his smile was straight and noncommittal. He reached to adjust his hat, which carried a round emblem of a golden star on a field of red and blue, the colors of the Provisional Revolutionary Government. Chi Kha stepped to his side and spoke in a lowered voice. "Anh Trong, here he is."

Anh Trong glanced at me standing five paces away but made no move to address me. Turning back toward Chi Kha, he spoke directly, seeming to presume I would not understand his language. "But sister, I don't understand. Why did you bring him up here? We were about to meet him down in the city."

Could it be! Mistaken communications! Could I have made it safely into liberated territory only to learn the PRG didn't even want me to come? Now what? Would they refuse to talk with me? Was this adventure all for naught? And Anh Trong said they were about to meet me in Quang Ngai city! About to—! That means they planned to storm Quang Ngai soon. Perhaps *very* soon!

I could not understand Chi Kha's response to him because she spoke more softly. Whatever she said, Anh Trong seemed to relax. He lifted his hand to tilt back his *bo doi* hat and scratch his head. I noticed several numbers written on his hand in ball-point ink. Down in Saigon-controlled territory students or civil servants often wrote on their hands to solve an arithmetic problem or make note of something to be remembered. Here on "the other side" the guerrillas apparently had the same habit. I made a mental note of the numbers on Anh Trong's hand: "357."

After a few more words with Chi Ka, Anh Trong turned toward me with his first genuine smile. Looking again at Chi Kha, he asked, "Does he speak our language?"

"Oh yes, Anh Trong, you can talk to him with no trouble," Chi Kha responded. Still, the thought of speaking directly to an American must have seemed too formidable for this man who had become accustomed to thinking of Americans as the enemy. One could imagine the only Americans Anh Trong had ever seen were GI's on operation. Just as my mind was spinning with this first encounter with "the Viet Cong," so also this hinterland guerrilla was perhaps needing some time to adjust to the presence of this unusual foreigner. Anh Trong smiled again but still did not speak to me. Instead he called an order to one of the younger guerrillas in the group who immediately disappeared into a high stand of elephant grass just behind Trong's back. Eager to present an approachable image, I turned to the young guerrillas at my side and commented about the beauty and peacefulness of the countryside. They too seemed overwhelmed with the strangeness of talking with a foreigner.

Presently the path into the elephant grass parted again and two men appeared. Dressed in blue and gray, these men did not wear the military uniform. These were the political officers, I presumed, the "cadres" who accompanied all military units. It was the political cadres who generally carried the greatest authority in the NLF units. The man in the lead was youthful-looking, about thirty I guessed, close to my age. His face was open and bright, eager and confident. He spotted me and flashed a warm smile. With brisk steps he walked directly toward me, not bothering to consult with Chi Kha or Anh Trong. The man enthusiastically extended his hand.

"Hello, I am Le Quang Vinh."

Le Quang Vinh! The man who sent us the note! So that note *was* authentic after all. And Chi Mai really was in touch with significant officials of the PRG. This man standing before me was actually Le Quang Vinh. I reached out to shake hands with the Communist official.

It had been an unlikely odyssey. On an autumn day fifteen years earlier I had ridden with a carload of fellow sophomores twelve miles from Garden Spot High School in New Holland, Pennsylvania, to the county seat of Lancaster. It was nearing election time and "our" candidate was coming to the city. It was a chance in a lifetime to see our hero, perhaps—if exceptionally lucky—even to meet him. I was probably not the only high-school junior who did not understand much about the substantive issues in that election year. But religious stereotypes were strong and I was much affected by the prevailing Republican concern in that "Bible belt" region to keep a Catholic out of the White House. More than that, this man coming to Lancaster, we were assured, would not be "soft on communism." I had been as impressed as any teen-ager by those films in which a world map showed a protoplasmic scarlet blob erupting in Moscow—even that city's name sent a chill down my spine—and pushing its oily red tentacles all over the Soviet Union, down into Eastern Europe, and then engorging the mass of China and a few other small victims over the map. (If North Vietnam was mentioned, it failed to register as I had never heard of such a place.) That blob had to be stopped and our candidate would stop it.

The throngs of people on the Lancaster streets prevented us from getting more than a glimpse of our hero as he sat waving from the back seat of his slowly moving open convertible. It was disappointing not to have been able to get closer to him. But, not easily foiled, my friends and I jumped into our car and chased after the motorcade, finally catching up to it outside town at the Lancaster airport.

We quickly parked our car in an open field and stood by the road that led into the airport. Within minutes our candidate's car approached. I stepped out on the curb and stretched my arm toward the man waving in the back seat. At that moment I felt the electric thrill of placing my hand into the hand of Richard Nixon!

But alas, the enthusiasms of high school must give way to the new questions and challenges of college. After two years at a Mennonite junior college in Hesston, Kansas, and a term at Penn State, my view of the world had broadened somewhat. I had come to see the world as big enough to contain Catholics and Jews as well as Protestants, Democrats as well as Republicans—and maybe a few folks who were none of the above! Still, like most other Americans of the era, I saw the world as being divided between the competing "Free World" and "Communist" camps. As a Mennonite I had been taught that war could never be justified. Hence, come draft age, I naturally registered "I-O," conscientious objector. Yet while I was unable to justify American military intervention in Vietnam, I saw the foreign involvement of the United States as essentially well intentioned and benevolent. The alternative, it seemed, was to allow communism to advance unchecked.

Becoming restless in academia, I dropped out in my junior year at Penn State and volunteered with the Mennonite Central Committee for Vietnam.

It would be an opportunity, I told myself, to experience life in its starkest form, to immerse myself totally in the sights and sounds of another culture, to witness the clash of international forces on a grand scale and to identify with human suffering and struggle at its fullest.

All that would come even more forcefully than I had youthfully anticipated. Shortly after I arrived in Saigon in 1966 my older brother Luke, who had been living there with his family for four years, drove me outside Saigon several kilometers to the sprawling military cemetery at Thu Duc. Slowly we walked from stone to stone, observing row after row of grave markers inscribed with recent dates. Many graves were freshly filled with packed dirt; many more stood open, waiting for an occupant. After watching us for some minutes from beside a large shed of corrugated steel, a Vietnamese soldier beckoned to us. As we approached he motioned us toward the shed. Without speaking, he pulled open the door. There, dumped in a twisted heap on the dirt floor, lay the mangled bodies of twelve young men. Fat black flies buzzed sickeningly over the bloodied forms. Stunned, we soon retreated from the heart-twisting scene. Momentarily, we watched as a middle-aged woman came in the lane and made her way fearfully toward the shed. Again without a word, the army man opened the door and the distressed woman forced herself to look upon the bodies. After moments of heavy silence, the woman shook her head and uttered, "Khong co." Her missing son was not among the twelve. She sobbed convulsively as she trudged out the lane.

Such experiences continued to punctuate our initial three years in Vietnam. One afternoon as Pat and I were talking with some youth in a refugee camp near Quang Ngai, we watched a handful of children playing a Vietnamese version of ring-around-the-rosie. I noticed one small child of perhaps five years stumble and fall, her forehead resting on the ground. When the child had not moved for some moments, I walked over and spoke to her. No movement. Then I noticed blood on the ground by her head. I gathered the child into my arms and carried her to a nearby house. While friends produced smelling salts and Pat administered artificial respiration, I felt in vain for a pulse. Flagging down an army truck we raced the child toward the province hospital. Squeezing the child in rhythm I tried to restore breathing and heartbeat to the limp form as we bounced along the rough roads. I prayed earnestly that the child would live. In the hospital emergency room nurses and doctors set to work immediately, but within moments they shook their heads. The child was dead.

Only later when we visited the grief-stricken family did we learn that the hospital had discovered a bullet had entered the top of the child's head. Apparently it had been one of the hundreds of rounds that were aimlessly fired into the air every day. An accident of war.

The "accidents" accumulated. At two o'clock one night a white-hot flare, dropped from a circling C-47 transport, crashed through a tile roof and fell onto an infant firstborn son sleeping between our close friend and his wife. The child was quickly burned to death. "One of those unfortunate accidents," said Colonel Grubaugh the next morning when I presented him with the charred "U.S. Navy" flare canister.

There was the village outside Quang Ngai incinerated to ashes by an exploding inferno of jellied gasoline called napalm. Upon being confronted, the military admitted it was a "friendly" village. The air strike had been a mistake. An accidental bombing.

There was the Mekong delta town under guerrilla siege that was bombed to rubble. The American commanding officer explained, "We had to destroy the town in order to save it."

Meanwhile, back in the United States, disenchanted academicians and even some Washington policy makers were begining to call the whole war a mistake, a blunder in American foreign policy, an unfortunate accident of history. The new liberal line seemed to be that the Vietnam War was an accident wrapped in a blunder inside a mistake.

But the longer we stayed in Vietnam, the less acceptable became the accident theory of the war. For all the accidents we observed, even more disturbing were the nonaccidents: the villages that were bombed to the ground because a guerrilla had sniped at a reconnaissance plane from that village; the 20,000 people who were tracked down and "eliminated with extreme prejudice," i.e., killed, because they were suspected of being connected with the revolutionaries; the farmers whose villages were surrounded with troops who forced them to board helicopters and be flown to "refugee" camps while their ancestral homes were burned to the ground and their farms were declared "free strike zones." All these were aspects of official policy.

Back in the United States for several years in a pre- and post-graduate program of East Asian studies at Stanford University and some months of research and writing at the Indochina Resource Center in Washington, another explanation for the war became more plausible to me. It was that American intervention in Vietnam, while certainly fraught with blunders, was not an accident at all. At the heart, it was a logical extension of a foreign policy presupposition that we had a right to intervene—diplomatically, economically or militarily—in the affairs of any country if American interest was judged to be at stake. Of course the official spokespersons would eventually attempt to clothe the brutalities of napalm and "body counts" in the lofty language of defending democracy and "giving the people of Vietnam an opportunity to determine their own future." But memories of hungry refugees and hospital wards crowded with artillery victims turned such justifications rancid and pharisaical. The official rationale had become but a whited sepulcher full of dead men's bones.

The man with whom I had shaken hands in that Lancaster motorcade had, of course, gone on to shake many more hands and finally to shake his way into the high office he had sought so long. But eventually Richard Nixon would come to represent not that bulwark that would save us from an encroaching scarlet blob, but a pitiful, helpless—but dangerous—giant that would stop at nothing to achieve its will in the world.

Although we had come to abhor the violence of American involvement in Vietnam, we did not become total converts to the cause of "the other side." There was no doubt about it: Enormous suffering had been caused by the guns of the revolutionaries. Although, on scale, their destructiveness paled in comparison with the military force of the United States, too much human anguish had been carried out under the revolutionary flag. But still, we wanted to meet and learn about the men and women on "the other side." At the very least, these were people struggling for their own land, their own nation, not flying 10,000 miles across the ocean to fight in another land. And more importantly for us, we were beginning to learn about the Viet Cong not as some faceless, formless enemy "out there," but as the fathers, brothers or sisters of many of our friends in the refugee camps. We had been encouraged by their policy that insisted upon differentiating between the majority of "peace-loving" Americans and the minority who enthusiastically supported American involvement in Vietnam. Going a step further, they maintained that their enemy was the American policy, not the American people. Ironically, it would be from reflecting upon this attitude that I would eventually come again to consider Richard Nixon a decent, well-intentioned human being. It was the policy, not the person, that was unacceptable. The person—each person—deserved careful and sensitive understanding.

Now, a decade and a half after meeting the candidate who had built a career on anti-communism, I was meeting a Communist guerrilla "behind the lines." Our warm handshake dispelled any doubts I had about being welcome here. My barely coherent response revealed my utter surprise at being greeted by the man who had sent us that mysterious note weeks before.

"Le Quang Vinh! You are! Uh—er—well, I'm very happy to meet you. Uh—oh yes, my name is Kien."

"Yes, I know. We were expecting you. We're happy you came to see us. And we're happy to welcome you to liberated territory. And may I introduce you to Anh Ai," he said as he nodded toward his partner. "But let's not stand out here in the hot sun. Let's go in and relax a bit."

Putting his arm on my shoulder, Le Quang Vinh led me along the riverbank to the path from which he had appeared. Walking up an incline through elephant grass, which grew above my head, I was impressed with how difficult it would be for a "spotter plane" to detect any guerrilla presence among the surrounding foliage. At the crest of the small hill, we were suddenly standing in front of a bamboo and thatch pavilion. I marveled at the ingenious camouflaging of this guerrilla hideout, which had been invisible to me only a few yards away. Even at close range, only the thatch roof was visible as the main room of the pavilion had been dug beneath the ground surface. In addition to the surrounding grass, clusters of tall leafy bamboo trees formed an arch high above us, making this redoubt virtually immune to detection from the air.

"Do come in." Le Quang Vinh's spontaneous cheer buoyed me considerably. We filed through a short trench opening into the pavilion. "Come sit down and tell us about your trip up here."

Only when I sat down did I notice the weapons. Neat rows of AK-47's, grenade belts, B-40 rocket launchers, mortar tubes and machine guns with circular magazines lined the opposite wall—all polished and obviously ready for use.

Guns and grenades in Vietnam were as commonplace as a broom in the kitchen. Down in Quang Ngai city I had seen much bigger stuff: 105mm cannons, 1,000-pound bombs, 175mm howitzers with a 20-mile range, bulbous canisters of napalm, super-sophisticated jet fighters—all bearing the stamp: Made in USA.

Yet now, actually coming face to face with this array of Chinese, Russian and locally made weapons lining the wall startled me a bit. What had I expected in a guerrilla hideout? Olive branches and chrysanthemums? No, but still, all the guns and mortars were stark reminders to this slightly idealistic pacifist that if "the Front" took control of Quang Ngai city, they were going to use more than sweet words of persuasion.

But my thoughts of guns were soon superseded by the hospitality of my hosts. "Tell us, how was your trip up here?" began Anh Ai, who conspicuously sat next to me and seemed to carry more authority than Le Quang Vinh. I told them of the walk past Hill 10 and through the fields verdant with the crops of corn, beans and manioc.

"Oh, you've not seen anything yet!" Le Quang Vinh replied with almost boyish eagerness. "Wait until you see the areas up farther, the ones that have been liberated for many years. Up there we have vehicles, trucks, electricity, roads—large roads—whole communities of people living peacefully. You must come and visit those areas." Then turning to Anh Ai, he continued, "Don't you think we ought to invite Anh Kien to stay in liberated areas for three or four days?"

Anh Ai hesitated for a moment, so I took the opportunity to respond. "That would be fantastic! I would love the opportunity to go deeper into liberated territory, although I should mention several things: One, my colleagues back in the city are really expecting me back this afternoon. There's another thing that worries me a bit: On my way up here, two soldiers spotted me and raised a protest. I don't know if they will try to make trouble or not, but if I return this afternoon, rather than several days from now, they would probably suspect me less."

"Well, we can talk about that later," Anh Ai's tone of voice signaled a change in subject. Then he leaned forward and looked toward the far end of the pavilion, which was dark because it was completely walled in, unlike the open-walled area where we sat. "Chi oi, prepare some tea, if you will," he called to a young woman with black silken hair flowing down her back to her waist. The woman who until now had been listening curiously to us immediately went to stir up embers glowing in a mound in the back corner of the pavilion. Then Anh Ai cleared his throat as if to announce a new beginning in our conversation. "How is your family? Are they well?"

I told him that Pat and the children had gone to Saigon because we were unable to defend ourselves from the heavy bombing that was predicted should Quang Ngai city be contested. I said that they would have liked to stay in Quang Ngai if we could have been assured it would not be too dangerous for the children.

"I see. Now, tell me about Chi Thuy. How is she?" He listened with much attentiveness.

"Chi Thuy? Which Chi Thuy?" My mind was grasping vainly for the person in question.

"Thuy. You know, she works at the Quang Ngai hospital."

"I'm sorry, but I can't say I know any Thuy who works at the hospital."

"But didn't Chi Thuy arrange for you to come up here to visit us?" Anh Ai queried.

"Plan my trip up here—?" Suddenly I understood. "Oh, you mean *Chi Mai*! Yes, Chi Mai planned my trip up here. Yes, she's fine! You call her Chi Thuy. I'm sorry. I had never heard that name for her before. In the city she goes by Mai! Yes, she's fine and, if I might add, quite optimistic right now!"

Anh Ai seemed momentarily disarmed that he had been ignorant of the common name of a person with whom he apparently had considerable communication. And yet it was most common for Vietnamese revolutionaries— and counterrevolutionaries as well—to operate under assumed names. The architect of the Vietnamese revolution, Ho Chi Minh himself, had sported no fewer than ten pseudonyms in his career. So apparently Chi Mai had been using one name in ARVN zones and another in her communication with the PRG.

"Good, I'm glad to hear that," Anh Ai responded after a moment's thought. "Now tell me, what's the situation in Quang Ngai city?"

The question left me a bit uncomfortable. I tried to determine his motive for asking. Was it just an "innocent" question or would my evaluation somehow be fed into the computations of when, or whether, the PRG should attack Quang Ngai city. The Mennonite Central Committee outlined a clear policy that its personnel should under no circumstances be couriers of information with military significance for any belligerent in a conflict. But the question there before me in that guerrilla hideout illustrated the dilemma we frequently confronted in Vietnam. In Quang Ngai I would occasionally visit the American "consulate" to learn any pertinent information they might have had on the situation of refugees or unexploded munitions in the province. The American personnel were invariably friendly and eager to converse with me. They often expressed interest in my work, which took me to villages they never dared visit. "Where have your travels taken you recently, Earl?" they would frequently inquire, or "What do you hear the refugees talking about these days?" Seemingly innocuous questions, asked to demonstrate their interest in our work. And yet I was conscious of the fact that these American officials could easily use any information or evaluations I might pass along in their intelligence calculations. For that reason I had learned to respond with the most nonspecific answers possible. And now sitting in that guerrilla redoubt, I felt the same reflex toward cautious generalities.

"The town? Well, a lot of people in town are wondering what will happen. Some have left town for other places, like Danang." Anh Ai listened closely but did not press for details. There was one other specific concern he had, however.

"How many foreigners are there in town right now?"

"I can only speak for certain of one. Hiro Ichikawa, my Japanese colleague. He is also with our organization. As for other Americans, I know of none besides myself. I don't know what the plans of the American government people are, but as far as I know none of them are in Quang Ngai right now. Of course, there are a number of Indian cloth merchants and Chinese businessmen and their families in town."

"This Japanese fellow—what's he like?" Anh Ai was pleasant, yet intense.

"Excellent! Anh Hiro works with me in Quang Ngai. A very good person."

"Very well."

The female guerrilla appeared wtih the pot of the tea and set it on another bench in front of us. Anh Ai did the honors. Again, the familiar rinsing of the cups and pouring of the guest's cup first. This simple unpretentious ceremony of tea dramatized a profound commonality among the Vietnamese people that reached across the divisive lines of war. "Communist," "capitalist," "pro-Soviet," "pro-American"—whatever labels had been pinned on the people of this country over the years, the men and women on *both* sides were, most fundamentally, Vietnamese.

As we sipped tea, Anh Ai and Le Quang Vinh reiterated their invitation for me to stay in "liberated territory" for several days. For me, it would have been the fulfillment of a long-held hope. But the risks seemed too great. I again expressed my concern that I should try to return to town before the police noticed my absence. In the end, the cadres accepted my judgment.

What surprised me most about my hosts was their seemingly unqualified acceptance of me. Certainly they must have had many secrets they were not divulging to me, but I was not given to feel as though I were "on trial,"

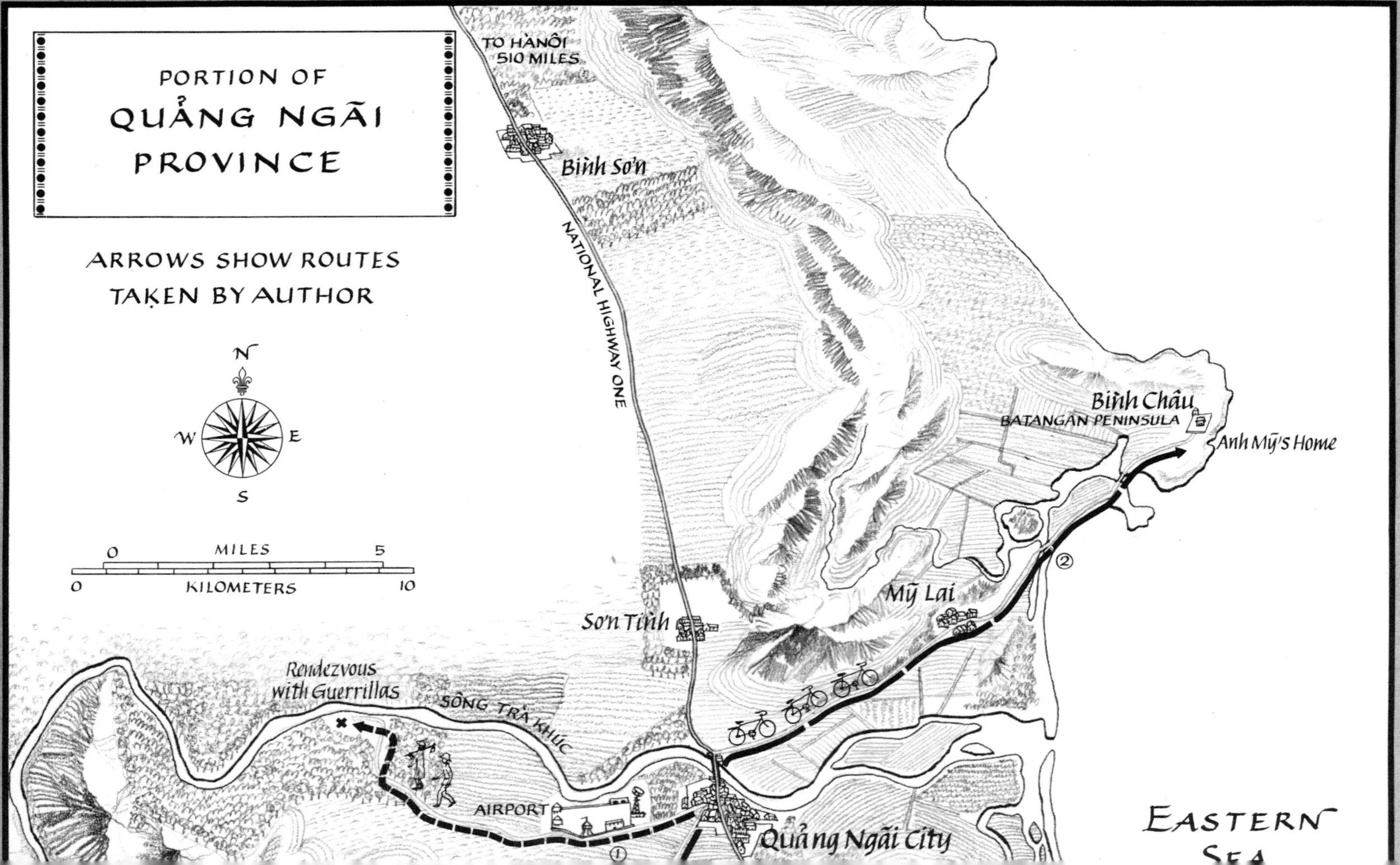

PORTION OF
QUẢNG NGÃI
PROVINCE

ARROWS SHOW ROUTES
TAKEN BY AUTHOR

N
W E
S

MILES
0   5   10
KILOMETERS

TO HÀ NỘI
510 MILES

Bình Sơn

NATIONAL HIGHWAY ONE

Bình Châu
BATANGAN PENINSULA

Anh Mỹ's Home

Mỹ Lai

Sơn Tịnh

Quảng Ngãi City

AIRPORT

SÔNG TRÀ KHÚC

Rendezvous
with Guerrillas

EASTERN SEA

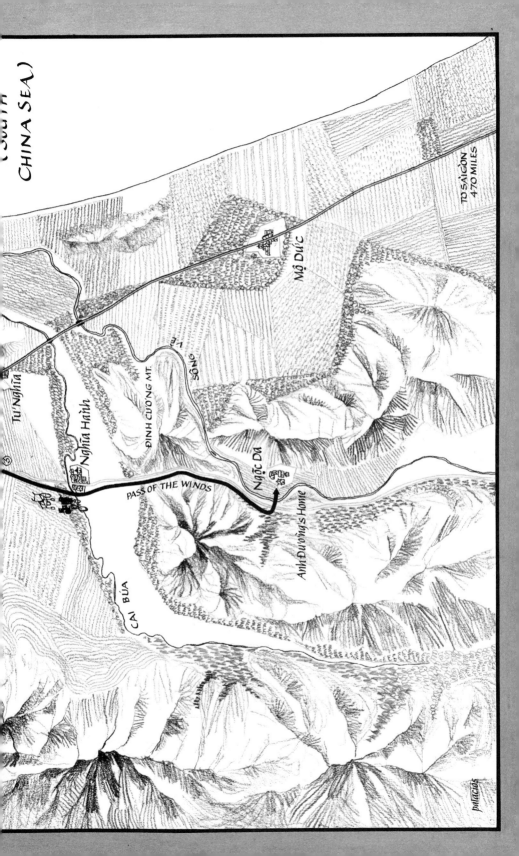

or that they were wary in any way. Their attitudes corroborated an impression about the Vietnamese revolutionaries that I had gathered from reading Liberation newspapers and meeting PRG representatives in Paris: These people were not racist in their conceptualization of the enemy. That is, they did not automatically place all Americans in the same camp. I had frequently heard their official line asserting that their enemy was U.S. imperialism. It was a small "clique" of war makers in Washington, not the American people. Indeed they knew that, at least in the later years, the majority of the American people opposed the war. It was easy for them, therefore, to jump to the conclusion that most Americans were actually sympathetic to the revolution in Vietnam. After all, had not the United States once fought against colonialists for its national liberation also? Although their assessment of American support for their cause may have been greatly inflated, it did allow them to approach foreigners open-mindedly, not automatically labeling them "enemy" merely because of their nationality. It was a far cry from the "gook-dink-slope" stereotype that poisoned many American views of the Vietnamese—all Vietnamese, friend and foe alike.

My main concern had been to raise with these PRG representatives the subject of my remaining in Quang Ngai if they would take control of the city, but the tone of our conversation obviated the need to ask. These cadres seemed to be *assuming* that I would stay in Quang Ngai. Anh Ai finally removed all doubt.

"When you go back into the city you must prepare plenty of film. You must be ready to take pictures as soon as the *bo doi* come into town! Your camera—do you have a movie camera?" he asked hopefully.

I did not tell him I expected to be deep in a bunker when the *bo doi* came into town! "No, just a regular camera," I replied.

In fact I merely had a tiny half-frame camera, which a friend had loaned me after my 35mm Ricoh had been stolen in Saigon several weeks before. If the PRG cadres were seriously counting on my staying in Quang Ngai to take photos, I was poorly equipped to fill the role.

"Well, it doesn't really matter," Anh Ai assured me. He looked at his watch and then put his hand on my shoulder. "Kien, if you are sure you should not stay with us here in the liberated zone, then you should be getting back into town before it gets too late. We don't want you to get into trouble. You know those police are sharp. They can make a lot of trouble for you. So you should probably be heading on back. We'll send an escort part way with you so you don't lose your way. All right?" Then after a pause he added, "Now, there's one other thing, but we'll have to talk about that outside."

As we stood, I noticed, walking up the hill past the pavilion, my guide, Chi Kha, who had tried to dodge any police tail by switching from her gray-flowered blouse in Quang Ngai to the navy blue one before she started our journey across the line. Here Chi Kha appeared again and—could I be seeing correctly?—now her blouse was white!

Anh Ai led me past the row of polished weapons, up the packed earth steps and outside to a clump of bamboos. I also had one more matter on my agenda.

"Anh Ai, I told you we were concerned about the safety of the children, so my wife flew to Saigon with them on Thursday. Now what do you think, would it be advisable for them to return to Quang Ngai?"

"Surely. Tell them to come back, but do it immediately. You've no time to lose. All right?" While the cadre paused, he glanced over his shoulder to make sure we were alone. "Now, Anh Kien, there's one more thing. When you get back into Quang Ngai, get together with Chi Thuy—or Chi Mai as you call her—and your Japanese friend in a place where there's a good bunker. There you must make yourself a small sign. It should be about so big." Anh Ai's fingers sketched in the air a rectangle about eight inches by six inches. "It should have a dark blue background." Now Anh Ai was whispering. "Paint on the sign the white numbers: three, five, seven. At the first sound of gunfire in the town, take this sign and hang it on the door of your house."

My mind grasped to pick up every detail of Anh Ai's instructions. Life, perhaps, depended on it! What could it all mean? Was this some secret code? Would many homes in Quang Ngai have "357" signs? Was this exclusively for us? Whatever the significance, it was imperative to remember the details.

"Hang it where? On which door? The front or the back?" The stakes seemed high enough to risk the impertinence of begging for clarification.

"Just hang it where it will be easily visible to our people. All right? Now are you sure you'll remember the number? Three, five, seven."

"Three, five, seven. Three, five, seven." I tried to burn the number into my mind. "Yes, I'll remember." Then it suddenly struck me that that was the number written on Anh Trong's hand! Of course. Anh Ai and Le Quang Vinh were political cadres. They would probably not be involved in the first assault on Quang Ngai city. Anh Trong represented the military command here at this outpost. He would coordinate the military attack on the town. He needed to know the number so that at the last minute he could inform his guerrillas to look out for—and, hopefully, to refrain from attacking—a house with a "357" sign.

"Now then, it's time to get on your way. And remember, do be careful. I hope you don't have any trouble with the police." We walked back toward the pavilion where Anh Ai introduced me to two young guerrillas. "These two fellows will show you the way back. You'll be returning a different route from the one you came." Then with a firm handshake, he and Le Quang Vinh bade me adieu. "Anh Kien, go in peace. We will meet you again."

I followed my two guides down over the side of the hillock through the elephant grass to the riverside. We started walking briskly along the coarse gravel that had been deposited along the river's edge. Within several minutes I had lost all orientation and for a moment actually thought we were heading west instead of east toward town. But I could only trust their knowledge of the terrain. After all, it was home to them.

I looked at the sun and judged it to be well after five o'clock. My pace quickened as I thought of trying to get back across the line before a suspiciously late hour. My escorts seemed to sense my urgency and soon we were actually trotting. Presently our route left the riverside and we headed across a wide sandy bank toward a wooded area. We slowed our pace somewhat when we reached a bamboo-lined trail. After a few more minutes I could see an open cornfield lying ahead. The lead guerrillas suddenly halted behind the last cluster of bamboos.

"We've got to stop here. Beyond this, the enemy could see us from Hill 10. If they saw us, they might open fire," the guerrilla said.

"Oh no, I don't want you to endanger yourselves. That wouldn't be good for any of us."

"You'll have no problem finding your own way after this. You see those thatched roofs over there in the distance? Just walk across this field toward those houses. When you get there you'll find the trail that leads back to the main road into Quang Ngai."

"Thank you very much, fellows. And I wish you peace."

"Good-by, brother. Go in peace."

With that I stepped out of the cover of the bamboos and started across the field of knee-high corn. Remembering again the lateness of the hour, I broke into a jog in the direction of the houses in the distance. Suddenly a shout came from behind. I turned and saw one of the guerrillas waving vigorously to me.

"What did you say?" I called back.

"Don't run! Hill 10—they might see you. You must *walk*—naturally—like a farmer!"

"Oh yes, of course. Yes, thank you very much. Thank you for warning me." There must have been a whole set of reflexes necessary for survival under these circumstances. My ignorance of those reflexes was dangerously apparent.

Soon I was back again in the "rice-bean" area between the two sides. As I neared the first houses, I again became concerned about my reentry into the Saigon-controlled zone. I hoped I could get back on the main road and be far from this suspicious territory before any troops or police would detect me. If I should encounter any troops along the way, what should I tell them if they inquired? I suddenly remembered that for a number of days I had considered precisely this area as a possible sanctuary should there be heavy shelling and bombing in Quang Ngai city. If I should happen to run into some ARVN troops, perhaps that would be a plausible explanation for my being in this *xoi dau* area.

I saw no people outside the first house I passed, but I soon came upon a courtyard where a man was washing his feet by an open well. The farmer appeared curious about my presence, so I called in a friendly greeting, "*Chao chu*, how are you?"

"Me? Fine. And you—are you lost?" The man seemed ready to help.

"No, I'm not lost. I live in Quang Ngai. You probably know that the town is pretty nervous right now. If the town should be shelled or bombed, do you suppose I might stay here in the countryside? I think it might be safer around here than in town."

"Well, I suppose so. I don't imagine there'd be anything wrong with that."

For all the suspicion and caution the war had created, many times Pat and I had observed a surprising openness—even instinctive friendliness—among the rural Vietnamese. Even foreigners, if polite, were treated with politeness. The term *xenophobic*—while sometimes used in foreign textbooks about Vietnam—had never seemed to us an apt description of the Vietnamese people.

Farther along the trail I sensed it might be leading me to the "International Crossroads" that I had noticed earlier in the afternoon. I was reassured by the thought that this path would enter the main road closer to the airport than the path I had taken to the aunt's hamlet earlier in the afternoon to rendezvous with Chi Kha. Certainly I was safe here. This area should not be considered suspicious by ARVN troops. Nevertheless, I was less than delighted when a handful of children spied me and came running with their familiar chant, "*Ong My, Ong My*, where are you going, Mr. American?"

"I'm going home. And you children, where are you going?" I strode quickly, hoping they would drop back.

"We want to follow you," they chorused back.

"That won't be necessary. Why don't you children go home too? All right?"

But the children and their chants stuck with me until the main road came into view. I breathed more easily, knowing that I had reached the Saigon-controlled area without detection. When I got to the main road, I would hopefully be able to flag down a Honda *xe om* and quickly ride back into town.

"*Ong My! Ong My!* STOP!" My body stiffened. That was not a child's voice. I glanced over my shoulder to see an ARVN soldier coming across a rice field from behind me. He held an M-16 in both hands, pointing it into the air.

"Where you go? Stop!" This time the order came in broken English.

Could I just ignore him? Make a break for the road? But he had a gun! No, I would have to give him at least some answer. "Home! I'm going home. To Quang Ngai. All right? It's getting late. I must be on my way. Good-bye, sir." I shouted back in Vietnamese. I turned and resumed walking slowly toward the road, hoping my pursuer would become disinterested.

The soldier's answer was emphatic. BANG! BANG! I heard the bullets whistle through the air somewhere over my head. I stopped.

"I told you to stop. I want to talk with you." He was speaking Vietnamese again as he emerged from the rice field onto the path behind me. When he came within easy talking distance, I reiterated that I needed to get home before it got too late. And once again I turned to go, desperately hoping a casual appearance on my part would dissuade him from pursuing the matter.

His response was again to cut loose with two shots over my head. As I turned to face him again, I noticed a whole squad of ARVN soldiers coming across the rice field toward us. I could see one short soldier talking vigorously into a telephone receiver connected to a field radio on his back.

The first soldier caught up to me and demanded, "Now tell me, what were you doing coming down this path?"

"I was talking to farmers out here. I was asking them if I could stay out here in the event Quang Ngai should be shelled." I was unable to keep the sharp edge out of my voice.

"What's that in your bag?" the soldier demanded.

"Bananas—just a bunch of bananas." I was thankful I had decided not to bring a camera or literature along with me, although perhaps the soldier expected me to be carrying a weapon in the bag.

"Here, let me look."

I pulled open the bag and lifted out the bunch of bananas that I had intended to give to the aunt earlier in the afternoon. Now, perhaps, the bananas would persuade this soldier of the innocence of my presence here.

The other troops were approaching me on the path. The shortest man was still chattering into the radio crackling with static. I suddenly found myself in the middle of fifteen soldiers all asking me and each other what was happening. One soldier with a brass flower on his lapel, indicating his rank of second lieutenant, stepped forward and quizzed the soldier who had stopped me.

"He speaks our language, ask him directly," the soldier told his boss.

"All right, what's the story?" the lieutenant demanded.

I repeated to the lieutenant that I had been talking with farmers along this path about the possibility of staying with them if the fighting should get heavy in the city.

"You were out in V.C. territory, weren't you?"

"Are you trying to tell me this is V.C. territory along this road?" I replied evasively.

"You're going to deny it, are you? Come with us. We're going to take a little walk."

"Where to?"

"The outpost. We've got some things to talk about. Besides, we got to wait for word from headquarters. We radioed them about you and we'll have to wait to see what they want to do."

"Well, all right, I'll go to your outpost for a short time, but to be honest,

I really have no interest in spending much time in a military outpost. I'm a civilian and I would be most uncomfortable staying in your outpost for long."

"What are you worried about? Afraid we'll be attacked or something?" one soldier taunted. "Well, just relax. If we live, you live. If we die, you die!"

The 200-yard walk to the outpost was cathartic. The physical exercise relaxed my emotions considerably. Conversation with the lieutenant became more casual. I explained our work in Quang Ngai, that we were interested in helping refugees plow up their fields. At that point I heard several soldiers murmur that they knew about the MCC work and had often seen Pat and me visit their refugee camp. Apparently they too were refugee boys who had been drafted into this unit of the ARVN militia.

The lieutenant seemed particularly eager to solicit my evaluation of the deteriorating military situation throughout the country and probable response of the United States.

"Will they bring the American bombers back in if things keep falling apart?" Now the lieutenant seemed as anxious as I had been a minute before.

"Hardly. The American Congress actually passed a law forbidding it. No American reintervention without the approval of Congress."

"Your Congress—I just don't understand. Here just recently they refused to approve the additional military aid we need to fight the Viet Cong. My unit here—well, they're pretty scared. It's hopeless if your country cuts off its support."

A private walking beside us chimed in, "Yeah, why'd your Congress vote against the military supplemental aid appropriation anyway?"

Military supplemental aid appropriation! An ARVN private—by background a peasant farmer boy who spent his time grazing the family water buffalo in the boondocks of the world where neither electricity nor few of the modernities of even the nineteenth century had penetrated—this fellow speaking the formal, up-to-date legal language of the Congress of the United States of America! Here was the lowliest soldier in one of the remotest outposts in perhaps the most "backward" province of a tiny country lost somewhere on the Asian land mass who actually believed his destiny lay in the hands of a collection of starched-shirted disputatious parliamentarians under a domed Capitol fully halfway around the globe!

Because he so believed, so it was.

Of course the anxious farmer-boy-turned-soldier had heard the "supplemental aid appropriation" language on BBC or VOA. The radio newscasts had recently been full of such talk. It was secret to no one that the Saigon military apparatus had come to be entirely dependent on the United States for its survival. More pitiful was the fact that this individual ARVN soldier felt personally and directly that dependence. He *felt* like what the Communist propaganda called him: a puppet. It was the hardest

71

pill of all for the ARVN soldier. This self-image of helplessness denied him life's blue ribbon: the ability to face one's destiny with dignity. Without that, how could he be expected to fight when the chips were down? He could only run, if but to seek a second chance to find his dignity elsewhere.

Of course, all the guerrillas I had met just an hour before also were equipped with foreign weapons. And while a congressional report had revealed that American expenditures in the war were twenty-five to thirty times those of the Soviet Union and China combined, yet the present *degree* of the NLF's reliance on foreign weapons was little less than the ARVN's. The difference was that the guerrilla believed he had additional resources available to him. Even as far as weapons were concerned, the hamlet guerrilla remembered the day when he did not have an AK-47 in hand. Or he had at least heard myriad stories from older comrades of the times when the only weapons were those captured from the French, or homemade grenades fashioned from tin cans and the TNT from dud American artillery shells. Hence he believed that if his supply of AK-47 ammunition was cut off, he could improvise again as he had done in the past. This ability to adapt, to remain flexible, to shift tactics as the situation demanded, enabled the guerrilla to avoid the debilitating self-image of dependency that sapped his ARVN counterpart.

This difference translated into that intangible stuff called morale. And never before did I understand its role so poignantly. The PRG officers I had just met were absolutely calm and confident. Here the ARVN troops walking beside me were apprehensive and confused. In spite of the fact that the troop and weapon ratios likely favored the ARVN, there seemed to be no doubt now, even before the battle, who would emerge victor.

We walked through the open gate in the barbed-wire perimeter of the Tu Thuan outpost. Inside the compound a single masonry building was divided into two rooms. The one on the right was marked by a sign: Vietnam National Police, Tu Thuan Station. We headed for the unmarked room on the left. It was the office of these "Popular Force" ARVN. Inside, the lieutenant invited me to sit down at a small table across from him. He produced paper and pen and had me write and sign a sentence saying that I was in Tu Thuan village inquiring of farmers if I could stay with them in the event of heavy shelling in Quang Ngai city. Then we waited.

They were not equipped with a stove to boil water, but their instincts led them immediately to search for tea to offer me, their unusual guest. One man had a belt canteen, which he offered. With grace and dignity the lieutenant poured the lukewarm tea into a clean rice bowl for me to drink. As always, I was moved by the unpretentious courtesy of the tea ritual. I pulled the bunch of bananas from my shoulder bag and offered them to the men around me. We ate and drank together, sharing the single bowl for the tea.

It was an unusual moment of eucharist. The tea quenched my thirst. More than that, the communion quenched my initial anger toward these men. Indeed, they were my captors, and yet the sharing evoked a common spirit among us.

A handful of young soldiers gathered around me at the table and spoke about their apprehensions of the future. Would the United States bail them out if things deteriorated more? If "the other side" seized control of Quang Ngai, what would happen to them as soldiers? Would they be killed in the fighting? Were these their last days?

I suddenly became aware that although I had considered myself a captive of these men, they were hardly free men themselves. They spoke at length of the corruption of President Nguyen Van Thieu and of nearly all the high-ranking officers in the ARVN. These young village soldiers knew that the Saigon generals had gotten rich from the war, and that if push came to shove the generals would be the first to fly off to some other country and cash in on their Swiss bank accounts. It was hardly the exemplary leadership that would instill enthusiasm in these dispirited soldiers. In their own way these troops were captives too. Captives in a war they never wanted. Captives of the majors, the colonels and the generals who forced them to take up these M-16's and fight. Captives of a generation in history when a nation on the opposite side of the globe had insisted it was "time to stop communism in Vietnam."

As we talked, darkness quietly devoured the countryside outside, leaving us stranded in the small island of light cast by a small unglobed kerosene lantern seemingly suspended from the ceiling by a black ribbon of smoke. The darkness made me anxious again. Earlier in the day Anh Trong, the guerrilla chief, had indicated they were "about to" take Quang Ngai. This Tu Thuan outpost where I now sat was located squarely between the guerrillas and the city. It would be the logical first target. A ghastly thought: to die by accident, by an anonymous piece of mortar shrapnel *in an ARVN outpost*—what an inglorious end!

I begged the lieutenant for clarification of my status. At nine o'clock he received a radio message that police from Quang Ngai city would come out to the outpost to pick me up. That, I decided, would be slightly preferable to spending the night in this vulnerable post. But an hour later the police still failed to show up. I was becoming more desperate.

"Look, how about letting me spend the night here in the village, outside the outpost. Maybe with a farmer family. Or in a vacant building. Anywhere. I'm just not comfortable here in the outpost." I was almost begging the lieutenant.

Several of the less sympathetic soldiers detected my anxiety and seemed amused at this cowardly American's discomfort. It was almost as if they believed the Americans were responsible for getting them involved in this dastardly war and, consequently, there was a certain sense of satisfaction in seeing an American hostage suffer their fate with them. One fellow taunted, "You say you would stay anywhere. How about sleeping up the road in the morgue with all the corpses!"

73

"I'd be delighted to stay in the morgue!"

The men were startled at my spontaneous response. For many of these men, the morgue would likely have been the least desirable place to spend a night. For me, I could think of no place more exempt from the possibility of attack than a morgue! After that exchange the lieutenant talked more seriously of my staying in the village. By this time, more than four hours since my arrest, he actually appeared to regret that he was responsible for me. But he was no longer free to release me. He would have to follow orders from his superiors. Another hour passed and he still was not ready to let me stay in the village.

"TA, TA, TA, TA, TA—" Suddenly everyone stiffened. Heavy machine-gun fire. From the west. *Oh God! The attack's on!* And I'm stuck in this God-forsaken outpost!

After the initial shock, the soldiers sprang to their feet and ran for their rifles. They rushed outside and jumped into bunkers and foxholes dug around the perimeter of the outpost. Their M-16's clanged as they rammed bullet magazines into the chambers. The lieutenant stood on the porch looking toward the west as another round of sustained fire shattered the night.

This is it! No time to lose! Get out of this outpost immediately!

"I'm leaving," I announced to the lieutenant. "I'm going right now !" I strode past him and out into the courtyard.

"Hold it! You're not going anywhere!" The lieutenant was firm.

"I'm sorry, but I'm getting out of here." I continued walking toward the gate that opened onto the main road. Once through the gate, I discovered that a section of the road itself was blocked off with barbed-wire obstructions.

"You can't go down that road. There are mines at the barricades," the lieutenant called from behind.

"I'm sorry, but I'm leaving. If there are mines out here, you've got to clear them away. If anything happens, you've got to accept full responsi-bility!" Naked bravado, these words, but I kept walking toward the barricade nevertheless.

The shooting from the west had just stopped and the mood in the outpost quickly relaxed. False alarm. There was no attack after all. The lieutenant came walking out through the gate and joined me on the road.

'All right," he said, "I know you don't want to stay in the outpost. I'll take you out into the village."

We walked a few more paces along the road toward the barbed-wire coils and the barricade pulled across the road. I was familiar with the way ARVN troops often set booby traps around their perimeters to prevent anyone from entering. But as we approached, the lieutenant merely pulled the barbed wire aside and opened the way for us to go. The booby trap threat, in this case, had been pure bluff.

The lieutenant sent one of the soldiers ahead of us into the village, pre-sumably to inquire where I might stay. As we wound our way between the thatch houses closed and darkened for the night, we came to a house where the front doors were open. The lead soldier announced to the lieutenant that the family had agreed to keep me for the night. The weathered farmer stood graciously in the doorway, inviting the lieutenant and me to come and sit down.

"No, no, it's no trouble at all," the farmer assured me when I apologized for inconveniencing them. "No one sleeps in that bed; you are welcome to use it," he said, pointing to a polished hardwood platform in the corner of the main room.

"I guess I'll be leaving you now. I must only ask you to report to the outpost when you get up in the morning," the lieutenant said obligingly.

"You have my promise. I am deeply grateful to you for making this possible. In fact, I'll be happy to give you my wallet or anything else I have as pledge of my intention to return in the morning."

"No, that won't be necessary. I trust your word. I'll see you in the morning. Have a good sleep."

"Thank you very much. And I hope you have a good night too."

The lieutenant gone, I relaxed considerably, knowing I was once again among unarmed and unthreatening farmers. Only then did I realize how exhausted I was. With the lack of a noontime siesta and the excitement of the afternoon, I was ready to collapse. But the farmer and more especially his fifteen-year-old son were eager to be cordial and visit with their unexpected guest. For the next thirty minutes I answered their curiosities: How come you speak Vietnamese? Do you have a wife yet? Vietnamese or American? Do you also have a Vietnamese wife? Children? What do you do in Quang Ngai? What do American people eat? ("Americans don't eat rice, do they? They just eat bread, isn't that right?") How long does it take to fly from the United States to Vietnam? Does anyone farm by hand in the United States? ("I suppose they all use machines.") I had answered those same questions literally hundreds of times in Vietnam and at this particular moment American dietary patterns or the state of U.S. agricultural technology seemed of little consequence to me, but if my hosts were eager to talk, it seemed a small price for their offering me a haven.

Finally, the farmer was kind enough to interrupt his son, "Perhaps this man would like some rest." And then looking at me, "You may sleep on that bed. No one else would occupy it anyway. We'll be sleeping over in that other room, out toward the kitchen. If there's anything you need just let us know. Oh, by the way, if there should be fighting or shelling, you're welcome to come out to the other room to use the bunker. Just feel free—"

The son reluctantly rose to shut and bolt the front door and follow his father toward the kitchen. The boy paused at the kitchen door, then turned. "Oh, there's something I should tell you. It has happened on occasion that in the middle of the night the guerrillas stop in here to pay a visit. But it's nothing to worry about. Now sleep well. Good night."

Guerrillas! That's all I'd need! If unfamiliar guerrillas were to come storm-

75

ing in here tonight and find an American sleeping in this farmer's house, who could predict their response?

Even though we were only a hundred yards or so from the outpost, I realized that it was possible that guerrillas would occasionally visit the houses in this hamlet. At night the influence of most ARVN outposts hardly went beyond their barbed-wire perimeters. And yet, I worried little about the frightening prospect. With 365 days in a year, there was little chance they would choose tonight to make their visit.

I stretched out on the plank bed, but in spite of my fatigued body, sleep was not to come. My mind—or was it my stomach?—refused to relax. What would the police have in store for me tomorrow? Should I have stayed on "the other side" as they had invited me to do? Should I be in Quang Ngai at all? Even if we should live through everything, would there be any positive contribution we could make?

Throughout the night the countryside resounded with explosions. Several times the artillery at the airpost just a half mile to the east would pierce the sleeping night. "Haa-rum. Haa-rum." Then there were the smaller explosions, the M-79 rounds, hand grenades, possibly booby traps, and the staccato of small arms and machine-gun fire. Nervous sentries, no doubt, shooting at their fears lurking in the darkness.

Hours later I realized I had hardly slept at all. Suddenly I was startled by a loud knock on the door. A voice tore through the black night.

"Open up! How about some breakfast for your revolutionary brothers!"

No, it can't be true! What now? Hide under the bed? No, if they found you hiding, you'd really be in trouble. My thoughts spun frantically. Pull a blanket over yourself. No blanket. Then just turn your face away. Maybe they won't notice. Maybe they won't even come into the house. Maybe no one will open the door for them.

But before long the farmer's son emerged from the kitchen into the main room where I lay. All was quiet as he went to pull aside the bolt on the front door. I held my breath as he slowly pushed open the door.

"Hey, hey, you were a little slow in letting us in, weren't you." The voice came from outside. Then two uniformed guerrillas stepped in through the door. Just enough light shone from the small lantern in the ancestral altar alcove for me to see the outline of their rifles. The two young men seemed to be in an expansive mood.

"Why don't you go to the kitchen with this boy and get some breakfast ready," said the taller guerrilla to his partner. "I'll see if I can find anything on the radio."

The shorter guerrilla followed the farmer's son into the kitchen and I could soon see a lantern and hear the mother chopping on a board, presumably preparing food for breakfast. The taller guerrilla stayed in the main room where I lay on the corner bed. Through my folded arms covering my head, I watched him walk toward the altar alcove and turn up the wick on the lantern. He turned toward the table in the center of the room and reached for the radio. Then he spied me! He hesitated for just an instant; then his eyes widened.

"American! What are you doing here!" There was a edge of glee in his voice. He stared closely at me. "American, do you remember me? I met you yesterday in the liberated zone!"

Saved! He knows me! I'm going to be all right. I turned over and looked at his face more closely but did not recognize him. He must have been among the group of guerrillas I had seen briefly along the riverbank the afternoon before. I felt so weak and confused I could hardly answer him. "Oh, is that so," I mumbled softly.

The young guerrilla seemed overjoyed to find me again. "Say, why don't we go out along the road and have some breakfast together. All right?"

Outside? Along the road? But we were only a hundred yards from the ARVN outpost. It was dark, to be sure, but it seemed an act of folly to take that chance.

"Well—er—thank you, but I'm rather tired. I really would like to sleep a bit more," I managed.

"All right, you rest a bit longer. I'll listen to the radio if you don't mind." He sat down on a bench by the table and turned on the farmer's shortwave Sony. Turning the dial from station to station he was apparently having trouble finding Liberation Radio on the unfamiliar dial. Finally he settled on a station playing instrumental rock, certainly not Liberation Radio! I was surprised at the "unrevolutionary" tastes of this young guerrilla who bobbed his head to the beat of the electric guitar. But at that moment I felt little inclined to fault him even though he had turned up the volume so loud that I feared it might attract the attention—and violent response—of the ARVN soldiers in the outpost. A dangerous lack of discretion it seemed to me. Perhaps he was actually taunting the ARVN!

Finally the guerrilla turned down the radio, looked at me and smiled. A smile of sublime arrogance, chilling in its cockiness. He had proved his point. He could act as he pleased and the ARVN in the outpost were too spineless to come after him. His behavior left me all the more nervous. So rash and unpredictable. So very unlike my stereotype of the disciplined no-nonsense revolutionary.

"Well, you ready to go to breakfast now?" It seemed as much a dare as an invitation, and I again declined, begging for more time to sleep. "All right, all right, I guess there's no hurry," the guerrilla replied flippantly. With that, he returned to the radio, again switching from station to station at nearly full volume.

After what seemed like a long period of time, I could see the first touches of dawn outside the open door. If these fellows expected to sneak back to "liberated area" before the ARVN could spy them, they had better get moving. In the kitchen, sounds of slurping soup indicated someone had succeeded in getting breakfast. The guerrilla by the table looked outside and turned off the radio. He stood up and walked over toward me. Now for the first time it was light enough for me to see his features more clearly. He sat on the foot of the bed and leaned toward me. Looking straight into my eyes, he asked firmly, "Why did you go visit liberated territory yesterday?"

The question hit me like a shot. I was confused. Something was wrong. I stuttered for a moment and then answered defensively, "Visit liberated territory? What are you talking about? I visited farmers in the village up the road to find a place to stay if Quang Ngai city should be shelled!" I cringed inside at my own evasiveness.

The guerrilla's eyes became more piercing than ever.

"Do you know who I am?" he asked.

"Who are you?"

He broke into a grin of smug glee. "I'm a sergeant from Hill 10."

My body went limp on the bed.

A trap! A setup! My mind raced madly over the exchange of the last hour. Miraculously, my confusion and anxiety had prevented me from playing into the suspicions of this clever sergeant. But what about the lieutenant who brought me here? Had he been informed of this sergeant's plot? Or could the lieutenant have even put him up to it? No, the lieutenant did not strike me as so devious a man. But then what about the farmer's son informing me that sometimes they got visits from the guerrillas? Certainly the boy was too innocent to be party to this sly deception. But how could I ever know?

It had all come so naturally to the sergeant. It was easy to imagine that this was not the first time he had played this trick. Might this have been a familiar ploy to try to get information or "confessions" from farmers in the "rice-bean" areas?

The ARVN "guerrilla" in the kitchen finished eating breakfast and walked out into the early morning light, carrying an M-16 under his arm. The "guerrilla" sergeant paced across the room and back, then said, "Come on, it's light outside now. How about going for some breakfast?"

Now I was ready to accept his invitation. By the time I washed at the well and combed my hair, the farmer had already left for his fields. His wife was slicing manioc to dry in the sun in large flat bamboo trays, but when I thanked her for the bed, she seemed eager not to talk.

I followed the sergeant out the path toward the road and as we passed the ARVN outpost, the lieutenant spotted us and joined us. He seemed friendly, but reserved, often deferring to the more boisterous sergeant from Hill 10. Our trio walked up the road toward a small open-air market where women lined both sides of the road with their baskets of rice, spinach-like *rau muong*, manioc, squashes and a great assortment of other foodstuffs and household items. The presence of an American, as usual, evoked a rallying cry from the village children. By the time we sat down in a small shop to have rice porridge with red peppers and *nuoc mam*, the odiferous but tasty fish sauce, the windows and doors of the small room were darkened with a screen of curious children. As we waited for the soup, the sergeant passed the time by issuing threats to the noisy children, making suggestive passes at the two attractive young women serving us and insisting that I should "take a Vietnamese wife." The lieutenant seemed hardly able to contain his amusement at the sergeant's antics, but several times he indicated flashes of embarrassment by engaging me in diversionary conversation.

My primary preoccupation at that point was the possibility that some farmer from the "rice-bean" region doing his or her morning marketing would sight me and burst out spontaneously, "Hey, there's the American I saw trotting off to the liberated zone yesterday." But if indeed among the scores of shoppers and sellers there were any who knew I had gone to "the other side," they chose to keep their peace.

After breakfast, for which the sergeant insisted on paying—that gave him more authority—we returned to the ARVN outpost. This time I was routed to the room on the right, the office of the Vietnamese National Police. The gray-uniformed policeman to whom I was introduced was polite and seemingly nervous, apparently not accustomed to dealing with American detainees. He gingerly placed in front of me a National Police Dossier form that bore the words I had written on the paper for the ARVN lieutenant the night before, that I had been inquiring of Tu Thuan farmers about a place to stay to avoid shelling in Quang Ngai city. At his behest, I signed the document.

"All right, now you are free to go," the policemen announced quietly.

"Free to go! Really! Well, that's wonderful! I thank you very much." I was surprised at my good fortune and turned to leave.

"Here we have a man ready to provide transportation for you to go into town," he said, motioning toward a stocky police sergeant on a Honda 50. The two policemen exchanged knowing glances, but said no more.

I climbed on the seat behind the sergeant and we headed toward town. As we passed the deserted ARVN shooting range just west of the airport the air was rent with an ominous whistle.

"Rrrrrr . . haWOOM! Rrrrrr . . haWOOM!" Two mortars exploded in quick succession, throwing up funnels of dirt a hundred yards to our left, just short of the airstrip. A small herd of cattle grazing close to the spot galloped across the field in terror.

"There! V.C. mortar! They're going to attack!" the sergeant called as he accelerated the cycle. All I could think about was how I could most quickly get to a bunker behind a door bearing a "357" sign.

Back in Quang Ngai city it was immediately apparent that the two exploding mortars had escalated the panic to a full pitch. People were running here and there, gathering children and possessions. Some were retreating into their houses, others were pushing carts or carrying baskets and running through the streets, presumably seeking a place of greater safety. I saw no activity at the Quaker house as we rode past.

I expected the sergeant would turn down Tran Hung Dao Street toward our MCC house, but he continued straight on Phan Boi Chau. I suddenly became aware that probably this man did not know where our house was located.

"I'll be happy to jump off right here. My house is down that street a little ways," I offered.

"Oh no, I must take you to another place," the driver replied.

"I don't understand. My home is down that street."

"But I have orders to take you to another office."

"Another office? Are you absolutely sure about this?"

"Those are my orders."

The man's insistence pleased me little and I considered jumping off the cycle and running toward our house, but I decided that move would create even more trouble, so I rode on, wondering where our destination might be. I was not long in finding out.

The Provincial Interrogation Center! I shuddered as the cycle took us right up to the high barbed-wire gate of this notorious compound. I thought I was free, and now the Interrogation Center! My eyes raced over the high fences of barbed wire, the surrounding dry moat planted with pungi sticks and mines and the watchtowers with armed guards on the four corners of the prison complex. I gripped the cycle seat as I remembered all the stories I had heard about the Interrogation Center.

It was here that Em Tu's cousin was interrogated and where they held her feet over a bucket of burning kerosene to force her to say she was a Communist agent.

It was here that a young ARVN lieutenant friend of ours had worked eight years before and refused to let us visit his work because "you might not be able to take it."

It was here that we heard 150 anti-Thieu students from Saigon had been brought and incarcerated in a small room for two years, many of them reportedly losing the use of their legs because of lack of exercise.

It was here that the "trusties," who had authority over a cell of ten or twenty persons, were local thugs or common criminals, chosen on the basis of who would be the most effective in beating and intimidating the other "political" prisoners.

It was from this Interrogation Center that we received reports of a whole catalogue of brutalities used to exact information from political suspects: electric probes applied to all parts of the body, kicking, beating, sexual assaults, especially on the women, forcing lime water down the nose of a suspect and then beating on the stomach to make the person vomit—the list went on.

And now here I was about to be ushered into the Quang Ngai Provincial Interrogation Center.

The barbed-wire gate swung open. Then the second gate opened too, the armed guards waving to my driver. We drove right up to the office and I was motioned to enter the building as my escort turned his Honda and drove off. Inside the barrackslike office building I was invited by a guard to sit down, but only for a minute, as I was soon being introduced to a Major Hoa, the director of this "Quang Ngai Police Office," as he called it. Actually the main police headquarters was a block up the street, but apparently the vernacular title of "Interrogation Center" used by everyone in town was not dignified enough for these officers.

Major Hoa was given the police document with my signed statement. As he read the document I glanced around the room where we sat. The major's office had the feel of a command bunker; perhaps it was just that. There was not a window in the room. The walls of concrete block looked solid, likely lined with sandbags on the outside. The three main walls were covered from ceiling to floor with U.S. Air Force maps of Quang Ngai Province. Each of the maps bore a different title: "Enemy Initiated Incidents," "Enemy Forward Positions," "National Police Positions." Each map was covered by a transparent celluloid sheet with a series of X's, O's, arrows and jagged lines written in brilliant red and yellow wax pencil.

"Now then, you say here you were checking with farmers about staying with them if the town should be attacked. Do you have any more to add?" As a spider to a fly caught in his web, the major could afford to be gracious and diplomatic in his approach. He seemed to enjoy the opportunity to interrogate his unusual prisoner.

After a few minutes of questions and answers, during which the major never asked directly whether I had visited "the other side," he finally left the room, leaving me to be entertained by a rotund assistant who had joined us. From outside the room I could hear the muffled voices of the major talking with some of his men. In a short time I heard static and voices from an adjacent building, calling out in what sounded like radio jargon.

". . . found walking in Tu Thuan village . . . what location? Over."

The middle-aged man in the room tried nobly to put me at ease. "Aren't you the person I see riding around town with two children? The one child sits on the rack behind your seat on the bicycle and you carry the other one in a carrier on your back. Isn't that you?"

The voice called into the radio again, "Roger. The Popular Forces station at Tu Thuan Village. . . ." Apparently the major or one of his men was trying to get more information from the ARVN Popular Forces unit that had arrested me the day before.

"Yes, that's me all right," I responded.

"Well, then I know about you. My daughter has visited your wife several times at your home. She has a great deal of respect for you. She says you wash your clothes at the well just like all the Vietnamese in the neighborhood. And she says your wife is beautiful, so much like a Vietnamese woman."

"Oh thank you, that's a very nice compliment."

For the following half hour the heavy-set gentleman performed yeoman's duty in trying to entertain me with conversation. I soon learned that he was not interested in interrogating me about the activities of the last twenty-four hours; indeed, he conspicuously avoided the subject. He seemed rather to regret that I had befallen the inconvenience of arrest and wanted to make my time in the Interrogation Center as pleasant as possible. He spoke of losing his considerable landholdings during the Viet Minh era when the precursors of the PRG controlled Quang Ngai Province, so his ideology took a decidedly anti-Communist bent. Still, he seemed to be a reasoned man. I could not imagine this man beating a suspect to secure information. And yet I remembered that my ARVN friend who once worked here was a professing Christian, among the most easygoing and considerate in the youth group at the local church. Either these men were capable of two profoundly different personalities or else the Center had other men hired specially to perform the "dirty work" of interrogation.

Exhausted, I asked the assistant if I might lie down to sleep a while. The man was eager to oblige and after bringing me a soft drink and a roll of empty sandbags for a pillow, he left me alone in the room. I lay on a long couch and fell into my first deep sleep in nearly thirty hours. Even so, my sleep was punctuated with dreams of screaming shells and exploding bombs. I woke with a start and sat up on the couch. In the moment it took me to gain my bearings, I found myself staring at a flip chart displaying an organizational schematic. Each major and minor box on the chart bore a title and an accompanying number, such as "F.6.32" or "F.6.18." A scanning of the chart soon revealed that all the numbers began with "F.6." I suddenly made an association. When the CIA's Phoenix program of tracking down and assassinating PRG suspects had been officially phased out because of criticism in the United States, several antiwar journals carried charges by former American intelligence agents that the United States was establishing a similar, but even more clandestine, operation under the code name "F-6." Here in the Quang Ngai Interrogation Center I was seeing my first corroboration of the existence of the "F-6" program! I considered copying the organization chart into my pocket notebook but decided that such action would hardly endear me to my captors in the event, say, that Major Hoa walked in unexpectedly. I was even able to resist the temptation of exploring a further curiosity, a folder lying in the center of the major's desk marked *Toi Mat.* Top Secret.

Being alone, I wandered to the door of the office. In the courtyard a group of men were huddled together under an overhanging roof to escape the light rain that had just begun falling. A visible strain was written on the men's faces. They paced nervously. Through the open door I could catch snatches of their conversation.

". . . the attack could come any time."

"The roads are cut north and south, they say."

". . . if we just took off and left this place."

"We couldn't do that, we don't have release orders yet."

Agonized men, these. These were likely the men who did the "dirty work" in the Interrogation Center. Here were the guards, the investigators, the interrogators, probably even the torturers. But now caught in the blue flame of the torch of history, these men were speaking less like executioners than like victims. There seemed a certain imminent fulfillment of the biblical assertion that "all they that take the sword shall perish by the sword." But while these men had likely performed a whole catalogue of brutal and in-humane deeds, could one just write them off as evil? What circumstances of war had pressed these men into the mold they now fit? What about their bosses in Saigon—even Washington—who had channeled them into this disgusting occupation? Where did responsibility lie?

At one o'clock the heavy-set assistant returned and persuaded me to join him for some lunch. Although food was not my primary concern, I could not help but respond to the man's sincere kindness.

"I don't really have the authority to do this, but I'm going to take you out of the center to the house across the street. We can get a bowl of soup there," he said.

He motioned to the guards to open the double set of gates and we walked across the street to a house that belonged to a furniture maker who was an acquaintance of the assistant. The assistant asked the furniture man if he could prepare a bowl of soup for the guest. The man immediately opened a package of instant noodles and soaked them in boiling water from a Ther-mos bottle.

I was suddenly overcome with the thoughtfulness of the gesture. All around us tension was building. It was as though the ground was rumbling and churning beneath our feet, as though the earth was threatening to burst with a volcanic explosion of fire and war. The men around me feared that they too would be smothered in the merciless lava of revolution. Yet on the brink of that awesome eruption, this man offered what he had: a bowl of noodle soup.

Back in the Interrogation Center I was eager to get further disposition of my status from Major Hoa, but the men there informed me that the major had left the compound. I learned he was ferrying boxes of police dossiers to the nearby athletic field to have them shipped out of Quang Ngai. And sure enough, momentarily, I saw an Air America helicopter rise from the vicinity of the soccer field and disappear over town. Soon a jeep came roaring into the compound and Major Hoa jumped out of the driver's seat. He issued commands to the men who immediately began loading cartons of documents and dossiers into the back of the jeep. When the major stalked through his office to pick up some folders, I accosted him.

"Excuse me, sir. I know you must be quite busy, but there's something I want to tell you. You know my wife and I have been living here in Quang Ngai for five years. We have attempted to see if there might be some small way in which we could assist the farmers of this province." The major was listening, so I decided to continue. "Now the situation is very unsettled, but I have decided that I want to stay here in Quang Ngai regardless of what happens."

The major listened without obvious reaction, but he could not have missed the import of my words. It could only mean that I hoped to stay in Quang Ngai even if his enemy, the Viet Cong, should take control of the province. The major turned to go; then, without facing me, said, "I'll try to have some answer for you by three o'clock."

An hour later the gates to the compound flew open once again and the major stepped out of his jeep. He hurried in and out of offices giving orders to his men to package more documents. Then he came over to his office door where I was standing. His voice was quiet and sincere.

"Sir, I'm sorry we created this inconvenience for you. I trust you will understand we were only performing our duty. And now you are free to go."

Before I could express my gratitude, Major Hoa's face indicated he had something more to say. "And as far as what you told me—about staying in Quang Ngai regardless of what happens. If that's what you want, I hope you can do it."

The barbed-wire gates swung open once more as I set my feet toward home. Free at last. But my soul churned on unabated. Perhaps the town was about to be stormed by attack, but I had to walk. Even though it seemed urgent that I get to the bunker quickly, I could not bring myself to flag down a *xe om* cycle to drive me home. The terror and hope of that moment had to be kneaded into my being by the exercise of my limbs. Barely conscious of the frantic movement of traffic on the street, I walked toward home.

The universe was tottering on the awesome fulcrum of time. What was the metaphor that could give meaning to this moment? Was it the crucifixion? Stretched on a rack between heaven and hell? With the very powers and principalities slashing about in that cosmic cataclysm of the ages?

Or was this the eye of the hurricane? That noiseless, vacuous interregnum dividing the winds that slash west from those that slash east?

Or was this that rapturous and terrible final moment when the mother's cervix dilates completely and all the force of nature groans in mighty contractions to bring new life into being?

My mind reeled with the memories of the preceding day. Within just a few hours I had met the antagonists on both sides of this bloody war. Men engaged in an all-out contest of life and death. And yet men—like Le Quang Vinh on one side and Major Hoa on the other—who had treated me with fairness and even magnanimity, even to the point of Major Hoa's supporting my staying if his enemy took control of the town. These men—all capable of decency—enemies in battle!

In this ultimate moment of truth it seemed irrelevant even to ask the question "why." It was as though in greatest extremity one needed not reasons, but only to be able to joy or grieve in what is.

When I walked back through the alley into our courtyard Hiro and Trinh were scurrying about packing up food and clothes to take with them to the Quaker house.

"Kien, you're back!" Em Trinh cheered when she saw me coming into the courtyard. Hiro looked up and murmured, "*Hay qua!* Beautiful! Beautiful!" But we were not to be allowed to discuss the past day. Just then the town resounded with two exploding mortar rounds. If shells were to be bursting all over town, we had no time to lose in getting to the bunker in the Quaker house. But there was one more errand to run before it was too late.

"Hiro, I've got to get hold of a better camera. That's the one thing they mentioned we could do: take pictures."

"Sounds good. Here's the money I brought from Saigon."

"No, I won't take the money now. I'll just see if I can find anything. I'll be back shortly."

I raced around town on the scooter, stopping at every photo shop I knew to inquire about a camera. Quang Ngai was hardly the photo capital of the world, although there were a number of shops that specialized in taking sentimentalized portraits of lovers and families. I had nearly completed the circuit of shops, finding nothing but a few ancient cameras, which would have been practically worthless for my purposes. At the last shop along the route the shopkeeper produced an old box camera and a Mamiya/Sekko single-lens reflex. The latter was used and the light meter did not work, but the lens looked good and the shutter seemed to operate well.

"Seventy thousand piasters and I'll throw in this flash attachment," the shopkeeper answered when I asked his price.

"How about fifty thousand?"

"No, I'm not overly eager to sell it, but since you ask, I'll give it to you for seventy thousand. You can take it or leave it."

That would be about $100. "I'll be back shortly. I've got to go get some money," I told him. Outside the shop I gave the scooter starter a kick and was about to speed home when someone called from behind. It was Major Loc, my ARVN friend who worked with the Joint Military Team in Chu Lai.

"You're still here!" he shouted as he ran toward me. "So glad to see you. Lots of people have left town, but I'm staying." The major, now standing by my side, swallowed deeply. "I'm taking my family out to the countryside so they will not be in the city if it's shelled, but I'm staying." I felt a certain respect for the major's decision, although for the time being the prognosis did not look good that Major Loc would soon get to build his "miniature Quang Ngai Disneyland."

Just then the neighborhood reverberated with an exploding mortar shell. Doors and windows rattled and the shrapnel and debris from the explosion clattered on the tin house roofs around us.

85

"I'll see you again, Kien," the major called as he raced down the street. I sped home and grabbed bundles of piaster notes and within a minute or two was back at the camera shop. The front of the shop was wide open but now the premises were vacant. I walked into the room behind the shop calling for the proprietor. There was no reply. I checked the desk drawer where I saw him place the camera I had bargained for. The camera was there. Should I just take it and pay the man later? I walked out into the open patio behind his shop to call for the man. I was about to leave when I heard a faint call in response. I could not imagine who could be answering from so great a distance. Shortly the man emerged from a mound right in the center of the patio. Only then did I realize the mound was actually a bunker. The man and his family had taken cover after that last shell exploded so close by.

"I'm sorry to have disturbed you. I know this is a strange time to buy a camera, but if you are still willing, here is the seventy thousand piasters."

"Certainly, certainly," the shopkeeper said as he hurried to the desk to hand me the camera.

"I would like to buy some film and flash bulbs too, if you don't mind."

In a demonstration of consumer protection unbecoming to the moment, the camera man carefully packaged the flash attachment, bulbs and film together with the camera to insure nothing would break. I ran out to the scooter. The photo man headed back to his bunker.

As I once again drove into our alley I saw our landlord, Mr. Chau, pulling shut the doors to his house. I waved but it seemed apparent that now was not the time for a casual conversation. I noticed several children through the door, so apparently all the Chau family had stayed in town.

Hiro, Em Trinh, and I loaded ourselves and a few belongings onto the scooter and sped up the road past the electric company, the pagoda, the military camp, police headquarters, and the hospital. Chi Mai and Anh My were waiting for us at the Quaker house. They had already learned of my arrest from a friend who had seen me escorted through town in the morning by the police sergeant.

"Those scoundrels. I hear they got hold of you. Are you all right, Kien?" Chi Mai called out when we walked into the house.

"All right? Sure, I'm just fine. But I must say, Chi Mai, you certainly do plan interesting Sunday afternoon walks for your friends!"

Chi Mai couldn't resist a laugh. She likely thought my run-in with the ARVN was healthy for my education. "I'm just glad you're all right," she said. "Now what do you have to tell us?"

"First," I said, "just what is your name anyway, Chi Thuy!" Chi Mai laughed again, enjoying the added sense of mystery that her pseudonyms gave her. "But now, down to business," I continued, "we ought to be fortifying our bunker. The offensive could be coming any time. And finally— get this, will you—we are to be preparing a sign, about so big"—I demonstrated with my hands—"with a blue background and painted with the white numbers: 357. Then, at the first sound of gunfire in town we are to hang that sign on the front gate! There, what do you think of that!"

The group murmured their astonishment. The announcement was just unusual enough to be a credible message from the PRG. A secret code. Chi Mai listened carefully without expressing surprise.

"Fine," she said simply, "we should prepare the sign right away."

Hiro and I went through the house and scrounged up a can of white paint and a brush. We found a key rack that could be converted into a sturdy and visible sign. After removing all the keys and hooks we painted a large "357" on the board. As extra insurance, we found several other small boards and made three "357" signs, one for every possible door.

Hiro and I prepared the signs in silence. When we did speak it became obvious that we were both thinking of the biblical image of the Passover, the "357" sign reminiscent of the blood on the lintel of the houses to be spared.

"I would like to place a '357' sign on every door in Quang Ngai city," I murmured as I watched Hiro painting the numbers on the board.

"Really?" Hiro exclaimed. "That's exactly what I was thinking."

That evening eight persons gathered around the dining-room table for supper. In addition to Hiro, Em Trinh, Chi Mai, and me there were four other staff workers from the Quaker Rehabilitation Center. Of the six Vietnamese present, three had artificial legs as a result of American or ARVN mines, at least two had parents killed by ARVN or U.S. shelling, and at least two had spent time in South Vietnamese prisons.

The tension in town built steadily through the early hours of the evening. None of us ventured from the house for fear that the remaining equanimity in the town would suddenly give way to irrational outbursts of violence and terror. My wife, Pat, had often commented that she never visited any country of the world, including the United States, where as a woman she felt so totally free of personal threat as in Vietnam. In spite of the war, which was the most inhumane slaughter we had ever witnessed, Pat had never feared that Vietnamese men would attempt to harass her in any way. And in spite of my arrest of the preceding afternoon, I could concur with that evaluation. Even with all the violence around us, we had never thought of the Vietnamese as a violent people. On the contrary, we had come to know them, even the soldiers in most cases, as gentle and reasonable.

But if the total social order should suddenly collapse, and if the thousands of troops around Quang Ngai were suddenly faced with the fear of imminent death, who could predict their reaction? Would the ARVN blame their loss on the Americans and look for the first white face on which to vent their wrath?

Darkness fell and I went to the upstairs bedroom to spend some moments alone with my thoughts and the journal, which Pat had mistakenly left behind when she and the children left four days earlier. The head medic of the Rehab Center appeared and saw me sitting on the bed. He apparently assumed, as Vietnamese often did, that a friend sitting alone is actually lonely and will be cheered by company. The medic sat beside me on the bed.

"You're thinking of Pat and your children, aren't you?" he said quietly.

"Yes, I guess I was. And what about your family. Where are they?"

"I took them to the countryside this afternoon, so I'm confident they'll be safe. I returned to town to be available for work in the hospital in case there is heavy fighting." He paused a moment. "It must have been hard for you and Pat to separate during this time, Kien. I must say that I have tremendous respect for Pat. I now understand how strong a woman she is— letting you stay like this. I know it was more difficult for her to go than for you to stay." I was moved by the medic's uncommon empathy.

For the next thirty minutes the medic gave an animated monologue on Vietnamese revolutionary history. With a familiarity as spontaneous as if he had just read of their exploits in the afternoon newspaper, he spoke of obscure historical figures from previous millennia down to the present. It appeared that this medic, who himself had spent several terms in prison on charges of supplying medical assistance to the PRG, viewed the American war in Vietnam and the present explosive moment as but one of many watersheds in Vietnamese history. As so many times previously during thousands of years of Vietnamese history, the people were rising up once again to expel the influences that divided them. He was sure the Vietnamese people soon would again be united in one nation.

Swept up by the broad strokes this medic was brushing onto the canvas of history, for the moment I felt a new relaxation, the personal liberation of seeing my own existence take on the significance of a mere droplet in a surging river. The fate of any particular drop became less important. Paramount was the flow of the river itself: the survival of the Vietnamese people as a strong united family.

We were suddenly jerked into the present with Anh My's excited voice calling up the staircase, "The soldiers are coming into town! The street is full of troops and trucks!"

Then it dawned on me that the noise level on the street had increased over the last minutes, but with the medic's captivating stories neither of us had paid attention to it. When we went downstairs and peered out the windows from the darkened living room, we could see the turmoil on the street. Truckloads of ARVN soldiers were roaring full throttle down toward the center of town. The truck beds were jammed with standing soldiers, while others sat on the hoods or hung onto the doors. Within minutes the street was congested with people—soldiers and civilians—running down the street, some trying to grab onto the trucks, some weaving their Honda cycles through the crowded street. Truck drivers leaned on their horns to plow a way through the surging crowds. Several tanks thundered down the street, narrowly missing people on foot and on bicycles.

Why the panic? We had not heard any fighting west of town. To the best of our knowledge, "the Front" had not even launched an attack. Where were the troops going? If they had given up the outposts west of town, that meant Quang Ngai was totally vulnerable to attack.

The panic-stricken troops continued their frenzied retreat for more than half an hour, sucking many townsfolk in their wake. Around eight-thirty the din subsided for a period, with only occasional women with shoulder baskets or men on bicycles rushing past the house.

About fifteen minutes later the street filled with people again—this time heading in the opposite direction! Now what? Had the retreating column run into an ambush on the opposite side of town only to turn around and head back toward the west? Trapped on all sides with no safe place to run?

But we soon observed that the ARVN troops were conspicuously absent from this crowd. This crowd had no trucks or tanks, no guns or uniforms, and while these people were excited, they were not as panicky as the previous crowd. All this made it seem safe enough to leave the haven of our darkened living room and venture outside.

Out on the street we noticed that nearly all the people were carrying large cartons or full bags of rice. On their shoulders, in their arms, on shoulder poles supported by two people, strapped onto the backs of bicycles and Hondas—bags of rice and boxes of C-rations! We soon got the story. After all the ARVN troops fled town, running north toward the port base of Chu Lai, the townsfolk broke into the military warehouse and were making off with the supplies! The people were laughing and calling to their friends and neighbors to cash in on the loot.

The uncontrolled panic of the previous hour was being supplanted by a new mood of festivity and bonanza. For the growing stream of people toting their booty of rice and C-rations, the absence of the ARVN troops had a bright side. There was something in it for them.

Hiro and I walked down the poorly lit street to absorb the excitement of the crowds. We encountered a group of Hre tribal people with baskets strapped on their backs and small babies sheathed to their hips with blankets. These darker-skinned people wandered about anxiously. As opposed to some tribes that identified more closely with the NLF, the Hre had long been a target of recruitment by the United States Special Forces. After the American troop withdrawal, many of the Hre became unemployed and were "refugeed" into Quang Ngai city.

"My family—don't know where go," one man with green army trousers and a plain khaki shirt said to us in broken Vietnamese. "Trucks go. They not take us. These people in street get rice. No rice for us. Now Viet Cong come in. What happen to us?"

An ARVN soldier apparently from the neighborhood saw Hiro and me along the street. He was sobbing as he spoke to us, "Say, brothers, do you think we can live? Where can I go? I'm so afraid."

After an hour or so of walking along the street Hiro and I returned to the house for our bicycles. As we rode down Phan Boi Chau, the crowds seemed to be dispersing somewhat. But when we approached the Hoang Hoa Tham military camp we had to push our bikes through the streams of people still milling in and out of the camp searching for any booty left behind. A green and white police jeep was stalled in the middle of the street and coils of barbed wire lay tangled over the road, making progress slow. After we negotiated our bicycles past the military camp, we had easy riding again. Here and there the street was strewn with paper and broken glass, the detritus of the retreating army. The Buddhist pagoda was closed and dark.

We pedaled on past the Provincial Interrogation Center—my place of detention just eight hours before. Now the watchtowers on the four corners of the barbed-wire perimeter were vacant. One set of double-barbed-wire gates stood open and the other set was unlocked. The guardhouse at the gate stood empty. In the open courtyard in the middle of all the detention barracks a large circle of flames silently lapped at piles of papers. Apparently Major Hoa had been unable to ship all his dossiers to Danang on the morning's helicopter flights. The rest were now going up in smoke. A yellow and red Saigon Government flag still hung on a short mast atop the southeast watchtower.

We pedaled on. The street was noiseless but for the rattle of our bicycle chains over the sprockets. Down in the heart of town shops and houses were closed up. The steel accordion doors were pulled over the entrances and padlocked in the center with heavy chains. On some of the houses the padlocks were on the inside, indicating that some occupant was still in the house. On others, the locks hung on the outside: The occupants had fled.

We reached the town square where the canopied pedestal of the traffic policeman lay overturned in the street. We turned right on Quang Trung Street, the section of National Highway One that ran through Quang Ngai. The restaurants, the *pho* soup shops, the radio stores, the bookshops, and the pharmacies were all tightly closed and quiet. We had no way of knowing the indescribable carnage that was, at that moment, taking place on that road twenty kilometers to the north.

At the Esso station two drunken or delirious ARVN soldiers staggered down the street, M-16 stocks dragging on the sidewalk, stragglers who had apparently missed or ignored the evacuation trucks.

We turned west on Tran Hung Dao, the hypotenuse that angled back up to Phan Boi Chau. Stopping at our alley, we pushed our bikes past Mr. Chau's house, which was shuttered and still. Our house was still locked and intact, just as we had left it at six o'clock that evening. We headed back up the street toward the Quaker house. That section of Tran Hung Dao had no streetlights. A "fulling" moon, though obscured by a filmy cloud, offered enough light to silhouette the coconut palms and motionless bamboos. A stray dog loped across the street in front of our bicycles and disappeared into a dark alley.

Behind the Quang Ngai Province Office tips of yellow flames danced into visibility above the surrounding concrete wall—more documents being deprived prospective new province chiefs. We pedaled past the Quang Ngai Electric Company. The diesel generators were humming as usual, monotonously oblivious to any changes in town. But the premises appeared vacant. Were the operators gone?

Tran Hung Dao joined Phan Boi Chau at the pagoda. The military camp was now quiet. The barbed concertina still snaked across the street forcing Hiro and me to steer carefully through the maze in single file. The disabled police jeep still occupied its conspicuous position in the center of the road.

We arrived back at the Quaker house and jumped off our bicycles outside the gate. It was still unlocked, but we paused, neither willing to break the haunting mood of the night. Hiro looked at his watch. "Seven minutes till midnight."

We both laughed softly. The irony of it all. Rarely before in five years in this town had I been on the streets past the eleven o'clock curfew. But now, at the close of March 24, 1975, the most tumultuous and fearful day in recent Quang Ngai history, we had casually ridden our bicycles all over town at midnight.

Yet it was obvious that the freedom we felt to move through town had nothing to do with legal curfews. The town at that moment was cradled in a strange peace. The town was free, devoid of any political or military power structure. For perhaps the first and last time in decades there was no army of any kind in Quang Ngai city. We stood in a vacuum, as on an empty bridge between two kingdoms. The most reassuring phenomenon in that nocturnal interregnum was as basic as every father's axiom to his bickering children: It takes two to fight. With the Saigon Army out of town, there would be no fight.

It seemed that at such a consequential point in Vietnam's history we should stay awake to witness the unfolding drama. But there was nothing to witness. The town was still. So for lack of anything better, Hiro and I locked the gate and went into the house.

Most of our group had already settled in for the night, but Chi Mai had waited up for us.

"How do things look downtown?"

"Quiet. Absolutely quiet. Looks like a peaceful night in the making."

"What about the sign? Who's going to put up the sign if we need it?" Chi Mai wanted all the details covered.

"Well, Anh Kien, that sounds like a good job for you," Hiro laughed.

Given the peacefulness of the night I saw no reason to protest. Certainly we could not expect Chi Mai to strap on her artificial limbs and negotiate her way to the front gate with a sign if there should be shelling or shooting in the town.

"Sure, no problem." I picked up the converted key rack and admired the bright "357." The paint was dry and then, suddenly concerned for detail, I penciled in a dark blue background around the numbers as Anh Ai had instructed. I tested the hanging wire of the sign for strength. Everything

91

was ready to go. I placed the sign in the center of the dining table where it would be easy to find.

"Good night, Chi Mai."

"Sleep well, fellows."

The four women were sharing the back bedroom adjacent to the kitchen and the head medic and Anh My were sleeping on sofa cushions on the living-room floor, so Hiro and I were left to occupy the upstairs bedroom. We stretched out on the single beds on opposite sides of the room. I had gotten virtually no rest in the last forty hours and now perhaps I could get a long stretch of sleep uninterrupted by warfare.

2:15 A.M., TUESDAY, 25 MARCH. Ta, ta—ta, ta, ta. Five shots in quick succession. Or was it just a dream? Hadn't all the ARVN left town? Who could be shooting? Wait—could it be! Through my mosquito net I could see that Hiro was also sitting up in his bed.

"Did you hear that!" Hiro muttered in a hoarse undertone.

"Sounded like shooting to me, but who would be—hey, you don't suppose—!" We both jumped out of bed and crawled out a small trapdoor that led to the front-porch roof. Crouching low so as not to be visible from the street, we propped on our elbows and peered down on the street in front of the house.

There they were! Three guerrillas with AK-47's, green uniforms and floppy cloth hats, standing calmly on the street not far from the Quaker house gate.

"The sign! Kien, the sign!" Hiro was already retreating toward the bedroom and I followed suit. I ran downstairs past the other occupants of the house who were also stirring and grabbed up the sign from the dining table. Unbolting the rear kitchen door, I soon found myself in the narrow corridor between our house and the neighbor's block wall. I walked quietly out toward the street, now wondering why I had so quickly accepted the honors of hanging the sign. Nearing the front of the house, I could hear voices coming from the street. Standing in the shadows at the corner of the neighbor's house, I could see a group of neighbors already gathering around the two young guerrillas. The third guerrilla had already left. The shorter of the two seemed to be doing most of the talking. I could hear him plainly.

"You need run no more! Peace has come to Quang Ngai! But if you want to travel anywhere, feel free to go. Just carry no weapons with you!"

A murmur of approval rose from the gathering crowd of people. I took the opportunity to dart across the patio to hide behind the large masonry gatepost. How would the guerrillas respond to the sight of an American? Would they know the significance of "357"? From my vantage point behind the gatepost, I fastened the sign onto the hurricane fencing of the gate. Then I turned and retreated into the house.

"They're here! Right out in front of the neighbor's house. What are you all waiting for?" I announced back in the house. Hiro was already walking out toward the front of the house and the others were crawling out of bed or putting on their sandals. Chi Mai was strapping on her legs.

"Did they see you?" Chi Mai's voice snapped with excitement.

"Not yet. But everything seems peaceful enough. I've got to get my camera." I grabbed up the newly purchased camera from the desk in the center bedroom and fumbled to push a bulb into the flash attachment as I ran out the corridor to the street again. Hiro unlocked the gate and then stood nonchalantly in the open gate, watching the guerrillas and the swelling group of neighbors who were coming out of their houses to meet the town's newcomers. One of the guerrillas was making his announcement to the people again.

"Hello friends, be at peace. Just stay calmly where you are. Tomorrow the *bo doi* will bring tanks into town to guarantee your security!"

Both guerrillas were equipped with AK-47's and belts loaded with grenades. Both the belts and the grenades appeared to be American made. Captured matériel, no doubt. But their manner was pleasant and expansive. The shorter guerrilla could hardly contain his elation.

"Look brother," he said to his comrade and to the group in general, "everyone is coming out to greet us. Isn't this wonderful!"

Hiro's curiosity could be restrained no longer and he wandered into the street with me close behind. As we approached the group, one guerrilla suddenly spotted us. He quickly nudged his partner with his elbow and both of them fell silent and stared at us for a moment. They turned to the group of neighbors and without saying a word nodded their heads toward us as if to ask who we were.

"Oh, don't worry about them. They just do charitable social work. They help the people. They're not like the other Americans!" One woman in the group volunteered heartily. Other neighbors echoed agreement and the guerrillas seemed to relax a bit.

"Well, if they help the people they're free to live here just like anyone else," the taller guerrilla finally ventured to the neighbors. He then continued talking with the group about how the *bo doi* would come and organize the total liberation of Quang Ngai city.

I was eager to photograph the event but was a bit apprehensive about bthe guerrillas' reaction to a camera, let alone a flashbulb illuminating the scene. I raised my camera to my chest where they could see it clearly. They seemed to be indifferent to the camera, so I pressed the shutter, sending a flash over the dark street. The taller guerrilla shifted nervously on his feet. But he did not appear upset with the camera, only embarrassed and bashful that he had been singled out for a photograph. When I aimed the camera in the direction of the shorter guerrilla, he broke out with a grin worthy of the elation he was feeling with his triumphal entry into Quang Ngai city. Yet his reservations concerning us persisted.

"This American probably has a lot of misconceptions about the revolu-

The boyish grin on this first "enemy" guerrilla in Quang Ngai was as surprising as his words: "You need run no more. Peace has come to Quang Ngai!"

tion," he announced to the people after I had taken his picture. "He might help the people, but he doesn't really know what we're all about. He's got a lot to learn." With that he picked up his AK-47 and made a move to walk up the street. "So long for now, good people, we must go spread the word to other neighborhoods."

Several of the group looked at Hiro and me for our reactions. I smiled, an exaggerated smile of self-defense. The directness of the guerrilla's comment sharply contrasted with the frequent deference Vietnamese paid to foreigners. Had his remarks not been directed at me, I would have been more admiring of his forthrightness.

One of the neighbor men tapped me on the shoulder and said, "Don't worry. They won't harm you. All will be well—I'm sure everything will be all right." I quickly saw that the man was even more nervous than I. "I'm a—well, I used to be a soldier. I am staying in this house," he said, pointing to the house behind us. "When I heard those shots and looked out to see those guerrillas in the street, my heart was pounding—pounding nine beats a second, brother!"

The neighbors around us chattered excitedly.

"Impressive, weren't they!"

"Tomorrow the tanks are coming into town!"

"So peaceful, it all was. No fighting. No shelling. No bombing!"

"They just walked right into town!"

Back at our gate Chi Mai was beaming with pride. She exuded the quiet ecstacy of a drama director who has just witnessed her actors perform a stunning coup de theatre.

"Nice looking fellows, weren't they," she said, assuming modesty.

The euphoria of the neighbors still assembled on the street was subdued momentarily by the appearance of a woman walking from the west, sobbing convulsively. On the ends of her shoulder pole hung two baskets, bobbing as she trudged along the street. In each basket sat a small child.

"*Oi, troi? oi, troi oi*—Oh God, what will I do? God, God, oh God, what will I do?" the woman wailed.

"Woman, woman, what is the matter?" a middle-aged man asked as he approached the woman to help.

"Oh, what will I do? No one will take care of me. My husband was a soldier. I got a little pension money after he was killed, but it's all gone. Now I have no rice to feed my children. *O troi oi, troi oi.*" Her sobbing filled the night.

The man by her side tried to comfort her. "Don't worry, friend, everything will be all right. This new government isn't like the old one. They won't let you starve. They will take care of you. Now go home and be at peace."

"Ohhh, but I have no rice for my children—my children," the woman sobbed. The two children looked frightened, but they sat quietly in the baskets.

"Well, we have rice, don't we?" Hiro said, already walking toward the house. He soon returned with a package of rice and placed it beside the child in one of the baskets.

"There,"the neighbor man said, "that rice will last you for a while. Now go back to your house. Everything will be all right."

The woman adjusted the pole on her shoulder and walked off into the night, her sobbing quieter now.

The activity in the street subsided and our group gathered together again in the central room of the house. Everyone was talking animatedly of the peacefulness of the event and expressing relief that the tense waiting period was over. Within a few minutes voices sounded from outside the house.

"Where is Chi Thuy?" a woman's voice called from outside. "I want to meet her right now." Chi Mai glowed, recognizing from the use of her pseudonym that the visitor must be someone from "the Front."

An impressive, straight-backed woman of forty stepped into the room where we sat. She was dressed in a black cotton blouse and trousers. She carried a zippered shoulder bag of olive drab, which I had seen only on the political cadres when I visited the liberated zone on Sunday.

"Which one is Chi Thuy?" she demanded with a smile of anticipation. "I am Chi Phuoc."

"Chi Phuoc, can it be! I'm very pleased to meet you," Chi Mai answered. There was a brief exchange, explaining to the visitor that Chi Mai and Chi Thuy were two names for the same person.

In the ensuing conversation we learned that Chi Phuoc had operated with

The moment of "Liberation" left this widow crying in the night: "No husband. No food. Oh God, what will I do?"

the guerrillas west of the airport and had been in clandestine communication with Chi Mai for several years.

Within minutes the room filled with other newcomers, acquaintances of Chi Mai or others in our group. One short woman on crutches had come with Chi Phuoc. The woman was ebullient.

"Isn't it wonderful. It's really liberation! We're free at last. No more worry about Thieu's police harassing us in the *xoi dau* areas. Did you all see the *bo doi?* Aren't they beautiful!" Her face beamed with the innocent enthusiasm of a country woman. Only after she spoke did she notice me sitting in the group.

"*Troi oi.* I know him," she burst out with a clap of her hands. "You were the one who went to visit the liberated zone on Sunday, weren't you! I saw you going!"

"You saw me going in?" I asked incredulously.

"Yes, brother, I live in that *xoi dau* area west of the airport, I saw you going by and I just knew where you were going. I hope everything worked out for you."

"Well, you know he was arrested by the soldiers and spent the day at the Interrogation Center," Chi Mai blurted out, almost proudly.

"*Troi oi,* I hope they didn't mistreat you, brother," the woman replied.

"No, everything worked out just fine," I said.

"Well, you just rest assured that won't happen again. The *bo doi* will see to that, won't they, Chi Phuoc?" Then to Hiro and me, she said, "We're so glad you brothers stayed here to witness and participate in the liberation of Quang Ngai."

It was three o'clock in the morning, but people kept showing up to celebrate the event. One youth burst into the room and rushed to embrace Chi Mai and Anh My.

"The prisoners have broken loose! The prison doors are wide open! We're free!" The youth spoke with quiet intensity, then he burst out. "Oh Chi Mai, it's so good to see you again." The youth had been a political prisoner until earlier in the evening when the guards had fled and the prisoners broke out of the cells and escaped. In the following minutes he animatedly reported on the events of the evening. At the same time Chi Phuoc and the woman on crutches were talking and laughing with the people sitting next to them.

I was able to reach my notebook, which was lying on the desk in the room, and penned a few lines:

2:30 A.M., MARCH 25, LIBERATION!

Until this moment I have used the word "liberation" with a touch of reserve, but that truly is the word to describe the mood of the people around us now.

The victorious din in the room was interrupted with the appearance of another woman at the door. She was identified as a relative of the head medic. "Oh, these guerrillas. They're just like Thieu's soldiers. It's disgusting!"

"Now what's wrong?" Chi Mai was obviously concerned.

"Oh, they came up to me in the street and made off with my Honda. They said they needed it! Needed it! Well, I need it too, and it's my cycle. Then they had the gall to look at my watch and ask me what brand it was! But I yanked my arm away and told them there was no way they were going to take my watch. The bastards!" With that the woman turned to walk out.

"Now wait a minute," Chi Phuoc called out, "that's none of our brothers. They don't act like that. That's one of Thieu's soldiers who took your cycle."

Chi Mai agreed with Chi Phuoc's assessment but felt it was a mistake to let the woman's anger go unmollified. "We must really check this out or it could be a loss of prestige for the revolution. We can't afford to have this kind of thing happen or even to have people thinking these things will happen. Someone should go with this woman to check it out."

The head medic went out with the woman, but we never did learn the fate of her Honda. The group in the bedroom continued exchanging stories for another hour, until someone announced that we should perhaps salvage a few hours of sleep out of the remainder of the night.

The next morning when Hiro and I awoke we could hear the street humming with activity. Again we opened the trapdoor in the wall and walked out onto the porch-roof patio. Troops, guerrillas, *bo doi*! The street was bustling with young men—and women too!—walking down the street with AK-47's slung over their shoulders and knapsacks on their backs. Some of them carried red and blue flags with a bright yellow star in the center. The colors of the Provisional Revolutionary Government! Right here in the heart of Quang Ngai city!

Then an army truck moved noiselessly into view. But there was a difference about this truck. Not the smoke-belching and clanging American "deuce and a half." Painted olive drab, yes, but smaller and quieter. As it passed by the house we could see Chinese characters stamped on the hood. Trucks filled with smiling but quiet troops of the Vietnamese People's Liberation Army!

Unbelievable! The truck must have driven down from the mountains straight into Quang Ngai city!

Just two weeks before it would have seemed unthinkable that this moment would ever come. Shelling of the city, yes. Sapper attacks, yes. But truckloads of *bo doi* driving nonchalantly into the center of town? Never!

"Well, Anh Kien, it looks like we're surrounded by Viet Cong!" Hiro was smiling so broadly that his gold-plated eyetooth glistened in the morning sun. I realized too how euphoric I felt just then. The panic of the preceding week had built to a frazzling pitch. We had feared for our lives and the lives of our friends. But now the terrifying moment of truth had come, and it was wonderful! The town was spared. The people were safe. We were alive! Standing calmly on the porch roof watching guerrillas file down Phan Boi Chau Street! The Viet Cong! These were the people who up until now were represented on propaganda billboards by paintings of vicious, demonic beasts or poisonous snakes who relished in spilling the blood of innocents. But here they were, walking boyishly down the street, looking like any other Vietnamese and appearing a bit overwhelmed by the large buildings and concentration of vehicles and people in what must have seemed to them a big city!

Hiro and I walked downstairs and joined the others for breakfast. Already Chi Phuoc and some of Chi Mai's other contacts from "the Front" had stopped in at the house. It was quickly becoming clear that although she had spent five years in Saigon Government zones after her mine injuries, Chi Mai had indeed maintained or developed considerable contacts with PRG cadres in liberated zones.

One fellow in his early twenties appeared, carrying an M-16 rifle, with a white strip of cloth tied around his left arm. "The white armbands are to be worn by anyone carrying a weapon. You have to get permission from some cadre before you can carry a gun. And red armbands are for people who want to indicate that they are joining with the revolution," he explained to us. We learned that he had actually been an ARVN draftee but had served as a liaison agent for the PRG even while he was in the ARVN ranks.

A few minutes later breakfast was again interrupted by a knock on the front door. "Someone wants to see Anh Kien," announced Anh My, who had answered the door. I walked to the door trying to imagine who in town knew I was staying at the Quaker house.

"Le Quang Vinh!" With all the activity of the last hours it had not occurred to me that I would so soon meet this political cadre who had welcomed me to the liberated zone just two days before. "Do come in and sit down."

"I just wanted to stop in to make sure that everything is all right with you. We heard you got picked up by the soldiers on your way back into Quang Ngai on Sunday. We were very concerned about you. That's why we wanted you to stay with us in the liberated zone for several days. But apparently everything worked out all right. You are looking well." Le Quang Vinh spoke with quiet confidence. Instead of the distinctive blue shirt of a political cadre he had worn the previous day, this morning he was dressed in a green military uniform complete with the *bo doi* pith helmet sporting an emblem of the PRG flag in the center. The zippered bag of a cadre hung from one shoulder and a pistol was strapped to his belt. Then his youthful face burst into a disarming smile. "Well, Anh Kien, how do you like the way we liberated Quang Ngai city! Pretty peaceful, wasn't it!"

"I think everyone is relieved there was no heavy fighting. After the ARVN fled town last night, we all relaxed. We're just happy there was no bloodshed through it all," I said as I prepared to pour tea for Le Quang Vinh and a guerrilla who accompanied him.

"That was the way we wanted it to be," he replied. "The reports are that not a single person was killed in all of Quang Ngai city. There was one *bo doi* who was injured in the leg at the military compound downtown. Apparently it was a mine, but I did not get full details on that. Besides that we do not know of any other injuries."

We drank tea together and then Le Quang Vinh excused himself. "I can't stay. There's much work to be done immediately. We are all very busy. We don't sleep very much now. We just keep working. But I did want to stop in to see that all was well with you. Do you have enough food and money?"

We assured him that for the foreseeable future we were well supplied.

"Well, just let us know if we can be of any assistance to you. Oh yes, in a day or two when we have time, we will prepare travel papers for you. But in the meantime, feel free to travel wherever you like within the city. Now, if you will excuse me, I must be going."

We walked Le Quang Vinh to the gate. Only then did we discover on the front porch a stack of M-16 rifles. A high-school student from the neighborhood was removing the magazines and pulling open the firing chambers to make sure no bullets remained in the guns. Apparently some ARVN troops had not fled town the night before and had turned in their weapons in the morning. A maintenance man from the Rehabilitation Center drove up with the small Quaker pickup truck, loaded it full of the abandoned American rifles and hauled them off to some collection point outside of town. It was the first time I had ever seen a Quaker vehicle loaded with weapons!

As I stood in the street watching the truck drive away, I felt a hand grab my arm. I turned to see Tran Quang, a twenty-one-year-old primary-school teacher, who had been a close friend of Pat's and mine since 1967. He had taught us many Vietnamese folk songs and had prepared a notebook of songs and poems for us as a going-away gift at the end of our first term in 1969. During our second term in Vietnam we saw less of him, since his school was located in another province. Although he had recently shocked us by confessing he suspected that Pat and I had connections with the CIA, our friendship had developed with a considerable level of trust. This morning Tran Quang's face was ashen.

"Anh Kien," he spoke in a tense undertone, turning to make sure no one was overhearing, "Anh Kien, take me with you."

"Take you with me?" My voice reflected my confusion. "But I don't understand. Where are you planning to go, Quang?"

"Don't you see?" Quang looked nervously around again. "The Viet Cong are everywhere. We've got to get out of here! Please take me with you!"

"But, Quang, I really had no intention of going anywhere."

"Yes, but when you go—you'll have a helicopter or something coming for you certainly—when you go, you must take me with you!" He was on the verge of tears. His younger sister and his father, who made a modest living sewing hats and cutting hair, appeared from behind him. The panic was written on their faces as well.

"Yes, you will take Quang, won't you. We can't all go with you, but you must take Quang."

"But I plan to stay in Quang Ngai. Everything is calm and peaceful now. And hopefully Pat and the children will soon be able to return to be with me here. We hope to continue working here as before."

Tran Quang was crestfallen. "But what will happen to me?" he asked urgently.

"Well, I guess I can't really answer that question, but I presume there will be schools under the new government. And I presume they will need teachers too. Maybe you can continue to teach school." Even as I spoke I realized that I was in no position to allay any fears he had. "Say, why don't you come to the house this afternoon and talk with Chi Mai? She knows some of the cadres personally. Maybe she can give you some idea of what to expect."

Tran Quang finally seemed to accept that I was not going to leave Quang Ngai and he promised to return in the afternoon.

By midmorning Hiro and I could contain our curiosity no longer, so we rode downtown to witness the activities of the town's newcomers. Several times I found myself gawking at the guerrillas as they walked along the street, these unusual visitors to Quang Ngai city. I soon realized that they were also staring at us—two strange-looking, bearded foreigners riding down the street! I often nodded a smile when a guerrilla's eyes caught mine. Sometimes they would return the friendly gestures, but more often they would self-consciously nudge a partner by their side and converse excitedly in whispers.

We rode past police headquarters, which still looked intact. The green and white sign over the gate still read: "National Police Command of Quang Ngai." But already a red and blue PRG flag hung from the sign. An International Scout truck pulled up to the gate of police headquarters. It was the Scout that David Harr, the "consulate" representative, used to drive about town. But now a uniformed *bo doi* was in the driver's seat! Mounted on the front bumper was a pole bearing the Liberation flag. On the rear bumper a somewhat faded sticker in English read: "Have a Nice Day!"

The Provincial Interrogation Center stood vacant with its gates wide open. A small PRG flag had been hung on the barbed wire. Farther down the street in front of the Quang Ngai Province administrative headquarters, the street was milling with *bo doi* and cadre running in and out, apparently being assigned to duties all over town. Barbed-wire concertina was pulled across the gate to the Province Office and only vehicles with *bo doi* drivers were permitted to come and go. As we paused for a moment to watch the activity, we caught sight of a man inside the wall waving for us to enter. After initial hesitation, the guards at the gate let us enter and we made our way through milling *bo doi* to the place where the man was standing. A tall, slender man of perhaps sixty years, his uniform was indistinguishable from any other *bo doi* in town. He strode toward us and smiled, revealing brown tobacco-stained teeth. Although he, like all the other PRG personnel, wore no epaulets or rank insignia, we sensed from the tone of confidence in his voice that he carried considerable authority.

"Hello, friends, I am Nham. And you must be the people we heard were staying here in Quang Ngai. I am very happy to meet you. Forgive me for not paying a visit to your house earlier, but I trust you will understand that on this first morning of liberation we are very busy. Please forgive us," he repeated.

We introduced ourselves to the smiling man whose suntanned skin had the appearance of tough leather. We explained that we worked with refugee farmers in the countryside.

"Yes, that was my understanding," the man replied, "and I just wanted to call you in here to tell you that you should continue to go about your work as usual. If there's any way in which we can help you, just let us know."

It was only later in the day that we learned that this man was actually the

First Party Secretary for Quang Ngai, likely the top position in the province. And yet cadres or *bo doi* invariably referred to him as *Anh* Nham, Brother Nham, using the familiar honorific rather than the more formal titles "sir" or "honorable chief of the province," which people were expected to use for officials of the Saigon regime. We soon learned that all PRG cadres of rank high and low employed the familiar titles "brother" or "sister."

Down in the marketing center of town *bo doi* and local townsfolk were scurrying about, some getting gasoline from the Shell station and others tearing down the propaganda billboards of the Saigon Government's Ministry of Information. Across from the gas station a sign lay broken on the sidewalk. Its message, intact, was now facing the sky:

"Don't listen to what the Communists say;

Watch carefully what the Communists do!"

I saw Mr. Hung, the aging major of Quang Ngai city, who, almost exactly seven years before, on the ides of March, had with much flourish and delectation pulled a well-worn ledger from a cabinet jammed with city records and presided over the signing and sealing ceremony that was to become the marriage of Patricia Faye Hostetter and Earl Sauder Martin. It marked the first nuptials of Americans in Quang Ngai and initiated a continuing friendship between Mr. Hung and ourselves. We had recently visited his home during Tet, the lunar New Year, where he entertained our children with his menagerie of fish, cats and monkeys.

Although Mr. Hung had grown up in the northern part of Vietnam, he had spent several decades as an official under the Saigon regime in Quang Ngai. In that capacity he was called on to give numerous public speeches in which he was expected to denounce the "Communist aggressors" and drum up enthusiasm for the Thieu government. Now, this morning he was wearing a red armband signifying that he had "returned to the revolutionary fold." He was demonstrating his willingness to cooperate with the revolutionary authorities by helping to tear down Saigon Government propaganda signs. When he saw us pass, he responded spontaneously with a jocular wave. The erstwhile mayor was losing no time in adjusting to the new realities in his town.

At the Esso station we encountered a Buddhist monk who had frequently visited our home. He had always been interested in political discussions and seemed to have an intimate knowledge of political and military developments in the province. He had surprised us on several occasions with his seemingly intimate connections with the Quang Ngai police, but at other times he spoke with apparent respect and knowledge of the PRG. I thought the monk might be quite enthusiastic about the developments of the night and I approached him from behind, saying, "Well, brother, what do you think of the liberation of Quang Ngai?"

Only then could I see the strained look of simulated indifference on his face. Without looking at me, he answered quickly, "Oh, I haven't done anything. I don't have anything to be afraid of!" With that, he kick-started his cycle and drove off.

Hiro and I pedaled up Tran Hung Dao Street and turned in our alley. Mr. Chau saw us coming and seemed eager to talk. His countenance was more relaxed than I had seen in weeks.

"Well, I see you fellows actually stayed here through it all. I must say, I have a great deal of admiration for you. That means you really are ready to work with the people regardless of which government is in power." Then, nodding his head toward the street, he continued, "It's all been very peaceful, hasn't it? I think it will be different this time. I think the revolutionaries have probably matured a great deal. They will not be as harsh as they were before."

Mr. Chau paused, then quickly added, "Oh, speaking of hard times, I was wondering if you fellows have any spending money on hand?" Mr. Chau asked.

"Yes, we do have some. Are you short right now? Could we lend you some?" I offered.

"No, I just thought that if you're short on food or anything, the vegetables will soon be coming in the garden, and you're welcome to use all you like. After this we'll all be sharing together." He laughed and then added, "You know, that's the way it will be under this new government—everyone sharing!"

In the previous year the one area of misunderstanding between the Chaus and us was the fact that they charged double or triple the rate of rent we believed a Vietnamese tenant would pay for our house. But we could understand his point that at the prevailing currency exchange rate we were paying only thirty American dollars rent per month, so we had never made an issue of it. But the attitudes we were hearing from Mr. Chau this morning were in sharp contrast with his position of the previous year.

"By the way," he added to our surprise, "you fellows are welcome to stay here in this house as long as you like. And you don't have to worry about paying rent after this."

Hiro and I checked through our house and found all was intact. We had received a report that a few houses in town had been looted by ARVN soldiers on their way out of town. We had seen at least two houses that had apparently been set on fire the night before and were still smoldering in the morning. But looting in town had been minimal and our section of town had been left completely untouched.

We were again preparing to leave when a man and woman whom I had known for several months came driving into our courtyard. With hardly a greeting, Anh Khiem blurted out, "They've arrested my cousin! What can I do? I'm afraid they'll do something horrible to him."

103

"Your cousin. Who is he? And where is he now?" I asked the distraught man.

"He's the hamlet chief of Tan My. They captured him this morning and I don't know what they'll do to him. Can't you come and help?" Anh Khiem pleaded.

Under the Saigon regime Khiem had learned that it was sometimes helpful to have the intervention of an American to secure favor from officials. Those same instincts had now brought him to the only American in town to seek assistance for his cousin.

But even under the Saigon regime, Pat and I had followed the policy of intervening in behalf of a prisoner only if the prisoner himself or herself indicated that our involvement was desired. We had always feared the possibility that our attempts to help would backfire on the prisoner. Now I feared that even more.

"But do you think I could really help?" I asked the man. "Aren't you afraid that if an American should show up in Tan My hamlet to plead the case of your cousin—well, that it might only create more difficulties for him?"

"Oh—yes, maybe it would. Yes—" he said, and he was gone as quickly as he had come.

The visit left me a bit shaken. Everything in town seemed reasoned and peaceful, but how could we know what was happening in the countryside?

Hiro and I rode on up Tran Hung Dao in the direction of the Quaker house. We came to an intersection called the Five Corners where a group of ARVN soldiers, mostly Hre tribesmen, were sitting on the ground in an open lot. Their hands were tied behind their backs and three guerrillas were standing guard over them with AK-47 rifles. Apparently these Hre troops had not been included in the mass exodus of the night before and had only surrendered to the *bo doi* this morning. We wanted to learn more, but the young guards were obviously not disposed toward conversing with us. We watched them for perhaps a minute before we turned around and were shocked to find ourselves face to face with a T-54 Soviet tank! The huge machine was parked in front of a small general store and camouflaged with coconut palm branches and a green tarpaulin stretched as a canopy several feet above the tank. So these were the machines the guerrillas had promised would come to provide security for the town! Strangely, their presence left me feeling quite insecure!

I was eager to photograph the tank, but the *bo doi* sitting by the antiaircraft gun on top of the tank frowned and waved his hand when I raised my camera. Assuming we did not speak Vietnamese, he explained to a person on the street that no one could photograph military equipment without permission from the authorities. I was not in the mood to challenge the *bo doi's* desire.

Tuesday afternoon after a much needed siesta, Hiro and I biked toward the Tra Khuc River at the north edge of town. Along the way we passed

Bo doi tanks roll into Quang Ngai supposedly "to guarantee the town's security."

several disabled ARVN vehicles abandoned in the middle of the road; likely they had developed mechanical trouble or run out of gasoline during the frenzied retreat of the ARVN the evening before.

A steady stream of forlorn refugees was walking back to town. The townsfolk who had been caught up in the panicked exodus were now returning to their Quang Ngai homes. Hot and exhausted, they were a haggard lot. Some of them had wrapped towels around their heads to shield them from the afternoon sun. Some had bundles of clothing and valuables hanging from their shoulders. Others were empty handed. Some walked barefooted, having lost their shoes or sandals in the mad rush through the night.

A group of enthusiastic *bo doi* also came walking along the street. One *bo doi* pointed at my camera and walked over to where Hiro and I were standing. "Hello, brothers, you must be journalists. What do you think of liberation?" he asked cheerfully.

"Most of all we're grateful that it all took place so peacefully. Practically no injuries or destruction, they tell us. Journalists? Well, not exactly, but we like to take pictures. Primarily we're involved in social service work," Hiro explained.

"Very good. I'm actually a journalist myself," the *bo doi* replied. "I take some pictures, but mostly I paint." He showed us his tablet, full of brilliant watercolors he had done of farmers threshing rice, destroyed American tanks, and townsfolk working cheerfully with the bright reds, blues and yellows of Liberation flags in evidence everywhere. "Hope we can get together sometime again," he said as he closed his pad, "but now I must go." We shook hands and he ran down the road to rejoin his unit.

At the bridge over the Tra Khuc we were met with a deluge of people walking into town. Most were peasant folk, in the familiar blacks and whites

The presence of an American photographer distracted these hinterland farmers in their jubilant march into town. "Our villages have been bombed too long. Now Quang Ngai is liberated and we're coming into the city to celebrate!"

of the Quang Ngai farmers. From our vantage point atop an empty oil drum at the side of the road, it appeared as though a river of conical hats was moving across the bridge. A white-shirted youth, perhaps a student, near the front of the crowd, carried a large Liberation flag, and a generous sprinkling of smaller flags fluttered over the conical hats. The group was virtually unarmed except for long bamboo staves, which many of the farmers were carrying. The crowd was raucous with laughter and chants in praise of the liberation of Quang Ngai. We asked an old man in the group what was the occasion of the demonstration. He quickly stepped out of the flow of people and with great dignity explained that these were people from the older liberated villages of western Son Tinh district.

"We have lived with this war too long. Our villages have been bombed and shelled too long. Now all of Quang Ngai Province is liberated, including Quang Ngai city, so we are coming into the city to celebrate."

As the people continued to move past us I remembered stories of the Tet Offensive in 1968 when the Liberation Army had predicted an uprising in the cities that would overthrow the Americans and the Saigon Army. At that time there were also groups of unarmed country folk from liberated zones organized to march into the cities to celebrate the anticipated victory of the Liberation Army. Em Trinh, the young woman who lived with us, told of one such demonstration initiated from her village to march unarmed into the district town. In fact, the Americans and the ARVN were still in control of the town, and when the ARVN guards just outside the district capital saw the people walking toward the town, they opened machine-gun fire on the group, leaving many of Trinh's fellow villagers injured or dead. But today these farmers appeared confident that the war for them was finally over.

Back in town Hiro and I noticed that the number of Liberation flags was

106

rapidly increasing not only on government offices but on private homes. Twenty-four hours earlier these flags would have provoked arrest, if not something more drastic such as a grenade thrown into the house, by Saigon Government police. Now the flags were appearing everywhere. We watched an old man crawl out through an upstairs window onto a porch roof above his storefront. He nervously looked up and down the street, quickly mounted a Liberation flag over the edge of the porch roof and then rushed back into the house.

Along Quang Trung Street a fellow clad in black pajamas similar to those worn by the Saigon Government's Self-Defense Forces was carrying a large Liberation flag over his right shoulder and in his left hand he was clutching a now disgraced Saigon Government flag that he was tearing with his teeth.

In the Community Center across from the Province Office the floor was strewn with bolts of red and blue material and freshly cut yellow cloth stars. A man was pumping a treadle sewing machine, and every few minutes a brand-new banner for the revolution emerged. His flags were then being taken away and raised on flagpoles in front of every public building.

At the time of the signing of the Paris Agreement in early 1973, the Saigon Government had ordered that a Saigon flag should be painted on the exterior of every house in its zone of control. Now people were painting over the Saigon colors or scraping them off the masonry with broad knives. It was time for new colors.

There must have been a shortage of plain red material in one neighborhood because a cluster of houses flew Liberation flags the top half of which were made of white jersey material printed with small red flowers, a delightful variation! In another neighborhood, folks had used green material instead of blue for the flag's bottom half. The word *xanh* passes for both colors in Vietnamese and apparently it was unclear to these folks whether to use "ocean *xanh*" or "leaf *xanh*." Still other flags were mounted upside down, presumably by mistake.

The new authorities lost no time in mobilizing the town's youth into an armed home guard. We rode past the Quang Ngai Senior High School where students and teachers were milling about. A few *bo doi* were on the scene as well. A huge banner stretched across the gate read: "Quang Ngai Has Returned to the Hands of the People!" A teacher explained that they were forming the Students' Uprising and Self-Defense Program. Each participating student had to wear a red armband. One student was tearing the three red stripes out of a yellow Saigon Government flag to use as armbands! Students who wanted to carry weapons had to wear white armbands. The latter group formed ranks and a *bo doi* explained to this self-defense group their new responsibilities. Occasionally the *bo doi* would call for some response and the students would enthusiastically chorus an answer in unison. After their instructions, each of the white-banded students was issued an M-16 rifle and sent out to patrol the town. There was no doubt that in the students the *bo doi* had tapped a tremendous reservoir of enthusiasm. One could only hope that along with their zeal these students would display an equal measure of discretion and skill in the handling of their firearms.

After we left the high school we stopped again at the Mennonite house on Tran Hung Dao Street. While we were there, we had a return visit from Mr. Khiem, the man who earlier in the morning had reported that his cousin had been arrested. Now his face was stony.

"I just came back to say that you needn't worry about my cousin anymore."

"Oh, is he all right?" I asked hopefully.

"He's dead."

"Dead! Are you sure? I mean—but what happened?"

Anh Khiem was in no mood to talk and he dismissed himself before we could learn any details about his cousin's fate. Had the guerrillas taken vengeance on this hamlet chief? Was this an indication that the killing was not yet over? There were, of course, other possibilities. The cousin could have put up armed resistance to the guerrillas. Or villagers could have taken "justice" into their own hands and done away with the hamlet chief without the guerrillas being involved at all. Whatever the case, the report was hardly reassuring.

On the way back to the Quaker house Hiro and I paused in front of the Provincial Interrogation Center where I had been detained just one day before. Again, I was gratified to see its gates standing open. One could only hope these gates would never close again.

But even there I found my thoughts drifting to Major Hoa and the heavy-set assistant who had kindly taken me across the street for a bowl of soup. What had happened to them? What would "liberation" hold for them?

Just then I heard someone call my name from the furniture shop across the road where I had been served noodle soup the day before. The furniture maker was beckoning us to visit him again. He poured tea as we sat down. The craftsman sat on one end of a polished wooden bed that he had likely made himself. On the other end of the bed sat a man of about thirty with a hardened face. By his age and his air of bravado, I imagined he might have been a policeman until he jettisoned his uniform upon the arrival of the Liberation Army. He was apparently continuing a discussion started before we arrived in the shop.

"Thieu? What a president! I always hated Thieu! You couldn't find a man more corrupt than Thieu. Soaked the people for his own personal gain. What a rat!" The man was attempting to appear revolutionary, but he sopke much too loudly and ostentatiously to be persuasive. "You know, one thing I've always observed about the Liberation Front is how much more honest and uncorruptible they are than the Saigon Government."

Shortly, another man appeared in the shop. He was clothed only in a T-shirt and undershorts. He had a white towel wrapped around his face so that only his eyes were visible. As he ran to the back of the shop he looked around nervously before cautiously removing the towel from his head. The man's eyes were transfixed in stark terror. The furniture maker explained to us quietly that the man had been a policeman.

"Here, have a cup of tea," the furniture man offered the newcomer. The man sat down and with woefully trembling hands finally managed to light a cigarette. He sat with his elbows propped on his knees and his head drooped toward the floor. He spoke not a word.

After tea, we took our leave. All the while, the man at the other end of the bed was loudly holding forth about the decadence of Nguyen Van Thieu and the virtuosity of the Provisional Revolutionary Government.

Back at the Quaker house we found Chi Mai engaged in conversation with a young, round-faced *bo doi*. "This is Anh Chien," Chi Mai said. "Anh Chien is a photographer for the *bo doi*."

"Terrific," I replied. "Finally I've found someone who can teach me something about photography. But how did you find us, Anh Chien?"

"Tell him your story. Anh Kien, Anh Hiro, you won't believe this," Chi Mai laughed.

"Well, I was just telling Chi Mai how I found your house," Anh Chien spoke with a decidedly northern accent. "Today as I was taking some pictures downtown I met some comrades who said there was an American photographer in Quang Ngai. They said I should walk up Phan Boi Chau Street and look for the number 357. So that's what I did. I walked until I found a tall white building along Phan Boi Chau Street with the number 357. The high steel gate was closed, so I knocked. I waited for a time and was ready to push open the gate when some neighbors came rushing up and calling that I should not go into that house. They said it was the house of the American CIA and most likely the CIA agents set mines around the compound when they fled. If I went into the compound I might be killed. What do you think of that!"

"Whoa, now just wait a minute. Are you talking about our house? Are you saying that some neighbors thought it was the CIA house?" Hiro and I were speaking at once.

Chi Mai tried to clarify. "No, Anh Chien is saying that the CIA house up the street from us actually has the number 357. He says it is written clearly on the gatepost: 357 Phan Boi Chau!"

"You must be kidding. You can't tell me the cadres told us to hang a number on our gate that was actually the street number of the CIA house," Hiro blurted.

"An amazing coincidence, eh?" Chi Mai laughed.

"I hope that's what it was, but it seems unbelievable that of all the numbers you could pick at random, they should coincidentally choose a number that just happens to be the house number of the CIA! But I guess all's well that ends well, so we'll not worry about it. I just hope no one goes wandering into a mined CIA compound looking for us!" Unfortunately, the "357" mystery would never be cleared up for us.

While we talked, Tran Quang, the frightened schoolteacher whom I had met that morning, showed up wearing a red armband to signify his readiness—nominal, at least—to cooperate with the revolution. He was already more relaxed than he had been in the morning. I introduced him to Chi Mai and mentioned that he had some questions about what to expect with the new government. Chi Mai was gracious.

"Surely lots of people have questions about the new government. The Thieu government deliberately tried to mislead people about the revolution, so you needn't worry if you have some questions or even anxieties about the new government."

Tran Quang breathed more easily as Chi Mai spoke. He was getting the support he was looking for. "I used to be a primary-school teacher. What do you suppose I'll do after this? Will there be any way for me to make a living?" he asked.

"Sure thing! You'll just go on teaching if you want to. Where was your school before?"

"In Chu Lai. There were no openings in Quang Ngai before."

"You may be expected to take some sessions to learn some new techniques of teaching, but the curriculum will not change much in the primary school. Besides, there's a good chance you'll be able to teach in Quang Ngai after this because the revolutionary government emphasizes using local talent."

The two continued to talk, and by the time he left an hour later Tran Quang had regained much of his normal optimism and humor. "Who knows, it might not be so bad after all," he smiled.

Tuesday evening people at the Quaker house ate in shifts. There was a steady stream of visitors coming through the house, many of whom joined us for rice, sautéed pork and *rau muong* (greens). Chi Phuoc and several other PRG cadre and guerrillas shared our meal. The table manners of the people from PRG areas were fascinating to Hiro and me. Unlike people in Saigon zones who used only one end of the chopsticks, the people from the liberated zones used one end of the pair of chopsticks to lift food from the serving dish into their rice bowl and the opposite end to move food from one's rice bowl into one's mouth. The "chopstick-two-heads" method was obviously more sanitary, but until we learned the new technique, we novices from Saigon Government zones were handicapped with a decelerated pace of eating!

After supper we received a visit from Anh Trong, the guerrilla chief I had first met on my visit to the liberated zone two days before.

"So this is where you live, Anh Kien," he began as he sat by the cleared-off table.

"Well, actually we're just staying here for now because this house has a semblance of a bunker; we have a smaller house down on Tran Hung Dao Street," I explained.

"When am I going to meet this Chi Thuy we've been hearing so much about?" Tonight Anh Trong was in an expansive mood.

I responded in kind. "Well, we could possibly arrange to have you meet her one of these days. In fact, Chi Thuy—or as we call her, Chi Mai—is sitting right across the table from you!"

"You?" Anh Trong raised his eyebrows and produced an almost imperceptible smile.

"I'm Chi Thuy all right," Chi Mai laughed. "What did you hear about me?"

"Tell me, what do you think of the way we liberated Quang Ngai? Pretty clever, wouldn't you say!" Anh Trong's eyes held that same enigmatic aura that I had remembered from meeting him on Sunday. But the straight noncommittal smile was more playful tonight, reflecting a sense of smugness about the man. An instinctual man. Whatever lofty aspirations he might have espoused of fighting for national independence or winning true freedom for the Vietnamese farmers against "foreign imperialist aggressors," one still wondered if perhaps the most powerful driving force for Anh Trong might not have been his own ego. The challenge of outwitting the enemy. Not primarily because the enemy was so despicable or treacherous—although he would surely say the enemy was all of that—but because defeating the enemy proved one's own superiority. In a very personal sense.

"Clever?" Chi Mai's eyes danced at the opportunity to fence with a comrade. "Doesn't look to me like you did very much. You just said 'Boo!' and the ARVN tucked tail and fled town. Any twelve-year-old farmer boy can drop a couple mortars into Quang Ngai city!"

"Yeah, it's a shame, isn't it. Thieu's boys just didn't have what it takes, did they?" Anh Trong could not restrain himself from breaking into a laugh.

"What I can't figure out is why you all were so poorly prepared for the liberation of Quang Ngai," Chi Mai chided. "When I was still in the hills, I remember how we prepared for the Tet Offensive. Flags, lots of flags, propaganda leaflets, announcement bills, the whole works. This time it seems you didn't have much of that stuff prepared in advance, so when you came into town you had to busy yourself making flags!"

Anh Trong cleared his throat as if to give himself time to form a defense. "That's because when we took the first step at Ban Me Thuot, the enemy got very frightened and withdrew from Pleiku and Kontum in panic. That was only a week ago. After that it all went so fast. The morale of the ARVN just collapsed. Events developed even faster than we anticipated. We had to run to keep up! So, frankly, that is why we were perhaps not as prepared as we should have been for coming into Quang Ngai city."

By ten o'clock the visitors had gone and we all headed for bed. I tucked in the mosquito net around the edge of the thin foam-rubber mattress and wrapped a light sheet around my feet so they would not get bitten through the net as they protruded off the end of the bed. Tonight the guns were silent. No artillery vibrating the countryside. All was still, except for a few dogs barking at shadows here and there over town.

WEDNESDAY, 26 MARCH. When Hiro and I got up on Wednesday morning, we again crawled out onto the porch roof to stretch and greet the new day. On first glance up and down the street I was again shocked by the profusion of flags. Just two days before flags like these would have spelled treason. Now they flew from every house. Even the horse carts and Hondas on the street were sporting Liberation flags. It took me just a second to orient myself in time and space, to remind myself that indeed the political universe had been turned on its head. Or on its feet, perhaps. It was a turning—yes, a revolution.

During breakfast Hiro and I discussed whether we should also display a Liberation flag in front of the Quaker house and in front of our Mennonite house on Tran Hung Dao Street. We decided that it was the prerogative of Chi Mai and the other workers from the Rehabilitation Center to decide policy for the Quaker house. But at our own house on Tran Hung Dao, we decided we would not fly the flag. It was, after all, a Vietnamese flag, and we represented an international community. We had avoided identification with the Saigon Government flag. We would do the same with the Liberation flag. Furthermore, for me at least, something there is that doesn't like a flag. Any flag. Flags made the complex simplistic. And national flags attempted to direct allegiance not toward the total human family but toward a particular nation-state. Flags separated people as surely as they united them.

It was, perhaps, the influence of my father. Pop had always held a great deal of respect for governmental leaders. He prayed regularly that God would grant them wisdom and guidance. Whenever we discussed the war, he would defend at least the good intentions—if not always the actions—of the United States administration. So while my father was certainly not an American chauvinist, he was a grateful and respectful citizen.

But years before, about the time I was ready to graduate from the little one-room schoolhouse where I had studied for six years, Boy Scouts had come to our house selling small American flags to plant in front yards for Memorial Day. I had been sorely disappointed when Pop told the Scouts we would not be needing any flags. Only years later would I come to appreciate the message implicit in his action. For Pop there was a higher allegiance. It was not God *and* country. It was God *above* the nation. Above all nations.

Hiro and I were eager to ride downtown again in order not to miss any developments. As we pedaled down Phan Boi Chau, we noticed a paper Liberation flag pasted on the deserted house of the Christian and Missionary

Alliance missionaries. Farther down the street the house purchased by the Baptist mission was similarly adorned. The Baptist compound had the further distinction of having a message in Vietnamese scrawled on its gatepost: "Down with the American imperialists and the Lackey Clique!"

New banners had also been stretched high across the street. One close to the pagoda read: "Long Live the Quang Ngai Victory!"

By Wednesday morning the town was already returning to normal functions. The hospital was active with many of its staff members, including several doctors who did not flee town, back at work. Many of the shops downtown were open for business, although customers were few. The marketplace was busy, however, with the same women peddling the same kinds of vegetables, fish, meat, scrubbing brushes, candles and the myriads of items that filled their stalls. Barbers were back to cutting hair. In fact, some people were predicting a bull market for barbers because the more puritanical *bo doi* would be little approving of the mod hairstyles that had become popular among the Quang Ngai youth.

Many of these youth were now swinging brooms in the street. I talked with one student friend whose father had left him as a baby with his mother while he traveled to North Vietnam to "regroup" with the Viet Minh in 1954 after the defeat of the French. In spite of his father's loyalties—or possibly because he had felt resentment at his father for abandoning him— the student had recently expressed alarm to me about the prospect of a Communist take-over of Quang Ngai. But now this morning, with some of his fellow students, he was vigorously sweeping the street and apparently feeling positive about the state of affairs.

"Our team's swept this whole block," he said, referring to the group of about ten high-school students with him, "and we think that's a pretty good accomplishment. I must say, at least the work of the revolution is practical."

By Tuesday night we began hearing stories of the panicked exodus of ARVN and townsfolk on Monday night. "Terrible." "Indescribable." "A trail of blood and horror." We caught only brief descriptions from people. Apparently the retreating column of ARVN and civilians had been ambushed en route fifteen kilometers north of Quang Ngai city.

Wednesday afternoon Chi Mai, Anh My and I decided to ride our Honda north to discover what had really happened on Monday night. We briefly discussed the fact that I had not yet received official identification papers from the PRG authorities, but we decided the likelihood of being stopped was minimal. It would be worth the risk.

The road was fairly clear for the first five kilometers north of town. After that began a trail of the rubble of panic. Here an army jeep sat diagonally across the middle of the road. There an International Scout pickup sat facing north on the left side of the highway—a front tire flat. A green and white police jeep balanced with its back wheels in the right-hand ditch and its headlights aimed at the western sky. Next it was an ancient black French Citroën, which a white-shirted youth and a *bo doi* were pushing, apparently trying to move it off the middle of the road. One could only imagine the terror of the people who were driving these vehicles two nights ago. Fleeing, they thought, to save their lives.

As we traveled along the road, we could retrace how the horror of that night must have escalated. For 200 meters the road was littered with steel helmets. Black boots. Green shirts and pants. Strewn—like an Army-Navy store after a tornado—all along the highway. Then we saw the reason: a six-foot crater right in the middle of the road. The guerrillas must have learned of the retreat and mortared into the fleeing column of troops. The ARVN troops, terrified of imminent capture, apparently jettisoned their uniforms and weapons and streaked incognito into the night.

A Saigon flag lay crumpled and twisted through a green army shirt. Two army boots lay on top of this collage of defeat. Farther along a body, covered with a straw sleeping mat, lay by the side of the road. We inquired of a woman along the road why the body had not been taken care of.

"Good heavens, probably nobody knows whose body it is. Besides, what happened on up the road is so much worse, no one is paying attention to this one body," the woman replied.

For the next several kilometers the road was relatively clear. An American tank had dropped headfirst into a deep culvert along the side of the highway. Dried blood splotched the driver's seat, suggesting that the ARVN driver had been injured in the crash or had perhaps been injured before the crash, thus causing the armored vehicle to veer out of control. Bandoleers of ammunition lay unused inside the tank. The symbol of the tank platoon, the White Stallion, still glistened in prancing form on the massive turret.

We continued north in the direction of Monday night's heaviest carnage. Suddenly, above the noise of the Honda, we heard excited shouting from behind. I turned to see a uniformed guerrilla driving a Honda toward us at full throttle. On the seat behind him another youth furiously brandished a revolver in the air.

"I think they want us to stop," Anh My said, gripping his arm more tightly around my waist.

"Halt. Stop immediately!" Now I could hear the agitated shout above the engine noise.

"They look like they mean business, don't they?" I said as I cut the throttle on the cycle.

"Yeah, we'd better stop." Chi Mai's voice was urgent.

"*Stop*, I said, for heaven's sake. When we say stop, you damn well had better stop!" The fellow with the revolver barked fiercely as he sprang off his vehicle and ran toward us. "Just where do you think you're trying to go with this American anyway? Trying to escape to Danang, eh? Well, I'll just have you know you're not going anywhere until we check you out. Who is this guy with you anyway?" He was talking to Chi Mai and Anh My, apparently assuming that I could not understand him.

Chi Mai tried to restrain her fury. "Now wait a minute, I think there is some misunderstanding here—"

"Misunderstanding! Now you're going to try to lie to me, I suppose. You're going to try to tell me you have joined the revolution!"

"Joined!" Chi Mai lashed the word like cracking a whip. "I've been a part of this revolution for as many years as you are old! Now tell us, why'd you stop us and what do you plan to do with us?"

"Let me see this guy's papers if you are all you claim you are," the fellow retorted, with a quick nod toward me.

"Look, lots of cadres in Quang Ngai know this brother. But it's just one day after liberation. They haven't had time—" Anh My was coming to my defense.

"Let's take 'em back to headquarters," the fellow interrupted.

"Yeah, follow us," the young guerrilla ordered as he turned his Honda around.

"Show us the way!" Chi Mai answered, biting off each word.

I kick-started our stalled engine, did a U-turn and followed our escorting cycle at a distance. Occasionally the fellow with the revolver turned to make sure we were following. He was wearing a white armband, indicating he was permitted to carry arms, but he was dressed as a civilian with a light blue shirt and blue pinstriped trousers flared at the cuffs.

"That rascal! What does he think he's doing anyway! He has no right to act that way. He can't do that. He's a disgrace to the revolution." Chi Mai clanged her metal walking cane on the Honda's luggage rack for emphasis. "What's he know about the revolution anyway? Look at the way he's dressed. He's probably one of these revolutionaries-come-lately, just trying to throw his weight around. The bastard!"

I was much relieved that I was not alone, that Chi Mai and Anh My could be spokespersons for me. Yet I was concerned that Chi Mai's bubbling wrath—as justified as it seemed to me—might only incur more trouble for us. "Maybe we'd better take it easy, Chi Mai. It is just one day after liberation. Everyone's a little jumpy. This guy's just doing his duty—checking out any suspicious-looking characters on the road."

"Checking them out! All right, I don't begrudge him that. But he doesn't have to be rude about it. Talking like that! Where's his *revolutionary discipline!* I tell you, Anh Kien, true revolutionaries don't act like that—he's a disgrace to the revolution!"

We followed our escorts for several hundred meters until we came to an intersection with a small dirt road. The guerrilla and the other youth conferred with several other guerrillas along the road and we pulled our cycle up beside theirs.

"So what's your verdict?" Chi Mai fairly spit out the question.

"Watch it, woman. You don't talk that way to the troops of the revolution," the guerrilla said, eying Chi Mai sharply.

"Well, I just asked what you wanted us to do?" Chi Mai said, obviously showing more respect to the guerrilla than to his pistol-swinging partner.

"You will follow us, that's what you'll do," said the youth with the revolver as he climbed back onto their cycle. "You are under arrest!"

"Who is under arrest, this fellow," Chi Mai nodded toward me, "or us?"

"All three of you! Now let's go!"

We again followed their Honda onto a dusty path, which led through a small collection of thatch houses. Some of the local residents heard the commotion and came to their doors to watch.

"Oh look! They've caught an American!" Several women standing in their doorways called out to their neighbors and were pointing at me. The children picked up the chorus.

"*Bat Ong My! Bat Ong My!* They've caught an American!"

We cut off that path onto an even smaller trail, which eventually led to a thatch farmhouse sitting in a grove of fruit trees and bamboos. The lead cycle stopped and the blue-shirted youth ran into the house shouting he had captured an American.

We pulled up our Honda and parked. The courtyard in front of the house was covered with waist-high stacks of M-16 rifles. Rifles everywhere, heaped like stacks of firewood all over the courtyard.

The fellow came running out of the house again with a rope in his hands. "Tie him up! Tie him up!" insisted an old farmer in the courtyard.

By that time I had already begun speaking to another guerrilla who was standing close to one of the piles of rifles. "Quite a collection of guns you have here, eh? Oh, I see you even have some mortar tubes over there. What a haul!" I tried my best to appear friendly and innocuous.

"Hey, this fellow speaks our language!" The guerrilla marveled to the farmer. "Who is he anyway?"

I took the opportunity to promote an unthreatening image of myself. "Oh, we're from Quang Ngai city. We have contact with the revolutionary cadres in the city. This afternoon we decided to visit this part of the countryside, and these brothers wanted to inquire about us, so they invited us in here."

The guerrilla was obviously surprised to hear a foreigner speak his language and he soon relaxed. The tension of the moment subsided and the white-banded youth was left standing with his limp rope.

"What's the story on this?" The guerrilla by the guns asked him. The fellow, in markedly more moderate terms, explained that he had spotted us driving along the highway and had deemed it his responsibility to find out who I was. It was his job, after all, to maintain security in the area, he explained.

"Well, I think we need to consult Anh Quang on this problem," the guerrilla announced.

"Say, Mr. American, who do you suppose made these guns? Do you think they were sent here to help us?"

"All right, let's go find Anh Quang."

The fellow wound up the rope and returned to his cycle at the gate where his driver was waiting. They rode off together out the path. Anh My and I continued to converse with the guerrilla by the stack of guns for several minutes. He explained that the rifles, mortar tubes and the piles of field radios stacked on the porch had been abandoned by the ARVN out on the highway the night of liberation. This farmhouse served as one of the collection points for the weapons. I walked through the mounds of weapons and received no protest when I raised my camera to shoot pictures of the American guns. As I looked through the range finder to focus as one stack of M-16's, I caught sight of a girl washing rice by a well across the courtyard. I could not help contemplating the juxtaposition. A bucolic hamlet scene of simple tranquillity beside heaps of the most highly engineered rifles on earth.

Nor was the irony of the situation lost on two old farmers who came falteringly down the path. When they spotted me they paused close by. They carried an air of confidence about them, a dignity that comes only with spending much time in the soil. The one man raised a polished bamboo cane and tapped it on the stack of rifles next to me. Then with a mischievous glint in his eyes he said to the American visitor, "Say, sir, maybe you could tell us—just where do these guns come from?" He paused, but just for effect, not long enough for me to answer. "Who do you suppose made these guns? Do you have any idea why these guns are here? In our country of golden-skinned people?"

117

He paused again but still would give me no mercy. "Do you suppose these guns were sent here to help us? Well, I don't imagine you would know the answers to these questions, but I was just curious!" Without waiting for a response, the older farmer nodded graciously and resumed walking down the path with his friend!

For the next half hour or so while we waited, Chi Mai stayed at the gate and captured a group of local residents with her vigorous explanations of how she had served with the revolution for many years and was personally acquainted with high-level PRG personalities. "And this American. He is not a soldier, like the other Americans you've seen. He is opposed to American intervention in Vietnam. He's a *progressive* American. And for that fellow to come up behind us and curse and yell at us—well, I just think it's a disgrace to the revolution! Don't you think so, uncles and aunts? Sure, if he has to carry out his duties, that's fine. But just let him be a little respectful and disciplined when he does it. I really don't think guys like that ought to be able to carry firearms around if they are not more discreet in how they throw their authority around."

I was still amused by Chi Mai's unwaning indignation. "Come, come, Chi Mai. The poor guy thought I was an American imperialist trying to escape to Danang or Chu Lai. He was only trying to do his job." The villagers seemed confused to find themselves agreeing with the remark of the captured American. But Chi Mai would not be assuaged.

Finally, a tall, lean guerrilla with a cloth hat and a cadre's bag appeared on the Honda with the guerrilla who had assisted in our arrest. This was presumably the Anh Quang they had spoken of. A man of perhaps forty-five, he quietly inquired of Chi Mai and Anh My our backgrounds and our purpose for traveling in that area. Chi Mai explained our story in a most comradely manner and in the process dropped the names of several high-ranking revolutionary figures she had worked with in Central Vietnam before she lost her legs. Anh Quang seemed duly impressed and promised he would help us as soon as possible. He said he would have to check with someone else about our status. Before he left, Chi Mai calmly related to Anh Quang her story of our being stopped, and ended by saying, "Now I grant that that fellow was right in checking us out, but his manner was most disgraceful. I am only concerned that action like that will lose prestige for the revolution, and I wonder if he should be permitted to carry a weapon."

"Well, I'll look into this and get back to you as soon as possible," the cadre replied.

Anh Quang returned after a half hour with word that we were free to go. "I want to say that we are very sorry about this misunderstanding. We are sorry to have caused you this inconvenience. But after this you really should carry some identifying papers with you from the province officials. That way you could avoid problems of this sort."

We thanked Anh Quang for his assistance and promised that we would try to acquire travel papers at the first opportunity. Before we left, Anh Quang spoke softly to Chi Mai and Anh My. "You must forgive that fellow who stopped you. He is not really a trained revolutionary as you could probably tell. You see, he actually used to be a Saigon Government soldier. Then he defected and was subsequently arrested by the Saigon Military Police and sent off to the front lines unarmed, as a battlefield coolie to carry ammunition for the ARVN troops. About a month ago he deserted again and this time he went to the countryside and turned himself over to the revolution. So now that liberation has come, we wanted to show our good faith in him by allowing him to participate in security-keeping missions. But I'll have to talk to him, and if he continues to be so undisciplined, perhaps we'll have to take his gun from him. But please excuse us, and please understand that he was trying to do what he thought was his responsibility. Now, have a safe trip back to Quang Ngai."

Bidding adieu to Anh Quang and the gathering of villagers, our trio jumped onto the cycle and as the Truong Son mountain range was preparing to engulf the giant orange sun, we sped back home to Quang Ngai city. We would have to wait until later to see what happened "on up the road."

On the Tuesday afternoon of the liberation of Quang Ngai, Hiro and I had seen a green and white National Police jeep driving up Phan Boi Chau. But instead of being filled with police in khaki camouflage fatigues, the two front seats of the jeep were carrying green-helmeted *bo doi*. Between the two *bo doi* sat Major Loc, our ARVN friend who had proposed the "miniature Disneyland" for Quang Ngai. Apparently he had been serious when he told me the afternoon before that he was not going to flee town. He had a red band tied around his right arm. When he sighted Hiro and me riding along the street, he waved broadly and smiled.

On Wednesday evening at supper Anh My reported, "Today I heard that Major Loc and several other officers have come forth with statements in support of the revolution."

"Oh, and what did they say?" I asked.

"Well, he got up at Province Council Office downtown and said something to the effect: 'I see that the path of the revolution is the right way. I am ready to serve the revolution in any way possible. I am ready and eager to help liberate those provinces still under Thieu's control.' That's about what all the officers said," Anh My finished.

There was little doubt that Major Loc's self-serving statement was contrived to please the revolutionary officials around him. Yet, that the new army had arrived with no bloodletting had produced an initial wave of relief and optimism throughout town. The fact that Major Loc seemed so relaxed when we saw him that afternoon indicated that at least he was not resisting what now seemed an inevitable shifting of the balance of power countrywide.

Mood of relief or not, it quickly became clear that the new authorities had a very clear plan for consolidating their victory. Dispatching high-school students throughout town with M-16 rifles was an attempt to prevent looting and other minor offenses during the days of transition. The larger problem was registering and demobilizing the remnants of the Saigon Army and police forces which still remained in, or had returned to, Quang Ngai city. Perhaps with an aim to capitalize on the initial wave of relaxation that swept town, the new authorities lost no time in setting up the registration procedures for each member of the army, police or civil service of the Saigon Government.

Wednesday evening the propaganda truck of the former Ministry of Information buzzed up and down the streets of Quang Ngai, now with several *bo doi* with a high-pitched chant reading a new kind of information into the microphone: "A-lo, a-lo—all civil servants and officials of the puppet administration and all troops of the puppet army shall report to the Provincial Council Building tomorrow in order to register with the authorities of the Provisional Revolutionary Government. A-lo. A-lo." The "o" of the last "a-lo" would invariably trail off in a falling pitch, giving a plaintive tone to the announcement.

"Puppet." We were hearing the term for the first time in Quang Ngai. It was hardly a flattering label, and yet certainly less harsh than the title of "enemy," which was used less frequently. Only the morning would reveal if the "puppet" troops and civil servants would heed the mandate to register.

THURSDAY, 27 MARCH. By Thursday morning the grounds of the Provincial Council Building were jammed with officials and troops, now dressed primarily in the whites, blues and grays of civilian clothes. Each registrant was handed a Self-Declaration Form to fill out and submit to the authorities. The form was thorough. In addition to name, birth, residence, religion, level of education, social class and so forth, it asked registrants to list all their affiliations with the PRG and with the Saigon administration. Each person was also required to provide such information about his father, mother, brothers, sisters, wife and children. Just above the line for the registrant's signature was a pledge:

> I pledge that the matters which I have voluntarily declared above are true and correct. I promise from this point to dissociate from the Saigon authority and to stand completely in the ranks of the Revolution. I will follow and approve every policy platform and guideline of the Revolutionary Authorities.

On the street outside the registration center I ran into Anh Den, a police lieutenant friend who with his wife and children had frequently visited in our home. We had known them since 1967 when his wife, Chi Xuan, taught in a sewing class Pat had established in a refugee camp. This morning Anh Den's eyes shifted with haunting anxiety. He bore the visage of a wraith.

"Anh Kien, you're still here." His voice was languid. "Chi Xuan and the children are gone. I don't know if I shall ever see them again."

"Gone? Gone where?"

"They fled toward Danang on Monday night, and you know what happened along the road. I fled too, but at a different time. And I just made it back into town."

"I suppose you will have to register with the new authorities?" I asked.

"Yes, we all have to register. I guess I'll register today. Kien, I'm afraid this is the end!" I could hardly hear Anh Den's voice as his head dropped toward the ground. "Kien, now I must go."

Anh Den was born in North Vietnam. After the French defeat in 1954, the twelve-year-old Den was encouraged by his Catholic parents to go south. It had never been clear to us why his parents had not come with him, but Den had heard many rumors of brutal treatment of landlords in the North, which had persuaded him to follow his parents' advice. Because of one eye that was nearly blind, Anh Den could have been exempt from military service in the South, but he voluntarily chose to join the National Police. It was one of few ways he knew to earn a living for his four children; then again, he wanted to contribute to the anti-Communist struggle. Den was not a vicious person. If anything, he had always seemed plagued with an inferiority complex, perhaps because of the bad eye, which he often covered with a pair of tinted glasses. With the salary of a police lieutenant, Anh Den and Chi Xuan, his particularly gregarious wife, had experienced tremendous difficulty in making ends meet. Pat and I had originally felt the problem was Chi Xuan's inability to manage finances, but we finally concluded their poverty was due to Anh Den's refusal to accept bribes in his job. They were living only on his salary, which amounted to thirty-five dollars per month.

The temptation to take bribe money had been tremendous. There hardly seemed enough money to provide clothes or food for their family, let alone to move out of their tight two-room house into more adequate quarters. Furthermore, nearly all Anh Den's colleagues in the National Police regularly accepted bribes as daily routine. But in conversations with Anh Den and Chi Xuan, various contradictory reasons emerged for his eschewing such payoffs. For one, Den was a Catholic, and he apparently felt it would be morally wrong to accept a bribe. Then too, Anh Den appeared to believe genuinely that the graft of Saigon Government officials was seriously eroding the effectiveness of the anti-Communist front. For him to participate in such corruption would be a negation of the cause for which he had abandoned his home in North Vietnam and would contribute to a Communist victory in the South. Finally, the village where Anh Den was station chief of the local police station was extremely poor, and there just were not many opportunities to exploit the local people for bribes. Then, within the last three months, Anh Den had been transferred to a more wealthy region, and although he never spoke about it, Chi Xuan said her husband had begun to come home occasionally with "supplemental income." Apparently the pressures to take bribes had gotten the best of Anh Den.

Now Anh Den's world had suddenly been turned upside down. His wife and children were unaccounted for, and he had to face a regime similar to the one he had fled twenty years before. I watched Anh Den walk up the street. He circled back and paced listlessly on the sidewalk opposite the registration grounds. He hesitated, then walked in toward the registration center. He seemed almost to be limping as he made his way through the crowd of reporting troops.

For all the Anh Dens who registered that day and the following days, there must have been at least some solace in their sheer numbers. If it was traumatic to face the uncertainty of placing oneself in the hands of authorities whom one had regarded as enemy, there was at least the assurance that one was not alone. In fact, so many ARVN troops and officials registered on Thursday that the authorities ran out of registration forms by the end of the day.

Late in the afternoon, after the registrants had all gone home, a few cadres were busy gathering together the forms and closing up the registration building. As Hiro and I walked into the center we met Chi Phuoc, the cadre friend of Chi Mai's who had visited us on the night of liberation. Chi Phuoc was one of the cadres assigned to register the "puppet" troops and officials.

"Good heavens, what a job! This is harder work than fighting in the countryside," Chi Phuoc sighed. Yet it was obvious in her tone of voice and the manner in which she worked that she was quite pleased with the responsibility she had been given. She introduced us to several other cadres who were working with her. One seemed quite pleased to have the chance to converse with several foreigners. He spoke at length about U.S. policy in Vietnam and ended on a note of explanation about the policy of registering the "puppet" troops, a policy that he obviously felt was most lenient and humane, "in keeping with our policy of national reconciliation and concord." He ended with a final word of advice to us.

"We're delighted that you stayed here in Quang Ngai. You will be in a position to tell many people around the world about liberation. But make sure you record things exactly as you see them. Don't be like some of those foreign correspondents who fabricated stories about us that were not true. You must tell the truth objectively."

Hiro and I talked with a number of ARVN troops who had registered, the majority of whom were taking the procedure well in stride. There were, however, at least some for whom confronting the "enemy" face to face remained deeply unsettling. Thursday evening around the supper table at the Quaker house, Anh My related the experience of an ARVN sergeant

Chi Phuoc (*center*) and her fellow cadres register three local ARVN soldiers. "Revolutionaries" and "puppets" sometimes turned out to be cousins or old schoolmates.

who lived next door to him. I remembered the unusually rotund neighbor of My's from an encounter several months before during a Tet celebration at My's house. After our dinner with My's family, the half-drunk sergeant had insisted that Pat and I visit his house for a few minutes. Seemingly eager to win the friendship of Americans, he had talked at length of the admirable contribution the United States had made to Vietnam in its fight against communism. The sergeant himself was a refugee of sorts. He had formerly been a wealthy landowner in an area toward the sea, which had come under PRG control. He spoke bitterly of having been dispossessed of his landholdings and concluded that he could "never live with the Viet Cong."

Anh My now related that this sergeant had fled town on Monday night with the ARVN evacuation but returned to Quang Ngai on Tuesday. When the revolutionary authorities decreed that all ARVN should register, the ARVN sergeant had complied. But after his registration was completed earlier in the day, the sergeant returned to his home and swallowed "some kind of pills." That night the sergeant was dead.

Thursday evening after dinner we received our first full account of Monday night's flight of terror when the ARVN had gone careering out of town. We had known that a number of townsfolk had been swept up in the wake of the ARVN exodus. Among those people were several workers at the Quaker Rehabilitation Center. Anh Quy, a longtime acquaintance of ours, was an unusually resourceful and levelheaded person. While Anh Quy had never expressed himself as explicitly supportive of the PRG, he was certainly not a partisan for the Saigon Government. He had relatives on both sides of the conflict. His wife, Chi Phuong, was from a farming background but now lived in town and spent her time taking care of their two small children. Finally, there was Chi Tuyet who, like Quy and Phoung, seemed to have nothing to fear from a change in government. They had been, nevertheless, swept up in the panicked evacuation of town Monday night.

"It was horrible," Chi Phuong related with wide eyes. "The trucks going north were jammed, literally layered with people. The truck beds were so full that babies were crushed to death. Mothers had to abandon their dead babies and run on. I saw one mother jump out of the truck, run into a rice field, push aside the soil with her hands to bury her baby and then run on.

"A soldier at the Tra Khuc bridge threw off his grenades as he was running. One exploded and killed a mother and child. At Binh Hiep—about twenty minutes north of Quang Ngai—soldiers were dead, lying along both sides of the road, and in the middle of the road too. I guess 'the Front' had fired in a couple of mortars and the troops panicked. They took off their uniforms and threw their guns and grenades to the ground. Some of the officers started shooting at these men to discourage others from throwing away their guns. One body lying by the side of the road had not a piece of flesh left on it. People walking had to climb over the dead bodies. Some of the bodies were still twisting and turning.

"Oh God, you wouldn't believe it. Quy and I were lucky enough to get in the cab of one of the trucks or my children would have been smashed to death. Oh God, it was horrible.

"One man along the way was stumbling with blood streaming out of his head. His wife had just been killed. He was carrying a baby in his arms and crying out, 'Please save my child. Please save my child,' but no one would take the child.

"We got to Binh Hiep about midnight and spent the rest of the night there."

Chi Tuyet had fled Quang Ngai before Quy and Phuong and she was able to travel the whole way to the former American port base at Chu Lai, 25 miles north of Quang Ngai. Tuyet picked up the story where Phuong left off. "It was like we were animals in a stampede. Just rushing madly in the night. When we got to Chu Lai, people fought madly to get onto one of the ships. The people had to wade through waist-high water to get to the ship, but everyone was fighting and shoving so much that old people and babies got trampled in the water. Somebody threw a rope down from the ship and a mother with three children tried to climb up the rope, but she dropped one of her children and it fell into the water while she was climbing. There was nothing she could do. A lot of soldiers pushed their way onto the ship. The ship was jammed. But other soldiers who couldn't get aboard threw grenades onto the ship to wipe out a layer of people so that they could climb in on top. Then they threw the dead bodies off the ship into the water. Then more soldiers began throwing grenades onto the ship and soon the soldiers on the ship were throwing grenades back at the ones trying to get aboard. Six or seven grenades at a time. By the end, the last people getting on the ship didn't have to wade through the water. They just walked over a ramp of bodies. It was so terrible, I didn't even try to get on a ship. I stayed in Chu Lai for the night and came back to Quang Ngai the next day."

The eight or ten people in the room were silent for a moment, and then Chi Phuong continued her story. "Anh Quy and I spent the night at Binh Hiep with crowds of other people. We all just huddled together there in the rice paddies. Soldiers had stripped off their uniforms and were going around begging clothes from civilians. From midnight to seven in the morning, everything was quiet. Then at dawn there was a brief gun battle. There was still one truck loaded with ARVN and their families. The ARVN started firing at some Viet Cong—I mean *bo doi*," Chi Phuong smiled as she quickly corrected her out-of-date vocabulary, "and the *bo doi* fired back. Nearly everyone in the truck was killed.

"Then the *bo doi* came out announcing that all of Quang Ngai Province was liberated and there would be no reprisals. The people should raise their hands or hold white flags in the air. You should have seen us. Everyone scrambled to find a white cloth. Some used white shirts or undershirts. Anh Quy and others managed to get the long skirts of the girl students' white *ao dai* dresses and tie them onto long sticks. *Troi oi*, we must have looked silly, a whole sea of people marching down the road with their arms reaching in the air and furiously waving white flags. And then somebody started a chant, which we were soon all yelling, '*Cach Mang Muon Nam*. Long live the Revolution!' Can't you see Anh Quy waving a girl's skirt in the air and calling out 'Long live the Revolution!'" The image was indeed an unlikely one, and even Quy could not help joining the laughter that broke the stunned silence of the people in the room.

"As you look back on it now," someone asked Chi Phuong, "what made you flee Quang Ngai on Monday night?"

"I was afraid for my children. There was no shooting when we left at eight o'clock and I was afraid the town would be mortared and everyone would be killed. I couldn't think of living in a bunker with my children for days, so I insisted we run. Anh Quy didn't want to go, but I insisted. Luckily I was sitting in front of the truck or my children would have been crushed to death. I didn't fear the revolution, I was just afraid of the shelling."

Chi Tuyet had a similar response. "I don't know," she said, "I just saw that everyone was running and I thought I'd better run too."

We were never able to learn the number of casualties in Monday night's flight of terror. Chi Phuong and others we talked to subsequently believed that from several hundred to a thousand people had been killed. In light of the utter peacefulness of the take-over of Quang Ngai city, one could not help feeling the tragic and unnecessary waste of that nocturnal exodus. One wanted to say, "If only—" But then all the unnecessary tragedies of this long war had been a long chain of blood stained "if only's—"

FRIDAY, 28 MARCH.   Friday evening Mr. Chau, our landlord, invited Hiro and me for dinner. The Liberation Army was in the process of taking control of Danang city to the north, and Mr. Chau seemed ready to accept the course of events. "All of this region is now"—he paused a split second as he grasped for the right word—"liberated, and as far as I'm concerned I hope the whole country goes along with it quickly. There's really no other way for this country now, so let's get it over with quickly. And now the radio talks about your country's plans to evacuate a lot of Vietnamese. If you don't mind my saying so, I think this is just another one of the many blunders your country has made in Vietnam. Who are they going to evacuate? The Saigon generals. Thieu and his sort. They're the ones who've sold out Vietnam. They're the only ones who got rich off American dollars and now your country is going to reward them with a ticket to the United States. They're the ones who should be forced to stay in Vietnam and face the consequences of their corruption.

"Vietnam's true nationalists won't be evacuated—but then your government never could tolerate them. The true nationalists would have refused to become American puppets like Thieu and his sort."

Mr. Chau suddenly stopped talking, smiled and then apologized, "Forgive me, Anh Kien, I don't mean to insult your government, but then I know you don't agree with their policy either. That's what I do admire about your country: If you disagree with your government, you can stand right up and say it. That has never been permitted here in Vietnam."

After this predinner conversation Mr. Chau invited Hiro and me to join him and a schoolteacher friend at the table. His older children served an elegant meal, which we knew was atypical for his family. It was the first time we had been invited to share a meal in his house.

"I'm delighted you fellows can join us for this meal," he said as he broke the crisp *banh trang* rice paper to open the meal. "You know I should have invited you all for a meal before this, but before this week there was always the possibility people would not understand. Now it's different." Mr. Chau did not expound on the differences. One could only suppose Mr. Chau's former hesitancy related to the suspicion among high-school teachers that we were connected with American intelligence operations and that now our having stayed through the change of government had finally dispelled that suspicion. On the other hand, because of our work in the remote countryside and the reputation of Mennonites and Quakers for opposing the war, perhaps Mr. Chau had felt our "anti-war" sentiments would have made too close association with us risky under the Saigon regime. Or it could have been a confusing combination of these factors, because during the war it was impossible for anyone to trust totally another person. In fact, the bungling and ineffectual nature of the United States intervention in Vietnam, together with President Nixon's sudden courting of the People's Republic of China, had actually caused some Vietnamese to suspect that the CIA in some cases might deliberately be assisting the Communists in Vietnam!

Whatever cause there might have been for past reservations, now there was a new freedom in our sharing. Over dinner we discussed the events of the preceding days. Mr. Chau told us that he had registered earlier in the day, since all public high-school teachers had been paid by the Saigon Government and were consequently considered to be civil servants. We asked him what he saw for his future.

"Well, I've had a long teaching career. I think I would like to retire now. You know, before, I used to write some poems. Well, I would like to concentrate on literature again. I think I could serve the people and the country well by writing, to inspire the people, to encourage them to rebuild our country. I would like to get back to writing more poetry."

SATURDAY, 29 MARCH. "We'll ride out through My Lai, down to the sea, and then north to my village. You'll see what the war really meant to the people of Vietnam. We'll spend the night in my hamlet. You'll see how peaceful it is in the liberated zone." Anh My, our paramedic friend from the Rehabilitation Center, easily persuaded Hiro and me to join him for a two-day bicycle trip to the remote villages along the sea in the northeastern part of the province. The area had been one of the cruelest battlegrounds of the war.

We felt much more free to travel now since we had received official papers from the new government. Friday morning, Le Quang Vinh, still cheerful and optimistic, though apparently getting only little sleep because of the press of duties immediately following Liberation, had stopped in at our house and filled out official identificaiton and travel papers for Hiro and me. The papers were standardized forms in which the issuing cadre wrote the name and the mission of the recipient. So on my paper after the first line, "We respectfully introduce Comrade _____," was written: "*Kien. American.*" Just above Le Quang Vinh's signature (actually he signed a pseudonym: Nguyen Vy Dai) and the official seal of the People's Revolutionary Committee, Quang Ngai Province, was the final statement: "Recommend all local agencies and personnel assist comrade *Kien* fulfill his duties."

Our new titles provided considerable amusement for all our friends at the Quaker house, so Friday night Anh My had concluded his trip proposal with, "Well, *comrades*, what do you think? Shall we set out in the morning?"

Saturday morning at a respectably early hour we were off, riding three abreast down Phan Boi Chau. Anh My's wife and children were still in refuge on the offshore island of Ly Son, but we stopped at the pagoda to pick up a mutual friend of ours from My's native hamlet who had requested to travel with us. Chi Sau was a woman in her late forties who had spent most of the last five years in prison after the Saigon Government police accused her of being a Communist communications agent. She had been released in June, nine months before, and since then had been cooking and serving meals to the teachers and monks at the pagoda.

After heading north out of Quang Ngai and crossing the river, we turned east toward the sea. We soon passed one of the many refugee camps built on the outskirts of Quang Ngai to house the people who had been driven off their farms by the war. This morning a man was swinging a heavy club, smashing the mud walls of his refugee house. Others were pulling the thatch off the roofs of other huts. In fact, most of the mud buildings in the camp were already demolished. Men were salvaging the bamboo posts that had formed the framework of the houses. Others were taking beds, tables, cooking pots, bamboo poles or a few sheets of USAID-supplied tin roofing and tying them onto bicycles or shoulder poles. Already the road ahead of us was streaming with people pushing their loaded bicycles or jogging to the rhythm of swinging shoulder poles.

"Where are you going?" we called as we biked past one group of refugees.

"We're going back to Son Quang," one called back.

"Just tell them we're going home," corrected another.

It had been a long time in "going home" for some of these people. Some of them had been in the refugee camps for eight or ten years. One group of refugees came from east of My Lai, from the villages of the Batangan Peninsula, which jutted out into the sea. The area had known a strong revolutionary presence for decades. During the "First Indochina War," the French were never able to make inroads into the province, and the people of Batangan, like other regions, had built watchtowers to scout for French bombers, which occasionally harassed the people of the province. After the French defeat in 1954 many of the men from this region were among those

(opposite and overleaf)
For refugee farmers, the war's end brought liberation from years of idleness and despair in the camps. They loaded everything they owned onto bicycles or into shoulderpole baskets, crying happily to one another, "We're going home!"

who had "regrouped" in North Vietnam under the provisions of the Geneva Accords. We had a close friend in Quang Ngai city whose native home was in the Batangan. As a lad he had often heard his mother relate to him the story of his father leaving with a party of men for North Vietnam.

"My mother said that she and Father knew for several months that he would be leaving, but no one knew the day. It had to be secret so that the French or the Saigon troops would not sabotage their trip. Then one evening, just as it was becoming dark outside, a knock came on the door. It was the men who had planned to go with Father. He picked up the cloth bandoleer of rice that Mother had prepared for him and slung it across his shoulder. He put on his conical straw hat and was all ready to go. Then Mother says he picked me up and embraced me. I was only three years old. He said good-bye to Mother and pulled his thatch-grass raincoat around his shoulders and walked out into the rainy night carrying a small lantern. That is really the only memory I have of my father, watching out the door of our little house as he walked the winding dike through the rice fields. I can still remember that lantern bobbing up and down."

Our friend, never having met his father again, stepped on a mine in 1968 in the Batangan and lost the lower part of his left leg. He left his native village to get treatment in the Quang Ngai hospital, then stayed in the city to work.

Batangan was the French and American variation of the Vietnamese name Ba Lang An, or the Three Villages of Peace. It was a misnomer of the first degree. They were three villages of war.

The American and Korean "allies" had spared little in their attempts to "pacify" the Batangan and the surrounding villages in this northeastern part of the province. In addition to the notorious My Lai massacre in 1968, there had been numerous other massacres in the region, most frequently carried out by Korean troops operating in the area. Diane and Michael Jones, former representatives of the Quaker Rehabilitation Center, researched this region and documented no fewer than twenty massacres by the Korean Blue Dragon Marine Brigade between 1966 and 1968. Each slaughter averaged about ninety persons killed—mostly old men, women and children.

Pat and I had worked with a Mennonite Central Committee program of providing financial assistance to students who would otherwise have had to drop out of school to help support their families. The home of one of our scholarship students, Anh Viet, had been in this region, and he retained particularly vivid memories of the Korean troops.

"I remember those times when the muffled shouts passed from house to house in the hamlet: 'The soldiers are coming.' We would run and look toward the distant hill. We'd watch to see if they were big—or small like the Vietnamese. If they were tall, we were not so afraid. We knew they were Americans. If they were small, that meant they were Koreans, and we ran for our lives.

131

"So savage!" Anh Viet shuddered as he reminisced one morning in our living room. "Sometimes it was like they were hunting wild game. They would shoot and injure a guerrilla. They then would track him. If his blood trail led back to a village, they were apt to kill all the people in the vicinity on the pretext that it was a Communist village."

We asked Anh Viet if the Koreans ever killed anyone in his hamlet. "No, not in ours, but in Lac Son, the neighboring hamlet, they herded the people into a field and just shot them down. About four hundred people. My father and some of the men from our hamlet went down the next day and buried the people. It took all day. They found one small baby still alive, lying amidst all the bodies. It was still sucking at its mother's breast, but the mother was dead." Anh Viet shook his head. "After that, lots of people around there left to join the Viet Cong."

The American military was more apt to rely on sophisticated equipment that put greater distance between the troops and the victims. "Spotter planes" constantly droned over the countryside. If the pilot detected any suspicious activity, he could hit the area immediately with phosphorous rockets or he could radio the coordinates to an artillery battery that would have shells bursting on the spot within minutes. Under this arrangement, the enemy could remain impersonal. The enemy never had a face. Only a body. That's what you counted. Any dead person was defined as an enemy and was included in the day's "body count."

Despite the danger, however, many people decided to stick it out in the countryside. It was, after all, home. The fields and the cattle were here, and that was the only way to support your family. To leave them seemed like a vote for suicide by starvation.

In the end, the "Allied" strategists finally decided that the presence of peasant farmers in the region meant increased support for the guerrillas. The oft-cited maxim was true: The guerrillas were like fish swimming in the sea of the people. After many frustrated attempts to "pacify" the Batangan region, the U.S. Americal Division operating out of Chu Lai launched what they hoped would be a final solution to the problem: Dry up the sea.

"Operation Bold Mariner" was launched in January 1969. It would—it was hoped—solve the problem of guerrilla harassment from the Batangan once and for all. During a four-day period six American and ARVN battalions—approximately 2,000 troops—circled the Batangan villages in a "soft cordon" operation. Leaflets dropped from planes ordered all the residents of the villages to assemble in open fields. From there the people were hustled aboard large Chinook helicopters, ferried six miles toward Quang Ngai city and dumped out on a barren sandspit along the Tra Khuc River. Into a two-acre area surrounded with barbed wire, the 11,000 villagers were corralled, but only after they had gone through intense interrogation by the Vietnamese National Police to weed out and imprison the "VCS" and the "VCC"—the Viet Cong Suspects and Viet Cong Confirmed. As the villagers were sent through the gate into the camp, they were greeted by several television sets featuring Saigon Government propaganda films. Over the entrance to the camp a large banner in Vietnamese read: "The People are Grateful to the Government for Emancipating Them, For Providing a Way of Escape from the Treacherous Communists."

I had visited the camp a number of times in 1969 and learned from the farmers that their "emancipation" had been in process for several years. In response to an inquiry about their rice yield, one farmer told me, "Well, we really haven't had a rice crop in my village for over a year and a half. One day the planes came and bombed the dikes we had built along the seacoast and our fields were flooded with salt water." A group of young boys in the camp had told me they had not been in school for the last several years. "It was too dangerous. We didn't dare get together in large groups. One bomb could have killed us all," they said.

After the people were all removed from Batangan—with the exception of the guerrillas hiding in the labyrinthine network of underground tunnels— the American and ARVN troops systematically destroyed all the houses and any other structures in the area. It was, an American official had explained, an attempt "to deprive these resources to the enemy." Once the "Viet Cong infrastructure" had been wiped out, many of the Batangan people were moved back to the peninsula. Not to their native homes, of course. They had been burned to the ground. But to "return to the village" camps on the pattern of the dreaded "strategic hamlets" in the early 1960s. Here the people were placed under sharp police surveillance and had to be within the perimeter of the camps by an early curfew each evening. Others of these "refugees from communism" from villages neighboring the Batangan were never able to return to the countryside because their villages were still regular targets of harassment and interdiction shelling—"H and I fire"— from American or ARVN howitzers.

Now today, the "liberation" of Quang Ngai Province meant literal liberation for these refugees from the camps that had contained them for five to ten years.

All along our route we passed the caravan of home-goers. Five miles to the east we came to the site of the most notorious symbol of the Vietnam War—My Lai. Today the hamlet was silent. It was exactly seven years to the month after Lt. William Calley and Charlie Company entered this hamlet one morning and demonstrated graphically to the world the logic that is war. Today the only memorial to the several hundred men, women, children and babies being gunned down in cold blood was the plaintive whisper of the breeze through the pine trees that line that ignominious irrigation ditch where many of the bodies once lay.

The tragedy at My Lai never was as talked about in Quang Ngai as it was in the United States, where it became a shocking revelation to many Americans. Pat and I were living in Quang Ngai city at the time of the My Lai massacre, but in the succeeding months we never once heard specific mention of My Lai from any of our friends. The only reference was a vague one about a month after the massacre from a fourteen-year-old boy who visited our home. I was sorting medicines in the small warehouse for our team nurse when Em Luan appeared on the scene, begging for a box of Band-Aids. I explained we could not just hand out medical supplies to everyone who asked.

"Oh, I know why you won't give me any. You think we'll take them home and give them to the Viet Cong, don't you, Anh Kien?" I explained to the lad that that was not a consideration for us, that we attempted not to differentiate political sympathies in giving assistance.

"Oh, I see," he replied. "Then you're different from the American soldiers. They go out on operations and kill little children like that fellow standing at the gate"—he pointed to a small neighbor boy at the gate—"and they kill old men with beards and they burn down houses and destroy everything. The Americans are imitating the Koreans in the way they destroy everything. I guess they don't love the Vietnamese people."

The primary reason we heard little about My Lai was that the Vietnamese were afraid to tell an American—or even another Vietnamese who might have been a secret police for the Saigon Government—for fear they would be accused of being *than-cong*, Communist sympathizers. Just as in the United States, so in Saigon Government zones, there existed tremendous pressures to cover up such atrocities. It was only in 1974, for example, that people confided in us that similar killings had taken place in other villages around Quang Ngai. The one about which we received the most corroborating reports was the Truong Khanh massacre. I once asked Anh Nhat, a close friend, why he and the other refugees did not return to their villages in PRG-controlled areas. He shook his head silently. The fine features of his face became fixed as his eyes glazed over. "Kien," he said finally, "the people are still too afraid. Especially the people from Truong Khanh." Anh Nhat went on to explain that a number of the refugees from Truong Khanh, ten kilometers south of Quang Ngai city, had returned to their homes after the Tet Offensive in 1968. A year later American troops launched operations in the vicinity of the Nghia Hanh hills. On the day the troops approached Truong Khanh they triggered a mine that killed four or five Americans. The guerrillas, who had set the mine, had, of course, fled to the mountains. In revenge, the troops stormed the hamlet, which was occupied mostly by old people, women and children.

"They went from house to house. If this family had four, they killed four. If that family had eight, they killed eight. In the end, sixty-two villagers were dead." Anh Nhat's voice became quieter. He gripped my arm and then concluded, "The people of Truong Khanh were broom-makers, so they had broom grass drying in the lofts of their houses. After all the people were dead, the troops put the bodies on a pile, covered them with broom-straw and set them on fire."

Only several weeks later did Anh Nhat call me aside after he had shared a meal in our home. His eyes were blurred. "Kien, there was one thing I didn't tell you the other day. You know, about the people of Truong Khanh—my aunt was one of those killed."

Hiro, Anh My, Chi Sau and I left My Lai and pedaled east another mile or so to the South China Sea. (Significantly, the Vietnamese revolutionaries drop the reference to China and call it the Eastern Sea.) The terrain was level. The only vegetation was an overgrowth of tough grasses and, here and there, a tree along the bank of the river we were following. Anh My informed us that before the war the river had been lined with coconut palms, bamboos and fruit trees. The fields by the path that had once been fructive now lay fallow. The reason soon became obvious.

At the juncture of the river with the ocean, we saw a series of charred posts protruding above the river's surface. It was all that remained of the dike-bridge that once prevented the seawater from intruding into the fields of the area. When this dike was bombed in 1967, the salt water backed up into the river, damaging agriculture in 3,000 or 4,000 acres of rice land in the surrounding villages. Furthermore, it cut land travel between these villages and those that lay north across the river. In 1969 after the Americal Division completed "Operation Bold Mariner," pacifying the region to their satisfaction, they rebuilt the bridges for strategic purposes, to facilitate the movement of trucks and tanks. But the American bridge, constructed over

Homecoming was often tragic. Where once were houses, now were ashes; where rice paddies, now shell-cratered waste land; where trees, the barren swath of a bulldozer's blade. Here even the land was gone, flooded with salt water through the bombed-out dike.

Anh Dong, a My Lai guerrilla, speaks of forgiveness. "Now that's all over. We can begin again."

In the Batangan Peninsula, all seemed scarred by the war except the faces of the young.

large culvert pipes, did not function as a dike, so the fields were still incapable of much production. High fields were able to produce one crop of sweet potatoes or manioc during the rainy season. Finally, even the culvert bridge had been destroyed, once again breaking the transportation route. So our passage across the river would have to be by boat.

Several dozen people gathered by the bank of the river, many of them refugees also waiting for a boat to return to their homes across the river. Among the group were several young guerrillas. Three young women in their early twenties carried American M-16's and one slightly older fellow had an American M-79 grenade launcher slung on his back. Anh My struck up a conversation with the young guerrilla who was cuddling a pudgy, tan puppy in his arms. Shortly, Anh My and the guerrilla were chatting about the area and the people whom they knew in common. Bui Tan Dong seemed a particularly fitting name for the guerrilla because his skin was the deep color of bronze, *dong* in Vietnamese. Anh Dong was so soft-spoken we had to concentrate to catch his answers to our questions.

"There. My home used to stand over there," he said quietly. We could only guess the location from the angle of his pointing arm. "The bulldozers came and then it was over. The trees, the houses. Everything." He explained that the destruction of the pine trees and bamboos created particular hardship for the returning villagers because now they had no shade from the tropical sun, no windbreak from the salty sea breezes and no building materials at a time when all three were most needed.

But the scar of human injury went much deeper. Anh Dong related how several close family members had been killed at My Lai. As a local hamlet guerrilla, he had been captured by the Americans in 1972 and was sent to the prison island of Con Son, infamous for its cramped "tiger cages." He was imprisoned until the end of 1973, when he returned to this hamlet.

Here in this village the effect of the American involvement in Vietnam was exposed in its rawest form. The American policy—ostensibly to assist the Vietnamese—had not only decimated the population but destroyed the very economic base of the people. One would have expected Anh Dong to issue a venomous diatribe against "American imperialism and the traitorous Vietnamese captains of state who sold out to the American policy." Instead, with a quiet earnestness, he spoke of forgiveness.

"Now that's all over. Now we can begin again. It's the policy of our government to welcome back those people who supported that policy."

Our conversation with Anh Dong was interrupted with the sudden appearance of a low-flying helicopter speeding in from the sea and following the river in the direction of Quang Ngai city. A visible alarm spread through the people. My mind raced irrationally. A war plane in a land of peace! Shoot it down! My anger boiled up so spontaneously that only after the helicopter disappeared from sight up the river did I realize that mixed with my rage had been a strong element of fear. In five years I had seen countless helicopters flying over Quang Ngai. During the Tet Offensive in 1968 I had seen helicopter gun ships strafe and fire phosphorus rockets from not a hundred feet over my head. That was frightening enough, but this was the first time I was standing in what these chopper pilots considered enemy territory. For the first time, I was in a position to be a potential target of that helicopter's 30-caliber strafing guns. For the first time, I stood where the Vietnamese villagers "on the other side" had stood. Had I been in this position throughout the war, I fear my pacifist principles might have gone up in smoke.

Anh Dong appeared as calm as ever with the appearance and disappearance of the chopper. It obviously was not the first time for him to be in this position. He speculated that the pilots were attempting to make a rescue of ARVN officers or police who were hiding out in some thicket and radioing Danang, which was still partially in ARVN hands. He said that it was the second helicopter for the morning. An earlier one had been shot down somewhere to the north.

While we were waiting for a boat to show up, an ARVN army jeep came driving toward us from the direction of Quang Ngai. From a distance I could see a red plate with the insignia of a three-star general mounted on the right-hand windshield. The jeep drove toward our group of people, then stopped. A man in civilian clothes jumped out of the driver's seat and a senior-aged *bo doi* emerged from the passenger's side. The *bo doi* strolled about without speaking. He surveyed the landscape and the bombed-out dike, and then, without a word to anyone, he and the driver climbed back into the three-starred jeep and drove off. Only then did Chi Sau whisper to me that the *bo doi* was Anh Van, "one of the highest-ranking party officials in Quang Ngai Province." Just where he had gotten the ARVN jeep with the three-star insignia remained a mystery, because the highest ARVN officer Quang Ngai had ever rated was a general of one star!

Eventually, we received word that a boat was available to ferry us across the river. We pushed our bikes down over a hill toward the water's edge where the sampan was waiting. Upon spotting me, the tall boatman jumped out of his boat and started waving his arms and yelling angrily, "American! American! Grab him! Grab him! Watch him! He's running loose! Get him!"

For a second we were all stunned. Then Anh My and Chi Sau, situated between the boatman and me, quickly walked up to the riled man. "No, no, everything's all right. This American is different. He isn't going to hurt anyone."

"But he shouldn't just be walking around loose like that. After all, just look at what the Americans have done around here. Look at this dike, look at our houses, look at our fields— Open your eyes, I say, and see what the Americans did to our village. Get him, I tell you, get him!" The man's arms kept waving as he continued. "Why, those American invaders even took their bulldozers and pushed the graves of our ancestors into the river. Into the river! Our forefathers' graves! And you say this American is not going to hurt anyone. Grab him, I say! He's dangerous!"

"No, you don't understand," Chi Sau spoke softly as Anh My placed his hand on the man's arm. "This American and his Japanese friend—they're different. They hate the war. They hate the bombing, the bulldozers. These fellows fought against the war. They're for *peace*. They want to help rebuild the countryside. They're our friends."

The lanky boatman ran his hands through his tousled hair. Anh My stood by his side quietly reiterating Chi Sau's explanation of us. The barefooted man eyed us carefully. One could tell he was straining to conceive of an American who was not bent on creating hardship. Could an American actually be friendly? Finally the boatman shook his head, threw down his hands and said, "Well, if they are who you say they are, if they really help the people, then let me lift their bicycles into my boat and I'll take them across the river."

American journalists and scholars had often typed the Vietnamese peasant as one whose interests revolved only around farming and fishing, maintaining good relations with the neighbors, paying homage to the ancestors and continuing the family line. This image saw the peasant as devoid of interest in political affairs and ignorant of the larger national scene around him. In short, he was "apolitical, just wanting to be left alone to farm his rice."

As with most stereotypes, there was a certain truth to this image. But the feelings expressed by these people along the sea in eastern Quang Ngai reflected those we had heard from farmers all over the province. To be sure, they did want to be free to grow their rice, but they had some pretty clear ideas about what and who had been keeping them from their fields and orchards. They were sophisticated enough to know who had bombed their dikes and who had bulldozed their villages. And that knowledge easily converted into some rather powerful feelings about the political forces that swirled about them.

Once across the river we bade adieu to the boatman who turned out to be quite friendly—and talkative—after he decided we were no threat. Now on the Batangan Peninsula we walked past some of the "return to village" camps, which had been set up after "Operation Bold Mariner" had been completed. Unlike the traditional Vietnamese village, which the noted Vietnamese artist Vo Dinh once described as "a garden within the larger garden of fields and hills, rivers and rocks," these camps were a series of hovels built next to one another with none of the saving graces of the individual wells or the tall coconut palms or shading bamboos that are integral to the traditional village.

An hour's walk along the white sands of the Eastern Sea and across the peninsula brought us to a second river to be crossed. Here the boats were in plentiful supply. So were the children. And the inevitable chant began

Returning home with Anh My and Chi Sau through the war-torn "Three Villages of Peace" along the South China Sea.

as soon as the children spotted us. *"Ong My, Ong My.* Mr. American, Mr. American—" When I had first arrived in Quang Ngai I found the thronging of the children most unsettling, but I had long since accepted it as an immutable feature of living in Vietnam. Actually, such discourtesies rarely occurred among children living in their traditional village habitat; but when they were crowded together in the refugee camps or the cities, the chant was sure to erupt. Whenever adults were nearby they would inevitably chide the youngsters for their raucous disrespect, but to no avail. The chanting would continue unabated.

Today, it was safe for Chi Sau to take an approach I had never heard used before. She turned to the swarm of children behind us and said kindly, but firmly, "Here, here—now you children are the nieces and nephews of Uncle Ho! And it's not polite to shout like that at our guests." The allusion to the national revolutionary leader Ho Chi Minh did the trick. The children immediately became silent.

Our boat across this second river was larger and we rode with several other passengers. Chi Sau recognized one of the women aboard. "Weren't you in prison the same time I was?" Chi Sau exclaimed. And in the following minutes the two women shared experiences of their time in the Quang Ngai jail. They reminisced about one warden who was especially heartless in his dealings with the prisoners, of the meager fare in prison, of the cold cement floors that served as beds for the prisoners. The two women were silent for a moment. Chi Sau's friend looked pensively up the river and then concluded simply, "Now there'll be no more prison."

140

"Yes, sister," Chi Sau affirmed, "prison's over."

The dock on the other side of the river marked our entry into Binh Chau village. I had previously heard only the name Binh Duc for this village but now learned that the Saigon Government had changed all the village names in 1954. Binh Chau was the name the Viet Minh had used before 1954 and the PRG side continued that name until the present day.

Perhaps eight square miles in area, Binh Chau was the "native village" of both Anh My and Chi Sau. This village was divided into many smaller hamlet areas, each comprising approximately one hundred to two hundred families and their lands. We had to push our bicycles up a steep hill, which gave us a clear view of the region. From this vantage point, we could see the river we had crossed and the long dike that had been built near the mouth of this river, similar to the one east of My Lai. Anh My explained that this dike had been built in 1931 to prevent saltwater instrusion over the 500 or 600 hundred acres of fertile rice land just behind the dike. It was this land that was the primary source of food for the hamlets of Binh Chau village. But today as we viewed the flatland behind the dike, it was entirely flooded with the salty ocean water. A 100-yard section of the dike was missing. In 1967 several strategically placed American bombs had wiped out the rice basket of Binh Chau village.

Although the embattled Binh Chau village had frequently changed hands through the war, Ahn My's father had always opted to stay, somehow working out an accommodation with the belligerents on all sides of the war. But eight months before, in July 1974, the two sides once again began shooting over Binh Chau. Anh My's father, a handsome and magnanimous person by My's description, was killed in the crossfire.

From the top of the hill we biked a winding course toward Anh My's hamlet of Phu Quy. Nearly all the farmer folk along the narrow path called out greetings to Chi Sau and Anh My as we passed. It was the first homecoming in three years for My, six years for Sau. As with a horse nearing its home stall, the pace of Anh My's bike steadily accelerated. We were soon bouncing over ditches, around hedgerows and through gardens until he turned a final corner and announced, "We're here!" He propped his bike along a squash arbor and ran toward the small house of mud and thatch. "Uncle, Uncle, are you home?" We were soon being introduced to this uncle and that sister and other cousins and friends, all of whom were being referred to as "brother so-and-so" or "aunt so-and-so."

Ecstatic with the sweetness of homecoming, Anh My forgot to invite us to sit down. But the uncle quickly did the honors. In a minute we were sitting around the bamboo bed in the center of the small, crowded room drinking tea. But Anh My and Chi Sau were already off in the neighborhood looking up old relatives and friends.

As we talked, it turned out that the "uncle" was not really a brother of either My's father or mother, but here that seemed irrelevant. In the confines of the hamlet there was a sense that everyone was part of one's extended family. Hiro and I were soon engaged in conversation with "Uncle Hai." Uncle Hai had grown up in Phu Quy hamlet, had farmed here for nearly all of his fifty-seven years. He used to cultivate land down in the valley behind the Binh Chau dike, but after that was bombed he had to depend on less productive garden plots closer to home. He grew a few vegetables and enough tobacco to supply his water pipe throughout the year. Even now, we could see some of his freshly harvested and shredded tobacco pressed onto woven bamboo racks drying in the sun outside his front door. Six years earlier, foreign soldiers had herded Uncle Hai aboard a Chinook helicopter and flown him toward Quang Ngai city. He was one of the 11,000 persons caught in the dragnet of "Operation Bold Mariner." Uncle Hai never even got into the refugee camp. Like most of the able-bodied male "refugees" in this operation, he was weeded out by the Vietnamese National Police as a "Viet Cong Suspect."

"They took me to the Quang Ngai Interrogation Center," Uncle Hai related in response to our curiosity. "Oh, I guess I didn't get treated any worse than any of the others. They beat me on the back with the casing of a mortar shell. Then they beat me across the knees. Two men in our group were beaten to death. Many others were injured badly."

Uncle Hai pulled a small wad of tobacco out of a stained plastic bag while he talked and stuffed it into the neck of his water pipe. Then he held the steady flame of a small cigarette lighter over the tobacco while he sucked several short breaths through the pipe. After the tobacco was glowing red, he took one long sustained draw, mingling the cosmic elements of fire and water and inhaling the smoky fury into the center of his being.

"They had a strange way," he said through the cloud of smoke he released around his head. "When they beat us, they said it was to teach us not to follow the Communists. But the more they beat us, the more we wanted to follow the Communists." Uncle Hai shook his head as he laughed aloud. Rather than expressing bitterness or even anger, Uncle Hai seemed almost to pity the Saigon Government for having to contend with such hardheaded prisoners.

The smoke evoked an added mellowness from the tough-skinned farmer. "They just didn't have a chance," he sighed with a lugubrious shrug of his shoulders. And then brightening, he added, "Now, as for the revolution—well, above all, it's virtue. In the revolution you've got to have virtue. Why did we win? Because we had virtue. *Duc luc nao cung thang!*" Virtue always wins!

Eventually Chi Sau and Anh My reappeared and we all sat cross-legged on Uncle Hai's bamboo bed and ate a meal of small fish and squash. Sliced manioc mixed with the rice indicated a more Spartan diet than the preferred all-rice meals of most Vietnamese who could afford it. By now, even Hiro and I were becoming fairly adept at serving ourselves from one end of the chopsticks and eating from the other, and Chi Sau called attention to it.

"See, Uncle, these friends even know how to eat chopsticks-two-heads."

"Have to know," Hiro grinned. "When it comes to eating we're ready to learn whatever is necessary."

After the meal we four sojourners took our leave of Uncle Hai and began a trek through the hamlet. One could tell by the relatively unweathered thatch on the roofs that the few houses scattered through the hamlet were of fairly recent construction. It had been less than a year since the NLF had retaken this village from the ARVN and only a valiant—or desperately hungry—few farmers had then moved back to the hamlet to begin planting their gardens. We walked stretches of several hundred yards where there were no houses. The paths cut through untilled fields grown over with high grasses.

Without the bicycles we were more in touch with the soil and with the persons moving along these paths who gave the soil its soul. In all likelihood these same paths had for centuries been trodden by the coarse feet of farmers whose basic instincts were much the same as Uncle Hai's. These paths had been the playgrounds for barefooted children spinning tops and flying kites in the cool hours of the evening. And certainly these paths had felt the nervous steps of the young groom escorted by father, uncles and matchmaker to the house of the appointed bride, to take her back to the family of the groom for marriage.

Then came the boots, leaving oversized tracks in these dusty paths. Government Issue (GI) boots, carrying men of giant proportions. Men with steel pots on their heads and rifles at their hips. And then other men of modest proportions and familiar almond-shaped eyes but wearing similar boots. Boots on the path.

And the sandals, cut from discarded tires, darting across these paths in the cover of darkness. Sandals carrying erstwhile farm boys each wearing a headdress of grass and carrying a small basket of TNT-filled tin cans topped with simple pull strings.

Then ominous shadows of airborne machines streaking over these paths at lightning speeds. And in their wake the paths lay broken with deep craters.

Then other sandals, even a pair of leather shoes, and a few bare feet moving slowly, almost in cadence to the wailing dirge of the procession making its way over these paths toward the distant plot with the hole freshly dug in the earth.

Then the flat, spread-toed footprints of women who never covered their feet, leading once again to the scattered gardens of squash, corn, beans and sweet potatoes.

These paths knew all. But today as our foursome walked through the remains of Phy Quy hamlet, the paths were silent.

At a juncture of our path with another, we could see the thatch roof of a small hovel rising inconspicuously above the grass that surrounded it. A young woman in front of the house called to Chi Sau as we passed. Chi Sau returned the greeting, "Em Duyen, is that you? *Troi oi*, you still live here? How's your mother? Is she well?"

"She's doing well, thank you. She's not here now. She's still in the mountains. But won't you all come in for a bit? How are you, Chi Sau? You know, we were all worried about you for a long time. We got word that you had been arrested. Do come in," the young woman implored.

"What have you been doing these years?" Chi Sau asked her friend.

"Chi Sau, do you remember my father?" Duyen's eyes glowed with admiration. "He's spending several days with us just now."

"Uncle Tan, of course—oh, but it's been so long. He was a regroupee, wasn't he? And now he's back already!" Apparently the father had "regrouped" to North Vietnam in 1954 with the Communist-led Viet Minh as stipulated in that year's Geneva Accords.

Then Chi Sau turned to introduce Hiro and me to Em Duyen. We all followed the radiant young woman into the small house comprised of a single mud-walled room. "Father, it's Chi Sau and Anh My, Uncle Quang's son, and their two progressive friends," she announced. Her father rose from a stool by a small table to greet us and then quickly cleared a space on the bamboo bed for us to sit down.

"Quang's son," he said quietly looking at Anh My, "yes, that's easy to see. And it's good to see you again, Chi Sau."

"You're looking very well, Uncle Tan," Chi Sau said. "Doesn't look like the North has been too hard on you!"

Vo Duy Tan was tall and slender. He was wearing the green khaki trousers and rubber-tire sandals of the *bo doi*, but his white threadbare civilian shirt and modest manner made him seem a natural part of this peasant setting.

After some reminiscing with Chi Sau and Anh My about relatives, Uncle Tan poured tea for us all. We had to drink in turn because there were not enough cups for us all. His pouring of tea was without flourish, as was his speech. As with a child, it was easy to meet his eyes, which were pensive and steady. Hiro and I were particularly eager to learn of Anh Tan's experiences because, while we had heard much about the 1954 regroupment of the Viet Minh, we had never before actually met a "regroupee."

Uncle Tan was thiry-two when he left his wife, a small son and daughter to go north. "We were just finishing a new house, hadn't yet closed the door and I went. It was a fine house. Stood right over there across the path," he motioned with his hand. "Actually, I had taken part in the resistance since 1945, during French occupation."

"And you were in North Vietnam until just recently?" I asked.

"I returned south for the first time in September of last year. In the mountains west of here, that's where I was assigned. I met my wife there and Duyen too. They had moved up there because it was impossible to live here. It was difficult to live in the mountains, but they were not as vulnerable to the bombing as here."

"You said you also have a son, Uncle Tan?" Hiro asked.

"Yes, I had a son, whom I met again just briefly when I returned to the South last September. He was serving as a guerrilla here in this district. Then just one month ago, as he was crossing over a road, he was shot by the Saigon soldiers."

"Shot!" the muffled exlamation echoed through our group. We sat in silence for a moment. Uncle Tan's eyes deepened. Then, as if eager not to burden his guests with a saddening silence, he continued, "I asked permission to have several days' leave from my duties in the mountains to come back to Phu Quy to visit the grave of my son. So this is the first time I've been here in twenty years."

We asked Uncle Tan if he would be staying in Phu Quy now that all of Quang Ngai Province had been liberated.

"Oh, no, there's much more work to be done. I'll return to my post and I'll continue working for the revolution until we have peace and unification for our whole country." He paused thoughtfully. "Phu Quy?" A slight smile played over his face. "Perhaps when I'm old, I'll return to Phu Quy to retire."

We commented that Phu Quy today must seem different from the hamlet he left in 1954. He nodded. "Everything's been destroyed. When I came back it was hard for me to get my bearings. I couldn't tell where anyone used to live. The houses are gone. The people are gone. The trees are gone." He paused again, as if ever conscious that he did not want to dominate the conversation, but then continued with reverence, "For me, I think it's the trees I miss most. Phu Quy used to be full of trees. Now, you have seen it for yourselves. I mentioned that I built our house just across this path out here. Well, right at the intersection of the two paths there used to be a huge banyan tree, centuries old. Our house was shaded by that tree. Phu Quy really had three of those great trees. There was a saying we had: 'Village head, a tree; village heart, a tree; village tail, a tree.' The tree that stood here marked the village tail. But now—the people here say the Americans brought in huge bulldozers and leveled everything."

He paused again, but no one spoke, so he concluded, "Those old trees, especially the old banyans, they provided shade and comfort for the villagers, a sense of well-being. For those of us who lived here, we believed a kind, protecting spirit inhabited those old trees. Now—now they're gone."

After we left Vo Duy Tan's house, we continued our trek through uninhabited areas ot the village. Along the route we encountered Anh Thoc, a hamlet guerrilla and longtime friend of Anh My. In fact, four days earlier, the day of liberation of Quang Ngai city, Anh Thoc had shown up at the Quaker house looking for Anh My. Hiro and I had met him then and he proposed we visit Phu Quy hamlet "sometime soon, while the wounds of war are still obvious." The statement indicated some of the zeal that characterized Anh Thoc. Thoc was born here, and his job throughout the war

Hiro and Chi Sau follow the guerrilla leader, Anh Thoc, through grasses where once he crouched in ambush. His battle now would be to restore the area to agriculture.

was to defend the home village. Now that the war was over for Quang Ngai Province, he was eager to see the hamlet rebuilt. He knew the job would be formidable, but Thoc seemed to thrive on hardship.

Today when we met Thoc, he was unarmed, wearing only a plain khaki outfit and a conical hat. He appeared delighted that we had come to visit his village, and he led us on an extended walk up and down long rolling hills, now entirely dominated by thigh-high grasses. Anh Thoc related personal and village experiences as we walked. Here and there he would point out places where groups of trees or houses had once stood. From the top of one hill we could see the Eastern Sea, lolling in the late afternoon sun. Thoc pointed toward the ocean and said, "You notice those few pine trees on that ridge that forms the sea cliff? Well, that whole ridge used to be lined with those trees. They were planted years ago to keep the sea breezes from destroying the gardens of the people in that hamlet. Now they're gone too."

We walked downhill toward the hamlet he had pointed out. Along the way I noticed an inconspicuous grave marker along the path. I walked around the stone, but it was impossible to read any inscription because the face of the marker had been badly pocked with rifle bullets. Thoc said he remembered when there were many other tombstones at that site, but most of them too had fallen victim to the bulldozer's blade.

We arrived in the nearby hamlet of Chau Thuan. Anh Thoc and Chi Sau explained our presence to the hamlet cadres. Chi Sau introduced us to "this comrade" who invited us to sit down in a small thatch room where he lectured us about "the crimes of the American imperialists and their lackeys" in the hamlet. But all had emerged well because of "the unswerving spirit of the people and the glorious leadership of the party."

After his rhetorical speech we asked him some specific questions about the welfare of the people in his hamlet.

At that point the "comrade" suddenly dropped his didactic manner and replied in a warmer, almost pleading tone of voice. "I must tell you that the people are hungry. There's just not enough food. Liberation has just come and there's so much to be done. But now the people don't have farm tools. Even hoes and shovels are scarce, let alone plows or water buffaloes. There are no cattle left in the village. And the people go to their fields, but they must constantly worry about explosives lying in the soil. And then, as far as this village is concerned, it's the dike—without the dike there is no rice. Without the dike, our people cannot live. We must rebuild the dike."

Earlier that morning west of My Lai we had heard that a helicopter had been shot down along the sea, and throughout the day we had heard people referring to the incident. Now someone again mentioned the downed helicopter. "Oh yes, that happened just south of here," replied one of the village leaders. "In fact, maybe you would be interested—come with me." We walked through the hamlet and came to a shuttered school, the only masonry building I remembered seeing in the settlement. A young guerrilla with an AK-47 leaned against one of the porch posts. The official pulled open one of the windows and motioned for us to look in.

Sitting on stools or on the floor of the schoolroom were twenty men in undershorts and T-shirts. They looked at us nervously. The horror in their eyes was compounded with their confusion at the sight of two foreigners. Toward one corner sat a frightened woman and a small child. Prisoners.

"They were trying to escape from Danang this morning," the official explained. "They were apparently following the coastline so they wouldn't get lost; that's why the guerrillas were able to shoot down their plane. They tried to escape, but we rounded them up with not much trouble, although there still is one man at large."

The explanation was plausible. For the last several days, Danang had been surrounded by Liberation Army units. These young ARVN soldiers—without their uniforms it was impossible to discern rank—had jumped on the helicopter and were making a desperate attempt to fly south to areas still controlled by Saigon. I wanted to speak to the men but could think of nothing to say that would relieve their obvious shock and fear for their future. Feeling a sense of shame for peering at my fellow men like animals in a zoo, I lamely turned away from the haunting faces.

On our way back to Phu Quy hamlet I asked Anh Thoc what he thought would happen to the prisoners. His answer was only partially reassuring. "They'll be taken to the mountains for a period of reeducation and then they'll be brought down here to live again, or wherever they go to make a living. They too are covered by our policy of reconciliation and concord."

Earlier in the day when I saw a helicopter flying over our heads east of My Lai, I had felt instant rage—and fear—at the thought of Quang Ngai at peace, once again being invaded by these machines from the sky, and I would have found it difficult to restrain myself had I had the means at hand to bring that helicopter down. Likewise, the guerrillas here in Chau Thuan who had shot down this "chopper" had no way of knowing it was not flying in to attack Quang Ngai. But now, face to face with the men and woman who had been shot down out of the blue, I found myself secretly wishing they had been successful in their flight to the south. When the machine had been predominant, the response was rage, an impulse toward violence. When the human face emerged, the response turned to empathy, an impulse to identify.

While Chi Sau and Anh My went off to look up old friends and relatives, Hiro and I had the opportunity to spend the evening with Anh Thoc. We sat on stools in the dirt courtyard in front of Thoc's small thatched house. Thoc reminisced about the days of American and Korean military operations in Binh Chau village; sometimes the foreign troops had even come as far as Phu Quy hamlet. An old farmer sitting nearby could not help interjecting, "It was frightful to live here during those days. When the Americans and the Koreans came through, they said everything that's got two legs is V.C. Bang! That was the end of you. What's more, they shot all the cattle too. They must have thought that anything with *four* legs was also V.C.!"

It had been the job of Anh Thoc—a genuine "V.C."—and two or three other hamlet guerrillas to sabotage such invasions into Phu Quy hamlet. Booby traps, hideous inventions that they were, played a key role. Whenever their village had been invaded they were, of course, grossly outnumbered. Sometimes, according to Thoc, two or three guerrillas had to contend with a platoon or a company of Korean, American or ARVN troops. But the mines and booby traps had been set in advance and the few guerrillas would scatter in separate hideouts over the terrain with which they were intimately familiar. So while the invader held numerical superiority—sometimes fifty to one—the guerrilla held the advantage of familiarity of locale and of the element of surprise in attack.

Ultimately, one of the most devastating strategies in the guerrilla's arsenal was the option not to fight back at all. He could stealthily sneak away if overwhelmed, then at a time of his choosing call in assistance from a larger guerrilla unit and strike back at the troops that occupied his hamlet.

Neighbors of Thoc's came and went as we talked. The hamlet was beginning to be reoccupied by refugee farmers who had been living in refugee camps near Quang Ngai city during the war and who were now returning to the hamlet. One man in his fifties came to plead his case with Anh Thoc. The man had been a member of the former Binh Chau Village Council under the Saigon Government. Now, with the defeat of the Saigon forces in Quang Ngai, this man feared for his welfare. Many members of village councils under the Saigon Government had earned notorious reputations for seeking bribes or siphoning off food or other commodities that were intended for the refugees. Whatever the background of this particular man, he obviously feared that he would suffer retribution for his former position on the Village Council. He knelt on the ground in front of Anh Thoc. His head drooped toward his knees as he mumbled, "Oh, most honored representative of the Revolutionary Government in Phu Quy hamlet. I implore you for understanding and mercy. Some of the people want to make trouble for me because I served on the Village Council of the puppet government. But let me assure you, most honored representative, that I was forced by circumstances to take that assignment and in all cases I dealt most fairly and honestly—"

"Enough. Enough. Stop your whimpering," interrupted Anh Thoc, obviously unimpressed with the man's toady servility. "Why don't you get up off your knees and speak clearly? Around here we're not so concerned about what you did as about what you're going to do from here on. You're welcome to come back here to the hamlet and live naturally, just so long as you work for your living and don't take advantage of people. A lot of folks around here are pretty hot about some of the tricks you Saigon Government officials pulled, but don't worry, we're serious about this policy of national concord. If some of the people give you a hard time or treat you roughly, it's because they've not lived with the revolution long enough. They don't understand the policy of reconciliation. I can assure you, you won't get treated like that by any guerrillas or cadres among our ranks."

The official started to mumble something else, but Anh Thoc cut him off, telling him to go home and get to work building a house for himself. The man climbed to his feet and left, perhaps reassured, but obviously less than elated. Even if he could believe Anh Thoc's words about "national reconciliation" it did not mean life would be easy. The days of bribe-taking and corruption were over for this official. He would now have to work—and work hard—for his own living.

The sun disappeared and darkness gradually rose out of the soil, obscuring first the trunks of the banana trees, then the fronds. Eventually the curtain of night rose to leave just the silhouettes of bamboos and an occasional jackfruit tree that had escaped the bulldozer's blade. It was a pure darkness, untouched by the cold lights of electricity. Anh Thoc invited us inside where we sat cross-legged on a bed and by the light of a small lantern ate together the meal prepared by Thoc's aunt in whose house he was living. Only after supper did we learn that Anh Thoc had spent five years in prison. He was captured in 1968, and after being routed through prisons in Quang Ngai and Danang, he was sent to the southern island of Phu Quoc, which served as a stockade for prisoners of war. There, Anh Thoc related, beatings and torture became a way of life.

"Finally they told all of us in our camp that they would quit beating us if we would drink water mixed with our own excrement." The lantern on the bed cast distinct shadows over Anh Thoc's lean face, which made his cheekbones seem all the more prominent. He wet his forefinger with his tongue to peel off one of the thin white tissues from his pack of cigarette wrappers. He spread a small wad of tobacco on the paper and rolled it between his forefinger and thumb into a slightly conical shape, leaving a triangular tab of paper, which he sealed against the cigarette by moistening it with his tongue. He lifted the lantern to the end of the cigarette, which soon pulsated with a glowing red.

"At one point we went on a hunger strike for twelve days to protest the death of a comrade who had died after they threw him into boiling water. In one camp when the comrades protested, the MP's shot into the camp, killing forty and wounding over a hundred. For comrades the prison authorities considered to be troublemakers, they had Camp 7. Camp 7 was a series of cubical cells, two meters square. They put from four to six prisoners in each one of the cells. There was a bucket for excrement. That bucket would be emptied once a week.

"And if we continued to protest our treatment, they only beat us all the more." Anh Thoc had apparently come to terms with the treatment he had received, because there was a conspicuous lack of hostility or revenge in his voice. He spoke matter-of-factly, refraining from elaborating the details of their treatment, almost as if he feared he would be rehashing what certainly must be common knowledge for anyone who knows anything about the Saigon Government prison system.

Humane considerations aside, I had always been puzzled, even on pragmatic grounds, by the Saigon regime's extensive use of beating and torture of its prisoners. Granted, over the years I had met some refugees who said they would not return to their farms in disputed territory, or young men who would not dodge the draft because they feared the flogging of the police. But for nearly all the people we knew who actually had prison experience, the brutality had only increased their determination to fight against the Saigon regime. When I suggested my bewilderment to Anh Thoc, his reply was simple.

"They had no choice but to beat us. They couldn't use reason because they don't have justice on their side. They're not fighting for a righteous cause. If they tried to use reason on us, we could easily answer them. So the only thing they had left was to beat us."

Thoc also gave Hiro and me an insight into an event we had previously only read about in newspapers: the exchange of the prisoners of war in the spring of 1973 after the signing of the Paris agreement. Anh Thoc was one of those exchanged prisoners. "The MP's at Phu Quoc said we should get ready for our release. They divided us into special groups. I was placed in a group with about five hundred other officers of the National Liberation Front. Actually, I wasn't an officer, but I think they decided I was hard-headed enough to be one"—Thoc gave a rare audible laugh. "Frankly, we didn't think they were going to release us at all. We just thought they were going to take us away for reasons of their own. We were prepared for the worst. In fact, only when we saw that Liberation flag at the exchange site in Tay Ninh did we believe we were to be freed. Oh, so many people came out to meet us. Many of the prisoners were sickly. The people took care of us just as though we were their own children. It was very moving."

Anh Thoc's eyes danced in the lantern light and his voice became more animated as he remembered the event. He pulled from his shirt pocket a ballpoint pen, which was printed with a Liberation flag and an inscription in memory of their prison experiences. "They gave each of us one of these pens," Thoc said with obvious pride. "After our release, everyone immediately volunteered for service in the most dangerous spots possible. Many of us wanted to form a fighting force made up entirely of released prisoners, but that idea was eventually vetoed. They decided that the prisoners were too gung ho to follow orders—in battles they always wanted to attack; they couldn't be persuaded that sometimes it was wise to retreat."

After his release, Anh Thoc stayed in the Tay Ninh region west of Saigon near the Cambodian border to recuperate for several months and then returned to his native home of Phu Quy hamlet. We remarked that he must have considered it fortunate to be able to return home.

"I guess I don't really think of any place as home; now as far as I'm concerned, wherever there is a place to serve, that is my home."

"Hard-core Viet Cong." That's the label American officers in Vietnam would certainly have pinned on Anh Thoc. And when it came to defending his hamlet from foreign troops and planes, there was no doubt about it; this native son of Phu Quy was determined to the core. There was no changing his course. But one sensed that Anh Thoc's hard-core-ness, his stubbornness, was of a species with a mountain stream that "stubbornly" insists upon running downhill instead of up. If in time the "stubborn" water actually wears down the hardest of rocks, what choice has it? What it is determines what it does.

To sit and converse with a Viet Cong guerrilla in his native setting, to see him as a rational—even sentimental—person was a perspective denied the American fighting man and policy maker throughout the war. Nor could the guerrilla ever really know the sincerity and generosity of the average American soldier in Vietnam. But then distorted perspectives have always been the fuel for the machines of war. Can one wage war if one credits the same degree of rationality and sensibility to the enemy as to oneself?

Seven years earlier I had found myself face to face with an American military advisor at a party in Quang Ngai. His eyes were intense, focused on me. He cut an impressive figure in his freshly starched uniform.

"What the hell are you doing over here anyway? What does a person with your kind of philosophy think he can accomplish over here? I mean, how do you justify your being in Vietnam?"

I had been in Vietnam for two years and was no longer accustomed to the American custom of direct confrontation. His sudden interrogation intimidated me, but I tried to disguise my feelings. "I'm afraid I'm not sure what you're talking about."

"Oh, don't worry about me, I've had a drink or two more than necessary, but you see, I don't agree with what you're trying to do here in Vietnam. It just won't work. People aren't ready for your kind of philosophy. See, I believe the vast majority of people in the world don't know what's good for them. And so you come along—you believe in loving people, and you respond to human suffering. But I don't agree with you. You've got to show people what's good for them and that's why I believe in the military. People just aren't intelligent enough to know for themselves.

I asked the major if he thought we—he and I—were intelligent enough to know what was good for us.

"No, no, we're not. Everybody's got different principles." He paused, his eyes jumping here and there. Then he brought up his hand. "Take this bread, for example." In his hand he bobbed the piece of French bread, served with the meal on the veranda of the home of the American Senior Province Advisor for Quang Ngai. "Now I think this is damn good bread. The French made this bread and they brought it to Vietnam and why shouldn't we all like their bread? And why do we think we have to fight because one group of people thinks one way and another group of people thinks another way? Take my mother-in-law, for example. Now my mother-in-law was a very good woman. She was bullheaded. I fought with her constantly. But she told me one day, 'Negroes are all right—if they are in their place.' Now, just what *was* their place? She didn't know, just so they were kept in their place. Well, I knew that place was just a little lower than the Caucasians. Just a little lower. But she was a good woman. She died hard. She fought to live. And I helped her for what that was worth.

The major took a bite of his French loaf. Not knowing where to take a mother-in-law conversation, I waited for him to continue.

"You and I are different. You've got a beard and I don't. You've got brown eyes and I've got blue eyes. But what's the difference? You eat and drink the same way I do. I smoke and you don't. I drink and you don't. But is there really basically any difference? No, we're essentially the same. You like good music and so do I. I don't know about you but 'Greensleeves' is my favorite. 'Greensleeves' can solve just about any problem for me, so we're basically the same. In your home you treat your wife the same way I treat mine. She makes you feel—well, she makes you feel better than you really are. So why do we have to fight each other? Why can't we accept each other and allow each other to be different?"

I asked the major if he felt he could accept the Viet Cong, to let them live according to their belief.

"Him?" The major straightened and he squeezed the bread in his hand. "Now, that's the enemy. I'm a soldier and I believe the best possible thing to do with the Viet Cong is to kill him. I've killed plenty of the enemy in my lifetime. I've killed Chinese, North Koreans. I've killed North Vietnamese and Viet Cong. That is, I've personally killed them. I killed two of them with my knife."

But were not these men also part of the common family of mankind?

"Yes, maybe they are. But in the army you act on orders, and if my commander tells me to go in there and kill the enemy, you can count on it, I'll carry out his orders."

I wondered out loud if our problems might not be resolved if we attempted to communicate with the Viet Cong in order to understand him.

The major's reply was quick. "I'll first kill him and then I'll understand him."

"And suppose the Viet Cong feels that way about us?" I asked.

"Then we'll just go on fighting each other."

Anh Thoc held the lantern up to another cigarette he had just rolled. We sat on the bed in silence for a moment, following the flame with our eyes as he set the lantern on the bed again.

"I'm ready to go wherever I can be of service to the people," the veteran guerrilla spoke toward the lamp, "but Phu Quy is special to me. I have a small garden here and I can grow all the vegetables I need—" Anh Thoc interrupted himself, looked at Hiro's watch and announced he had to leave to attend a meeting that would be held at the hamlet office. He invited us to accompany him.

Anh Thoc led our trio, walking single file through the darkness, following the winding paths. After we had walked about five minutes, we began to see glowing balls of light bobbing along the tributary paths converging into the main path that led to the hamlet office. When we arrived, a group of perhaps forty or fifty people—it was too dark to see well—were milling about on the path outside the office, which was a small thatch building not unlike the village homes. In the courtyard stood a bench behind a table, illuminated by only a single lantern. Three men took their seats behind the table: a hamlet representative, a man we understood to be a Party cadre and Anh Thoc. Hiro and I sat on the ground with the other villagers. We quietly declined Anh Thoc's invitation for us to address the group. The Party man addressed the assembled villagers for several minutes with a denunciation of American imperialism and a platitudinous tribute to the "perceptive leadership of the Party in the fight for independence and freedom."

Then it was Anh Thoc's turn. His tall, lean body took on an impressive starkness in the light and shadows cast by the flickering lantern. He spoke clearly and firmly, occasionally cutting the air with his hand for emphasis. From his speech we gathered that many of the assembled persons had just returned to the hamlet within the last several days. Some were apparently former ARVN soldiers. Thoc's purpose was to welcome them back to the hamlet, to instruct them to register with the authorities—"and make sure you are thorough and honest on your declaration forms"—and to mobilize them for the urgent work of rebuilding the hamlet.

"The kith and kin of Phu Quy who never fled to the enemy zone during the war, but stuck it out here in the countryside, faced incredible hardships," Thoc declared to the barely discernible faces of the group. "But we welcome those of you who have just returned. There's a place for you in this hamlet. There is also work for you in this hamlet. I know that most of you will be busy building some kind of homes for yourselves in the coming days. But eventually we will be asking each family to provide one person for public-service jobs a day or two a week. There's lots to be done. Roads to be repaired and waterways to be rebuilt. We expect full cooperation from everyone."

After the meeting we followed Anh Thoc home in silence as a gigantic apricot moon emerged from the sea cliff in the east. The path twisted and branched in a confusing labyrinth through the grasses. But to Anh Thoc, who was leading, the way was clear. He had, after all, walked this way many times before.

MONDAY, 31 MARCH.   "Down with the American Imperialists!"
"Overthrow Nguyen Van Thieu!"
"Uncle Ho Lives Forever in Our Endeavor!"

The long cloth banners waved above 10,000 conical hats in the Quang Ngai Athletic Field. Hiro and I had just managed to pull ourselves to the top of the wall surrounding the back end of the athletic field to discover a sea of people standing at attention while tribute was being read to the inimitable Father of the Vietnamese Revolution, Ho Chi Minh. Peasant farmers, pedicab drivers, shopkeepers, students, children, market goers—it appeared that the whole city of Quang Ngai had turned out for the victory celebration and the formal installation of the Quang Ngai Military Management Committee.

It was not the first political rally to be held on these grounds, of course. I remembered standing with some friends in this same soccer field in 1967, and after a thunderous pass by escorting "Sky Raider" bombers, we watched a bevy of Huey helicopters appear out of the blue and land in formation by the eastern goalposts. With much pomp and the sounding of bugles, there emerged from the lead helicopter the moustachioed figure of Premier Nguyen Cao Ky, complete in his black flight suit and hat and purple ascot. He stepped briskly between two phalanxes of Military Police and ARVN Honor Guard as he made his way toward the nearby Provincial Headquarters. Stepping close behind him were the Chief of State, General Ngueyn Van Thieu and finally the renowned Commander of American Forces in Vietnam, General William Westmoreland. They had descended upon Quang Ngai to celebrate "a brilliant victory," in which they boasted "847 Viet Cong dead by actual body count, and an estimated several hundred more, which were dragged away before the count." They decorated ARVN troops for bravery in battle and predicted many more victories over the Viet Cong. In front of the town library were displayed the spoils of battle: long racks of AK-47 rifles, hand grenades, 82mm mortar tubes, Chinese-made rockets, machine guns and booby traps.

Finally, the crowds of Quang Ngai spectators had been presented with the most spectacular booty of all. As I stood with my bicycle on the fringe of the crowd, I could hear loud gruff commands like rustlers herding cattle. And then they emerged through the crowds: dirty, unkempt, in black shirts and shorts, hands tied behind their backs, a long row of men and boys tied together by a wire to prevent escape. Prisoners of war. The Viet Cong, twenty-one of them, prodded along by shouting armed guards. The chain of captives was herded through the crowds and up toward the Quang Ngai Interrogation Center for "exploitation."

Now today the Quang Ngai Athletic Field was once again the scene of a "brilliant" victory celebration. The cheering crowds were composed of many of the same people who had attended the victory celebrations of former years. The Viet Cong were back too. Only today, instead of being tied together like animals, the Viet Cong were lined up on the grandstand, smiling and waving to the chanting crowds.

It was the first time that the average Quang Ngai citizen had had an opportunity to be introduced to what American advisors had once referred to as the "V.C. Province Chief." Actually, it was a ruling council of nineteen men and two women who would form the primary leadership for Quang Ngai Province. In the central position stood a broadly smiling Anh Nham, the avuncular Party Secretary whom Hiro and I had met the morning of Liberation. At one end stood Anh Ai, the political cadre who had given the instructions for the now-forgotten "357" sign. The grandstand—built several years before with cement from the U.S. Agency for International Development—was decked in Liberation flags and pictures of Nguyen Huu Tho and Huynh Tan Phat, the respective heads of the NLF and the PRG. On a pillar to one side stood a white plaster bust of the revered "Uncle Ho."

"We may not look as fancy as the former Quang Ngai officials, but when it comes to politics, we stand second to none!" The Quang Ngai People's Revolutionary Committee.

The celebration was eloquent testimony to the complete collapse of the "Saigon puppet authority" in the province. A week before, any guerrilla in Quang Ngai city would have been shot on sight and now here, standing openly in front of thousands of people, was the whole rank of leadership of the Quang Ngai Provisional Revolutionary Government. Here and there *bo doi* stood with AK-47's, but security precautions seemed unusally relaxed for coming so close on the heels of the ARVN defeat in Quang Ngai. But if the new authorities seemed unconcerned about sabotage attempts from the people, they had apparently not foreclosed the possibility of a retaliatory air attack on Quang Ngai. On both sides of the grandstand were two antiaircraft guns with their flared muzzles camouflaged with leafy branches.

After the rally terminated, the new province authorities were not whisked away in a convoy of jeeps or a waiting helicopter as in former days. Today they waited patiently and respectfully until the thousands of people had walked past the reviewing stand and filed out of the stadium. Only then did the new ruling council disband and return to its respective offices.

Monday afternoon, a week and a half after Pat and the children had gone, I decided to try to find some way to communicate to them my well-being. The primary problem was to determine a channel the message could take. We had Quaker friends in Laos who had been in touch with the North

Vietnamese embassy there and we decided to route the following message through them:

MARTIN AND ICHIKAWA CHEERFUL BUSY STOP HOPE
PATRICIA RETURN QUANG NGAI STOP WAIT WHERE HAPPY

When we reported to the Province Office with this message, the *bo doi* guards at the gate were chary about allowing us to enter. We explained our mission and said that if nothing else was possible we would have them deliver our message. One of the guards ran into the province building and talked with several men standing at the entrance to the building. The guard returned and announced that we were free to enter. We walked through the entrance toward the Quang Ngai Province Office.

One of the last times I had visited the Province Office, two months before, a visitor from the United States and I had paid a call on Paul Daly, the quick-witted chief of the American "consulate" team in Quang Ngai. Daly had worked in nearly every country in Asia in the last twenty years and he saw the direction of history. " 'What about the other side?' you ask. They've turned off the clock in Hanoi. They'll fight on forever until they've taken over the south." At the same time Paul Daly was not giving up without a fight. In his office he proudly showed us a new wall map of Quang Ngai Province covered with Plexiglas, which he was rigging up for briefings. "I'll have people sit down there and when they ask about the security situation in the province, I'll flip on a switch and red dots will appear all over the map. 'Those are the enemy positions,' I'll explain. They'll say, 'Oh, that's bad. That's bad.' Then I'll flip on the second switch and a whole raft of yellow dots will appear under the Plexiglas. 'There, the positions of the friendlies,' I'll announce, and they'll say, 'Oh, that's great. That's great.' "

I complimented Daly on the fresh paint and refurbished decor in the previously drab office suite. "Yeah," Daly replied, "we're trying to give the place a look of permanence."

Today, two months later, the American advisors were out of town. The only apparent hint of their former presence was an International Scout sitting beside the Province Office. A sparkling white Mazda, abandoned by a bank manager who fled Quang Ngai, sat directly in front of the freshly whitewashed office headquarters. The grounds were nearly vacant, perhaps because it was late in the afternoon. When we approached the front door we were greeted by Anh Nam and his right-hand man, Anh Nga. Both men were at least in their fifties and their complexions evidenced their having spent much time in the sun. Dressed in rubber-tire sandals and plain khaki work uniforms with no identifying insignia, on the street they might have passed for itinerant peddlers or ordinary farmers. In fact, we learned that Anh Nam was now the Chairman of the Quang Ngai Provincial Revolutionary Committee.

The two veteran revolutionaries greeted us and invited us to sit down at a table in the lobby of the two-story office building. The four of us appeared to be the only occupants of the huge building, and Anh Nam and Anh Nga, who likely spent most of the last twenty years in thatch hideouts in the mountains, seemed out of their element in these spacious halls. Hiro and I introduced ourselves as the Mennonite representatives who had worked in Quang Ngai for several years.

"Oh yes, I know about you," Anh Nam interrupted. In fact, I stopped in at your house yesterday morning, but you were not home. I had forgotten that it was Sunday and you would be celebrating mass at the church."

"Oh, we're sorry we were not at home. No, we do attend church, but this weekend we happened to be visiting in Binh Chau village with some of our friends," I explained.

"It was nothing pressing. It's just that there are several Japanese technicians who worked at the Quang Ngai sugar mill. They can't speak any Vietnamese and no one here can speak Japanese."

"I'll be happy to help in any way possible," Hiro offered.

"We'll be in touch one of these days about that," Anh Nam said.

There was a lull in the conversation and we took the opportunity to present him the message we had prepared. He looked at it a bit while we explained the content and the address. Anh Nam took the message but made no promises. "We'll see. When we were in the hills it was quite easy to handle messages like this. Now that we're down here, liaison is more difficult." We all sipped tea that Anh Nga had poured for us from a teapot and cups so ornate that I suspected they had been found in the premises of the Province Office. After offering us a smoke, the two men shared tobacco and paper and rolled cigarettes together. Vietnam was finally becoming Vietnamized. The Winstons and Salems of a former era were absent even from the highest office in Quang Ngai Province.

Then, almost as if to cast further question on whether they would transfer our message, Anh Nam said, "Now our highest priority is to provide for the general welfare of the people. We concentrate on collective affairs rather than individual needs. For example, there is that large orphanage at the east end of town. Hundreds of children need food and we must get it to them. And we want to get schools started, but we're lacking books. We also need more teachers. Now, some subjects won't change much: mathematics is the same everywhere, but other subjects, like geography and history, will be quite different."

We asked Anh Nam if he had encountered any surprises in coming into Quang Ngai city.

"The town seemed terribly dirty to me. With so few trees. We must begin planing trees all around town. And I found it amazing that in the twenty years I was outside of Quang Ngai city, so little development has taken place. With all the American involvement, there's been no development at all except the sugar mill west of town."

Anh Nam, new province head, did not mind unmatched teacups or hand-rolled cigarettes. "My first concern is to make sure the children in the orphanage have enough to eat."

Hiro took an opportunity to inquire about Anh Nam's personal history, whether he had a family.

Anh Nam brightened. "Family? Oh yes, but I've been separated from them since 1954."

"You must have regrouped to the north in 1954, did you?" Hiro asked.

"No, no. Quang Ngai is my home, and this is where I've always been," the province chairman replied proudly. "But my family—I have seven children—they're in the north."

"You haven't seen them for twenty years?"

"I saw them last in 1970. I went to visit Russia that year. And India and China too. So I had some time in Hanoi with my family then. But when you talk about family, the people of Quang Ngai are my real family. It's the Quang Ngai people who have supported and sustained me."

Talking personally evoked increased casualness from Anh Nam. Staring at the stub of his simple cigarette, he seemed suddenly struck by this encounter with two persons from industrially advanced countries. "You probably notice things are a bit more plain in this regime than in the Saigon regime. I probably don't look quite like the old Quang Ngai Province chief, do I?" He was smiling at the thought. "The shirt I'm wearing—and I guess the old province chief didn't wear rubber sandals or smoke hand-rolled cigarettes, did he? No, there's no doubt about it, I'm just not as fancy as those Saigon officers were on the outside—on the outside. But when it comes to politics"—Anh Nam paused for emphasis—"we stand second to none!"

159

TUESDAY, 1 APRIL. The sky threatened rain. Hiro and I wondered if we should postpone the whole venture. Several days before, we had visited Anh Duong, our friend in the refugee camp in Nghia Hanh. All his neighbors were busy dismantling their houses in the camp and heading back to the long-abandoned farms in the countryside.

"I want to go home too," Anh Doung had told us, "but I guess I'll have to wait until the authorities are free to help me. There's no way I can get myself—let alone our beds and things—over the mountains and back to Song Ve valley." It was then that we had promised to rendezvous with him on Tuesday to help move his family home. But now that Tuesday morning's sky was overcast, the thought of rain made the project seem formidable. We decided we would ride the ten kilometers to Anh Duong's camp at least to honor our commitment and perhaps to set a rain date.

When Hiro and I pulled our bicycles to a stop in front of Anh Duong's hovel in the camp, however, there was no turning back. Far from being discouraged by the threatening clouds, Anh Duong was excitedly issuing packing instructions to his two young boys and to Chi Ba, his wife.

"Oh, it can't matter if we get a little wet," Anh Duong replied quickly when we mentioned the weather. "Besides, raining water is surely better than raining bullets." With that, he pivoted his wheelchair toward our bicycles and asked, "Which of those vehicles is stronger? That one? All right, take the chain off the sprockets so it doesn't get snagged when you push the bike. See those two bamboo beds there? Place one on either side of the bicycle in an upright position, sandwiching the bike between them. Then tie the two beds together through the bike frame with these bamboo strings."

By the time we had finished with Anh Duong's instructions, the beds were firmly strapped onto the bike somewhat in the form of a "V." In the open part of the "V" above the seat, we piled in the baby's bamboo basket, several boxes, numerous other baskets, two plywood boards, a child's blackboard, and three cooking pots. The rest of the family belongings Chi Ba packed into two baskets tied to her shoulder pole.

Finally onto the bicycle's handlebars we tied a bamboo pole, which extended beyond the bed on the left side. With that we were to steer this two-wheeled moving van as we pushed it down the road. It was just such contraptions as this, I remembered from photos, which the North Vietnamese Army had used to ferry tons of supplies over the Ho Chi Minh Trail during the earlier days of the war.

Chi Ba scurried about stuffing miscellaneous items into already full baskets. The excited six- and ten-year-old boys paced back and forth between the bicycle and the house, not wanting to miss any of the activity. Finally, everyone was ready to go. The boys would walk; Chi Ba shouldered the pole with the two swinging baskets; Chi Ba's mother had the baby on her hip; Hiro would take the first shift on the marvelous moving machine; I would push Anh Duong in his wheelchair.

"Everyone ready?" It was impossible for Anh Duong to keep the excitement out of his voice. "Let's go home."

Duong and his family and a hundred thousand other refugee farmers in Quang Ngai Province had waited many years for this day. For most of his thirty-eight years Duong had been a farmer. He had often reminisced with me about the *que huong*, the native hamlet where the sweet potatoes grew "so-o-o big"—he would gesture with his hands—and where there were always enough papayas to send to market. Beans? "We had black beans, green beans, white beans, soybeans, mung beans—there was nothing that wouldn't grow back home. And the sugar cane—and the tales spun on as long as a friend had time to listen.

That all ended suddenly for Anh Duong ten years before. With the escalation of American involvement in the war, Duong, like many of his compatriots in rural Vietnam, was faced with the decision of sticking with the soil—which was under NLF control—or fleeing to the cities, which were more immune from bombing and military operations. But surplus jobs and housing in Quang Ngai city were virtually nonexistent, and Duong had a wife and newborn child to support. So he chose to stay with the land.

On an afternoon in late 1965 Duong saw troops coming up the valley toward his village. As he had related it, even in the distance he could tell by their size that they were not Vietnamese soldiers. Panic swept the village. There was no time to waste. Duong helped his wife and child into the deep hole they had dug in the earth beneath their bamboo bed. Certainly the troops would not harm a woman and a child, he hoped. Then he ran out in the yard and coaxed his two oxen into another bunker, which he had dug for them. Finally Duong himself ran across a field to a thicket where he had prepared a camouflaged hole for himself. As he ran he noticed a droning reconnaissance plane flying high above the hamlet. Apparently the "spotter plane" saw Duong racing for his secret bunker. Within minutes, jets were whistling over the village and a large bomb exploded close to Duong's hiding place. The violent concussion threw him high into the air and out onto an open field. He lay there, blood oozing from every opening in his body.

As the jets sped back to their air base, several local guerrillas came to Anh Duong's aid. Although he suffered no broken bones or shrapnel wounds, he was unable to move and needed treatment immediately. The guerrillas told him that he could go to the Quang Ngai Provincial Hospital, but they would be unable to provide transportation for him because that was enemy territory for the guerrillas and they would run a great risk of being captured. On the other hand, they would gladly carry him to the NLF hospital deep in the mountains.

"That night in the district NLF clinic my body was racked with unbelievable pain. The next day they carried me into the mountains to their clandestine hospital, so secret they didn't even permit my wife to accompany me.

161

"The care in the hospital was fantastic. The doctors and nurses were so considerate, always trying to find some way to help me. They had a sign hanging on the wall of the ward reading 'The doctor is the parent of the patient' and they treated us just that way. And the nurses were very conscientious. I think they knew they would be transferred to the battlefield if they were charged with giving patients shoddy care."

But medicines in the mountain hospital were scarce and after several days there, Anh Duong's legs swelled to double their normal size. The two doctors—who did patient care in the afternoons and evenings and planted rice in the morning—became so alarmed at Duong's situation that they went out into the forest to gather special leaves, roots and herbs. Back at the hospital they cooked their collection for several hours and condensed from it a cup of syrupy black distillate. With a long needle they pumped the herbal juices into Anh Duong's spine. His pain during the operation was so acute that they had to give him a dose of their scarce anesthesia.

By morning the swelling in Duong's legs was gone and he was on his way to recovery. Partial recovery, that is, for though his body was reviving, Anh Duong would never walk again; he was paralyzed from his waist down.

After four months of convalescence in the jungle hospital, Duong was sent back to his home village. But farming for him was now impossible. More seriously, he would not be able to run for cover if the jets should return. The local NLF official gave him and Chi Ba written permission to travel into Quang Ngai city—by NLF reckonings, the enemy zone.

"The Front permitted us to bring our cattle with us, but our rice crop was in head and needed harvesting. They said not to worry about that, so we went. A month later while we were in the Saigon Government zone, the Front sent me the money for our rice crop, which they had harvested and sold. All the money was there except for a bit that was deducted for transporting the paddy to market."

That marked the beginning of what was to be ten years in a Nghia Hanh refugee camp for Duong and his family. Camp life was hardly pleasant. The physical conditions were bad enough; mud and thatch row houses with only a low incomplete wall separating families. Water supply was inconvenient and sometimes inadequate, and the refugees often did not know where the next meal would come from. But the emotional atmosphere of the camp was worse. There was little employment possible since all the surrounding farmland was tilled by local farmers. Formerly independent and self-supporting farmers were doomed to sit idle, waiting prayerfully on the government for the next handout of food. Sometimes it came; sometimes it was siphoned off by officials in the province seat.

Then, in June 1967, huge Chinook helicopters descended onto Nghia Hanh camps where Anh Duong lived. Within several days, the choppers had disgorged another 7,000 "refugees." The American generals had decided that the Song Ve Valley, where Anh Duong formerly lived, was the

Like ten million refugees countrywide, Anh Duong's family (*bottom*) was sustained by the dream of returning to the native hamlet where the sweet potatoes would grow "so-o-o big."

source of too much "hostile activity." Reconnaissance planes, such as the one that had spotted Anh Duong, were being sniped at from Song Ve Valley and American patrols in the area were being ambushed. The valley would have to be "pacified." The strategy to bring peace to the valley was to take the people out of it. That was the purpose of Operation Malheur II in mid-1967. Again, it was the theory that if the guerrillas were the fish that swam among the sea of people, then removing all the people would let the guerrillas flounder helplessly on dry land.

An American correspondent, Jonathan Schell, witnessed this operation from spotter planes and command posts of American military strategists and described it in a moving account called *The Military Half*. We were on the ground and witnessed the civilian half, what was happening to the people who were yanked off their farms and away from their kinfolk who fled to the mountains before the American helicopters descended on their valley. Any able-bodied man or woman without children who had not previously been an active guerrilla now was likely to become one. The valley was laid waste of its houses. Rice granaries were destroyed or confiscated. The "refugees" were promised that their cattle, their chief investment, would be herded to the camps and returned to them, but only a small fraction arrived. Most were shot or confiscated by ARVN troops who cooperated with the Americans in the operation.

The 7,000 new "refugees from communism" lived in tents and vacant schoolhouses until new camps were built. Then families were awarded "houses" in the camp. In a survey of the camp, I had discovered an average of thirteen people living in each of the four- by five-yard rooms in the long mud row houses.

Then there was the problem of food. These dispossessed farmers had nothing. Those who had attempted to bring baskets of rice with them often saw their precious grains being spilled on the ground by the foreign troops under the pretext that there might be explosives hidden in the rice. Because of a lack of interpreters, many of the refugees did not even understand the pretext. At any rate, they were hungry.

That's where we fit in. Pat and I and four other volunteers were working in Quang Ngai with Vietnam Christian Service (VNCS), an umbrella organization for Church World Service, Lutheran World Relief and our own sponsoring agency, the Mennonite Central Committee. James May, the American Senior Province Advisor, came to our VNCS team and appealed for help in feeding the "refugees." The United States Government would provide the food. We were essential, he argued, for organizing and executing the "feeding program."

It was a bitter decision. If we helped, we could be seen as acting in complicity with an operation that had manipulated thousands of civilians for the military aims of one belligerent. Some months before in an unrelated setting, the top American military advisor in Quang Ngai stated the issue more starkly in conversation with several of us on the VNCS team. "Our first job is to kill V.C." Lieutenant Colonel Brown had told us, "but it's important that at the same time we carry out programs of social and economic reform. Here's where organizations like your own fit in."

It was precisely to demonstrate that we did not "fit in" with a system that had wiped out the homes and livelihood for 7,000 civilian farmers that some of us resisted becoming involved in the feeding program.

On the other hand, if we had the food at our disposal and personnel to feed the people, would not refusal to do so only contribute further to the misery of the uprooted farmers?

With reservations unresolved, we launched the feeding program. We bought kerosene stoves and cooking pots. We set up kitchens in each camp and daily provided a bowl of American CSM—corn, soya, milk—gruel to 7,000 people. The foreign concoction was unpalatable, but the people had no choice. For many, it was all they had.

For the Hre tribal people, it was not enough. Along with the 7,000 Vietnamese farmers, there were 512 Hre mountain people swept up in Operation Malheur II. Vietnamese officials argued against settling them with the Vietnamese refugees but the American Senior Province Advisor insisted otherwise. It would be, the advisor was to argue, a progressive experiment in racial integration. The advisor's dream notwithstanding, camp life for the tribal people looked less like integration than genocide.

The tribal people were used to living in houses on stilts and drinking directly from mountain springs and streams. In the camp they had to sleep on the ground and drink from a contaminated well. They were not used to boiling their drinking water. Besides, they did not have the firewood to do it. Above that, these people of the mountain were heartbroken. One after another became sick—mostly the old people and small children.

We visited them day after day. We stepped up the feeding program with specially prepared foods for the tribal people. A VNCS nurse visited the people daily. We took all who could be persuaded to the Provincial Hospital. It was not enough. Gradually they started to die off.

One afternoon I had squatted down in the dusty hut of a woman who swung a twelve-month-old wraith of a boy in a small hammock. Palid skin draped from bone to bone like curtains hung from chair backs to dry. The child's head was normal size, but one wondered if the brain had not already been shrunk by famine and dysentery. With tears begging to be understood, the mother appealed to anyone who would hear for deliverance from the slow death she and her people were suffering in this camp.

"Why don't they take us back to the hills where we can hunt and farm and drink from the mountain streams and live in our own houses? They say bombs are dropping on those hills, but we would find a place of security. They bring us here and spill us onto this dry land; they give us some rice and some corn, but not enough for us and our children. Now our children are dying; soon they will all be dead. We are thrown here and left to die. And when we die, there is no one to provide funeral clothes or coffins for our burial and we are buried like dogs.

"Let us go back to our hills."

Eventually some of the tribal people did clandestinely return to their homes in the hills, leaving 350 behind in the camp. Of these remaining, fifty-four died of disease in the four months we were working with them.

In addition to our feeding program in the camp, Pat established sewing classes for the young women in the camp. It was in one of these classes in 1967 that we first met Anh Duong's wife. But even though Chi Ba learned machine sewing, she was never able to find enough tailoring business to support herself, her child and her paralyzed husband. So whenever possible she hired herself out as a day laborer to transplant or thresh rice for local farmers.

For Anh Duong and Chi Ba, as for the majority of the refugees, the overriding preoccupation was thinking about the day they could return home: back to their own paddy fields, their own orchards, their own thatched houses landscaped inconspicuously among gently swaying bamboos and palms. Home was so close—not more than a half day's walk—and yet so far, in the "free strike zones" where anything moving would be subject to aerial bombardment. The separation from the homeland—the *que huong*—was especially painful each Tet season, which was the time for each Vietnamese family to follow the centuries-old tradition of cleaning the ancestral gravesites and paying homage to the spirits of their forebears.

But it was obviously more than emotional or spiritual attachment to the land that made the call to the *que huong* so powerful. For many, it was sheer hunger. As the years dragged on, the Saigon Government took nominal responsibility to feed the refugees. But even when the government handouts were not siphoned off by corrupt officials, the dole was not enough. It was then that a valiant—and hungry—few began the trickle back to their homelands on "the other side."

Eventually nearly one-third of Anh Duong's fellow camp members sneaked across the lines to the *que huong*. Saigon Government officials, who feared this movement would result in greater support for the guerrillas, attempted to arrest refugees they suspected of trying to return home. The stream of hungry returnees increased nonetheless. For the paralyzed Anh Duong, however, a clandestine flight to the home village had always been out of the question. Now the Saigon police were gone and finally Anh Duong was free to return home.

"Come on, let's be on our way." Anh Duong was already tugging at the wheels of his wheelchair. "We've got a long trip ahead of us."

Hiro led the way, pushing the stack of beds and baskets on wheels. Then came the two boys with capes of green plastic pulled over their shoulders in case of rain. Anh Duong and I followed, while grandmother with the baby and Chi Ba shouldering the baskets rounded off our home-going caravan.

I quickly learned that Anh Duong's American-made wheelchair was not designed for rocky, muddy country roads. The two small wheels in the front snagged in small ruts, causing near upsets for Duong and me. Presently I learned to balance the chair on the large rear wheels to negotiate the more difficult spots. It was Hiro, with his wonderful moving machine, who received the most attention, however. "He's terrific, the way he balances that load, and he never had any experience with the 'pushing vehicle' before," Anh Duong would marvel to himself and to anyone within earshot.

We pushed past Mr. and Mrs. Dat's house. Seven years ago Pat's sewing classes were taught there. In those former days we would regularly see a handful of ARVN soldiers sitting on the porch chatting with Mr. Dat and— more interestingly—with two of Mr. Dat's lovely daughters who subsequently married ARVN and left home. Now, in the wake of the revolution, the scene had changed, but only slightly. Today I noticed Mr. Dat sitting on the porch with his two younger daughters, who were engaged in conversation with three handsome *bo doi* guerrillas!

We passed the headquarters of Nghia Hanh district. I had visited those headquarters many times before. It was here where interrogators tormented a neighbor of Anh Duong who had tried to slip back to her *que huong* just two months before. Back in 1967 we had sometimes come here to meet with district government officials concerning our work in the Nghia Hanh refugee camps. Major Al Fraley of the American advisory team here had always seemed genuinely concerned about what the war was doing to the people. He, too, had seemed baffled over what to do with so many refugees.

It was also from this spot that Pat and I had watched shirtless GIs sitting in lawn chairs on the roof of their sandbagged command post. They were drinking beer and shouting and whistling into a radio that was on the same frequency as radios in the cockpits of two Phantom jets diving up and down beyond a stand of bamboo trees a mile and a half to the west. "Zingo, what a hit!" one cheered into the microphone. We could see the cloud of smoke and debris shoot above the trees, and seconds later we felt the mighty explosion as it vibrated doors and windows around us. "Now bring in the firecrackers and wipe out the whole damned valley," another bellowed into the radio. The scene was reminiscent of Saturday afternoon football games I had watched at Penn State. We learned that they were gunning for several guerrillas who had taken advantage of the one-day Christmas truce to come into Saigon-controlled zones to hold a "political propaganda" session for some local villagers. A small reconnaissance plane had watched the guerrillas head back to the hills and at 6 P.M., when the truce ended, the Phantoms were already on hand to "wipe out" the valley.

Now, over the same building that had once served as the American command post fluttered an enormous Liberation flag.

Heading south, the muddy road passed through open fields of emerald rice. For the first kilometer or so there was an occasional settlement of a few houses. Beyond that the farmers had not dared to settle because occasional guerrilla traffic through the area had attracted dangerous "H and I" fire from ARVN howitzers. We splashed through several small rivulets that ran across the road. Em Cao, the six-year-old, complained that he was tired. "Why do we have to walk so far?" he grumbled.

"Just keep walking," the home-bound father prodded. "If you lag behind, the tigers will get you."

We came upon a 50-foot bridge that had collapsed into a long slanting "V." It was not clear if the metal span covered with American imported "PSP"—perforated steel planking—had been mined or had just dropped under the weight of a civilian lumber truck that now sat in the bottom of the "V."

Hiro and I had to team up, first to inch the loaded bicycle and then Duong and the wheelchair across the slippery slopes of the bridge. Just on the other side of the bridge lay a huge pile of American land mines and 30-caliber machine-gun ammunition, which the *bo doi* had apparently confiscated and stacked there for the time being.

Half a kilometer further down the road, we could see six T-54 Soviet-built tanks parked in the middle of the road with *bo doi* probing the dirt at the sides of the road with tools that looked like long ice picks. The reason for their probing soon became obvious. The lead tank had hit a land mine that blew off one of its tracks. Several *bo doi* with shovels were beginning to fill in the small crater in the road. As it formed a rather unusual sight, I decided to take a picture of the tank and the crater with damaged track lying beside it. The several *bo doi* who saw me snap the picture initiated a flurry of protest. Soon a man with the green canvas bag of a political cadre emerged and addressed me.

"Why did you take that picture?" His voice was quiet but firm.

"Well, I thought it an interesting picture and didn't realize there would be any problem," I replied.

"But this is military equipment, and you've got to get permission before you photograph anything like this. I'm going to have to ask you to destroy that film," the cadre declared.

His order sounded strangely familiar. Just two months before this, a friend of ours from the United States visited us in Quang Ngai. During his stay he had taken many pictures of the countryside and of the effects of the long war. He had snapped several shots of 155mm howitzers during an ARVN firing mission. As we were leaving the firing site, an ARVN major came rushing toward us in a jeep and demanded to know why we were photographing military equipment without first securing permission. He demanded the film. In spite of our most fervent protestations, the major succeeded in securing the wanted film.

But now, faced with this determined cadre, I decided to plead the case. "It would make me most unhappy to have to destroy this film because I have many other nonmilitary pictures on this roll."

"I'm sorry, but I cannot let you have the picture of this tank. Besides, why did you take a picture of this tank? There are five others that are not damaged."

By that time I myself had begun to wonder why I had taken the picture of the tank, but I made one final appeal. "How would it be if I reversed the film in my camera and then reexposed that frame to the open sunlight?" I pointed out to the cadre and the circle of *bo doi* gathered around exactly how it could be done. The cadre was satisfied with the proposal and nodded affirmatively. I reversed the film and reexposed the frame. (Upon developing the film several days later, I discovered I had mistakenly reversed the film two frames instead of one and the relatively uninteresting picture of the disabled tank came out intact.)

After we left the tanks well behind us, the road started to climb the first range of hills. Along the road we occasionally saw small craters left by exploding mines. It was always a bit disquieting to travel roads that might be mined, but at this point we were not unduly concerned. Any possible mines along this road were likely set for tanks or truck and our small vehicles would not detonate them. Furthermore, those six tanks and much civilian foot traffic had already traveled this stretch of road, so most of the mines on the road should have already been removed or exploded.

The climb up the steep ascent was arduous. We were now thankful for the clouded day, which brought relief from the tropical sun. We stopped to rest when we reached the summit of the mountain at the place the local people called the "Pass of the Winds."

It was hard for me to believe that we were sitting down to rest on the shoulder of Dinh Cuong Mountain, which ran a mile east from the Pass of the Winds. Not two months earlier this hill had been the scene of one of the bloodiest chapters of Quang Ngai history. Several hundred men were slaughtered on and around this hill and approximately 1,000 were maimed within the space of thirty days. It had been the ARVN's last desperate offensive. Dinh Cuong Mountain was considered strategic to the defense of Quang Ngai city. Lying just 15 kilometers from the province capital, Dinh Cuong, when held by the PRG, was a potential base for the easy shelling of Quang Ngai city. When held by the Saigon forces, it served as a base for excellent surveillance and possible shelling of the large Song Ve Valley, which was held by the Liberation Front.

Because of the hill's crucial position, in July 1973 the Saigon forces took advantage of the lull in fighting that occurred after the Paris Cease-fire Agreements to seize control of Dinh Cuong and most of Song Ve Valley. The PRG had put up only minimal resistance at that time. In October 1974 the PRG launched surprise counterattacks and were able to retake the Dinh

Cuong region after only two days of fighting.

By January 1975 the Saigon generals decided they would seize the hill again—"at any cost." First came the crack Twelfth Regiment of Rangers probing the northwest flank of the hill. Then the Fifth Regiment of Saigon's Second Division moved into position on the northeast side of the hill. The Fourth Regiment completed the ground forces by marching in from the southeast of Dinh Cuong. All told, Saigon frontline and support troops assigned to the operation numbered well over 3,000 men.

Saigon forces threw restraint to the wind and rolled in eighty pieces of 105mm and 155mm artillery, even a battery of the biggest guns in the war— the 175mm "Long Johns" with an effective firing range of twenty miles. When the assault on Dinh Cuong got in full swing, they also flew from ten to thirty bombing strikes a day.

The intent of the Saigon generals, in addition to occupying a strategic hill, was to restore the sagging morale of the Saigon forces who had been on the defensive for the previous six months. I had talked with Paul Daly, the American "consulate" representative from Quang Ngai, about the operation.

"If the ARVN take the hill, it will be a big morale boost," Daly had told me. "It will debunk the myth that the V.C. are twelve feet tall." He went on to explain that the PRG were very well dug in, that a whole network of tunnels and bunkers now laced the mountain.

"Those bastards dig like moles, the sons of bitches," he said. "They don't have any P.S.P. [perforated steel planking, which the Americans used to make bunkers]; they just use alternating layers of bamboo and dirt. Bamboo, dirt, bamboo, dirt. Then their bunkers will absorb the concussion of bombs. Everywhere they are, they dig. Even on the level ground, like along the sea. You're walking along the flat sand, and—boom!—up jumps one of the bastards out of a hole in the sand. He's in there all scrunched up, waiting for hours. What you have to do is walk along, open each little trapdoor, drop in a grenade and slam shut the trapdoor."

The Saigon command was determined. On February 3, my wife was awakened at five in the morning by rapid-fire explosions that shook the earth for more than ten miles. Within fifteen minutes she counted 500 separate explosions. Later that morning I spoke to an ARVN lieutenant who was in charge of four 105mm howitzers. He explained that they had a "TOT mission"—time on target—when all eighty howitzers in the region were firing in rapid succession for two hours on the same target: Dinh Cuong Mountain. In that one morning he said they fired more then 2,000 artillery rounds and then they had to cease fire so they would not strike the planes that had come in to bomb.

I asked the lieutenant how many guerrillas they suspected were holding the mountain. His answer had caught me off guard. "We think there are about thirty or forty Viet Cong in the hill." (In talking with PRG guerrillas after the change of government, I learned that indeed they did have only one company of approximately fifty men defending the hill, with a battalion of about 400 support troops deeper in the mountains.)

Many times in my visits to Anh Duong's old refugee camp I had heard the artillery shells whistling over our heads. In fact, for one week of the operation an ARVN artillery battery had been positioned about a hundred yards from Duong's camp. That made the refugees nervous. They feared that if the PRG fired back to knock out the artillery site, a short mortar round might fall into the camp. I had watched the small jets dropping their payload on the hill. The pilots would push their planes into a dive but drop the bombs and pull out of the dive while still at considerable altitude, because as soon as the bomb exploded there was the sound of antiaircraft fire. The guerrillas were shooting back at the planes.

The casualties during Dinh Cuong Operation were heavy. I was not able to learn how many troops on the PRG side had been killed or injured. Later the only incident I was able to learn about from that side concerned one *chot* of three guerrillas in the hill. *Chot*, in revolutionary parlance, is a small group of men who are committed to defend a particular position at all costs, a kingpin that cannot be jarred loose. The NLF strategy was to establish such *chots* all over Dinh Cuong hill. In this particular *chot*, two men had already been killed. The remaining troop was reported to have written in his diary a two-line verse:

"*As long as I have breath,*
This chot *will not be lost.*"

On the Saigon side, the casualties were in the hundreds. Several times I had gone to visit the military hospital where lay row after row of patients, the young men who had been marched up Dinh Cuong Mountain only to be fired on by the NLF defenders or chewed up by the frightening constellation of land mines the NLF had set prior to and during the operation. The day I visited Quang Ngai's military morgue, the "House of Eternal Separation," not only was the main building filled, but the porch outside was lined with another row of caskets. Another building was filled with bodies, still in plastic sacks, which had just been flown in from the battlefield. And the attendants at the morgue confirmed the report that there were at least nineteen more dead men lying in a huddle close to Dinh Cuong Mountain. Apparently in the course of the operation the guerrillas captured an ARVN field radio and learned the frequency and code of the jet bombers. In a gruesome *coup de main* the guerrillas established radio contact with one jet and successfully instructed the pilot to bomb coordinates which happened to be an ARVN position near the base of the mountain. Four days later the ARVN had still not dared to return to the position to recover their nineteen dead comrades.

In the end, this month-long Dinh Cuong Operation, originally designed to be a morale booster, proved to be the lowest point of the war for the Saigon forces in Quang Ngai Province. One afternoon during the operation, a longtime friend who was a draftee in the local militia came to see Pat and me. His normal buoyancy was gone.

"All my friends are so discouraged. I have never seen morale so low. Even if the ARVN take the hill they've lost the battle.

"The people now are hopeless," he had told us. "Peace? It's hopeless even to think about peace. The only way would be for one side—any side—to win. But nobody can win. We'll just keep fighting on for years.

"I think it would be better if someone dropped an atomic bomb on us all. Or if God sent a plague and wiped all of us out at once. That way we wouldn't have to go through this slow piecemeal death: losing one family member, then another—the suffering of not knowing who it will be tomorrow."

By the end of February the ARVN finally gave up in its attempt to seize Dinh Cuong Mountain. That a virtual handful of guerrillas had been able to stand off the combined power of three regiments and an estimated 30,000 bombs and artillery shells seemed only to confirm the myth "that the V.C. are twelve feet tall." Worse, a thousand men suffered broken bodies from this operation, which left the military line of control absolutely unchanged.

Now, hardly more than a month after the end of the operation, Anh Duong's family, Hiro and I sat down to rest on the shoulder of Dinh Cuong Mountain. The bloodbath that had been the war was finally over.

Other farmers had also paused on the Pass of the Winds to catch their breaths before continuing the journey. Several women passed a canteen of tea among themselves and two squatting farmers helped each other light hand-rolled cigarettes. Some of these people had lost their homes three or four times in the preceding decade. This time—and no one seemed to have any doubts about this—they were going home to stay. But would "home" really be home?

"What's the place going to look like when we get back there?" one woman asked, looking past her husband into the gray rain clouds over the still not visible Song Ve Valley. "Do you suppose the betel nut trees will still be standing?"

"All the water buffaloes are gone," I heard a farmer say. "That means we'll be plowing by hand for several years unless the authorities bring some in from other places."

After our brief rest Hiro took his turn at the wheelchair and I tried my hand at the two-wheeled moving rig. True to its name, the mountain pass was blowing with stiff gusts of wind, making it difficult to keep the load of beds, baskets, and boards from overturning. As we descended the hill into the Song Ve Valley, Anh Duong became less talkative. Several times he wondered out loud how we would manage to cross the Song Ve since the bridge had been bombed many years before. (*Song* means "river" in Viet-namese.) We bounced through several rocky-bottomed streamlets flowing across the road and several times got bogged down in mud. But by midaf-ternoon we neared the banks of the Song Ve.

Underneath a towering jackfruit tree near the river's edge we noticed a hovel set in the side of a grassy hillock. A wrinkled, bronze-skinned woman emerged from the lean-to. When she spotted the seemingly out-of-place American and Japanese visitors, a betel-stained smile played over her face as she taunted, "Hey, aren't you fellows afraid of the V.C.? You know around here we're all V.C."

"You don't seem very ferocious," we responded in kind.

Perhaps to clear his own reputation as well as ours, Anh Duong quickly explained to the woman that Hiro and I were volunteers in a relief assistance agency, that we were not soldiers or government representatives.

"What do you think of this guy?" Hiro pointed toward me mischievously. "I'll bet you never saw a real American before."

"Saw Americans! They marched in and out of this place like they owned it. I lost my house so many times I can't remember. They came. I took off for the hills. They blew up my house. They left. I came back and built another shelter for myself. They came again. I left again. That's the way it went. Over and over. One month I lost my house four times. They hapen't come for several years now, and I'm still here." She grinned widely.

We soon learned that the only way to get across the Song Ve was to go through it. The bridge had not been repaired and no boats were available. We unloaded the bicycle and piece by piece carried the family belongings above our heads as we waded through the waist-high waters. After the two women, the children and all the beds, boards, baskets, blankets, bicycle and wheelchair were safely on the other side, I returned for Anh Duong himself.

Anh Duong lay against my back and wrapped his arms around my shoul-ders. As I embraced his impotent legs, I could feel the pulse of this crippled man of Vietnam. The end of the war and his ability to return home could not make him totally whole. But he was a resourceful man and determined. He had reminisced to me so often of his *que huong*, how life could be when there was peace in his land. He always had believed the day would come when he could return to this soil, which gave him the giant sweet potatoes. I stepped carefully on the river's bottom so we would not stumble. The moving waters bathed Anh Duong's dangling feet.

Once across the river we entered Ngoc Da hamlet. I had heard much about this region from the refugees, but since this region had always been controlled, as the woman said, by the V.C., I had never been able to visit it before. Ironically, now that the whole of Quang Ngai Province was con-trolled by the V.C., we were able to travel more extensively than ever before. But my eagerness to see what had been considered "enemy territory" throughout the war was but a pale reflection of Anh Duong's excitement as we moved toward the spot where his old home had been.

The path into the home hamlet was arched by bamboos and more jackfruit trees. As we wound along the shaded path we could hear the hammers and saws of Duong's neighbors who had returned home several days earlier. Already we could see the bamboo frames of several new houses. There were also numerous complete houses with weather-darkened thatch, indicating that some people had been living there for at least a year or so.

We stopped at the house of Anh Duong's cousin. Although the cousin was not home, Anh Duong invited us in. He pulled a canteen from his wheelchair seat and poured tea for each of us. Even without his saying so, we knew this was a toast to the home soil. How many generations of Duong's ancestors had sipped tea over this very soil!

Teacups aside, Anh Duong pivoted the wheels of the chair and pushed himself out the door. We followed him around the side of the house and back through a small path in the garden to the spot where Duong's house had stood before the war. Now exactly where the old foundation had once been was a deep hole, the crater of a large bomb. Sweet-potato vines tangled through each other on the bottom and sides of the crater. Anh Duong was silent.

Back again in the cousin's house, we sat cross-legged on the bed to feast on a fare of rice with river fish and pork, which Mrs. Duong had sautéed in *nuoc mam* (fish sauce) and carried with her in the shoulder baskets from the refugee camp. While eating, I happened to notice a rough wooden table made from discarded shell crates. I was fascinated to notice Chinese characters stenciled onto the boards. Hiro and I deciphered the characters: "Three Rounds Mortar Explosive: 82mm."

After the fine meal I leaned back against the woven bamboo wall to relax. My eye caught some other boards making a little loft above us. I had seen boards like this many times before in Quang Ngai city. Also from shell crates, these were stamped with an inscription from my native country: "Ammunition for CANNON with Explosive Projectile."

At dusk the cousin returned home. An ebullient woman of approximately twenty-five, she greeted the Duong family cheerfully.

"Where have you been all day?" Duong inquired of the cousin.

"I was carrying thatch and bamboo for the revolutionary government to make a rice storehouse. You know, up here it's not like it used to be in the enemy zone. There in the Saigon zone, if you wanted to work, you worked. If you wanted to rest a day, you rested. Up here, if there is one person, one person works; if there are two people, two people work." The cheerful and spontaneous way in which she spoke made me uncertain whether she intended her statement as a complaint or a boast.

Mrs. Duong announced that Hiro and I should go with her to report to the hamlet revolutionary authorities. She seemed anxious to explain to the hamlet leaders why an American and a Japanese should be spending the night with them.

Along the way we met a neighbor whose house was already partially constructed. Beside the bamboo frame stood a simple thatch lean-to. In it a lantern flickered alongside a few smoking joss sticks. The neighbor explained.

"The day before yesterday old Mr. Khanh was burning some brush over here. While the fire burned he walked down and stood on the path over by that tree. Suddenly there was a terrible explosion. I don't know what it was—must have been a dud grenade or something in that brush pile—but a piece of shrapnel struck him in the chest and went out through his back. He died almost immediately. We built this small altar for Mr. Khanh."

Nguyen Khanh, aged fifty-one, died March 30, 1975, one among what would inevitably be a long list of casualties of a delayed-action war.

At what was apparently the hamlet chief's office, but what appeared to us as a simple thatch dwelling like all the others, we met two men who were working over a fire, preparing their evening meal. The men were obviously healthy, hardworking farmers. We soon learned, however, that these men had been armed with more than hoes over the past decade. Similar to the colonists during America's War of Independence 200 years earlier, these men had wielded hoe in one hand and rifle in the other. They were the farmer-guerrillas.

The men were polite. They motioned for us to sit down and offered us tea. Their manner was that of the average Quang Ngai farmer, but there seemed to be an unusual quiet confidence about the men. They did not demonstrate the spirit of deference to us as foreigners that we had become accustomed to with the troops from the former Saigon Government. They seemed to accept at face value Mrs. Duong's explanation of why we were visiting the hamlet, although it soon became apparent that they had never before seen foreigners in their hamlet in quite that capacity. We inquired of them how life had been in the hamlet over the years. They told stories of the war, stories they had likely related to each other around campfires a hundred times before. The older man explained how, if they were grossly outnumbered by "enemy forces," they would retreat to the mountains and wait.

"One day the Americans came to Me Son, the hamlet next to us. There were too few of us who were armed. We had to leave. The Americans went from house to house and rounded up all the people. They herded the people into a big bomb crater and made preparation to gun them all down, but their interpreter—uh, an enemy soldier, ARVN—intervened and persuaded the Americans that the people were innocent, so the enemy didn't shoot." It was a rare tribute to an "enemy interpreter."

I stared into the fire as this farmer-guerrilla picked out a glowing ember with a pair of chopsticks to light a cigarette he had rolled while he was talking. Although I had always considered myself to be an opponent of American military involvement in Vietnam, I nevertheless felt some strange emotions when I became aware that these men, who showed us nothing but warmth and cordiality, were unconsciously interchanging the words "American" and "enemy."

The somewhat surprising fact that they seemed to make no mental association between me and "the American aggressors" did not sadden me in the least. Then, on second thought, it occurred to me that these guerrilla farmers would likely have been just as friendly to the average American foot soldier if they only had had the chance to meet him over a cup of tea rather than on the battlefield. Likewise, I had difficulty thinking of any American worker, soldier or politician who would not have responded positively to these two simple farmers if given the chance I was having.

The two farmer-guerrillas invited us to join them for supper, but we declined in order to return to Anh Duong and the children, who were waiting for us back at the cousin's house. A heavy rain had begun to fall over the now totally dark hamlet. As we stepped toward the door the men insisted we take their two conical hats and raincoats. They would pick them up in the morning.

Mrs. Duong hesitated at the door. "It's so scary walking around out there in the dark," she worried.

"If you're afraid of mines and booby traps, you don't need to worry. Here within the hamlet everything has been cleared away," replied the hamlet representative.

"No, it's not that," Mrs. Duong said meekly.

"Oh, the con ma!" the men nodded knowingly. I thought that perhaps to these men who had become accustomed to worrying about booby traps or ambushes in their nocturnal missions, Mrs. Duong's fear of "the spirits" may have seemed trite. If so, they hid their feelings well. These men too may have accepted the common belief that sometimes the spirits of the dead come back to haunt—or bless—the living. It is considered especially unfortunate if a dead person does not receive a proper burial because his soul will then be doomed to wander aimlessly.

Throughout the war there were thousands of men who were lost on various battlefields—missing in action. Many of these men never were given proper burial, and Mrs. Duong seemed well justified in her concern that this region might not be exempt from some of these wandering spirits.

The men tried to be reassuring. "There will be four of you walking together and the con ma don't usually trouble groups. It's the isolated person that sometimes get harassed."

We groped our way back through the rainy darkness without incident. In the cousin's house we dried and warmed ourselves by the coals still glowing from the supper fire.

Anh Duong did not have to coax long to persuade Hiro and me it was time for bed. But in spite of my exhaustion and the soporific rhythm of the rain trickling off the thatch, sleep came sporadically. Scenes of tender sweet potatoes, bomb craters, new thatch houses and exploding grenades raced through my thoughts in that tiny hut a world and a half removed from my ancestral *que huong* in New Holland, Pennsylvania. Though all was quiet around us except for the rain, I realized that back home in America on this day in early April people were reading banner headlines denoting the worsening fortunes of the American-supported government in Saigon. I wondered if my parents in New Holland were worried about my being "behind enemy lines" as the daily paper likely put it. I wondered if Americans would ever again want to hear about the Anh Duongs and Mr. Khanhs of Vietnam. Or were all these persistent thoughts just a troubled dream that would not go away?

WEDNESDAY, 2 APRIL. Sitting by the bombed-out foundation of Anh Duong's old house the next morning, I was most impressed by the birds. During the five years we had spent in Quang Ngai city, Pat and I frequently commented about the scarcity of birds. But here in Ngoc Da hamlet by the Song Ve there was no dearth of these feathered creatures of all colors and sizes.

There, of course, being no toilet built, I walked out toward the edge of the cousin's garden in search of an appropriate spot. The grass was trampled into a barely discernible path leading out of the garden, down over a bank and into the longtime fallow field beyond.

"Over there," Mrs. Duong called after me, "but be careful, don't go too far. And don't get off the path." A strange force gripped my stomach. As I walked I carefully scrutinized the ground for anything metallic, any trip wires, any unusual protrusions from the soil. The path into the field was still discernible, but the tall damp grass brushed my legs from both sides.

"Stop right there," Mrs. Duong called, "right there on the path." But I knew that stopping on the path would be most inconsiderate for anyone who might come this way again, so I carefully examined the tall grass to my right and ever so gingerly took two steps off the path. As I squatted I shuddered to think that farmers in the Song Ve Valley would have to live daily with these same gnawing fears.

Retreating toward the garden I made sure that I stepped only on soil that had been tramped before. Safely back in the garden, I wondered for how many more Mr. Khanhs this hamlet would burn incense in the coming years.

Back in the house Anh Duong expressed his gratitude to us for helping his family return to the *que huong*. He tried to assure us that now they could work gradually on the building of a house and that neighbors and hamlet authorities would provide rice and building assistance until their family became self-sufficient once again.

Unfortunately Hiro and I could not stay to help the Duongs start their house. We had failed to inform anyone in Quang Ngai city where we had gone, and if we did not soon return, our friends there might become concerned about our absence. There was another reason, which I left unspoken: I was afraid. To stay and help Mrs. Duong chop down bamboos for their new house with the possibility of unexploded grenades or forgotten booby traps lying hidden among the undergrowth was too frightening to contemplate. But to have admitted that reason—even to myself—would have given the lie to the measure of altruism and selflessness I usually like to attribute to myself. But I suppressed the thought of my cowardice by persuading myself I would return within a week or two to help the Duongs build.

The Anh Duong we left that morning was a powerful symbol of the 10 million refugees the war had created in Vietnam. There still remained so many awesome uncertainties, and yet a deep-seated optimism persisted. To me, it appeared that Anh Duong's life was one hardship upon another. And yet he always had found ways of bringing joy into his own life and the lives of others. As we parted with the Duong family that morning and walked out the hamlet trail, I recalled a visit that Pat and I and our two children had made to the Duongs in the refugee camp three months earlier. There never had been enough land in the camp for gardens, but Anh Duong had found a small spot of soil where he had planted ten stalks of sugar cane. He had watched the cane grow for a year. Before we left that day, he sent his oldest son out to cut the sugar cane. Then Anh Duong had tied up six stalks and sent them home with us.

We headed back to the Song Ve where we had waded across the day before, but this morning the river was swollen with the night's rain. After an exploratory probe brought the cold swirling water up to my chest, we decided that to get ourselves, let alone our bicycle and camera, across the river would be too hazardous.

We had two options: wait for a boat or walk downstream on the south side of the Song Ve. Thirty other persons were waiting to cross the river, but no one knew when a boat would show up. So Hiro and I headed east, on foot. Very shortly, we met a friendly *bo doi* who helped us find the trail that he said would bring us to National Highway One.

"Keep following this main path," the *bo doi* offered, "but make sure you don't step off the worn trail." We started walking at a brisk pace. We had not gone more than 200 yards when we stopped short. I felt the same flash of fear that I had experienced years before on a backpack trip to California's High Sierra when I had heard the buzz of a rattlesnake by our campsite. Now, half buried in the rain-washed path, I saw an egg-shaped object of copper and aluminum colors. I immediately recognized it to be a small, but lethal, M-79 grenade dud.

When Pat and I went to Vietnam for the second time in late 1973, our primary mission was to investigate the problem of unexploded munitions left lying in the farmers' fields and orchards. Even before we left for Vietnam, we had spoken with explosive ordnance disposal (EOD) experts who warned us that EOD was "an inherently dangerous game" and that "in this business many people who know what they're doing get blown away." One EOD expert had told us, "You can drop a bomb from 10,000 feet in the air and it won't go off; then you can come along and kick it and have it blow up in your face."

Our study in Quang Ngai revealed that the specific dud that caused more casualties than any other was the M-79 grenade, "a medium-range weapon in the American arsenal," according to munitions manuals. The M-79 launcher, which looked like a fat, stubby shotgun and fired the egg-shaped grenade up to 400 yards, was used extensively throughout the war in the defense of American or Saigon Government outposts. Any noisy saboteur— or dog or bird—in the darkness beyond an outpost's perimeter was apt to be answered by an anxious sentry firing an M-79 grenade into the vicinity of the noise. For technical reasons, many of these grenades failed to explode on impact as intended, yet they would often blow up much later if struck by a plowshare or a farmer's hoe.

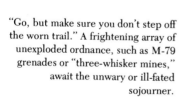

"Go, but make sure you don't step off the worn trail." A frightening array of unexploded ordnance, such as M-79 grenades or "three-whisker mines," await the unwary or ill-fated sojourner.

179

I had witnessed the effects of M-79 duds on peasant farmers, and on children who sometimes picked up these curious shiny objects and innocently played with them like toys. I had recently visited a refugee hut where the mother sat on the dirt floor by the side of the bed that held the stilled body of a thirteen-year-old boy. "My son, my son, oh my son—" the mother wailed as her fist pounded her knees in anguish. But her son, Le Van Dan, was gone. Pierced through by the steel pellets of an M-79 grenade just an hour before. Another of her sons, Le Van Vu, and two other schoolboys were wounded by the same exploding grenade. On their way home from school the boys had taken a shortcut across a paddy dike. One of them had spotted the shiny object in the grass and the curious boys huddled together to analyze their find. Hoping to take the mysterious device apart, one of them pounded it on a stone in the path. The instant explosion claimed Dan's life. Vu excaped with minor injuries. The other two boys died within three days in the hospital.

But most of the casualties from M-79 grenades occurred when farmers were tilling their fields and struck the unexploded rounds with a hoe. For example, Pham Thi Luan was the mother of a student friend of ours. Mrs. Luan's family were refugees and food was always in short supply. When a local farmer offered Mrs. Luan and some other refugees nearby the privilege of farming some of his fallow land free of charge, Mrs. Luan was eager to take up the offer. There was only one hitch. The land lay close to what the local people called "Artillery Hill." Earlier in the war, Artillery Hill had been an American "fire base" for their biggest cannons, the 175mm "Long Johns." But Mrs. Luan felt she had no alternative. She would take the chance and hoped to grow a little rice for her family. So one morning she set out with a broad blade hoe over her shoulder. She arrived at the field and began cutting the hoe into the moist soil, turning over the sod that had not been cultivated for years. She had not been working more than thirty minutes when her hoe slammed into an M-79 grenade dud lying invisibly beneath the cover of grass. When I visited the field several days later I found a battered conical hat and a splintered hoe handle lying on the freshly turned soil. Mrs. Luan was already buried in the hamlet cemetery.

It was for fields precisely like this one that we had formulated the project of "plowing up swords." We learned that M-79 grenades would not pierce heavy metal, so we tried renting tractors from a few local landlords to plow up the fields surrounding outposts where the incidents of M-79 casualties were high. The Rototiller-type plows would chew up the soil and in the process they would detonate or uncover any dud grenades in the ground. But for obvious reasons, the few tractor owners in Quang Ngai Province were not eager to plow such fields. At that point the Mennonite Central Committee decided to buy a tractor of its own and equip it with steel protective armor beneath the tractor and behind the driver. That was the tractor we had recently bought in Saigon but were unable to truck to Quang Ngai before the roads were out.

On hands and knees this farmer
combed twelve grenades out of his
grassy field. His hoe struck the
thirteenth, hidden in the soil.
Miraculously, he survived.

Most farmers never had access to tractors to open up their fields. I talked
with one farmer near Artillery Hill who had tilled a field the size of a
basketball court. But before he set hoe to the soil he had felt through the
grass with his fingers and found twelve M-79 duds. Ever so gingerly he
dislodged them from the grass and—for lack of a better place—dropped
them down an abandoned well. A neighbor of his commented to me, "It
sure takes guts to handle those grenades like he does. And he's a specialist
in guts!" But the "guts specialist" failed to find the thirteenth dud. It found
him. He struck it with his hoe and the explosion ripped off his hat, knocked
him to the ground, and sent his hoe hurtling through the air. Miraculously,
the hoe struck the grenade's near edge and the broad steel blade prevented
the shrapnel from striking the farmer. When I met the farmer a week after
the explosion, he said with a wry smile, "I guess I'm getting lazy; I haven't
done any hoeing all this week."

Now there on the path, not five feet in front of Hiro and me, lay an
unexploded M-79 grenade round. I suddenly was feeling short in guts myself. We talked of digging around the grenade and taking it away for disposal
at some safe place, but the words of an EOD specialist rang in my ears:
"Never touch or disturb an M-79 dud. They're very dangerous." I wished
I had had a quarter pound of TNT with me to "BIP" (blow in place) the
grenade as an ARVN expert in EOD had once taught me to do. Soon we

181

were surrounded by people on the trail who noticed our preoccupation with the half-buried death trap. One man broke off some small branches and pressed them into the ground in a circle around the grenade to warn succeeding travelers of the potential danger. Several people asked what it was, but everyone seemed to know it was dangerous even if they did not know its name.

I tried to intercept a young *bo doi* soldier on the trail. "Say, do you have any way of disposing of this grenade?" I asked. He looked at me with barely veiled surprise mixed, perhaps, with some suspicion of what an American was doing up there so deep in "liberated territory" talking about grenades. He looked at me a second time, said nothing, but turned and hurried down the path. His action seemed irresponsible to me. But after some thought, we decided there was nothing we could do either, so we too turned our backs on the marked—but still dangerous—grenade and continued down the trail toward home.

We were walking through sandy terrain where many Vietnamese farmers and fighters—and unwitting American soldiers—had spilled their blood. The tough waist-high grass with which the local folks thatched their houses grew ubiquitously, hiding the little gullies and trying to suppress memories of the days when the blood of Nguyens and Smiths mingled in these fields. Now the only remembrance to all that was the eerily deserted fields with artillery and bomb craters sprinkled about like a great and terrible pox over the face of the land.

Just across a rickety bamboo bridge spanning a small stream, we spotted a dud 175mm artillery shell lying in a patch of sweet potatoes. But this shell was safe. It had been neatly sawed open and the highly explosive contents had been removed. The explosive had probably been recycled by some resourceful guerrilla. The guerrillas were known to dig such shells out of the soil and unscrew their detonating fuses. They would cut the shell in half with a hacksaw to remove the TNT or other explosive "filler." Knowing that a blast rather than heat detonates the explosive, the guerrillas would liquefy the TNT by cooking it over a fire and then pour it into Coca-Cola cans salvaged from an American dump. Finally the cans were capped and topped with pull-string detonators to form deadly hand grenades or satchel charges. On other occasions the guerrilla would leave the dud American shell intact and merely replace the dud fuse with a new trip-wire fuse or pressure fuse and set the shell in a strategic location as a booby trap or land mine against advancing American or ARVN troops.

In the middle of the war the United States military took some measures to prevent being hoisted with the petard of their own duds. In some cases they introduced more complicated fuses such as the Mark 36, which could only be disarmed with nonmagnetic beryllium tools because it would explode if its magnetic field was entered by any steel object such as a truck, a rifle, or a hacksaw—or, for that matter, a woodcutter's ax or a farmer's plow. Another variation designed to make life difficult for the guerrilla was the bomb fuse that would detonate when it was unscrewed over three-quarters of a turn. In this case, the guerrillas—apparently after some trial and fatal error—learned they were safe if they held the fuse stationary and unscrewed the bomb!

Farther down the path we spotted what on first glance appeared to be a farmhouse courtyard. Intrigued by the earthen mounds at three of the four corners of the 40-foot-square space, we cautiously stepped into the courtyard, keeping an eye open for any deserted trip wires or telltale protrusions such as the metal prong of the infamous "three-whisker mine," the M-16 mine in the American lexicon. Upon further inspection, it became apparent that the three structures had been used as hideouts for local guerrillas until just recently. The mounds, each somewhat hidden under an arching clump of bamboo trees, were actually bunkers. Each was dug deep with a roof made of a layer of heavy bamboo topped with a layer of earth, more bamboo, then more earth. Each bunker had two entrances or, perhaps more to the point, two exits. If one end of the bunker collapsed with a direct hit of artillery or bomb, the occupant guerrilla could escape at the opposite end and run to another bunker. It appeared as though the complex had been shelled, perhaps during the Dinh Cuong operation. The bamboo trees arching overhead were badly splintered, likely by "air burst" bombs or shells set by tiny altimeters to explode 30 feet or so above the ground. And here, as before, were indications that the defenders of this position were farmers as well as fighters: Still growing in the center of the courtyard was a patch of leafy sweet potatoes.

A bit farther on we met a young lad with an AK-47 slung over his back. When he inquired about our destination, we explained the predicament of our not being able to cross the river. His face brightened and with an "Oh, that's no problem, come on, follow me," we headed back toward his house along the Song Ve. As we walked, Anh Thang (Victor in English), hardly more than twenty years old, told stories of his life as a guerrilla. He said his father and three older brothers were killed "fighting in the revolution" and now only he lived with his mother.

"In fact," he said, "why don't you come and have lunch at my mother's house before you cross the river?"

Anh Thang's mother was a handsome bronze-skinned woman of few words. Yet the way she stood, with her feet apart and a hand on her hip, suggested a strong independent person. White rice with fermented shrimp paste is considered to be one of the most spartan of Vietnamese meals, but it was all they had and she served us with dignity. There were none of the effusive apologies we had sometimes received when dined by city officals of the Saigon regime. Furthermore, given our hunger, the meager fare was honestly delicious. Five bowlfuls each and we were replenished after the long march of the morning.

After lunch Thang took us to the riverside and helped us into the family sampan. On the other side of the Song Ve, he pointed out the trail that would take us back to Nghia Hanh and Quang Ngai city.

Through a steady rain we retraced our path back past Dinh Cuong Mountain and over the mountain pass, pausing en route to have a friendly chat with the *bo doi* who were still working on the damaged tank.

We stopped in at Anh Duong's deserted refugee camp to pick up Hiro's bicycle, which we had left with a neighbor before the trip, and pedaled silently toward Quang Ngai city. Nearing town, we passed over a rise where the once-operating railroad crossed the road. Looking back toward the southwest, we could see the sky clearing over the Pass of the Winds.

THURSDAY, 3 APRIL. "It's Anh Nam." Hiro had noticed the town's only white Mazda stopping in front of the Quaker house on Thursday morning and announced the arrival of the chairman of Quang Ngai's People's Revolutionary Committee.

After greetings, the province leader waved off our offer of tea. "I wonder if you might be able to accompany me to visit the Japanese engineers from the sugar mill. I need your help in translating," he nodded toward Hiro.

In our meeting we learned that the three young men had been sent by their Japanese corporation to Quang Ngai for two months to inspect the sophisticated machinery in the new sugar mill west of town. Suddenly one night the Vietnamese around them, with whom they could communicate only by sign language, began to run. The engineers were motioned to follow. That move proved nearly fatal, for they were soon caught in the middle of the panicked ARVN retreat and guerrilla ambush. Miraculously, they lived through the night but were captured by the the guerrillas in the morning and sent to the hills for several days. Being brought back into Quang Ngai city was only small relief because they still could not communicate with anyone and feared only the worst.

Today, in understandable language, they heard Hiro translate Anh Nam's message not to worry, that all would be well. Would they be permitted to return home to their families in Japan, they asked Anh Nam politely.

"That's a foreign affairs problem," Anh Nam replied. "At least now that you're here, you are not prisoners, which you would be if you'd been involved in political or police work. And in the meantime—while you're still with us—we would like you to return to work. The local technicians don't know everything about the mill yet, and you could teach them while you're here." The engineers quickly nodded their consent.

Thursday afternoon Hiro and I checked in at our MCC house on Tran Hung Dao Street. All was intact and we stayed but a minute. As we were leaving we met Mr. Chau's son Dieu, who was one of the high-school students who had volunteered to serve as "home guard" to keep order in the town. Chin high, this ninth-grade student displayed his white armband prominently and swung his M-16 rifle with a flourish. He seemed not the least unhappy with his newfound power.

"Anh Kien, Anh Hiro, don't you worry about your house here. Nobody will touch it. I'll see to that. You know? I've really been busy. I've been given responsibility to keep order downtown. Now nobody gets away with anything." With that Dieu clanked the stock of the M-16 on our cement porch.

"Wow! I suppose everyone in town's afraid of ol' hawk-eye Dieu!" Hiro's eyes were wide with pretended alarm.

Dieu scrambled to inject more authority into his story. "No, seriously, Anh Hiro, yesterday I nabbed this kid who was stealing five thousand piasters from a woman at the market. I grabbed him just like that." Dieu snapped shut his fist in the air as though he was snatching someone's shirt. "The party told me I should shoot someone like that if I had to—dead on the spot! But I caught him alive. He confessed everything."

"Oh thank God! I'd hate to think what Quang Ngai would do without you, Dieu!" Hiro shook his head gravely as we mounted our bicycles to leave.

"No really, Anh Hiro"—but then, giving up on his merciless skeptic, Dieu turned to me—"really, Anh Kien, and yesterday I also caught these two guys who were raping a girl down at—" But Dieu's audience, already riding out the alley, never caught the end of his sentence.

Thursday evening about nine o'clock I jumped on my bicycle and pedaled around the streets of Quang Ngai. Nine o'clock Indochina time. Saigon time would have been ten, but everyone had already changed their clocks to the time of the revolution. It was my favorite hour of the day in Quang Ngai. A time to be alone with your thoughts. Or your friend. It was at this hour that Pat and I had often "happened" to find each other at the same place—sitting by the well or waiting near the bougainvillaea arbor—back in that special period in our friendship when only "the spirit" could ordain our rendezvous. One summer night eight years before, we "found" each other at the front gate of our house at about this hour. We ambled down the dusty unpaved street to the edge of town where the absence of streetlights permitted the intimacy we sought. Hand in hand we strolled along a bamboo-lined path toward the river north of town. In simple, but romantic, thatch houses by the path's side we could see by flickering lanterns young students poring over copybooks or mothers with flowing hair swinging infants in knitted hammocks. Forgetting the war, we walked on, beyond the last houses, close to the river's edge where we sat in the grass and talked of life and love.

"*Who goes there!*" The voice shot out of the blackness. We heard the metallic rattle of a rifle just yards to our right.

"Just us! Just taking a walk. Friends! Civilians!" We stood motionless as we waited for a reply.

Two forms approached and became faintly visible in the darkness. "Kind of risky to be walking around out here at this hour, isn't it? You might get shot." The local militiamen came close enough to see us more clearly and then without further word disappeared back into the night.

It was also about this hour of night when the gongs from the town's pagodas would bathe the town in their pure resonance. And when the calls of invisible peddlers would lure the town's denizens from quiet conversations to go to the street for a treat of half-hatched duck eggs or freshly baked bread.

"Breeeeeeadioooo . . . hot bread . . . breeeeeeadioooo . . . hot bread. . . ." The plaintive cry from the street sent a shiver of anticipation through me. We had just returned to Quang Ngai after nearly five years in the United States and the thought of sinking teeth into one of those hot crisp loaves was too much to resist. Postponing bedtime, I pulled my shirt back on and walked out toward the street. From the fire base west of town I heard the cannons. "Haaa-rum. Haaa-rum."

At the gate I called to the small lad silhouetted by the distant streetlight. "*Em oi, lai day,* I'd like to buy some bread." A small urchin. Hardly more than five or six. His shorts and shirt were soiled and ragged, but the child stood erect.

"Have change for a two-hundred-piaster bill?" I asked through the gate.

"How many loaves do you want, uncle?" His voice was soft. Bashful.

"I'll take two." The boy let his sack fall from his shoulder and he started routing for the bread. "Where are you from, little brother?"

"Down the way." He handed me the warm loaves through the gate and began digging in his pocket for change.

"How much is a loaf by now?"

"Twenty piasters apiece, uncle."

"Where are your parents?"

"Dead."

"Dead?"

"Cannons."

"Oh, cannons—. Where do you sleep?"

"On the street. Uh—here, how much is that?"

By the distant fluorescent light I could barely decipher the bill he handed me. "It's a fifty." He kept digging and handed me two more fifties. "That'll do, little brother." He kept digging. "That's all right, you just keep the rest."

"But uncle, I still owe you ten piasters." He sounded as though his sense of fairness had been offended.

"That's okay. What's your name?"

He found the coin and handed it to me. I had to accept.

"Xuan."

"How old are you?"

"Eight."

"What was that?"

"Eight. Eight."

"You go to school?"

That wounded him. "How you to go to school when your parents are dead?"

"Oh—uh, hope you can sell all your bread tonight."

"Good night, uncle."

"Night, little brother."

He gathered the neck of his sack in his hands and swung it over his shoulder. His bare feet shifted in the sand and then pattered softly as he walked down the street. The bag of loaves swung like a pendulum over his straight back. His cry was more plaintive than ever. "Breeeeeeeadioooo . . . hot bread . . . breeeeeeeadioooo . . . hot bread. . . ."

The distant cannon fired again into the night. "Haa-rum. Haa-rum."

Now, in a Quang Ngai liberated from cannon fire, it was once again that time of night. I pedaled slowly through the ill-lit streets. It was a time when one could allow the subconscious to play delightful tricks. I could imagine Pat appearing on a bicycle, pedaling in cadence beside me. In the back streets all that was visible was the quivering flames in kerosene lanterns or candles. From courtyards here and there one could hear the voices of scampering invisible children eager to postpone bedtime. The guns, the flags, the propaganda banners dissolved in the darkness. Ah yes, let them go! Pray, let them be gone forever. Let the world be conquered by lanterns and children's voices!

FRIDAY, 4 APRIL. Friday afternoon, ten days after the Liberation of Quang Ngai, Em Tu, a high-school student friend, stopped in at the house to chat. It was at the house of Tu's aunt that I had met with Chi Kha before my journey across the lines less than two weeks before. Em Tu had had relatives in Thieu's army and relatives in Thieu's prisons, but primarily his family had attempted—with considerable success—to dodge conscription from either side and to continue farming their sugar cane and peanuts. Em Tu's primary preoccupation before Liberation was the ARVN draft. As a small boy Tu had lived in the countryside and started school a year late. When his family "refugeed" closer to Quang Ngai city, Tu lost another year in school, leaving him two years older than most of his classmates. But as many other students in his predicament, Tu had paid to have his village chief issue him a falsified birth certificate that subtracted two years from his age, so when the military police stopped him on the streets or made a nighttime raid on his village to nab draft dodgers, his papers indicated he was seventeen years old instead of a draftable eighteen or nineteen. However, Tu's school records had not been changed to correspond to his new birth certificate and the high-school principal was apparently uncorruptible. Hence, Tu feared that he would be discovered by the police and drafted at the end of the school year. That gnawing fear had badly demoralized the normally buoyant and optimistic Em Tu.

When Em Tu visited us Friday afternoon his boyish spark of enthusiasm had returned. "Kien, Hiro, I knew you guys would stay! Well, what do you think about this place now? Pretty exciting, eh!"

"Pretty exciting, all right. And I suppose you've joined the *bo doi* by now, eh Tu?" Hiro laughed.

"Not if I can help it! But who knows, maybe someday I will. Right now they're getting things organized, all right. Every night there are meetings out there where I live."

"Meetings?"

"Sure thing, They're not losing any time. Everyone is included in some kind of group. I guess you'd call it a cell or something like that. Each cell's got a leader—someone who shows revolutionary potential, even though he's not necessarily been in the revolution before."

"How large are these cells?"

"About ten to fifteen people in a group. Yeah, nearly every evening you hear some guy with a bullhorn walking around the village, 'Hear ye, hear ye. Everyone from sixteen to thirty-five years of age is to attend a meeting tonight at the house of Uncle X to discuss village activities.' "

"So what do you talk about at the meetings?"

"Oh, you sing a lot and the cadres talk. And we discuss what we're going to do to implement the revolution in our village. For example, everyone is supposed to volunteer for something. We volunteer for things we like so we won't be 'volunteered' for jobs we don't like. Me, I don't want to carry a gun and so far I haven't had to. But I don't know, these guys are incredible. You wouldn't believe how effective they are at the art of persuasion. You know, after a while, you just volunteer to go. They never beat you like under the Thieu regime. They're really good at it. It's just like they open up your mind and make you want to do what they want you to do!"

Em Tu shook his head and whistled to emphasize his point. "The big thing now is to erase the signs of the old regime—like propaganda banners and flags and billboards. But even the *way* you do things—they want to change that too. You remember how whenever you talked to a superior, like a teacher or an official under the old regime, you always addressed them with that special 'sir' title. Well, now everybody's just 'brother' or 'sister' or 'comrade so and so.' "

Anh Tu also related that some individual cadres were encouraging changes in personal habits that appeared to them as not "appropriate for the revolution."

"For example, you remember my brother Anh Ba?" I had met his brother on several occasions and was always intrigued at his success in evading the Saigon draft. It may have been partly due to a handsome beard he sported, a feature generally marking an old man in Vietnamese custom. "Well, after Liberation, when the head cadre in our village met Anh Ba, he said, 'Say, brother, about that beard. I know you grew it so you wouldn't be pressed into Thieu's army, and that's all right. But those days are over, so now you may go home and shave.' Oh Anh Ba, he kind of liked his beard by now, but he went straight home and shaved."

Although no order had been given concerning clothing, Em Tu observed that none of his friends now wore the transparent flowered shirts that had been all the rage the last year in Quang Ngai, and that girls with super-flared slacks had taken them in. Em Tu reported that now the hottest item on the attire market was the rubber-tire sandal. The sandals had always been available from a few sidewalk peddlers in Quang Ngai, but since Liberation, the price for the sandals had doubled or tripled because of increased demand.

Hiro and I had obviously not put much credence in predictions by American and Saigon officials that there would be massive reprisals after a Communist victory in Vietnam. Had we believed the "bloodbath" predictions, we most certainly would not have considered it a reasonable risk to stay in Quang Ngai for the change in government. Nevertheless, for a war so long and bloody, it did seem credible that there would be some "score settling" on the low levels, especially between guerrillas and former Thieu officials. In the ten days since the Saigon administration in Quang Ngai had collapsed, we had made a point of asking former acquaintances from various districts about the fate of officials in their regions. In that time the only report of violence we received was the one concerning the hamlet chief of a fishing village who apparently had been killed the morning the PRG took over. Who killed him or for what reason, we were never able to learn. There was no doubt about it, the transition had taken place with a remarkable lack of recrimination.

I was especially eager to ask Em Tu what had happened to the officials in the area west of Quang Ngai city where he lived. A simple trust had developed between us, and in the past Em Tu had candidly reported positive and negative events about both sides. He answered my question by going down the list of all the officials he could think of.

"In Tu Quang village, the Security Officer committed suicide. He had a reputation of forcing limewater down the stomachs of suspects to get information, and on one occasion he shot prisoners at the Am Bo market near my house, so he probably was afraid. The former village chief of Tu Quang reported to the PRG and he is being detained. The more recent Tu Quang chief had been associated with the National Reconciliation Force, that Buddhist group, and he was not even detained.

"Then I know of a contractor who used to work close to the sugar mill.

He had fled to Danang with piles of money and when he returned he was detained and his money taken. The old village chief of Tu Thuan committed suicide, the more recent one was detained.

"And the Security Officer from Tu Thuan—a bunch of local people ganged up on him right after Liberation. He had a terrible reputation for torturing people in Tu Thuan village and a lot of people were really mad at him. They started beating up on him. Even broke his nose. Maybe they would've killed him, I don't know, but some Liberation Front cadres around there saw what was going on and they quickly intervened and sent the people home. They said the policy of the revolution does not permit individual reprisals. They took the man into custody."

We asked Em Tu if anything about the events of the past weeks had surprised him. He gave a snappy nod of his head and blink of his eyes, which was characteristic of Em Tu when he became excited. "Oh, the crazy man was a surprise! Actually his name was Anh Ba Yen, but everybody in Tu Quang village knew him as the crazy man. He would do all sorts of weird things. Like he would get up in the middle of the night and storm out into his yard in a rampage. He'd take a machete and slash down banana trees and plants. And he'd go to the pig sty and slice open the throats of little pigs. At one point he got drafted, and he was an ARVN soldier at the military headquarters here in town for a while, but then they decided he was mentally unstable and sent him home, but he still pulled an ARVN salary most of the time. He had a family. Five children, I believe. And his wife would get so upset by her husband, she often cried.

"Well, three months before the revolution came to town, this guy was wandering around in the rice-bean area and some guerrillas came and nabbed him. They tied him up and led him away. Some of the farmers saw it happen. Now, when the Liberation Forces came to Quang Ngai, who should be with them but the crazy man! Carrying a sidearm and a cadre bag. Calm and collected. Not crazy anymore. Here it turns out that he was an intelligence agent for the Front the whole time. He kept records of everything that happened in that village. He knows exactly who made trouble for the people. There's not a thing they don't know!

"Isn't that incredible? I tell you Hiro, Kien, the tactics of the revolution give you the shivers."

Em Tu also said it was his understanding that a woman who had in recent years been a vendor of sugar-cane drinks at the entrance of the ARVN military compound now emerged as one of the top People's Revolutionary Committee for Quang Ngai Province. "Their eyes were everywhere," Em Tu concluded. "There's nothing large or small they don't know."

Em Tu observed that prices of imported goods had risen sharply in the days since Liberation. Bicycle tires had doubled in price and gasoline quadrupled. Obviously, merchants were operating on the supposition that these items would be difficult to procure in the future. When Em Tu spoke about inflation in the price of cigarettes, he laughed. "The other day in a Quang

Ngai shop a fellow came in to buy several cigarettes, loose. The old price was four cigarettes for a hundred piasters. The new price, three for a hundred. The guy was upset. He cursed, 'Mother fuck, these cigarettes are sure expensive.' Well, a cadre happened to be sitting in the shop. He called the fellow over and asked him to sit down and quietly started talking to the guy. 'Don't you realize it was your mother who gave birth to you? Do you think you ought to talk that way about your mother? Remember, now the revolution has come. You don't have to talk like you did in the old society any longer. All right?' The fellow walked away without a word."

Official corruption at levels high and low had virtually become a way of life under the Saigon regime and Em Tu said that he had heard some people were now confronting former Saigon officials and demanding they return bribe money. He knew of several "popular force" militiamen who had to pay off an ARVN captain to avoid being transferred to a more dangerous post in the "regional force" militia. Now they had gone to that captain and demanded that he return their bribe money. The captain, on fear of being reported to the revolutionary authorities, returned the money.

"My brother-in-law really got taken by bribes," Em Tu went on. "You remember him, Anh Kien, the one you and Pat met at our house a month or so ago."

"You mean the one who was on crutches?"

"Right. You remember, I told you he had deliberately set up a small 'toad' mine and stepped on it to blow off his toes so he'd be discharged from the army. Well, after he did it and he was lying there in the field with the blood pouring out his foot, the lieutenant in his unit demanded a promise of thirty thousand piasters before they would carry him to the hospital. Then he got to the hospital and the doctor apparently assumed it was a self-inflicted wound, so he demanded twenty thousand piasters to amputate the foot. Then another doctor at the Military Field Hospital demanded seventy thousand to keep him out of Room Ten. Room Ten is the ward for patients with self-inflicted wounds. Those fellows eventually wind up in military prison. Then after he was mobile again he started working on his discharge papers. The officers at the military compound demanded one hundred thousand piasters to issue papers certifying this was a 'hostile injury.' So he lost his foot and a couple hundred thousand piasters, and then they transferred his case to the regional military hospital in Danang where he was to get his final discharge papers. Well, out there they demanded another hundred thousand piasters, but he hasn't gotten around to paying that one yet. And now the revolution's come and he's free. Most of one foot is gone and he's much poorer, but free!" Em Tu fell silent. I would not have been surprised if Em Tu himself would not have taken some such desperate action if he had been drafted into the army, but now that day was past.

Friday afternoon after Em Tu left, Hiro and I pedaled to the nearby open-air market to buy some vegetables for dinner. Along the way my eye was caught by a tall handsome fellow working on a garbage crew along the street. He dug his shovel into a pile of debris in the gutter and threw it onto a large two-wheeled cart. He was dressed in soiled clothes and was wearing a battered conical hat. His pant legs were rolled halfway to his knees, revealing muddied calves beneath. As we neared the garbage crew, the young man's eyes met mine.

"Hiep!" I had first met Hiep just two months before on a bus trip to Saigon. Midway to Saigon, when our bus stopped at a roadside inn for the night, I had been singled out by this dashing young man. Assuming—or perhaps hoping—that I spoke no Vietnamese, he had tried out some English on me, seemingly quite eager to impress this American. He had gesticulated grandly and managed to produce a few intelligibile sentences. When he discovered I spoke Vietnamese, he had begun to speak proudly of his various exploits. He had introduced himself.

"Hiep. Captain Hiep. Twenty-eight years old—yes, very young for a captain, I know, but I'm a pilot. A bomber pilot."

I soon learned that Captain Hiep was one of the pilots who were flying bombing missions during the Dinh Cuong Mountain operation in Quang Ngai, which was in full swing at that time. He went into a long discourse describing his American A-37 bomber and the 1,500-pound bombs they regularly dropped on the hill. He was quite pleased with his performance.

"We kill ten or twenty V.C. every time we bomb. Sometimes fifty," he boasted. I did not mention that an ARVN artillery lieutenant had estimated that no more than fifty guerrillas occupied the Dinh Cuong Mountain at any one time. I did ask if he thought the ARVN would soon take the hill. He threw back his head in an air of glib confidence. "No problem. We have the Rangers, the Airborne, the Second Division, Artillery and the Air Force—all in there." Then he suddenly became more thoughtful for a second and in a muted tone of voice said, "Those V.C., I don't understand how they eat. We have that mountain virtually surrounded, and I don't understand how they get their food and water."

But the baffled Captain Hiep preferred not to dwell on the tenacity of his enemy and quickly changed the subject to his anticipation of meeting his girl friends in Saigon.

"You know, we Air Force pilots have the reputation of being butterflies and, uh, as you know, butterflies do like to have lots of flowers." With that he whipped out a packet of pictures from his jacket pocket and started introducing me to his garden of flowers. Among them he identified one as his fiancée, whom he would be marrying in several months. He was quick to assure me, however, that his marriage would not prevent him from cultivating relationships with the rest of his friends as well.

Now, ten days after the Liberation of Quang Ngai, I was surprised to encounter Captain Hiep once again. Today the "butterfly" bomber pilot had been given new employment. He leaned against the garbage cart as we exchanged a few words. Now his air of arrogance was gone. His tone was subdued, resigned. There was no mention of the bombing raids or the "flower girls." Today Hiep was meeting face to face the people he had been bombing just a few weeks before. For me he had only one request. "Say, brother, could you spare me a little rice? I'm hungry." We invited him to stop in at our house when he had opportunity, but we were never to see Captain Hiep again.

Friday night we again listened to the BBC and VOA broadcasts. The check marks on Anh My's map pressed farther south. The Liberation Army had taken the highlands and was pushing relentlessly down across the coastal provinces. The BBC reported that the ARVN had even withdrawn from Nhatrang! That bastion of unassailable ARVN supremacy, now fallen!

Very unsettling was the report from Saigon that the world's largest air transport plane, the American C5A, was flying out of Saigon loaded with Vietnamese babies and American women volunteers when the huge plane crash-landed killing nearly 100 children and many of the women. The tragedy was only heightened by the dubious moral underpinning of "Operation Babylift." One wondered if Americans had now foisted onto innocent Vietnamese babies the irrational premise of the cold war: better dead than Red.

SUNDAY, 6 APRIL. Sunday morning Hiro and I pedaled down Phan Boi Chau to the Tin Lanh church. Tin Lanh—"good news"—was the name of the main body of evangelical Christian churches in Vietnam. Tin Lanh membership countrywide numbered less than one hundred thousand, far smaller than the Catholic church, which could claim two million adherents, or the Buddhists, who were in the majority in South Vietnam. But we were well acquainted with Tin Lanh because Mennonite Central Committee had established working relationships with the church for over two decades. Several projects in Vietnam had been sponsored jointly by MCC and Tin Lanh.

Yet the relationship had been an uneasy one. Some Mennonite personnel became impatient with Tin Lanh's preoccupation with avoiding any action that might be labeled "political." Tin Lanh's strong emphasis on personal salvation often had the effect of precluding any effective testimony or action against the brutalities of the war.

Actually within all the religious groups, Tin Lanh included, there was a minority of the believers whose faith propelled them into self-sacrificing missions of service. For example, concerned zealous Tin Lanh youth had formed a social-welfare organization, which became active in working with refugees and orphans. A small collection of Catholic priests and a larger number of Buddhist monks had been very involved in campaigning for an end to the war and greater justice for poor people and political prisoners.

Still, just as Catholicism had been viewed by many to be a French religion, Tin Lanh was considered by many to be the religion of the Americans. This view was given further credence by the fact that Tin Lanh pastors, thanks generally to introductions from certain American missionaries, regularly cultivated close ties with American military chaplains who bestowed copious material benefits on the Tin Lanh congregations in the form of church buildings, church schools, or more dubious favors such as rides on U.S. Army helicopters or Christmas parties with the American chaplain. Whether or not one argued in defense of such practices, there was little doubt that to the Tin Lanh Christians who continued to live in North Vietnam or in PRG regions such alliances throughout the war must have appeared "political" indeed.

But if the Tin Lanh voice was conspicuously absent in protesting against the injustices of the old Saigon regime, there was no sign now that the church had any intention of protesting visibly against the new regime either.

When Hiro and I entered the church on Sunday morning, forty persons, fewer than half the normal number, were already assembled for worship and prayer. A number of Christians, including the pastor and his family, had fled to Danang in the day or two before the PRG take-over and had not yet returned. Our small group was muted, more pensive than normal for the Tin Lanh services in Quang Ngai. A young seminarian led the group in prayer for the Christians not yet accounted for. Then he opened his Bible to the fourteenth chapter of the Gospel of John.

" 'My peace I give to you, not as the world giveth, give I unto you. . . .' " For twenty minutes the young man simply, but eloquently, challenged the congregation to find peace and solace in God. "What is peace?" the pastor asked the assembled believers. He related the illustration of two artists who were commissioned to depict on canvas the meaning of peace. The first, he said, painted a scene of a tranquil lake in the woods where not a ripple broke the glassy surface of the water and not a leaf moved on the surrounding trees. The second artist painted a turbulent waterfall crashing on cold jagged rocks below. Merciless gales of wind tore at a battered pine tree growing beside the thundering cascade. On the end of a lone branch that extended in behind the surging falls sat a small sparrow—still and unafraid. "This, beloved," the pastor's voice quieted, "is the peace of a Christian in the world."

Sunday afternoon Chi Mai and I rode west out of town in the direction I had taken to cross over to "the other side" exactly two weeks before. To my delight, Chi Mai led me to the refugee home of Chi Kha, the multi-bloused guide who led me on that journey. It was our good fortune to find her at home, or what remained of her largely dismantled home. Her family was beginning to move back to their native home in the countryside in the vicinity of that guerrilla hideout she had led me to. Chi Kha had apparently been a refugee woman indistinguishable from the thousands of other refugees around Quang Ngai, and yet she had continued to perform important liaison missions for the PRG whenever the need arose. I wondered how many of our other refugee acquaintances performed similar functions throughout the war. There seemed to be two fallacies in the American and ARVN strategy to isolate the "sea" of people from the "fish" of the guerrillas. For one, tributaries of the sea always found their way back to the fish, and furthermore, the sea that had been scooped up itself contained many fledgling fish that would come to "contaminate" the waters of South Vietnam's cities.

We wished Chi Kha well in her new life and took our leave. I did not notice the color of her blouse. Now it no longer mattered.

TUESDAY, 8 APRIL. "We longed for the day of peace when liberation would come—but now that day has come, and things just aren't so rosy." The feisty old woman gesticulated broadly as she spoke. She identified herself as a refugee woman who was short of rice and wanted us to help her out. "We have to go back to our homes in the countryside and start all over again. We have to build from nothing. And it's not certain peace means we're going to live. Those old fields are just popping full of explosives. The dying's not over for us yet." The woman stamped her bare foot on our living-room floor to dramatize how easily a person could be blown to pieces by stepping on a mine. And then, one hand on her hip, she snorted in a flurry of indignation, "And that vicious plane that flew over here yesterday—that thing made me shake like a leaf. When I heard that machine, I hit the floor in a flash!" Jumping as she spoke, the woman landed in a crouched position by the living-room couch.

We couldn't help laughing at the woman's comic-horror. "People around here have been saying that plane was from North Vietnam, so it won't drop any bombs here," I offered reassuringly to the crouching woman.

That brought the woman back to her feet in a hurry. "Humph! North, South, East, West! I don't care where the blasted thing was from. It scared the wits out of me! Tigers from the north scare me just as much as tigers from the south!"

It was exactly two weeks since the ARVN had fled town and the guerrillas had placidly entered. From this vantage point Hiro and I felt totally vindicated in our decision to remain in Quang Ngai. To have left would have been to miss our once-in-a-lifetime opportunity. And now that we had stayed, perhaps we would even be able to participate in reconstruction projects in central Vietnam. Although it would likely be several months before we would know, perhaps Pat and the children could return and we all could serve as MCC representatives in central Vietnam.

Our plans were abruptly modified, however, by a surprise visit from a top-level NLF official.

"Hello, hello, friends. You must be Anh Kien."

"That's right, won't you come in?"

"Oh thank you, thank you. My name is Tran Duc Doanh. Doanh. Tran Duc Doanh. I've been meaning to visit you for so long now, but I hope you will understand that as Chairman of the National Liberation Front for Quang Ngai, I've had to attend to the affairs of consolidating security for the province. And you, are you well, friends?"

"We're just fine, thank you. And Anh Doanh, this is Anh Hiro."

"I'm glad to meet you, friend Hiro. We have known about friend Kien for some time. We are happy to learn to know you, Hiro."

"Won't you please sit down?"

Hiro left to bring hot water for tea, while our visitor and I took seats facing each other over the coffee table. A grand man in stature and style, this Tran Duc Doanh. Dressed in military uniform, he moved with vigor and spoke with gusto.

"Chairman of the National Liberation Front for Quang Ngai? Yes, we have heard your name. We are pleased to have the opportunity to meet you. I'm sure you must have a fascinating personal history."

Tran Duc Doanh settled back into the cushioned chair and swung one leg over the other. His feet were clad in the familiar rubber-tire sandals, but he seemed the type of man who would not have been uncomfortable in boots. He immediately reached into his shirt pocket where he procured a Western-style pipe and an ornately engraved silver tobacco case.

"Personal history? I used to be a teacher. An intellectual. Lived in the Saigon-controlled zone for a time but had to leave because of Diem"—Ngo Dinh Diem was Premier and later President of the Saigon Government from 1954 to 1963—"leave and fight for national independence. Had to leave my family—"

"So you have a family."

"A wife and six children. Had to leave them in the Saigon zone for fifteen years."

"A teacher by profession you were." I enjoyed injecting an element of grandness into my own style. After all, a man of this carriage must come with a clear mission and we would do well to create a favorable impression.

"Education is of prime importance, you know. For us revolutionaries, there's nothing more important. Unfortunately, because of the long war, the level of education among the guerrillas is not ideal, but now there will be quick progress." Hiro returned with the hot water Thermos and began arranging teacups on the table while the NLF leader continued talking. "As you know, we had a long, difficult struggle against American imperialism.

But you must understand," he added with calculated diplomacy, "we know not all Americans are imperialists." Tran Duc Doanh packed tobacco into his pipe while he spoke, but his words were not idle musings. Already there seemed to be a definite progression to this man's speech.

"Indeed, we are grateful for the contributions you and your friends have made in Quang Ngai," he continued. "I met your three friends who were captured last year." (He was referring to Sophie and Paul Quinn-Judge and Diane Jones of the Quaker team who were picked up by guerrillas and detained for ten days in early 1974 when they were visiting a refugee camp near My Lai.) "We appreciate the contributions all of you have been making." He paused just long enough to light his pipe. "Yes, we know how to be grateful to our friends, and, mind you, we know how to distinguish between a friend and an enemy. That is crucial to the success of our struggle, that we accurately differentiate friend and enemy."

I was grateful that his words—leaping with rapier-like precision—were cutting in our favor rather than to our condemnation. For loss of a grander response, I merely replied, "Thank you. Yes, thank you."

"Anh Doanh, please have tea." Hiro nodded his head and motioned with his hand.

"Yes." Tran Duc Doanh acknowledged the offer, but continued talking. "But I must tell you that as Chairman of the National Liberation Front for Quang Ngai, we have to be concerned about the security of our city. As you know, Quang Ngai has a great revolutionary history. Many revolutionary heroes. Historic revolutionary landmarks—Ba To, Ba Gia. Because of Quang Ngai's example, many people all over Vietnam took faith that we could stand up against the American imperialists. And"—he paused to puff his pipe— "and we have the strength to preserve the fruits of our revolution."

"No one accuses Quang Ngai of lacking determined people," I affirmed.

"You should know"—he leaned forward slightly and his voice lowered— "right now we are preparing for an American response to the great defeats they have suffered over the past weeks. We have reason to believe the United States will not be content to let South Vietnam be liberated without making some response. We expect they will bomb—perhaps using B-52's— and we must be ready to guard against that. Let me assure you, we are prepared for that. We have antiaircraft equipment in place. We are ready and capable of defending our province."

Tran Duc Doanh took several puffs on his pipe, but it was obvious he intended to continue. "But we are worried for your security. You understand that we feel a special responsibility to insure your safety as foreigners."

Suddenly I thought I understood the purpose of the visit. This high official had come to advise us to build a sturdy bunker. Or perhaps to have us take refuge in the mountains for a week or two, I surmised to myself.

"For that reason," he continued, "we at the upper levels are suggesting that you, Kien and Hiro, evacuate to Saigon."

Evacuate to Saigon! It was as if a bomb had exploded in our living room. Certainly, I did not hear this man correctly. Go to Saigon! But Saigon was still in ARVN hands. Across the line of battle. Hanoi, perhaps, but certainly not Saigon!

"We will make papers for you to travel through the liberated areas," he continued calmly. "You may travel by sea or overland. Sea may be easier for you, but we suggest you go as soon as possible, probably leaving tomorrow morning."

Tomorrow morning! That's only one day! Why the rush? How could it have been so safe in Quang Ngai for two weeks and suddenly become so dangerous for us to stay?

"This will be temporary only," I heard him say through my spinning thoughts. "After this we will invite you to return if you desire to do so." The official had delivered his message. He sat back in his chair and puffed in silence.

Then, after a conspicuous silence, I began to speak. "We would like to thank you for your visit and for your concern about us. Uh—we had hoped that we could stay in Quang Ngai to continue serving the people here and to help Americans and other foreigners attain a better understanding of the revolution. We have been interested in trying to mobilize interest among Americans to contribute toward healing the wounds of war as indicated in Article 21 of the Paris agreements. But" —I could hardly bring myself to say it— "but if the Revolutionary Committee feels it would be better for us to go to Saigon or some other place at this time, uh, I suppose we are ready to cooperate with that plan."

"I want to emphasize that this is temporary, and that we hope you can return to Quang Ngai again." Now Tran Duc Doanh was quick to be gracious.

"Evacuate to Saigon—" The sheer danger of the prospect suddenly eclipsed my disappointment at having to leave Quang Ngai. "I must confess I do wonder how it will be crossing the battle line into Saigon-controlled area."

"Oh, no problem," Doanh was quick to dismiss the concern. "You will have papers from us to move freely in the liberated zone and when you get to the Saigon zone, it will be easy for you because you are foreigners."

Foreigners. The word presented a fascinating test proposal to present to Tran Duc Doanh. "During the last several days Hiro and I have been spending time with the three Japanese engineers from the sugar mill. They cannot speak any Vietnamese, and if you plan to suggest that they travel to Saigon in the coming days, we'd like to offer to travel with them, to assist them along the way." The proposal was diplomatic enough, I thought, but it caught the official off balance.

"Uh—you mean the three Japanese who work at the sugar mill? Uh—I haven't had the opportunity to meet them yet. It is my understanding that they will be, uh, will be staying at the sugar mill." Then, with recovered conviction, he added, "And we will defend that mill at all costs! After all, it belongs to the people! And we will have a plan to defend the mill and the people working in the mill. If necessary, we will evacuate them with the other employees of the mill to a safe place. The contribution of the Japanese engineers will be important to the production of sugar in Quang Ngai."

Now feeling that their "concern for the security of the foreigners" was directed specifically toward us, I again became concerned with the potentially explosive situation we might encounter in Saigon. "Reports on the radio recently make the Saigon scene appear quite volatile, Anh Doanh. If fighting in the city should break out, it would hardly seem the most secure place to be." And then, mustering all the levity possible, I added, "Are you sure we shouldn't be heading for Hanoi instead?"

Tran Duc Doanh shook his head. "Oh, don't worry. Certainly we shall liberate all of South Vietnam, but we shall do it in an amazing way, especially Saigon—even more peacefully than Quang Ngai's Liberation."

Hiro diplomatically presented a new tack. "We appreciate the concern of the Revolutionary Committee for our safety and we certainly do not want to be a burden on anyone. As far as bombing of the city is concerned, we considered that possibility before we decided to stay. We had prepared ourselves to accept that risk—"

"Our committee has weighed this matter very carefully," our visitor interrupted. "We have discussed it very much. We had to weigh the benefit of your staying with the possible risk to your lives from American bombing. But we have decided that it would be better for you to go and to go soon, leaving tomorrow morning."

Hiro was not ready to concede. "Could we possibly have a bit of time to think this over?" he asked.

"Certainly, why don't you think about it and I will return at eleven o'clock—that's about two hours—but I hope you will have no reservations about our goodwill. And I hope you will have no difficulty in deciding your course of action. As I say, you may either go by ship or overland. But many bridges may be out and it may be difficult for you by road. You may have to walk long distances. It would likely be easier for you to go by ship." And then, looking around the room, he added, "Have no reservation about your belongings in this house. We will guard them for you."

"Oh no, that is not our concern," I quickly assured him.

Tran Duc Doanh stood and moved toward the door. "Let me repeat, I hope you have no doubts about our goodwill, and we hope you will have no hesitation about your course of action." With a bow, he closed, "Good-bye, Friend Kien! Good-bye, Friend Hiro!"

Out on the porch Tran Duc Doanh was joined by a guerrilla guard who had been standing quietly outside the house during our conversation. The two climbed into a leftover white American Falcon and drove away, Tran Duc Doanh waving courteously.

Hiro and I sat for a minute in stunned silence in the living room.

"Kien, I feel like crying."

"Yeah, so do I."

Whatever the real reason for our being "invited" to head toward Saigon, we could not help feeling a deep disappointment that our welcome in Quang Ngai had expired. Did they not trust us? Did they suspect us of undercover activities? Or were they genuinely worried that, with all our traveling over the countryside, something might happen to us? That we might become victims of a hidden land mine, a disgruntled ARVN soldier or a nervous guerrilla. Then they would have the embarrassing job of explaining what had happened to us. Or could the bombing rationale have been serious? It hardly seemed likely, but there certainly was no guarantee that the American or Saigon air force would not carry out retaliatory bombing. Whatever the reason, it would not be our privilege to share the future with our friends in Quang Ngai.

But I quickly found myself contemplating a positive angle to our leaving: With this turn of events, I might rejoin Pat and the children sooner, if we survived the trip to Saigon! Hiro and I again discussed the hazardous nature of the trip Tran Duc Doanh outlined for us. We would be expected to travel over roads possibly harassed by defeated ARVN soldiers turned highwaymen, through the contested zone where bombs and rockets were apt to be exploding, into a capital city that was boiling with frenzy and panic. It hardly seemed the route anyone "worried about our security" would suggest. But Tran Duc Doanh's instructions left little room for equivocation.

Regaining his humor slightly, Hiro asked in English, "Is that what you would call an *imperative suggestion?*

We discussed every angle of the "imperative suggestion" in the next two hours. Finally we decided we would present Tran Duc Doanh, upon his return, with one final request. At eleven o'clock sharp the NLF chief was climbing out of his Falcon in front of our gate.

"Yes, we are ready to accept your advice for us to move toward Saigon," I began, after we were all seated in the living room again. "But we do have one final request. It concerns Hiro."

Hiro nodded. "Yes, I worked in the province north of here, Tam Ky, for five years. I have many friends there whom I've not seen since Liberation. I would like to say farewell to these friends before I go to Saigon. I don't know when I might get to see them again. I would plan to go to Tam Ky this afternoon and return tomorrow, Tuesday afternoon. Then we would be prepared to leave Quang Ngai Wednesday morning for Saigon. It would be just one extra day. So if there is no objection, I would like to—"

"There is objection." Tran Duc Doanh interrupted with finality. He paused, then looked at me. "So—what is your decision? When will you set out?"

Our decision! The gall! Foreclose all options but one, and then insist on calling it "our decision"!

"Uh—well then, I guess we'll try to be ready to leave in the morning," I replied with insincere graciousness.

"Fine, if that's your decision. Then you should probably report to the Security Office sometime this afternoon where they will issue travel papers for you and arrange for any other details. Ask for Thuan Vinh. He will take care of you. Now, if there is nothing else, I will excuse myself." Reaching out to shake hands, he said, "Anh Kien, Anh Hiro, have a good trip."

"Yes, Anh Doanh, a good trip—thank you, thank you very much."

Hiro and I immediately laid out plans for our last day in Quang Ngai. Visit Chi Mai and the people at the Rehabilitation Center. Visit Mr. Chau, our landlord, and our house on Tran Hung Dao Street. Sell my Mamiya/Sekko camera, since I now had a Minolta I had found in a dresser drawer at the Quaker house. Dispose of my books on unexploded munitions. If they did not know about our "plowing up swords" project, persons going through our library after we left might have difficulty understanding why we should have had munitions manuals. Finally, we would visit all the friends possible.

Monday afternoon, after a lengthy wait at the gate, we were ushered into the PRG Security Office. Just two weeks before, Hiro had come to this same office, then the Saigon Government's National Police Command, to intervene for my release while I was being held at the Interrogation Center. Old regime or new, it was not cheerful business that brought us to this office.

"Thuan Vinh. That's my name. Sorry to keep you waiting. Please sit down."

"Thank you." We sat in silence while our host, the top security officer for Quang Ngai Province, prepared tea for us. He worked noiselessly, with finesse. He poured tea and, without a word, motioned for us to drink. We nodded our acknowledgment but, in custom, did not drink on the first offer. He took a fresh pack of imported cigarettes from the table, opened them, and extended them toward us, still without speaking. We again declined. Thuan Vinh smiled warmly. His eyes emitted an unusual magnetism. He hardly fitted the image of top province cop.

"Friends," he said finally and the address seemed sincere, even warm. "Do I hear that you are planning to head toward Saigon?"

"That's right. That's the way it looks."

"We will remember you. The contribution of progressive friends from around the world such as yourselves has meant a great deal to us. We remember Anh Dung and Chi Anh." Those were the Vietnamese names of Jane and David Barton who had previously co-directed the Quaker Rehabilitation Center and who had exchanged written correspondence with the PRG while they were in Quang Ngai.

Thuan Vinh asked what we would do after we arrived in Saigon. We suggested that we would probably leave the country because we had no

PRG acquaintances in the capital who would be able to distinguish us from American embassy or military personnel, in the event the Liberation Army would take Saigon.

"Then you'll be going back to your home countries? You to Japan? And you to the United States?" He nodded toward each of us respectively.

"Yes, probably so."

"Well, you have an important mission to fulfill in your countries—to tell the world about the Liberation of Vietnam." Thuan Vinh seemed to imply it was for that "mission" we were now being sent to Saigon. But he was careful to add that the issue of our "personal safety" was also involved.

He was meticulous in inquiring what we wanted done with the possessions we would leave behind, both in our Mennonite house and in the Quaker house. He discussed our travel to Saigon in detail and we informed him that we would prefer going overland rather than by boat. That was fine by Thuan Vinh, but he added, "You should be prepared to walk some long stretches. There are probably a number of bridges out, making transportation unreliable." Finally, the Security Office chief said they would provide travel papers for us that would indicate to all PRG cadres and guerrillas along the route that we were to be given expeditious travel. He would send his assistant to our house at nine in the morning to help us on our way. We thanked Thuan Vinh for his concern with the details of the trip.

"Oh, we just want to make sure that you'll want to come back to Quang Ngai again sometime!" he answered with a smile.

By the time Hiro and I left Thuan Vinh's office we were incredulous. Out on the street, Hiro looked at me and smiled. "The shivers, eh!"

"Honestly! That's exactly the word I was thinking of!" I too was remembering our student friend who had used that word to describe the PRG cadres' way of getting you to want to do what they wanted you to do. "First they hit you hard—bam! You've got to get out of Quang Ngai! Then this guy comes along with the soft touch. Good heavens, he almost has me believing it's my own choice to leave Quang Ngai. Oooo, the shivers! Brrrr!"

While Hiro returned to the Quaker house, I rode down to our house on Tran Hung Dao. I sorted through our belongings to choose the few items we could carry with us. If we were going to have to walk long distances, we couldn't take much with us. We limited ourselves to one knapsack apiece. I chose one change of clothes, my sneakers in addition to the rubber-tire sandals I was wearing, some suntan lotion, my pith helmet, the Minolta, and a small half-frame camera, all my notebooks, and Pat's journal. The rest of the stuff: Our library, my files, our clothes, our household goods, our souvenirs—we could only hope that someone in Quang Ngai would make good use of them.

As I closed the door of our house, I was filled with memories of lovely friends and playful children of the past year. I walked across the courtyard to say good-bye to Mr. Chau and his family. Mrs. Chau, who had returned to Quang Ngai from Danang with her asthmatic daughter a week before, was standing on their porch looking extremely nervous. The tall woman's eyes revealed that she had been crying. Then I noticed in Chau's living room two uniformed men with the red and blue armbands of the Security Office. They were rummaging through Mr. Chau's library. Something had gone wrong. It obviously was not the time to talk.

"They've taken my husband," Mrs. Chau said in a quiet, broken voice when she saw me.

"They've taken him?"

"They have him out at their jeep, at the end of the alley," Mrs. Chau said thinly.

"Hiro and I will be leaving for Saigon in the morning. I just came to say good-bye to Mr. Chau," I explained, anxious not to make Mrs. Chase uncomfortable with my prolonged presence.

"Leaving for Saigon?" Mrs. Chau was confused. "Yes, Mr. Chau would want to say good-bye to you. You'll find him out at the street."

I nodded silently to Mrs. Chau and pushed my bike out the alley. They've taken Mr. Chau! Why? An honorable man. True, he had once been affiliated with the anti-Communist Nationalist Party, but that was years ago. True, just before the take-over Mr. Chau had been haunted by the fear that blood would flow profusely if the Communists took control; but he told me that he was not fleeing, that he would stay to deliver one message to the new authorities: "Spare the blood of our brothers." And after that he said he would be ready to die. Those aren't the words of a criminal. That's a man of honor speaking! After the take-over, when Mr. Chau saw the way the cadres performed, he was convinced he had been wrong. The blood would not flow after all. There wouldn't be any recriminations. The revolution had matured. He would write poetry to inspire people to support the new government. And now they've arrested him! It seemed a foolish move for the revolutionaries. In two short weeks they had earned so much respect and goodwill from Mr. Chau. Now, how could he help becoming embittered once again?

Out at the street I saw the People's Security Office jeep, green and white, commandeered from the former police command. A guerrilla, armed with an AK-47, stood guard at the driver's side of the jeep. Mr. Chau, eyes anxiously transfixed, sat in the passenger seat. He saw me.

"Anh Kien." I could hear the nervous resignation in his voice.

Eager not to embarrass the anguished man, I spoke softly. "Mr. Chau, I just came to say good-bye. Hiro and I will be leaving—"

"Speak up, Anh Kien, so that he can hear." Mr. Chau nodded his head toward the guard. "I'm under arrest. It's not permissible to speak to an arrested person. I have nothing to hide. Speak loudly enough that he can hear. You're leaving?"

"Yes, the authorities have suggested that we make our way toward Saigon." The guard on the other side of the jeep listened but showed no reaction to our conversation.

"I see. Yes. May you go in peace. I don't know when we'll meet again." Mr. Chau paused a moment, then added with feeling, "Anh Kien, all I've ever done I've done because I love my country—" His voice broke just slightly. "When you go to Saigon tell my brother Huong to return to liberated Vietnam. Tell him to put no faith in the American government. And my son, you know him, you met him here once—tell him to come home to his family in liberated Quang Ngai."

Our eyes met in a moment of silence. "Good-bye, Mr. Chau."

"Good-bye, Anh Kien."

I pedaled back to the Quaker house in a daze. Liberation! The word had lost its luster. Was it liberation or domination? But look, my reason argued with my emotions, hadn't thousands of prisoners been liberated from cold wet cells in the last weeks? And the refugees—hostages of war in those miserable camps for a decade—hadn't they now been freed to go home! Yes, but oh God, was it the writ of Almighty Heaven that the liberation of some required the suppression of others? Must the freedom of some mean the domination of others? Mr. Chau. A counterrevolutionary, I suppose. A dangerous element. An oppressor. Well then, you say, down with the oppressors! But then, don't you become an oppressor yourself? Where does the cycle stop? True, the revolutionary officials and guerrillas had displayed far more discipline, far more constraint than even their supporters had predicted. True, these men and women had lived under the most barbarous bombing and shelling in the history of mankind. And they had been tortured and assassinated by foreign and local interrogators. All because they had stood up in the face of a foreign power, which they believed was trying to dominate their land. After all they had endured, how could anyone expect anything but an orgy of bloodletting when the revolutionaries took over? Revenge! Revenge! It would take a river of blood to avenge those "ten-to-one kill ratios" the American, Korean, and Saigon troops had for years been racking up against the revolutionaries. A mighty river of blood. And yet in these two weeks since the take-over, there was an astonishing absence of blood. No raping. No pillaging. True, true, the *bo doi* must rank among the more disciplined armies in military history. But now, how could it be in the interests of even the new authorities to take Mr. Chau away from his wife and children?

Later in the afternoon I returned to our Tran Hung Dao house and learned a few more details of the arrest. Mrs. Chau said the People's Security Office cadres had come and in the presence of the family read an accusation that Mr. Chau had failed to confess everything requested on his Voluntary Declaration Form. He had not admitted to having been a member of the "reactionary Nationalist Party." For reason of his untruthfulness, he would have to be arrested. After they had led Mr. Chau out to the jeep, the two remaining cadres began a thorough search of the house. They were especially meticulous in going through his library. Mrs. Chau mentioned they paid particular attention to an illustrated world cultures book that Pat and I had inscribed and given to the Chaus. Finally they took all the books and carried them to a small upstairs room, which they sealed shut. No one would be permitted to touch the books. During the course of searching the house, Mrs. Chau said they found money in several places, but they did not take a piaster. At one point Mrs. Chau, upset with the proceeding, began to cry. The cadres reproved her, saying that if she cried, then the children would cry and that would make the offense greater. After the search was completed, the cadres called on a neighbor man to come and sign a paper to certify that nothing had been taken out of the house.

After leaving the Chaus I stopped in to say farewell to friends at the Tin Lanh church. While I was there, Chi Xuan walked into the churchyard with her children. Chi Xuan had headed toward Danang the evening the ARVN had fled town. A week after the change of government in Quang Ngai, her policeman husband, Anh Den, had still not heard any word of her. He feared she and the children had fallen by the way.

"Chi Xuan, you're alive! You look well! I'm so glad to see you. We were afraid you were dead!"

"Never!" the young woman answered triumphantly. "The Lord takes care of me. Oh Kien, the Lord has been so good. When I got to Danang, the *bo doi* had not taken over yet. I prayed to the Lord that if He opened the way, I would board a barge and go toward Saigon. But the Lord closed the door. I was not able to get on that barge. And now I hear the barge is floating off the shore of Danang without a motor. The *bo doi* went out to tow the barge back to land, but there are some Marines on board who shot at the *bo doi*. The *bo doi* couldn't shoot back. They would have hurt the people. So they're still floating out there. And they've run out of water and food and the babies have all died and some of the older people are dying too, but the Marines won't let them come in to shore. But the Lord didn't want me and the children on that barge. Isn't He wonderful, Kien!" Then, with barely a pause, the always-loquacious Chi Xuan changed pitch. "Anh Kien, they've taken Anh Den away—"

"They've taken him?"

"He left yesterday. They call it *hoc tap*. You know, reeducation."

"Where did they go?"

"I don't know. I suppose to the hills somewhere. But, Kien, I am concerned not for his body. I only pray the Lord will keep his soul."

"Oh, but certainly he will return to you again after this *hoc tap*."

"Really, Kien, do you really think so?"

"Well, I have no way of knowing for sure, but I know of one person who was captured by the guerrillas a year or so ago—he was an ARVN soldier.

For some, "reeducation" merely meant sitting through a few lectures in a schoolroom or town plaza (*top*). For others, it was months, even years, of grueling labor in the hinterlands. (*bottom*) ARVN troops head home after six weeks of "reeducation" in the hills.

They put him through reeducation for about half a year. It consisted primarily of working the fields along with the cadres—physical work—as well as lots of intense discussions with the cadres, political education. Then he came back to his family in the Saigon zone."

"Yes, I know that's what they often do, but it's hard to know—. Anyway, that's in the Lord's hands," Chi Xuan concluded. "Kien, I really believe that everything that's happening now is the Lord's will. I believe He has brought us these times to make the church strong. And to give us new opportunities to witness for the Lord. For example, on the way back from Danang I was about out of money. Part of the way I came in a bus, but the driver only took a fraction of the fare from me. Praise the Lord! And then another stretch, a truck loaded with *bo doi* came along and picked me and the children up. They are so considerate and disciplined, Anh Kien. Not like the ARVN used to be. Well, as we were riding along I had a chance to witness to them. I told them they needed to believe in God. They said, 'Our doctors and nurses are the only God we have.' I said that we must respond to God because He created us and they said that we are descendants of monkeys. Well, I just told them flat that I'm no monkey!" Chi Xuan shifted her baby to the opposite hip as she burst out with a laugh.

"How is it now, Chi Xuan, with you and your children?"

"Oh just fine. I've got only eight hundred piasters left"—little more than a dollar—"but I'm not worried. The Lord will take care of us. Kien, I ask you not for money, only that you and Pat will remember to pray for us."

Tuesday Hiro and I ate supper with Chi Mai at the Quaker house. We reported that this would probably be our last meal together, explaining the proceedings of the morning's "suggestion" that we head toward Saigon. The news took Chi Mai by surprise. She failed to have an immediate explanation, as she usually did for most other developments. Although she seemed disturbed by the news, she was careful to emphasize some potential advantages of the decision.

"This way you'll be able to tell the world about the Liberation of Quang Ngai. And let them know what the revolutionary government is really all about. That's what the Revolutionary Committee must have had in mind when they asked you to go."

I mentioned to Chi Mai the arrest of Mr. Chau. While she was gracious enough not to applaud the arrest, she obviously had a greater emotional distance from Mr. Chau than I did. She knew him not as a next-door neighbor but as a former—and, she thought, perhaps continuing—advisor to the Nationalist Party in Quang Ngai. "If only you knew the full history of dealings between the Nationalist Party and the revolutionaries," she said, "you might not be surprised at the arrest. The Nationalists, many of them large landowners, were implacably against an agrarian revolution. Not to restrict their influence now would likely mean a new outbreak of war. During this transition period between the two regimes, it will be important to watch them closely. And surely the Security Office would be suspicious of Mr. Chau if he failed to report his Nationalist Party connections on his registration form."

Indeed, that was a likely explanation for what had happened, but unless there were surreptitious facets of Mr. Chau's activities I did not know, it was still difficult for me to feel that the arrest was justified.

The evening was filled with friends who had received word of our imminent departure and had come to wish us well. Most of the friends of the MCC program, including our closest friend Em Trinh, were country folks, who had already returned to their outlying villages to begin rebuilding their houses and fields. But a number of the staff of the Quaker Rehabilitation Center and other friends stopped in. Finally, a small band of enthusiastic young guerrillas whom we had met around town in the last two weeks showed up. In previous days I had taken and developed pictures of several of them and they were delighted to receive the prints. These young fellows and girls, in their teens or twenties, reminisced into the night. Although our days with them had been brief, we were much indebted to these young revolutionaries for offering us at least an introduction to "the other side" of this country's war.

After they left, Hiro and I did the final packing of our knapsacks and by two in the morning we were ready to catch some sleep.

The last night. For me the last of more than a thousand nights in Quang Ngai. As I lay in bed I contemplated the trip ahead. It could be the most dangerous undertaking of our lives. The unknowns were legion. But while several million people had been killed in this war, the fact remained that the *majority* of people lived through it, I reasoned. That law of averages was comforting. Feeling equipped with a liberal measure of common sense, precaution, and what there was of unseen forces affecting my life, I was ready for the journey.

WEDNESDAY, 9 APRIL. As per Thuan Vinh's promise, by nine in the morning a jeep from the People's Security Office had pulled up at our gate. Thuan Vinh's assistant hopped out, typed travel papers in hand. We read over the permit curiously:

Temporary Travel Permit

In order to guarantee the safety of these foreigners with the approval of the higher echelon, we issue this certification for the foreigners:

1) Earl Martin, alias Kien, aged 30, American citizen
2) Yoshihiro Ichikawa, alias Hung, aged 29, Japanese citizen

Be permitted to travel from Quang Ngai to Qui Nhon to find their way to Saigon.

Hence be it suggested that the Military Management Committee of Binh Dinh Province create every favorable condition to help them along the way and provide accommodations for Messrs. Earl Martin and Yoshihiro Ichikawa so they will be able to travel easily and conveniently.

> Quang Ngai, 9 April 1975
> People's Security Committee
> Provisional Revolutionary
> Government
>
> (signed) Thuan Vinh, Office Chief

On a separate paper signed and stamped with the seal of the People's Security Office, the assistant meticulously listed each item of value that we carried with us. It would, he explained, be our claim against any loss we might incur along the way. Papers completed, we said good-bye to the assistant and to Chi Mai, who delayed going to work until after we left. The jeep at the gate would transport us on the first leg of the journey. After that, we were given to understand, we might have to fend for ourselves. We would travel as far as Binh Dinh, the next province south, where we would report to the Binh Dinh People's Security Office before continuing toward Saigon.

Accompanying us in the jeep would be a cadre of the Quang Ngai Security Office, a guerrilla guard and a driver. Hiro and I scrambled in beside the young guerrilla in back of the jeep which then headed down Phan Boi Chau toward the center of town where we turned south on National Highway One. Mounted on a pole in front of the jeep, a large Liberation flag flapped toward the windshield. The highway soon led us out of Quang Ngai city into the lush countryside of emerald rice paddies.

After two hours of traveling, punctuated by a lunch stop, for which the Security Office cadre insisted on paying, our jeep halted behind a long convoy of army trucks loaded with *bo doi*. We learned that a bridge several hundred feet ahead was out, making the road impassable. It might be much later in the day or even the following day until we would be able to proceed.

The cadres from the Quang Ngai Security Office asked if we would mind proceeding to Qui Nhon without escort. The idea struck us favorably. We would learn more along the way if unescorted. So we bid adieu to the men in the jeep and walked across the rubble of the blown-out bridge. On the other side we had to walk through a checkpoint where a guard escorted us into a cottage to meet a cadre who immediately seemed most suspicious of us. But after he examined our travel papers, we were free to proceed.

There were no civilian buses or taxis running on that deserted stretch of the highway and the *bo doi* in trucks that were traveling on the south side of the bridge showed no inclination to pick up hitchhikers. Finally we settled on a lonely *xe om*, a Honda 50, that could taxi us to the next town where the driver said perhaps we could catch a bus to Qui Nhon. With the driver sitting on the gas tank and with knapsacks dangling from the back and side, the small cycle managed to bring us safely into the district town of Bong Son. After pausing for drinks of coconut milk, we were picked up by a small Honda bus that was already jammed with people and loaded with baggage on top. But the driver shifted some of the cargo on the roof and made enough space for Hiro and me and our packs. We tightened the drawstrings of our hats and clutched the side rails as the vehicle sped down the road.

Soon our minibus was winding through a craggy mountain pass. On both sides of the road stood the naked forms of tall trees stripped of their greenery, their very life, by powerful poisons sprayed from giant airplanes. The toll of defoliation had been great. An estimated 5 or 6 million acres of land had been sprayed with the potent herbicides throughout the war. In Quang Ngai and other provinces farmers told us that sometimes rice fields in remote areas were sprayed, presumably to starve out any guerrillas—and, perhaps coincidentally, any farmers—who lived in that area. The damage to the foliage in those cases was temporary. Within six months new growth would emerge. But most of the spraying took place in jungle areas to facilitate air surveillance of any activity on the ground. Here again, the initial effect was often the same. Within months a new crop of leaves would push out. But if those trees were defoliated twice, the effect was fatal. Often, as we flew from Quang Ngai to Saigon, Pat and I had noticed the stretches of jungle where the sun-bleached skeletons of the great hardwoods stood starkly above the green undergrowth below.

Back down in the rice-growing plains of Binh Dinh Province, it soon became apparent that this area was run by a different administration from the Quang Ngai Province we had just left behind. In the 50 kilometers we had traveled in Quang Ngai there had not been a single checkpoint, but here our vehicle was being stopped every several kilometers. Young guerrillas—and sometimes un-uniformed volunteers—would check through the vehicle, presumably searching for any weapons or ARVN soldiers with travel papers. On several occasions the checkers did not notice Hiro and me on the roof until after we had pulled away from the checkpoint. Other times they noticed and were perplexed by our presence. Once the checker was a young woman guerrilla who upon examination of our papers glowed warmly.

"Oh, I understand," she smiled. "You brothers are on mission for the revolution!" We smiled and nodded, eager not to disillusion her. As the minibus pulled away, she called to us. "Go well, brothers, and best of luck!"

Not far north of Qui Nhon we were stopped at our twentieth checkpoint in 60 kilometers. This post was crowded with *bo doi* and townsfolk. The young guard, marked by his civilian dress and white armband as a revolutionary-come-lately, checked out the vehicle. He suddenly became quite boisterous when he spied us atop the minibus.

"Get down off there immediately," he demanded curtly.

"You must be interested in seeing our papers," we replied as we handed our documents down to him.

He looked at them for a second and then called, "You're under arrest. I'm going to take you over to the office."

"But we have orders to travel to Qui Nhon People's Security Office. What's wrong with the papers?" we insisted. A *bo doi* soldier nearby heard the commotion and walked over, taking the papers from the youth. The *bo doi* examined the papers and handed them back up to us.

"Everything's in order. You're free to go." The minibus buzzed on down the road, but the youth was still angry. Scowling, he gripped his M-16 at his hip and gave it a bayonet like thrust through the air in our direction. The *bo doi* at his side grabbed his arm to restrain him. We speculated that the youth was attempting to prove his virtuosity to the *bo doi* by demonstrating his "revolutionary" outrage toward Americans. Or perhaps the fellow had lost a close relative to American bombing and this was his chance to express his true indignation. At any rate, it was comforting for us to have had the disciplined *bo doi* close at hand.

The sun was dropping behind the Truong Son range in the west as our minibus entered Qui Nhon, a city several times the size of Quang Ngai. Our journey ended at the main bus depot downtown, where we scrambled off the roof, paid our fare, and started looking for someone who could direct us to our destination. A Honda taxi driver, eager for patrons, pulled up and asked where we wanted to go.

"The Qui Nhon People's Security Office," we requested.

The driver looked confused. He turned to several persons standing nearby, but no one had ever heard of the People's Security Office.

"It's probably where the National Police Command of the old government was located," we suggested to him.

"Oh that. Sure, I'll take you. It's across town. Jump on."

We were about to take up his offer when a uniformed *bo doi* with a red and blue armband approached our group. We decided to confirm with him our destination.

"People's Security Office?" he echoed. "It's right here. Follow me." We left the taxi driver, disappointed without his passengers, and followed the *bo doi* across the bus station lot, in through a high barbed-wire gate to a compound marked by a newly painted sign, "Qui Nhon People's Security Office, Station Five." The place looked too modest to have once been police headquarters for Binh Dinh Province, but at that point there was little we could do but follow our escort. Through the last traces of twilight we made our way around the low barrackslike office building, past sandbag fortifications to a house in the back of the compound. We were introduced to a cadre who listened to the story of our journey from Quang Ngai. He looked at our introduction papers and suddenly appeared to understand who we were, almost as if he had been expecting us. Even more surprising was the appearance of a man introduced as the head of the Qui Nhon People's Security Office. His presence made us wonder if this post was perhaps the city's main office after all. We related our understanding of our trip to the chief, and he assured us that he would provide new papers for us to continue our journey.

"But it's late," he concluded. "You won't be traveling any farther this evening. Have you had dinner?"

"No. We'll just go out to some shop and find our dinner," Hiro responded.

"Oh, certainly not." The chief turned to his assistant. "Go bring these men some food." Then turning back to us, "You're welcome to spend the night here in this house—it's vacant now—and if there's anything we can get for you, please let us know. I'll have to be going along soon, but I'll be back in touch with you later this evening. I'll take your papers with me."

The chief stayed a few minutes, until we were served an impressive meal of rice with two meat dishes and several vegetable dishes to boot. Mighty fine spread for five minutes' notice. Likely it was food remaining from a meal served before we arrived. Even after the security chief took his leave, his assistant remained to make sure we were comfortable and provided for. He shortly noticed that we had nothing to drink, and while most Vietnamese do not drink during meals, save a thin green tea at the end, he sprang to remedy the situation for his guests. From a back room in the house he produced two bottles of Biere Larue. As he poured, I noticed the beverage was leftover government issue, bottled especially for the Saigon military. The bottle in the hand of this Viet Cong cadre was boldly printed with the yellow and red flag of the Saigon Government and the words: "Determined to Fight Dictatorship, Preserve Freedom and Democracy!"

After the meal the assistant showed us a well where we could wash and informed us of a toilet in a house across the street along Qui Nhon Bay. Then he too excused himself to allow us to relax after the day's trip. After a bucket shower at the open well, Hiro stretched out on an unmattressed platform bed and I on the cushioned sofa in the house while we waited for the People's Security Chief to return.

THURSDAY, 10 APRIL. We awoke with the sun already climbing over the buildings lining Qui Nhon Bay. Incredulous that the night had slipped by us unaware, we jumped up and washed at the well. Now we were restored and eager for the new day of travel toward Saigon. Presumably the Chief of Security had returned the evening before but had chosen not to disturb us when he found us sleeping.

Shortly we were greeted by a young woman carrying an aluminum tray with dishes of rice, fried tuna, and the spinachlike *rau muong*. An attractive woman, probably in her late twenties, she lingered in the room with us for a moment, seemingly waiting to make sure the meal pleased us. We were quick to assure her that it did, but she excused herself immediately as soon as we tried to strike up casual conversation with her.

Now, being rested and fed, we anticipated action. Since receiving the "suggestion" to leave Quang Ngai, our single goal had been to reach Saigon as quickly as possible. We estimated it might take three or four days. Perhaps when we arrived in Saigon Pat and the children would still be waiting for me. Crossing over the battle lines still posed considerable threat, but if we were to do it, let it be sooner rather than later. Some of the guerrillas and cadres in the post we talked with Thursday morning expressed grave reservations about the wisdom of a trip to Saigon while there was fighting along the route. We replied that we had raised this concern in Quang Ngai and had been assured all would be well. Several Qui Nhon cadres suggested we should spend some time traveling around countryside areas of Binh Dinh Province before proceeding to Saigon. Whatever their decision, we decided our worst fate would be to sit idly in this Security Office post while they deliberated over what to do with us.

By noon we were becoming impatient. We learned that indeed this was not the main Security Office but a small precinct post. The main office was across town just like the Honda driver had said the evening before. This "Station Five" had, until two weeks before, been a petty police station for the Saigon regime. The house we were now occupying had until recently been the private residence of the head police officer attached to the station.

In our impatience, Hiro and I toyed with the idea of simply walking out of the post and catching a bus or taxi from the adjacent bus station and heading toward Saigon. That, we soon decided, would constitute an act of folly, since the security chief had our travel papers. If we were snagged at a checkpoint without proper authorization to travel, we could find ourselves in more than a petty police station for a day or two!

Midafternoon I opted for a brief diversion from our idle waiting and I walked out a side gate of the compound toward the bus station where I sat down to have a glass of coconut milk at a vendor's table. I struck up a conversation with a local Qui Nhon man and a *bo doi* who were also having refreshments. I was glad to learn from them that indeed buses were moving on the road toward the south. After ten minutes I returned to our compound only to be met at the gate by a stoop-shouldered security cadre who seemed to be in charge of the post.

"Who gave you permission to leave this compound?" he demanded, hawk-eyes peering at me.

"Uh, er—excuse me, but I didn't realize I would need permission to go have a drink on the street," I managed, my ire—and apprehension—rising.

"That house," he pointed to where Hiro was waiting, "is where you belong."

"Could you possibly tell me," I was trying to be diplomatic, "what is the status of our departure for Saigon?"

"We'll let you know when we have anything to report, but for now"—his ire was rising too—"you go back to your house and wait there. Do you hear?"

I turned lamely and walked toward our house. A more kindly cadre came up behind me and politely tried to explain that the responsible officials were probably trying to arrange transportation and an escort for us, and that it might be the following morning before all the arrangements could be made, so would we please bear with them and wait a bit longer.

That helped. But the picture did not look bright. Back in our house, Hiro and I tried to analyze exactly what measure of power we possessed in this situation. Back in Quang Ngai our position had been stronger. The terrain was familiar, many local people knew and trusted us, and, most importantly, we had made the acquaintance of a few local PRG cadres who might have bailed us out in a pinch. Yet even in Quang Ngai our prerogatives were extremely tenuous as demonstrated by our inability to plead for even one extra day in the town. Here in Qui Nhon among strangers we were even more powerless.

Under the Saigon regime, while that government possessed the ultimate power to evict us from the country, we—especially I as an American—felt a certain immunity. After all, a government that was as economically and militarily dependent on the United States as Saigon was would be ill-advised to take any drastic action against an American citizen.

Here, since the tendency of PRG officials must have been to suspect the intentions of an American, I felt more vulnerable. If Hiro and I should become too insistent or obnoxious with anyone, it would only serve to fan any suspicions they may have already had of us. Consequently, our only defense in this predicament would have to be a generous dosage of patience, a willingness to be misunderstood and a sense of humor. In a word: wait.

We utilized the delay to prepare for a disturbing contingency. If we should continue our trek toward Saigon, we feared not only the corporal danger in crossing a line of control being contested by mortars and bombs. Even if we should make the crossing safely, we would most likely run into Saigon Government police or ARVN troops. In the few cases in the past when foreign journalists had visited PRG zones and were then detected by police on their return to Saigon zones, their films and journals had frequently been confiscated. In many cases the materials were later returned to the reporters, but it seemed too great a chance for us to take with the invaluable records of our experiences in Quang Ngai. We would hide the records on our bodies.

The films would be simple. Strips of negatives would be placed in the large fold of cloth underneath Hiro's belt. Our notebooks and journals, with notes of conversations with Quang Ngai people, would be too bulky to hide.

So we set about the task of recopying these records in minute printing on loose-leaf pages, which we would, when necessary, stitch inside our undershorts before crossing the line. The project was cathartic for its diversion. It injected at least a modicum of meaning into our delay.

FRIDAY, 11 APRIL. Prison!

No one said so. In fact, we had a beautiful house to stay in—the former police chief's residence!—and fine meals three times a day. Our "guards" were eating much more meager fare than we were served and they had to sleep in the barracks-type police station. There were no visible bars around us. The door to our house was open, and with no trouble we could have jumped over the back wall and been gone. But without papers we didn't stand a chance. So bars or no, it felt like prison nevertheless.

Our tuna-*rau-muong*-rice breakfast looked less appetizing this morning. In fact, the sight of food evoked a new option in my mind: a hunger strike! Don't announce it. Just don't eat. If they ask, just tell them we're not hungry. That ought to bring some response from somebody.

On second thought, I was surprised to find myself contemplating such dire measures after having been detained only a day and a half. Once again I tried to gear myself for an extended delay. I would memorize my journals to prepare for the possibility of confiscation. We would make a chess set. I would write. I would get Hiro to teach me Japanese. That ought to keep me busy for a while!

A midmorning visit from the stoop-shouldered cadre eased our misgivings. He came with the message that "high level" persons were making arrangements for our travel to Tuy Hoa, the next province capital south, but that presently it was impossible to proceed because of possible danger at one mountain pass. Finally he informed us we could expect a visit from several cadres of the Provincial Security Office.

The substance of his message was less than ideal, but the fact that he came at all, and was even pleasant, was tremendously reassuring. At least we were not forgotten.

The visit from the Security Office cadres was not long in coming. Two men in full uniform and familiar shoulder bags knocked at the door. We invited them in and exchanged introductions. Probably in their forties, they projected greater maturity and finesse than many of the younger cadres we had met. Politely, they began to inquire about us: Where were we from, where were we going, why were we in Qui Nhon, and where were our travel papers? (They appeared not to know our papers had been taken by the Chief of Security.) What were our activities in Quang Ngai? Our ties to the American Government? The Japanese Government? Our organization? Our religious affiliation? How was our association organized and what liaison had we with the Saigon Government? The Revolutionary Government? For a time it all seemed as though the cadres were merely fascinated with these two foreigners and were asking questions out of a simple curiosity about us. But then many of the questions came back a second time, rephrased and in a slightly different context, but essentially the same inquiries. It was more than a casual interest these men had in us.

"Mennonite. What does that really mean?" Anh Mien, the taller and more inquisitive of the two, asked with keen interest.

"Well, Mennonites began as a movement of people in the early sixteenth century, people who wanted to take seriously the life of Jesus as a model for how they would relate to others. People who felt the established church of the day was often using its power for selfish ends, to keep people under its jurisdiction rather than to truly free them. They believed there should be a distinct separation between the powers of the church and the powers of the state. Today Mennonites emphasize simplicity of living, service for others, an identification with disadvantaged people, and a—"

"But you talk about the Mennonite Central Committee. What is that?"

We explained that MCC was the service and relief agency of North American Mennonites, which sponsored approximately 500 volunteers—doctors, nurses, teachers, agriculturalists, therapists, and generalists—in about forty different countries.

"Five hundred volunteers. Forty countries." Anh Mien repeated the figures as if to seal them in his mind. "You mentioned your agency operated in four locations in southern Vietnam. What were those projects?" We told him about our unexploded munitions project in Quang Ngai, our medical clinics in Nhatrang and Pleiku, as well as our program to assist poor families and families of prisoners in Saigon.

"Quang Ngai, Pleiku, Nhatrang, and Saigon—and you said you sent aid to the North and to the Revolutionary Government in the South?" Anh Mien threw his leg over the arm of the chair with a nonchalant air, but the concentration of the cadres did not lag.

We detailed the history of MCC assistance to persons in the North and the PRG areas in the South, beginning in 1969 with a shipment of medical supplies to a Hanoi hospital in cooperation with the American Friends Service Committee. We detailed the various medical shipments MCC had made to the revolutionary zones in the South. We explained it was the goal of MCC to offer assistance to anyone who was hurt by the war regardless of the side on which those people lived.

"Where did you make these contacts with the Revolutionary Government? And with the Democratic Republic of Vietnam?" The latter was the formal name of the government in North Vietnam.

I took the opportunity to answer with specific data, which they could verify independently, if they so chose. "Several places. My wife and I visited the PRG delegation and the North Vietnamese embassy in Paris several times. In 1973, on our way back to Vietnam, we discussed our munitions project with Nguyen Thi Minh of the PRG and with Truong Si Phan at the DRVN embassy. The major projects of assistance to the North and the PRG were discussed in Hanoi. Doug Hostetter, who happens to be a brother of my wife, visited the North in, I believe, 1970 and again in 1974. Another MCC representative, Atlee Beechy, visited Hanoi in 1973. On that occasion the MCC agreed to help build a school and clinic in a province north of Hanoi."

"Duc Ho-te-to. A-ly Bi-chi." The cadres picked out the strange American names with uncanny alertness, even though they laughed at their Vietnamized pronunciation of the words. Then they quizzed us at length about who was team leader of the MCC project in Quang Ngai. We attempted to explain that we did not really have a leader because the team was small and we tried to work as equals. They balked at that answer and pressed us to commit ourselves to a definite answer. Certainly one person had to have final authority!

They were interested in hearing about our activities in the anti-war movements in the United States and Japan. That stimulated a question we had heard frequently from PRG cadres and *bo doi*. "Do you know Jane Fonda?" Every revolutionary knew the name of this American actress who had visited Hanoi during the war. I could only reply that I had once heard Jane Fonda speak at an anti-war rally at Stanford University where I had studied.

After an hour or so the cadres wrapped up the session by inquiring about our food and lodging situation in Qui Nhon. They asked us to let them know if there was anything we needed. We told them our only hope was to move toward Saigon or, if that was impossible, to return to Quang Ngai. Their response was that the road to Saigon was still the scene of heavy fighting, so that our trip might have to be postponed a bit longer.

As the cadres left, they hinted that they would be visiting us again. Their visit left us ambivalent. On the one hand, they seemed to respect us as friends. On the other, it looked as though we might be sitting in Qui Nhon for at least several more days. More disturbing, as Hiro and I reflected on the exchange with the cadres—friendly and innocuous as it seemed—it was difficult to escape the conclusion that we were under some type of investigation.

Investigation! What had gone wrong? All had seemed so positive just days before, and now it appeared as though we might be suspected by the revolutionary authorities. We tried to speculate about the cause of the detention. If the representative of the Quang Ngai Security Office who had turned back at the downed bridge had been able to come to Qui Nhon and vouch for us, would all this delay have been avoided? Or was this rather part of a scheme of the Quang Ngai office to get us out of town so that they could investigate our belongings and connections in Quang Ngai while the Qui Nhon cadres interrogated us? If so, what would it mean? A protracted period of checking us out? Days, weeks, months? Years? Whatever the truth, in our disappointment and uncertainty, it was possible to imagine the worst.

Investigation or not, there was little we could do to alter the state of affairs. Much of the time Hiro and I were alone in the house, but we did get occasional visitors. Most regular was the young woman who served our meals. We learned from two friendly guerrillas at the post that her name was Chi Huong. She would appear punctually three times a day carrying the tray with rice bowls, chopsticks, a pan of rice, some cooked green vegetable, fried tuna and a pot of hot tea. After the first day or two she became less self-conscious around us. When she brought our meals she would regularly bring with her a large black comb. In the main room of the house where we slept, ate our meals over a coffee table and did most of our writing and talking, stood a tall, handsome chiffonier with a full-length mirror on one door. After Chi Huong set our fare on the coffee table she would take her comb and walk over to the mirror. Raising both arms she would undo a bun chignon, letting the black silky hair fall to her thighs. While Hiro and I ate, Chi Huong would stroke the comb through her raven glory. Completing her mesmerizing ritual, she would once again roll the stream of hair up into a tight chignon behind her neck. After several days she would even sit down for several minutes and talk with us while we ate. We learned that Phu Cat, a former American base town in the northern part of the province, had been Chi Huong's native home. In fact, a number of the guerrillas assigned to this particular post were from Phu Cat. We asked Huong about her family.

"My father's dead."

"Oh?"

"He was killed by the Americans in 1965. Then my brother got killed too."

"Also in the war?"

"Yes, so after that it didn't seem as if I had much choice but to go to the mountains, to join the guerrillas."

"When was that?"

"Oh, let me think—that was in sixty-seven. After that the police arrested my mother, accused her of being a Communist because I was in the hills. They beat her and held her for eight months."

"Then she was free?"

"Well, they released her, but she was often harassed by the police after that."

"As a guerrilla, what did you do?"

"Whatever needed doing. All kinds of things."

"Did you carry a rifle?"

"Oh yes, I would always take my turn at guard duty."

"Were you ever afraid?"

"Oh no."

"Never afraid?"

"Oh no, because I believed in our righteous cause. Why should I be afraid?"

"But it must have been dangerous. Weren't you afraid you would be killed?"

"Oh no, if I died, I would die for an honorable cause. I would gladly give my life for the fatherland."

The sturdy young woman spoke with religious spontaneity and sincerity. One had the feeling she would have given this same answer under interrogation if she had been captured by Saigon police or American soldiers. One could label Chi Huong's drive fanaticism. Or it could be called commitment, or purpose. Whatever its name, it was the trademark of nearly every guerrilla we had talked with during the last three weeks. It was an unshakable conviction that their cause was "just" and that, regardless of the obstacles, it would eventually prevail. The cause would *have* to prevail because it was a "righteous cause." *Chinh nghia.* It was an undauntable belief in the mission that I had rarely encountered in five years of meeting ARVN soldiers. Even more seldom, as I remembered, among American soldiers in Vietnam.

In addition to Chi Huong, we received occasional visits from two guerrillas in their late teens who served as guards at this security post. The first time they dropped in on us they marveled at the "luxurious" furnishings in "our" house. These fellows guffawed excitedly as they propped their AK-47's in the corner and sank into the foam-rubber cushions on the chairs.

"*Troi oi,* is it ever plush down here in the city!" one fellow bubbled.

Hiro chided the young guerrillas. "You'd better watch out, young man. If you're not careful, you'll lose all the discipline you learned up in the hills. You'll get lazy!"

"Hey! He speaks our language like a Vietnamese!" The boys' eyes widened. "But you're not really—are you Vietnamese? Where's your native home?"

Hiro teased them as they guessed through the list—Chinese? Korean? Taiwanese? Japanese! "Say, Anh Hiro, what are you doing here in Qui Nhon anyway?" Hiro and I couldn't help smiling at their local Binh Dinh pronunciation, which sounded even more twangy and nasal than the countrified Quang Ngai accent.

"We're on our way to Saigon. Would you like to go along?" Hiro responded.

"I think your partner here is an American, isn't he?" The slender, narrow-faced lad was emerging as the spokesperson.

"Have you ever seen an American before?" Hiro asked tauntingly.

"Lots of them. I used to live in a village near an American base. They were crawling around there like ants. That was before I became a guerrilla. Your friend here"—he nodded toward me, apparently assuming I spoke no

Vietnamese—"he was fighting against us until Liberation, wasn't he? An American soldier. The brothers are holding him here to check out now, I suppose."

Hiro and I chuckled at their spontaneous assumption, but I let Hiro defend me. "No, I'm afraid you're wrong there."

"But then why's he here?"

Hiro explained. "You see, this American is different. He didn't support the war. He fought against the war."

"Fought against the war! I suppose! Fine story to be telling after Liberation! After all, he is an American, isn't he!" The young guerrilla apparently felt no great compunction to be diplomatic.

Hiro loved such verbal duels with persons his junior and he soon had the boyish fighters agreeing with his basic syllogism that just as the Vietnamese took various positions on the war, so Americans could also differ on their support of the war. Hadn't they ever heard of Jane Fonda! That clinched it. Maybe it was possible I could be an acceptable American after all!

The young guerrillas shortly launched into their theory of why their revolution had been successful. "It's this way. All the super powerful nations in the world are like men, masculine. Vietnam is like a woman, feminine. But what do you know, the woman—who is supposed to be weak—defeated the man! That's because our women are strong. Like Chi Huong. You know, the sister who brings you your meals. She's not afraid of anything. Our army even has women commanders"—perhaps a reference to Nguyen Thi Dinh, Deputy Commander of the NLF—"and look at Madame Binh, going to Paris to negotiate the peace agreement. In the revolution, the women are equal with the men."

While their words did not necessarily prove their point, their attitude of undisguised pride and respect for the women in the revolution struck one in sharp contrast to the overtly sexist references to women we had become used to hearing in the Saigon zones.

In addition to the guerrillas and cadres stationed in this security post, an occasional townsperson or out-of-the-war ARVN soldier wandered in through a side gate to the compound and on noticing us would accept our invitation to sit down and pay a visit. We learned from these folks that Qui Nhon, like Quang Ngai city, was spared heavy civilian death tolls and property damage during the take-over, although several hundred ARVN troops had been killed near the city's seaport when the panicked army converged and fought to get onto the few available boats. Several boats sank in the harbor.

Sunday, our fourth day of delay, finally produced a second visit from Anh Mien, the cadre from the central Security Office. This time he was alone and, as two days before, he seemed as casual and relaxed as his baggy *bo doi* pants. Inquiring about our welfare and our food, he was the epitome of friendliness and courtesy. But soon our conversation was covering topics we had discussed with him on Friday.

"Our women are just like Vietnam—strong, not afraid of anything."

"This Mennonite Central Committee, you say it has no attachment to any government whatsoever? Where do you get your operating budget?" Anh Mien seemed puzzled that an organization with a substantial budget could be so totally devoid of any governmental ties. Clearly, there were parts of our story that seemed incredible to this revolutionary cadre.

We explained that the MCC's budget came primarily from voluntary contributions of concerned persons, most of it from Mennonites in Canada and the United States.

"Tell me again where you had your projects in South Vietnam," Anh Mien quizzed.

"In Quang Ngai, Pleiku, Nhatrang and Saigon," Hiro reiterated.

"Hmmm, let's see, that makes one office in each of the Saigon Government's four military regions, doesn't it?" Anh Mien squinted enigmatically, obviously on the alert for anything that seemed conspiratorial.

"Anh Mien!" I was quick to express my dismay at the insinuation. "We don't arrange our service projects with a mind to any military regions. Those four places were chosen because it was deemed that the need was greatest there. Besides, those locations do *not* correspond with the four military regions. We have no representative in the Mekong delta, which is Saigon's Military Region Four."

After a half-hour conversation with us, Anh Mien raised a specific request. "In addition to your travel papers for your trip to Saigon, you said the other day that you had been given travel papers for movement in Quang Ngai Province itself. I would like to borrow those papers so we can process your travel permits for Saigon."

Those were the last papers we possessed with an official PRG seal and we were loath to relinquish them. It was like the last shred of identification and legitimacy was being stripped from us. "But Anh Mien, you wouldn't want to take from us a valuable souvenir of our stay in Quang Ngai, would you?" I protested as amicably as possible. "Besides, those papers can't be of any value to you. They were issued specifically for Quang Ngai Province and this is Binh Dinh Province."

"Oh, don't worry," Anh Mien laughed. "We'll make sure you get them back. We'll just borrow them so we can process your new travel papers." We gave him the papers.

"There is still difficulty along the road to Saigon," Anh Mien concluded as he stood to leave. "So we'll have to ask you to wait here another day or so."

Anh Mien's visit had again brought welcome confirmation that we were not forgotten by the People's Security Office, and yet it seemed only to confirm further our suspicion that we were under investigation. True to his advice, we had no choice but to wait "another day or so"; Monday, Tuesday, Wednesday—that marked a whole week with no movement toward Saigon. Thursday, Friday, Saturday, Sunday. One day dragged into the next. Something had gone seriously awry. With our detention well into its second week, Hiro and I were jokingly referring to our house as the Qui Nhon "non-prison." The joke, of course, had its sharp edge as reflected in my notebook:

Each new morning without any word of our next step brings that edge of disappointment, concern for Pat and the children, and yes, even a sense of betrayal. After having received such positive indications from the cadres in Quang Ngai before Liberation that they would applaud our staying, and now to be detained for a week and a half with no communication other than an occasional rationalization about the roads not being clear, which is totally implausible, it is hard to avoid a feeling that we have been betrayed. In my less guarded moments my imagination even torments me with thoughts of some terrible mistake—such macabre scenes as seeing myself being brought before a people's court, being denounced, and then being taken off to be thrown into a dank prison cell or finding myself staring down the muzzles of a stony-faced firing squad!

Thank goodness such thoughts are not an obsession with me; basically I am at peace. In fact, when I look at it from the PRG authorities' point of view, I see the fundamental question is: Would the United States Government stoop to using seemingly anti-war, friendly, even revolutionary-sounding young fellows to serve as intelligence agents under the guise of social work? The answer to that question is, no doubt, easy for the PRG to come by. Has not even the American CIA itself admitted that they sometimes disguise their agents as professional people or journalists? And that they frequently use missionaries and church people as sources of intelligence? That being the case, it is the unkind, but perhaps inescapable, responsibility of the revolutionary authorities to do as thorough an investigation of us as possible. I nevertheless hope it does not take them forever to complete.

In our more generous moments, Hiro and I could even chuckle at Anh Mien's dilemma. His assignment, or so it appeared to us, was to interrogate us to discern whether we were foes of the revolution, while at the same time he was to be diplomatic in case we really were friends. If that was indeed his task, we had to concede that he was performing with remarkable adroitness.

Hiro and I would discuss how taxing it must have been to Anh Mien's imagination to accept that we were exactly who we said we were. After fighting for a decade or more against rifle-toting Americans in green, Americans in bomber cockpits, American spies and CIA, Anh Mien was now being asked to believe two foreigners—one American—who spoke Vietnamese fluently and knew intimately the local scene in Quang Ngai, when they said they had no connection with, indeed abhorred, the American war effort in Vietnam. It would have been like a German social worker in France in 1944 trying to get to German occupied terrain and expecting sympathy and assistance from Allied troops!

Hiro's and my moods fluctuated from day to day. It seemed that when one of us was particularly discouraged, the other was more optimistic. Having a comrade gave mooring for otherwise free-floating emotions. For example, one day I was painting one of the many possible scenarios of our fate.

"Hiro, can't you see it, they comb through all the files we left behind in Quang Ngai and all the correspondence and documents they find points to the conclusion that we were actively opposed to the United States intervention in Vietnam and that our work was truly to assist the farmers of Quang Ngai Province. Yet, in the end, their suspicions get the better of them and they decide these files are part of an elaborate smoke screen for our real work in Vietnam: spying! Then—let's see, what will it be? Prison or hard labor? Four or five years? What do you predict?"

"Why not make it ten, for round figures?" Hiro was less than mortified by the prospect.

"And then we'll be used as bargaining chips in future negotiations with the United States. That's it! They'll use us to persuade the U.S. to implement Article 21 of the Paris agreement!" That article committed the United States to contribute toward postwar reconstruction throughout Vietnam and Indochina.

"Say, that would be terrific!" Hiro actually seemed to relish the idea. "They could use us as hostages to encourage the U.S. to help rebuild this country. Seriously, I would be willing to be used in that way." Then, after a pause, he added, "But shucks, I'm afraid we might not be very valuable bargaining chips for the Vietnamese. Too bad we're not U.S. agents!"

"Yeah, I can see it now." Hiro's levity was beginning to be contagious. "Hanoi's representative Le Duc Tho phones Henry Kissinger and says, 'Henry, we've got these two guys over here. We'll give them back to you for five hundred million bucks in reconstruction aid.' 'Two guys? What two guys?' Henry'll ask. 'You know, Martin and Ichikawa, Henry. How could you forget?' 'Martin and Ichikawa? Here, let me check my files. Yes, yes— *those guys*, now I remember. Yes, Brother Tho, uh, delighted to hear you've got them. Uh, Brother Tho, you just go ahead and dispose of those clowns in any way you wish. Thanks for the call, Brother Tho. Have a good day. So long.' Click."

"Oh well, it was a nice thought anyway," Hiro sighed.

Over time, we sensed an increasing coolness toward us on the part of the neighbors who lived in the vicinity of the security station. Originally we had told anyone who inquired that we were just stopping off in Qui Nhon on our way to Saigon, but as the days dragged on they likely wondered if there were other reasons for our delay. We never knew if the cadres in the security post spoke to the neighbors about us or not. The first several evenings we chatted with one friendly neighbor who loaned us a radio to listen to the evening news. One day the stoop-shouldered cadre asked where we got the radio and the next evening when we went to borrow the radio again, the neighbor self-consciously apologized, saying that he had loaned the radio to a relative in another part of town.

Another afternoon, when I was washing at a neighbor's well, a small girl, perhaps six years old, was catching flies and putting them into a jar. When she saw me she began a soft "Mr. American" chant.

"*Ong My, Ong My, Ong My—*"

"Oh little sister, do you know my name really isn't Mr. American. My name is Kien. You may call me Chu Kien." *Chu* means uncle.

"Chu Kien, where do you live?"

"Chu Kien lives in that house right there for now." I pointed toward our house.

"How long will you stay there, Chu Kien?"

"Oh, Chu will stay for a time."

"You stay here because you shot a lot of people, isn't that right, Chu Kien?"

The accusation—especially from a child—struck deep. "Oh no, Chu doesn't shoot—Chu Kien loves people."

"Maybe you just love your own children, not other children, right, Chu Kien?"

"Oh no, Chu loves all children—and all people."

"What about the other *chu* over in your house? He doesn't love people, does he?"

"Oh, his name is Chu Hiro, and he loves people very much."

"Look, Chu Kien, I caught six flies in my jar."

"You must be very skillful, little sister," I managed as I painfully tried to determine the source of the child's suspicions.

"Look, now I have eight flies—"

The child's grandmother appeared at the door and groused at the child to get back into the house and quit playing with the flies.

Being without a radio, Hiro and I were virtually dependent on the guerrillas or cadres in the security post for any outside news. Every morning about thirty minutes of Liberation Radio was broadcast from the bus station lot, but given the distance and the raspy static of the loudspeakers, it was difficult to decipher much. Nevertheless, on Tuesday morning, April 22, we did hear that Xuan Loc, the second to last province north of Saigon, had been "completely liberated." That meant the Liberation Army was practically on the doorstep of the capital city itself, with only the large Bien Hoa air base remaining between. But the radio had even more startling news that morning: "Nguyen Van Thieu resigns!"

The news was greeted with pleasure but little surprise by the cadres around the security post. Tuesday afternoon an older cadre, probably in his fifties, came to visit the post. When he peered into the open door of "our" house, we invited him in. The man's face was kind and his eyes smiled with avuncular warmth. He sat down in the cushioned chair opposite the sofa where we sat. He propped his shoulder bag against the chair leg. Totally unpretentious, he did not even carry the side arm of many senior cadres. As we talked, we offered him tea from the pot that Chi Huong always brought with her at mealtime. When we solicited his opinion on the resignation of President Thieu, he responded immediately.

"Thieu. A puppet of the Americans, of course." Then shaking his head in puzzlement, he added, "But I don't understand it. Why did the Americans pick a man of so little skill?"

Skipping from the morning news, we were soon discussing a wide range of topics with the seasoned cadre. He asked about our work, and when he learned we worked with a church-affiliated agency, he was quick to express his fascination. "That's very interesting. You probably know that it is often said the proletarian revolution is atheistic. But is it really? There are many in our revolution who believe in God. To believe or not to believe can only be decided by each individual, don't you agree? It is an old saying: *Tin tai nga; bat tin tai nga.* Belief lies within oneself; unbelief lies within oneself."

225

The cadre did not divulge to us whether he "believed" or not. "Besides," he added, "it has never been clear to me that people in capitalist societies really have faith in God. If they did, why would they use the threat of nuclear bombs to frighten the rest of the world?"

The man's eyes brightened as he continued. "But there's another day coming. In fact, you're seeing that day coming right now. That's what the revolution means. I think some people in the West do not understand revolution. There is a bourgeois revolution like you had in France and the United States many years ago. That's when the class of people who own land and the industries seize power and benefit from the revolution. But that revolution will eventually lead to a propertyless revolution, the proletarian revolution. Then society will be organized to benefit not the rich, but the poor. When that happens all over the world, everyone will have enough to eat and wear. The great potentials of energy, such as atomic power, will be used not to destroy mankind but to serve mankind."

Morale became a major preoccupation as the fourteenth day of detention rolled around. Two whole weeks with no positive movement. Not even a decent explanation.

To our encouragement, Anh Mien showed up again on Wednesday afternoon. It did not take long for him to get to the message. He announced it with a flourish. "In a day or two, you'll be heading for Hanoi!"

"Hanoi! Wow! Anh Mien, come now, you can't be serious!" The mischievous glint in Anh Mien's eyes left us unconvinced.

"Well then, if you don't want to go to Hanoi, how about Saigon?" Anh Mien had us eating out of his hand.

"Or how about another month or two in a Qui Nhon security office will be your next offer, right, Anh Mien?" I was preparing myself for the crash.

"Come now, Anh Kien, you wouldn't think we would want to inconvenience you, would you?"

"Oh no, Anh Mien, we would never think anything like that!"

Anh Mien smiled. "No, seriously, all is in order for you fellows to proceed toward Saigon tomorrow or Friday at the latest. Just as soon as your papers are completed. There—does that make you happy?"

"Well, this place was beginning to feel like home to us. It'll break our hearts to leave," Hiro quipped.

Anh Mien laughed, then became almost apologetic. "I do have one final request. You once mentioned that you have with you negatives of pictures you took after Liberation in Quang Ngai. I would like to borrow those negatives so I can make a copy of the photos. All right?"

"Give you the negatives! But they are a unique record of the Liberation of Quang Ngai. Now what self-respecting photographer would give up his negatives?" My protest was at least half serious.

"Don't worry. I'll return them to you intact. I would just like to print copies of them—you know, as a souvenir!"

I knew there was no point in protesting. Besides, there was nothing to hide. I was only anxious for fear I would lose the precious photographic record. I dug the negatives out of the knapsack and handed them to Anh Mien.

Thursday morning came, as did Friday morning, with no progress. Instead of staying only overnight as we had anticipated when we came to Qui Nhon, we had already spent sixteen nights in this "non-prison." Finally, late Friday afternoon, Anh Mien returned.

"Anh Kien, here, your negatives. You didn't think you'd see them again, did you? Now see, don't we keep our promises? You must trust us, Anh Kien!" Anh Mien chided with a knowing smile. "But I want you to check through them to make sure they're all there."

Now I felt a bit embarrassed for having expressed doubt that the negatives would be returned, so I was ready to be obliging. "Oh no, I'm sure they're all here. In fact, if there are any frames that are sensitive material, I want you to take them, becuase it is the policy of the MCC not to transmit any kind of military or politically sensitive information from one side of a conflict to another."

"No, no. You have some shots of military matériel, but I intend to stick to my promise of returning them all to you. Now—as to your departure, your papers are all prepared. I will come here at seven o'clock in the morning, that's Indochina time, to give you the papers and get you on the road. Tomorrow you will be heading to Tuy Hoa, the next province capital south."

We were expressive in our thanks for his help. Anh Mien responded with an apology. "I hope we did not inconvenience you fellows too much. You realize that in this period immediately following Liberation, the situation is a bit unsettled and there is much work for all of us to do. But we did not forget about you. And the cadres in Quang Ngai now know that you'll be moving on—one of our cadres from the Security Office went to Quang Ngai this week and informed them." This revelation was our first confirmation that there was communication between the Qui Nhon and Quang Ngai authorities. Perhaps it was that cross-checking with the Quang Ngai office that had finally produced the breakthrough here in Qui Nhon.

Having travel papers in hand with the signature and seal of the Qui Nhon Security Chief affixed restored lost identity to us. It was as though we had been put through the fire and been found worthy. We were legitimate once again!

And yet, when I pondered the fact that the new papers gave us permission to travel only as far as Tuy Hoa, the next province south, I could not help feeling terribly disappointed. Might that possibly mean another long wait in Tuy Hoa? Maybe months? Until the Saigon Government fell? Who could know? And might it possibly mean more investigation? What could come of that?

Ironically, it was now, with new travel papers in hand, that I reached my lowest point since the Liberation of Quang Ngai. For the first time I decided it might not have been worth it all to have stayed behind when Pat and the children left. My mind began to whirl with the possibilities of the unknown. Once again the murky domain of the imagination possessed me. Inexplicably, I felt as though I was staring into the face of death. Tomorrow, the day of our release, would be the end. Dead. My mind twisted and groaned in agony. I thought I should pray, but the despair was even too great for that.

Will! The will to live! I must force myself to swim upstream.

Providentially, Hiro was feeling particularly optimistic—or resigned—at this moment. When he sensed my depression, he fell into a long philosophical discourse.

"We're floating on a river—no, we are the river, just flowing along. And then something comes to change our form. We evaporate, and we float into the sky." Hiro's arms arched toward the dark, star-studded sky as we sat on a mattress in the small courtyard in front of our Qui Nhon non-prison. It was in moments like this, naked from the waist up, with his untrimmed beard and flowing mane of raven-black hair, that Hiro especially took on the aura of a Zen master. "We float through the air." Hiro rippled his hand above his head and let forth a laugh so thin as to suggest he was indeed drifting in an ethereal bliss. "And then we might change form again and become rain. And—who knows?—maybe we'll end up exactly where we started!"

Floating! How different from swimming upstream. Hiro seemed to be saying there are times when the course of strength is to be weak! The greatest power is in realizing your powerlessness. Was it coincidence that Hiro, like his fellow Asian Lao-tzu over two millennia earlier, spoke in the metaphor of *water*—that most yielding and supple of elements—when he wanted to portray the epitome of strength and power. If you would be strong, you must know when and how to be weak. It was a lesson difficult for me, an American, a Westerner. It was a lesson rarely included in my American textbooks, especially my political science texts. It was, perhaps, a secret of the guerrilla. To be powerful, he had to take full account of his weakness. As in judo, his weakness would overcome another's apparent superior strength. It was, perhaps, the crux of this tiny, technologically backward country's endurance under the bombs, strategies and sophistications of history's most heavily armored nation.

FRIDAY, 25 APRIL. Anh Mien showed up on schedule the following morning and escorted us across town to National Highway One. After a fraternal farewell, Anh Mien arranged for us to ride in a Ford Econoline civilian taxi heading south. It was refreshing once again to sit among weather-worn farmers and betel-nut-chewing market women.

But our reprieve ended five minutes after the van began rolling. Just several miles out of the city our vehicle was flagged to a stop at a checkpoint and the guards demanded an explanation for our presence. We handed them our new travel papers and the driver explained that a cadre had put us on the taxi, but the guards insisted we dismount while the taxi rolled on to Tuy Hoa. By that time, however, Hiro and I were emotionally prepared for almost any contingency and we thoroughly enjoyed mystifying the guards with the truth of our story. Within minutes they seemed apologetic that they had detained us, but they nevertheless said they would have to get in touch with the Qui Nhon People's Security Office to verify our papers.

The clearance came within an hour, after which the guards approached a truck driver loading furniture into a large blue *camion* to ask if we could ride south with him. The next two hours had us on the bed of the truck cruising delightfully along Highway One between scrubby fields and coconut groves. The highway was strewn with the leftovers of war. We counted thirty-two vehicles—trucks of all types, jeeps, private cars and an occasional armored vehicle—disabled along the route. In most cases they were wheelless. Likely some enterprising local entrepreneurs now had impressive collections of truck tires. The other leftovers in evidence were ragged bands of ARVN soldiers plodding slowly and quietly toward the south. Our truck stopped to make a furniture drop at a small hamlet along the route and one ARVN soldier begged a ride on the van. He explained that he had been walking for more than three weeks. After his unit had been defeated in Hue, nearly 400 kilometers north, the PRG authorities had issued travel papers for him to return to his home in Saigon even though the capital was still on "the other side." It was conceivable that if these ARVN soldiers should manage to cross the battle line, they could once again join units of the ARVN and fight against the Liberation Army. One could only speculate that the PRG rationale was that even if these defeated troops did arrive in the capital before the Liberation Army, the effect would be only to demoralize further the dispirited ARVN units in Saigon.

Not all the troops on the road were from the defeated army. The highway buzzed with convoys of uniformed *bo doi* streaming toward the battlefront in the south. Among those in uniform were some women, often strikingly beautiful with long black braids hanging from under their green helmets. Other convoys of olive-drab Chinese trucks or blue-cabbed Russian trucks carried green crates of ammunition toward the front. Occasionally military taxis sped by, likely carrying the top military commanders toward the scene of action.

Arriving at the outskirts of Tuy Hoa, Hiro and I jumped off the truck and asked the local shopkeepers where we might find the People's Security Office. As in Qui Nhon no one could tell us. So, as in Qui Nhon, we asked for the former Saigon Government police headquarters and we were directed to the opposite end of town. It would be within walking distance because Tuy Hoa was quite a small town. With its quiet wide tree-lined streets, it was reminiscent of a small Wyoming town. Tuy Hoa was immaculate, absolutely unscarred by fighting. With practically no military trucks or tanks in the town it was barely perceptible that anything had changed from the "old days" in Tuy Hoa. The only indications were an occasional *bo doi* along the street and the revolutionary movie advertised on the theater's marquee: *Military Victory of the 1968 Offensive.* As in the old regime, the theater featured war flicks—only now with a new victor! Still, if the medium is the message, it seemed little had changed in Tuy Hoa.

We stopped at a bookshop to buy a simple bamboo flute and instruction book. Fully anticipating another detention of several weeks or even months, I decided I would while away some time by learning to play the popular Vietnamese instrument. When we arrived at the former police headquarters we learned that indeed this did now serve as the new People's Security Office. It was early afternoon and the place was enveloped in a languid siesta mood. A handful of people sitting near the gate hardly seemed to notice our presence. A guerrilla guard at one side made no move to approach us when we paused in front of the gate, so we started to march into the compound. At that, the guard swung around and abruptly ordered us to halt. What was our business? And didn't we know no one could enter the compound without permission? We explained our problem and showed him our papers. He ordered us to wait under a thatch lean-to outside the gate while he took our papers into the office.

We waited to be invited into the compound, but the invitation was not forthcoming. While we sat, we took stock of the tree-shaded compound, surrounded by open fields. We could tell by the salty breeze that the sea was not far to the east. If we were to be detained another period of time, there could be worse environments than this, we decided.

A half hour later someone finally emerged from the office and walked out to the gate, but even he did not invite us in. He merely handed our papers back to the guard who in turn handed them to us. We were not sure what our next step should be until we noticed that these were *new papers*, freshly typed with orders to travel on to Nhatrang, the next province capital south!

The move caught us totally by surprise. We thanked the guard, who seemed happy to have us off his hands, and we fairly waltzed back through town. We considered finding a room at a local hotel for the night so we could gather a few stories of the Liberation of Tuy Hoa and take in our first revolutionary cinema in the evening. But when we learned from townsfolk that Nhatrang was only three or four hours south, we couldn't restrain ourselves from skipping right back to Highway One to hitchhike a ride south.

We were soon in another taxi-van heading for Nhatrang. The scenery complemented our sense of newfound freedom. The road wound through lush mountain passes and then plunged to level stretches along the lolling

Eastern Sea. The sun set over the hills and darkness claimed the land, but—unbelievably—we kept driving! For the first time in a decade it was safe to travel at night. No danger of guerrilla ambushes here! As the reflection of the rising moon shimmered across the sea, we pressed on toward Nhatrang.

Hiro and I had both spent time in Nhatrang before because an MCC-sponsored clinic was located on the idyllic coral beach just to the north of the city. Fearing we might forfeit any possibility of learning the fate of the clinic if we reported directly to the People's Security Office in downtown Nhatrang, we requested that the driver drop us off at the clinic road just north of the city. Thankful for the cover of darkness to give us anonymity, we made our way down the long dusty path toward the clinic. In the nearby Tin Lanh orphanage children were singing hymns before retiring for the night. Moonlit waves lapped at the sandy apron of the sea.

The gate to the clinic grounds was locked, but we were able to enter a side entrance through a neighbor's yard. The low red-tiled clinic building was dark and the house where the expatriate MCC personnel had stayed was abandoned. Peering in through a broken window we saw that the doors had been forced open and nearly everything movable had been removed from the house. Even the blades of the ceiling fan were bent out of shape. We were attracted by lights from the house of the clinic's chaplain-administrator, but we soon discovered the house was no longer occupied by the chaplain. The living room was now filled with a coterie of *bo doi* engrossed in conversation. If we were planning to spent the night at the clinic, we would eventually have to report to these *bo doi*, but first we wanted to talk with any acquaintances we could possibly find in the area. We were fortunate to find the old caretaker with his wife and a former MCC cook in their house nearby.

"Anh Hiro, Anh Kien—you're safe!" Co Mai, the cook, grabbed our hands when she met us at the door. "We heard from the MCC folks that you stayed in Quang Ngai for—for Liberation, but then no one heard anything more about you. Oh, I'm so glad to see you. I miss the MCC people so much."

Co Mai went on to explain that the other MCC personnel had left Nhatrang nearly a month before when the ARVN security forces were beginning to disintegrate around the city. Co Mai said that although she missed the MCC people, she was happy they had gone to Saigon. "It was terrifying. The main ARVN units fled town and then the place went to pieces. The ARVN troops who had been routed in battles in the highlands—they converged on Nhatrang and simply terrorized the place. Then the deserters and drug addicts broke out of their military prison, got guns and went from house to house demanding money at gunpoint. And if you didn't give them any money, they could shoot you at will. Before the MCC folks left they paid us five months' advance salary. That was a godsend. If I hadn't had that money—well, the money's all gone now, but at least I'm alive."

231

The elderly caretaker was eager to introduce us to the PRG cadres in the administrator's house before they could form any mistaken impressions of us. The caretaker explained that nearly all of the Vietnamese staff of the clinic including the doctor had fled to Saigon before Liberation, so the clinic had been turned over to a Dr. The, who had come with the *bo doi*.

The caretaker introduced Hiro and me to Dr. The as representatives of the organization that had previously sponsored the clinic. Dr. The, probably about our age, was of slight build and soft-spoken, a very serious and conscientious air about him. He wore the blue shirt, green pants and tire sandals typical of most cadres. Feeling a need to explain our presence, we presented the young doctor with our travel papers. Apparently Dr. The felt a need to explain his presence in the MCC clinic as well. He said that the Vietnamese pastor at the nearby Evangelical Bible School who took charge of the clinic after most of the staff had fled had subsequently turned it over to the PRG "for lack of personnel or finances to continue operating the facilities." We could only assure him that the Mennonite Central Committee would be grateful to learn that the facilities would continue to serve the medical needs of people in the area.

Several of the recent MCC volunteers in Nhatrang had—to the chagrin of some of the Vietnamese staff members—gained a reputation of being opposed to the American policy in Vietnam. Murray and Linda Hiebert, a Canadian-American couple, had particularly been viewed askance by some of the staff, but the caretaker was happy now to take advantage of the legacy. "The Americans who worked here at the clinic, they didn't support Mr. Thieu and his government in Saigon. No, no, they were different," the caretaker explained a bit nervously to Dr. The. "In particular, the fellow who lived in that house over there"—pointing to the house where Murray and Linda had lived—"he wanted to go out into the mountains and help poor refugees. We asked him if he wasn't afraid of"—the caretaker groped for the right word—"of—the other side. He just said he wasn't afraid of the main force units. His only concern was that some local guerrillas who didn't understand who he was might give him trouble."

"His fear was well based," Dr. The replied seriously. "The revolution distinguishes carefully between our friends and our enemies. And we realize that many Americans are our friends. But American spies and counterinsurgency agents have frequently used the guise of social work or medicine to gather intelligence to sabotage the revolution. So it was necessary for the guerrillas to be most cautious."

Dr. The invited Hiro and me to spend the night in the former administrator's house with his team of *bo doi*. We talked into the night about his training as a doctor in Hanoi and the practice of medicine in the North. He explained that under the socialist government the first priority was placed not on curative medicine but on preventative medicine. Mass innoculations and public health education were central. He said the Three Clean Campaign—eat clean, drink clean, live clean—avoided a lot of diseases. Acupuncture and herbal medicines stood side by side with Western medicines in the North. When Hiro and I took out our notebooks and scribbled notes of what he was saying, Dr. The spoke with added fervor as though he was taking seriously the responsibility of every cadre to engage in political education at any opportunity.

The clinic by the sea, built by MCC in 1957—an interesting place to meet a "Communist doctor." As we talked, my eyes wandered around the living room of the former administrator-chaplain. Mottoes with scripture verses in Vietnamese hung on the wall. Above the chair where Dr. The was sitting hung a picture of the thorn-crowned Christ on the cross with the inscription, "Father, forgive them. . ."

SATURDAY, 26 APRIL. It happened that Dr. The was expecting a friend from the Nhatrang People's Security Office to visit him Saturday morning. It was decided we would ride into town with him. While we were waiting for the man to arrive, Hiro and I strolled around the clinic grounds. Everywhere was evidence of the mayhem that Co Mai had talked about the evening before. Not only had the MCC unit house been ransacked. In the clinic building the expensive X-ray machine, too heavy to move, had been partially smashed. The medicine warehouse was pillaged. Apparently the medicines that were recognizable, such as antibiotics and aspirin, were stolen. The remaining jars and vials were dumped on the floor or the ground outside, often smashed.

On the grounds we met Pastor Ong Van Huyen, dean of the nearby Evangelical Bible School. The pastor, perhaps in his late fifties, seemed relaxed and accepting of the recent political changes in Nhatrang. Pastor Huyen never had been plagued by the irrational fears of a socialist government typical of many Vietnamese church leaders. Several decades before, he had lived in a zone controlled by the Viet Minh in central Vietnam. Throughout the war he had advocated doing what was necessary to survive *despite* the political regime in power. A good example of his ability to accommodate occurred a year before when at a clinic board meeting a Vietnamese administrator proposed that the clinic erect a flagpole so they could fly the yellow and red flag of the Saigon Government. North American Mennonites at the meeting reflected their misgivings about identifying with *any* government. Pastor Huyen took the pragmatic approach: The director should erect the pole to fly the government's flag. And looking at the Mennonites, he smiled, "When the 'other side' takes over the country, we will fly their flag!"

Now, although there were still no Liberation flags on the clinic compound, Pastor Huyen seemed at peace with the situation. He also related to us the terror of the few days when the ARVN forces crumbled and the scattered troops and bullies terrorized the town. In fact, even after the *bo doi* arrived in Nhatrang city the looting continued in the region north of town where the clinic was located. In a desperate attempt to save the clinic and the Evangelical Bible School, Pastor Huyen finally hurried into the city and begged the *bo doi* to come to their rescue. When the *bo doi* arrived, the looting ended. "We were fortunate," Pastor Huyen concluded. "If the *bo doi* hadn't come when they did, the Bible School might have been wrecked."

As I walked along the beach that morning my mind went back to the several times before when our family had come to these waters for vacation and renewal. Many were the hours we had splashed in this clear inlet of the sea and played in these white sands with our small children. And there were whole mornings when we snorkled around the boulders at the point, surrounded by the underwater paradise of coral and multicolored tropical fish. Nhatrang had always epitomized for me—and many Vietnamese—the impregnability of the Saigon Government. During the American heyday in Vietnam, and even up to several months before now, it had been unthinkable to many people that Nhatrang would be shaken by revolution. Even during the nationwide Tet Offensive in 1968, Nhatrang and the surrounding province had been virtually untouched by the sounds of war. But now, just weeks after the collapse of the old reality, it was difficult to remember the old perceptions. Already the inclination was to convince oneself that the change had always been inevitable.

Looking out over the sea I spotted a helicopter flying in toward the city from the northeast. For a moment I thought of the possibility of a sabotage mission by the Saigon Air Force, but then decided from the direction of approach that it must be a "revolutionary" helicopter. As I followed the flight of the chopper, the town suddenly reverberated with the crisp barking of antiaircraft guns. Within seconds we saw the puff of white smoke as the helicopter plummeted below the tree line. It was a dazzling spectacle, but no one seemed to know whose chopper it was.

The car from the People's Security Office finally arrived by midmorning. As we drove into Nhatrang proper, it quickly became apparent that this city had not been as fortunate as the other province capitals we had visited. The marks of war abounded. Close to an ancient Cham temple on the northern edge of the city a neighborhood had been demolished by bombs. The bombers had apparently hoped to destroy a nearby bridge on Highway One to impede the flow of convoys from the north, but the bombs had hit the houses instead. People reported that nearly 100 persons were killed in the bombing raid. In town we rode past the main market, which had been pillaged and burned by ARVN troops on the rampage before the *bo doi* entered the city.

The security office cadre who was driving the car spotted a *bo doi* friend along the street and pulled off to the side. "Did you see that helicopter?" the man outside shouted.

"Sure did, what's the story?" our driver called back.

"It was ours," the *bo doi* returned. "Our antiaircraft units hadn't been notified that it was coming. The thing crashed, then bounced, then hit the ground again. Several comrades were injured, but no one was killed."

At the Nhatrang People's Security Office a stern cadre probably in his forties looked at our papers and without listening to our story insisted that it would be impossible for us to continue toward Saigon.

"Everything is blocked," the cadre announced firmly, seeming to enjoy the authority of his words. "There would be no problem traveling through the liberated zone, but at the border, ragtag Saigon troops would make trouble for you. Besides, there's a problem here with your papers. Normally when foreigners are traveling like this the previous post notifies us in advance. We were not informed of your coming, so we'll have to confirm this with them."

If indeed that was PRG policy, perhaps that was at least part of the explanation for our two-week delay in Qui Nhon. Maybe there had been no formal investigation of us at all. Perhaps the Qui Nhon office had merely been waiting to get direct word from the Quang Ngai security office. There was no way we could know.

The humorless cadre continued his lecture by giving a running account of the recent news reports. "I guess you heard that some of the embassy personnel in Saigon are leaving. The time has come for no more foreign intervention in Vietnam. We welcome the exit of all foreigners." It was hard not to think that we too were included in that rubric. When he heard we carried journals with us, he frowned, "Just so you write the truth. If you really write the truth, that's fine, but we don't want you to write—" He broke off the topic and switched to report the two-week-old news that a pilot in the Saigon Air Force had turned on Thieu and bombed the Presidential Palace in Saigon. "After he bombed the palace he flew to liberated territory and we praised him, raised his rank to captain. That's our policy. If someone performs some action in support of the revolution, he is praised. If he opposes that policy, he will be punished."

Finally the cadre terminated his political peroration and sent us to "the house next door" to wait for clearance. The house happened to be the plush seafront villa of a now-absent Saigon army colonel. But if actions in support of the revolution rated praise, this colonel deserved high marks. Upon fleeing, he left behind his spacious hallways, his wood-paneled bedrooms, his terrazzo patios, his air-conditioners, his hot and cold running water bathrooms, and his finely manicured gardens of tropical flora—all to be placed in the service of the revolution!

The colonel's fine estate now served as the dormitory for forty enthusiastic local young people who had volunteered to "learn the ways of the revolution" and work along with cadres of the security office in policing operations around town. A spirit of camaraderie was evident between the cadres and the new recruits. The high morale evoked memories of teen-age summer camps.

Saturday night Hiro and I sat cross-legged with the other youth and, following the phrase-by-phrase leading of a young cadre, learned the songs of the revolution.

"Everyone ready? I'll sing the first phrase and then you sing after me. All right? Here we go." His arm swung to the beat as he started singing. *"Di ta di giai phong mien nam. . . ."* ("On we go to liberate the south . . . one, two. . . ."

The group chorused after him: "On we go to liberate the south."

The leader picked up the next line: "Smash the jails, sweep out the aggressors . . . one, two. . . ."

The room rang with the repeat, "Smash the jails, sweep out the aggressors."

"For independence and freedom . . . one, two. . . ."

"For independence and freedom."

"Take back our food and shelter . . . one, two. . . ."

"Take back our food and shelter."

"Take back the glory of Spring . . . one, two. . . ."

"Take back the glory of Spring."

The leader beamed. "That was tremendous. Now, are there any volunteers to sing the song by memory? Remember, I want you to have this one memorized by tomorrow night. Yes, here's a sister who's volunteering. Come up here, sister, and give it a try."

"On we go to liberate the south . . ." the sister sang perfectly. I had not seen such fervor since Youth for Christ rallies in my high-school days!

For being an adjunct of the People's Security Office, the colonel's villa had a remarkably relaxed atmosphere. On a number of occasions visitors dropped in to talk with the cadres or just to idle away time unemployed. Sunday morning there appeared two middle-aged men with clothes finely enough tailored to suggest they were of some means under the Saigon regime. They chatted several moments with the cadres who were about to head downtown. Then the two visitors turned to Hiro and me. Over tea, served in ornately decorated cups of the colonel's estate, one gentleman told us that until the change of government a month before he had been a captain in the ARVN. When we asked his assessment of why the Liberation Army had made such striking advances in recent weeks, his analysis was simple.

"We had matériel. They had spirit."

The other man never did identify himself, but he perked up noticeably when he learned we were associated with a church-related agency. "There's one thing I can't figure out," he began earnestly. "Why did all the missionaries leave us? I personally knew a number of the missionaries here in Nhatrang and they always said they were here only for religious purposes. If they were truly committed to their faith, why did they all run off? Even if they were afraid of the Communists, they had always given the impression they would be willing to die for the sake of Christ. Now that they're gone, it makes us wonder why they were really here in the first place. Oh, I understand why some of them left. Some of them had a pretty fancy life-style; they were afraid they would lose all those comforts if the revolution came. But many of them did not live like that. Many of them lived very simply, like the Bible translators, for example. They were making a significant cultural contribution. They didn't have anything to fear from the new government, did they? Unless they were doing things they weren't telling us about."

Given the surly response of the cadre we had met the day before in the Security Office next door, Hiro and I anticipated a protracted stay in the colonel's villa. So be it. We would get to learn more revolutionary songs and maybe even take some lessons on the flute from the song-leading cadre who, with a few minutes of his plaintive warbling on the simple bamboo instrument, could make everyone within earshot hopelessly homesick.

But it was not to be. Midmorning on Sunday an exceedingly gentle and thoughtful cadre from the Security Office next door showed up with our travel papers in hand. As he drove us to the bus station he wanted to make sure that we had been well cared for and that we had enough money and provisions for our continued trip south. When he noticed townsfolk at the bus station paying inordinate attention to these two foreigners, he quietly apologized. "Please forgive us. You must bear with us if people look at you strangely. They mean no offense. And do be careful with your camera. You'd better keep it with you at all times." He offered to pay our bus ride to the next province south, but we assured him that would not be necessary. "Be careful you don't pay too high a price for the ticket. Sometimes they will try to take more money from a foreigner. You must understand that not everyone here understands the way of the revolution yet."

More straggling ARVN troops making their way toward Saigon, demolished bridges and disabled vehicles marked the road from Nhatrang to Phan Rang, the next province capital south. Most of the bridges, we were told, had been dropped by the retreating ARVN, who sought to deny the easy passage of National Highway One to the advancing Liberation Army. Apparently close to one bridge the guerrillas had ambushed an ARVN column. We counted sixty-five trucks jeeps and tanks lying burned and battered around the bridge and in the ditches and fields. One was left to imagine the grisly scenes of bleeding men and dismembered bodies that must have been strewn around among the vehicles just weeks before. Several towns along the way showed fresh scars of shell holes and B-40 rocket explosions on the village buildings. Here was the first evidence of the two armies engaged in open warfare that we had seen since we left Quang Ngai 450 kilometers to the north.

Phan Rang, our next stop, was the birthplace of Nguyen Van Thieu, the recently resigned chief executive of the Saigon Government. Phan Rang's former province head was the nephew of Thieu's wife, so the province had seemed a veritable bulwark of Saigon Government strength. But even months before the earthshaking advance of the Liberation Army, some Phan Rang residents had begun to question the stability of their native son's administration in Saigon. When I had last visited the town three months earlier, I was told of an enormous rock formation that had for centuries been a landmark on the beach of the Eastern Sea just outside the city. The formation, because of its appearance, was known to the local people as the Devil's Face Rock. But to the surprise of everyone in the area and for no apparent reason, in mid-1974 the rock fell on its face. During my January visit several people had vaguely wondered out loud if the falling of the rock would possibly presage falling fortunes for their hometown boy in the Presidential Palace in Saigon!

Over lunch in a café at the Phan Rang bus station Hiro and I listened to an old man relate the story of the fall of President Thieu's hometown. Just three weeks before our arrival the ARVN defenders of the town had fled in disarray. There would be no medals for heroism under fire for these troops because at the time of the panicked retreat there were apparently no guerrillas, let alone main force *bo doi* units, within kilometers. In fact, the avalanche of retreating ARVN troops countrywide had picked up such momentum by this time that the *bo doi* were unable to keep up! So for three days Phan Rang was without any military force of either side. At that point a chagrined Saigon command ordered an ARVN contingent back into the city. The ARVN set up a temporary command post, which was to last for just over a week; one morning *bo doi* tanks suddenly appeared outside the post and caught the occupants by surprise. The commanders ran for their helicopters to escape, but their terrified pilots had already flown away, leaving the hapless officers at the mercy of the encircling Liberation Army. Hardly a shot was fired. Two ARVN generals, several colonels and majors and an American advisor were easily captured by the *bo doi*.

We quizzed the old man in the soup shop as to whether there had been any reprisals taken by the revolutionary army in the Phan Rang area.

"Reprisals? Not a soul. No one was killed around here. Why, the old village chief and hamlet chiefs are still running around free. Yes, they shot a couple hoodlums who kept on looting after they came in. Here they shot eight and it's said they shot twelve in Nhatrang. But thank heavens they did. Those guys were terrorizing the place before the *bo doi* took action. I lost thirty-seven thousand piasters. Thirty-seven thousand. Those rascals just made off with it like they owned it! And my cousin, my God, he fared worse yet. He had five hundred thousand piasters, and about a dozen ARVN

Rangers barged into his house and took all his money. And that's not the worst of it. Those Rangers took turns raping his two daughters right there before his eyes! *Troi dat oi*, the government used to scare us by saying that when the Viet Cong came they would rob and kill. But when they did come I didn't so much as lose a whisker off my beard! But these Saigon troops storming around, stealing and raping—tell me, how can you support them? Troops like this, who is their commander?"

Not all Phan Rang people were so convinced. One white-shirted youth in the soup shop had overheard the old man. When the old man was out of earshot, the youth spoke to us in undertones.

"I didn't see any soldiers stealing. It was the prisoners who escaped and picked up the soldiers' guns. And the local people stole from each other."

We asked the young man what he thought of the new government. "They say their policy is to 'erase rancor,' but in fact they have come in and killed the village and hamlet officials at My Tuong, not far from here." Eager to get more documentation, we asked if he knew any names or backgrounds of the officials or exactly what had happened. "Well, no I don't really know. I just heard these reports, but I have no doubt they're true." When we asked his background, it turned out this youth was an ARVN soldier himself. We asked his opinion of the Saigon Government. Did he consider it repressive as some people had alleged? He was quick to reply, "No, the regime was not repressive. Hopelessly corrupt, yes. Repressive, no!"

After lunch we managed to find the Phan Rang Security Office on a back street. We were met at the gate by a sleepy guard who in response to our request meandered into the abandoned National Police Station to find someone to help us. After a half hour's wait a bashful cadre about our age finally appeared. He read our travel papers, which called for "every accommodation" to be granted us, and seemed to take the instruction at face value. He apologized for their rustic facilities, but within an hour he arranged to spread a veritable banquet on the table before us. Replete with dishes of beef, pork, eggs, soups and Biere Larue, the meal was obviously prepared especially for us.

Hiro and I came to the conclusion that there would be marked regional differences in the way the new revolutionary leadership would function. The cadres in Quang Ngai and Qui Nhon were paragons of efficiency and discipline. Even their humor often had its political point. Immediately after Liberation in Quang Ngai, a whole setup of cadres who had already been organized in the hills stepped in to assume control. If their organization and enthusiasm were any indication, the Quang Ngai cadres would doubtless effect radical land reform and nationalization of the economy at a faster pace than some other regions of the country.

Here in Phan Rang the spirit was more benign, less controlled. But then there never had been the fierce battles in Phan Rang that had characterized the provinces farther north. The cadres told us that in years past they had virtually conceded the province to the Americans and the Saigon Government. One cadre told how he and a tiny band of hearty guerrillas had roamed the hinterlands of the province for years, but they never attempted to provoke encounters with American or ARVN troops. As a result, there never had been much bombing or shelling in the province. The cadre told us their primary enemy was not planes or ARVN ambushes but hunger and thirst. Many of his fellow guerrillas had died over the past years, not from warfare, but from having eaten a poisonous tuber or drinking contaminated water during dry summer months.

Survival demanded ingenuity. The cadre revealed that one trick they devised to throw an occasional ARVN patrol off their tracks was to camouflage their footprints. Most farmers or woodsmen in the province wore the molded rubber "thong" sandals similar to American shower shoes. The guerrillas needed the sturdier rubber-tire sandals, but their typical notched treads would have left tracks easily spotted by ARVN sleuths. With a smile, the cadre raised his foot to show us his sandal. It was the rugged type made from a rubber tire, but the sole was meticulously hand carved to imitate the ripples of the commercially made "thongs." Even the rectangular thong trademark was carved into the sandal's instep.

Survival demanded ingenuity. To escape police detection, this guerrilla carved his rubber-tire sandals to imitate the molded thongs worn by farmers.

The less combative nature of the war in Phan Rang went to produce a markedly different spirit among these men. In Quang Ngai the list of grievances against the enemy was long and bitter. Although the PRG's policy of "national reconciliation" seemed to be preventing the reprisal killings that many had predicted, it was not because there was a lack of rancor or an absence of the urge to settle some scores. Here in Phan Rang, however, one got the feeling that those "scores" did not even exist. The more benign character of the resistance struggle here promised to color the nature of the local administration for Phan Rang in the future.

While we ate we quizzed this official for stories of the take-over of Phan Rang. When we asked what had happened to the political prisoners in the local prison, he suddenly brightened. "Oh, that's quite a story! It seems that after the ARVN first fled Phan Rang there was an ARVN sergeant who had a father in the local prison. As we got the story, the sergeant came to the prison gate—a few guards were still around—and asked if he could enter to visit his father. The guards said no, but the sergeant shot his M-16 into the air to threaten them. The guards backed down and let him in. Once on the inside—the guards all stayed out in the outer compound—the sergeant found his father and then he and the prisoners went around opening up all the individual cells, breaking down doors and so forth. All this time the sergeant was firing his rifle inside the prison. After he was sure all the prisoners were out of their cell blocks, he returned to the gate where he yelled to the guards that they should leave because he had killed all the prisoners. At that point the sergeant grabbed hold of the heavy machine gun at the gate and started firing in the direction of the guards. The guards ran for their lives. Finally, the sergeant shot open the main gate and released all the prisoners!"

It was, of course, impossible for us to double-check the accuracy of this extraordinary account, but the cadre's final comment intrigued us. "Now we are trying to locate that sergeant. His heroic deed must go on his record. He must be rewarded!"

We were put up for the night with two armed guerrillas in the recently abandoned villa of the Saigon Government agricultural chief for the province. We were not used to having armed guards over us, but the guerrillas' congenial attitude and casual handling of their weapons convinced us that their presence was intended to insure our safety rather than to prevent our escape. By morning, a cadre showed up at the villa with our newly typed travel papers, duplicates in every way of the papers we had received in each of our other stopping points except that this version authorized travel from Phan Rang to the next province capital south, Phan Thiet.

A hot dusty trip, punctuated by our walking over several downed bridges while the bus forded the rivers, finally brought us to Phan Thiet. It was late afternoon when we jumped off the bus and looked for a place to eat. We had eaten nothing since breakfast except a bag of cookies we had bought to celebrate my thirty-first birthday. We located a small roadside restaurant and washed in a basin outside the shop. Suddenly the afternoon sky was pierced by the screaming of five jet fighters overhead. Jets! Over liberated area! And they looked like American jets at that. A-37's! And flying south! The diners in the shop talked excitedly, trying to speculate about the origin of the planes. The Liberation Army did have some Russian MiG fighters in the North, but they had never been used for combat in the South. But these were clearly American planes. Why were American planes flying from liberated area toward the Saigon area? No obvious answers were forthcoming, so we and the other diners settled down for our evening meal.

With the help of a high-school student walking along the street, we found our way to the Phan Thiet People's Security Office, housed in a magnificent French-built office building atop a hill and surrounded by towering banyans. We were met in the courtyard by a young cadre who greeted us very cordially. The kind-faced fellow listened to our story, nodding believingly. As he took our papers, he motioned toward the building. "Come, there's someone here whom you might like to meet." We followed him into a side room and found ourselves face-to-face with two husky Caucasians! Prisoners? Stranded Americans? Russian technicians?

"Hello. How are you?" The speaker's English was heavily accented but friendly. Then I noticed the badges on their shirts: *Bao Chi Duc*. German journalists! East Germans who had followed the *bo doi* from Hanoi? No, they soon filled us in.

They told us they were reporters for the West German magazine *Stern*. They had left Saigon several days before to travel to the seaport of Vung Tau, still under Saigon control, where they negotiated with a local fisherman to have him sail them under cover of night north to "Viet Cong territory."

"The boatman was hesitant at first," the undauntable Klaus Liedtke recounted. "Everyone was telling us we were out of our minds. The ARVN would shoot us. The Saigon navy would shoot us. The air force would bomb us. The Viet Cong would shoot us. We would get mugged by—what do you call them?—sea pirates. But the guy took us when we showed him two hundred thousand piasters. It was early in the morning when we got here to—what's this place called?—Phan Thiet. The guy in the boat cut his engine. It was still dark. And we floated in to the wharf. He motioned for us to get out and there we were, standing on the dock in the dark, and the boatman started his engine and took off out into the ocean!

"Nobody was around, so we walked to the nearest house, knocked on the door and asked the people, 'Where can we find the Viet Cong?' "

The mystified villagers led the journalists up the hill to meet the "Viet Cong" at the People's Security Office, which had been the journalists' residence since then. "We were hoping to go to Danang and check out the story Kissinger keeps repeating of three hundred or so officers being executed there. But now things are happening too fast. Saigon's a madhouse, I tell you. Everybody's running around trying to get out. It's wild! The

North Vietnamese are getting closer to Saigon all the time. So now we think maybe we'd like to march into Saigon with the Viet Cong. We'll be on the first tank that rolls into the city! Taking pictures, eh Hans!" Klaus looked at his photographer and laughed lustily. "Duck, here, is going to arrange it for us, aren't you, Duck!" Anh Duc, the interpreter cadre who had met us, smiled politely and said nothing.

Our conversation with the reporters was suddenly interrupted by the screeching sound of jets overhead. We ran outside in time to see planes flying over town. North this time! The same American jets that had been heading south just an hour before. But now only three instead of five! They were flying low enough to bomb the town. In a second, rifle shots pierced the air. "Shoot 'em down!" someone shouted in the distance. The short, crisp staccato of AK-47's stuttered from all over the city. Suddenly sharp cracks far louder than the rifles rent the air. Antiaircraft fire!

"STOP! Stop the shooting. They're our planes!" The Security Office cadre was shouting at the top of his lungs. "Stop! Don't shoot!" But no one was paying attention to him.

The jet pilots must have seen what we saw: white puffs of antiaircraft shells exploding high in the air around the planes. The plane on the left rolled on its side and peeled off to the left and then quickly back to the right in sharp evasive action. The other two planes were banking and dipping in dodging maneuvers of their own. The guns resounded all the louder, but within moments the planes streaked past town and back north in the direction from which they had originally come.

"*Troi oi*, what a spectacle," the head cadre murmured. "Where did those planes come from anyway? I'm sure they must have been our planes. They must have been." For several minutes we discussed the dazzling air show, but no one could be certain of the origin or mission of the mysterious jets.

As darkness claimed the quiet city the Security Office cadres, models of congeniality, set out soft drinks and cookies on an open patio for their unlikely quartet of foreign guests. As we exchanged stories, Klaus, the reporter, always with an ear for news, turned on a shortwave radio he had brought along in his suitcase. Soon we were hearing the VOA's familiar "Yankee Doodle" jangle peeling forth and we fell silent: "Eight o'clock. Twelve hundred hours, Greenwich mean time." Reception was excellent tonight. "The Voice of America brings you the news. First the headlines: *Planes of unknown origin bomb Tan Son Nhut airport on the outskirts of Saigon.* North Vietnamese troops move. . . . "

Planes? Bomb Tan Son Nhut? An attempted coup? A mistaken bombing?

"Ah, there you have it—" Klaus was first to make the association. "The planes, the planes we saw!"

I was not so used to hearing international news report events I had witnessed just an hour or two before, but Klaus was right. A week later we were to learn that the planes were, indeed, American-made A-37 fighters that had been captured by the PRG and flown by Liberation Army pilots. They had taken off from an airfield not far north of us and surprise-attacked Saigon's main airfield, leaving many Saigon planes destroyed. The mission had apparently been so secret that not even the antiaircraft units of the Liberation Army had been informed! In fact, since we saw only three return, we wondered if perhaps two had been shot down, perhaps by "friendly" antiaircraft fire!

With the attack on Saigon getting into full swing, our trip to the capital looked all the more hazardous. The line was shifting every day. To move across the battlefield when one did not even know who controlled what seemed the height of folly. But by now we had gained a bureaucratic momentum that swept us closer and closer to the front. In Qui Nhon we were detained two weeks without explanation when we wanted to be on the move. Now when it was beginning to look wiser to stay put and let the dust and shrapnel settle somewhat, the Security Offices were automatically approving our travel orders and sending us on our way. So we were rather ambivalent Tuesday morning when the cadres handed us our new papers and cheerfully wished us a good trip.

As Hiro and I walked through Phan Thiet to the bus stop at the southern edge of town, we stopped and asked a teen-age boy along the street if he knew anywhere we could buy a radio. We had decided that if we were going to have to cross a battle line within a day or two, we were going to do it with our eyes and ears open, with all the information possible, including radio newscasts. The lad didn't know of any shops that were open, but he had a friend, and just so quickly he was running down the street. In moments he returned with his friend's radio for our examination. Within five minutes we were surrounded by a crowd of townsfolk who had heard of our request. Soon we were examining radios of all shapes, colors and sizes. We picked one that looked to be in good shape and pulled in VOA and BBC with no trouble. We handed the delighted man 20,000 piasters—about twenty-five dollars—and set off.

Buses were not moving. We were already in territory that had been taken by the Liberation Army just ten days before and civilian traffic south was almost nonexistent. But near the bus stop a lumber truck was being loaded with local traders and their baskets. And soon we too were aboard, bouncing along on the bed of the truck toward Binh Tuy, the next province south.

Scrub country. Contrasting sharply with the lush paddy fields of Quang Ngai and other provinces to the north, here the land lay dry and uncultivated. Village settlements came only infrequently along the way.

We would try to stay put in Binh Tuy for some days, maybe even a month, we decided. Perhaps we would not even report to the Security Office in Binh Tuy upon arrival. Just find a boarding room and hide away for a week or two—anything to avoid being thrown into the middle of a battle outside Saigon.

Our plan worked. Once in Ham Tan, Binh Tuy's province seat, we checked ourselves into a quiet inn on a side street, and then set out to find a place to lunch. Though it was the province seat, the town seemed more like a large village. The place was now as tranquil as on the other two occasions when I had visited Binh Tuy in the previous year. People were calmly going about their normal routines. We learned at the sidewalk restaurant that there had hardly been a skirmish when the *bo doi* entered town. "Seven or eight soldiers were killed in a little battle west of town. That was it! The rest took off on boats for Vung Tau and Saigon," the shopkeeper told us. It was the story we had been hearing at each stop. Wherever there existed an easy escape route, the ARVN always took it. The towns, as a result, could not have been more fortunate. Had the ARVN stood up and resisted, the toll on lives and property would have been immeasurably greater. As it was, the towns were intact and life went on.

After lunch Hiro and I changed our minds. We had better report to the Binh Tuy Security Office after all. A confused guard at the gate finally ushered us into the run-down office building and had us sit down. Eventually there appeared a gray-haired cadre of over fifty who introduced himself as Binh. Even before we identified ourselves Anh Binh politely inquired, "You gentlemen just arrived in Binh Tuy?"

"Yes, just got here."

"Well, gentlemen, I trust you're in good health; that all's going well with you." His relaxed warmth relieved us. There seemed to be something of a pattern emerging. The farther south we got, the more casual the PRG cadres became. There was an honest contentment about the man's creased face, testimony to his having spent many years in the backwoods, perhaps much of the time alone.

"Mennonite Central Committee, you say?" Anh Binh had listened carefully as we related our story. "I'm afraid I don't understand foreign languages. Can you explain to me this term 'Mennonite'? Could it be that a man by the name of Mr. Mennonite founded your group?"

"Well, matter of fact," I nodded, "the name does come from one of the early leaders of the movement, a man by the name of Menno Simons. He lived in the early sixteenth century."

We chatted for perhaps an hour; he asked about the work of MCC and we asked about his life as a guerrilla in Binh Tuy. Anh Binh, as were the majority of cadres we had been meeting on our trip, was native to the province where he was now serving. As with the Phan Rang guerrillas, the primary enemy here in Binh Tuy had not been the ARVN or the American military, but the dry, barren woodlands which had become their home. Anh Binh's lanky frame and bony fingers attested to years of meager diets.

"There never were many of us in Binh Tuy province," he related. "In fact, it all started back in early 1960 when Ngo Dinh Diem was still President in Saigon. Here in Binh Tuy, Diem's police arrested a man and accused him of being a Communist. They executed him. That made me upset. So

I and about forty-two other men took off to the woods. We formed the core of the resistance force in Binh Tuy Province ever since. But in the meantime many of our group died, not from bullets but from bad water, or they got sick from lack of good nutrition." Anh Binh paused reverently in his reminiscing, then shook himself back to the present with a laugh. "Oh, enough of that! You shouldn't let me bore you with my stories. Tell me, gentlemen, what can I do to help you? Our facilities here are pretty plain, but we'll do anything we can to make you comfortable."

We explained that we had already checked into a room and had enough money with us to provide our own meals. We only sought his permission to stay in Binh Tuy until the fighting around Saigon subsided.

"As long as you like!" Anh Binh replied warmly. "And if you run out of money or need a different room, let me know. We'll see what we can do to help!"

For all the surging currents of war and revolution that we had witnessed in the weeks gone by, in Binh Tuy we were especially impressed with the feeling that more remained the same than had changed. Our perceptions over recent weeks had been so attuned to looking for the new—the flags, the *bo doi*, the Chinese trucks—that we often failed to notice what remained the same. It struck me with new force that afternooon as Hiro and I were sitting on the patio behind our boardinghouse. At the far end of the terrace, a young woman, likely in her late teens, plucked a tune on her guitar as she sat under a shading mango tree. With one leg folded under her on the bench, she was dressed in the simple cotton pajamas so customary for younger women. Although we never spoke, one got the clear impression that the spirit of life for this young woman had not changed significantly in the last several weeks. What the future would hold, of course, remained unknown, but it was not hard to imagine in the simple villagelike setting of Binh Tuy that this woman would be plucking tunes on her guitar for many years to come.

Along the street trudged an old woman with wrinkled skin and salt-and-pepper hair pulled back into a knotted bun. From her shoulder pole swung two wire baskets full of green *rau muong* and bright orange pumpkin.

A cook in the open kitchen behind the boardinghouse squatted flat-footed on the floor as her broad cleaver sliced carrots in rapid rhythm.

In the far corner of the patio a man adjusted his belt as he emerged from the inn's single squat toilet.

Even the propaganda billboard along the street still stood. Painted in red letters on yellow, an old Saigon Government slogan, "Only with Real Economic Strength Can There Be Freedom, Independence, and Peace," was still barely visible. Now the board had been repainted, yellow letters on red, with a famous quotation from Ho Chi Minh: 'Nothing is so Precious as Independence and Freedom." Different? Yes, but—

"All American personnel are evacuating Saigon at the request of General Duong Van Minh to comply with a demand made by a spokesman for the Viet Cong." The Voice of America broadcast went on to describe scenes of panic on the streets of Saigon: Vietnamese forcing themselves onto American buses only to have American Marine guards shove them off with rifle butts. Helicopters landing on rooftops and people scaling the high wall of the American Embassy in a desperate search for passage to the United States.

The implication for Hiro and me was clear. With the Americans having been evacuated, there was now likely no way for us to leave Vietnam. Even if we should successfully make our way through the battle line and get to Saigon, all routes out would be blocked. Strangely, that realization gave us a peace we had not felt for weeks. Now that the urgency for getting to Saigon was gone, we might as well relax and enjoy ourselves in Binh Tuy. We counted up our remaining piasters and calculated a budget that would hold out for a month. With care we could stretch it to a month and a half. If we were still in Binh Tuy after that, perhaps we could appeal to the Security Office for assistance.

WEDNESDAY, 30 APRIL. Hiro and I listened to FEBC, a Christian radio station in Manila. It reported that the last Americans had left Saigon with Ambassador Graham Martin, flying out at about five o'clock in the morning. No, a handful of Americans had chosen to stay, the news report continued. Several American journalists and a few volunteer relief workers were not leaving. Hiro and I perked up at that announcement as the radio continued: "Among them is Max Ediger of the Mennonite Central Committee. . . . "

"Max!" I shouted excitedly, then listened to catch the rest.

" 'We have talked about this for years,' Ediger said, 'and now we realize that having talked of love for our Vietnamese friends, and told them not to yield to fear or ignorance, we cannot leave them in this hour of need.' "

"Fantastic!" Hiro beamed. "Good old Max. I knew he'd do it!"

"And if Max is staying, I'll bet you my last piaster Jim's sticking around too!" I predicted.

Both Max Ediger and Jim Klassen were single fellows about our age. Presumably the other families with children had already left the country.

The news of our colleagues in Saigon sharply escalated our desire to get to the capital, but with the possibility of heavy fighting between here and there, that prospect still seemed out of the question. We geared ourselves again for the long haul.

Hiro and I filled up the morning hours by strolling through town, taking pictures and talking with folks along the street. We were invited to lunch by the man who yesterday had been guarding the gate at the Security Office. Far from being a revolutionary cadre, he turned out to be a top figure in the anti-Communist Nationalist Party. But he said he wanted to express his willingness to participate in the revolution by guarding the office. The cadres were apparently ready to allow the man to demonstrate his goodwill!

After lunch we returned to our room for a siesta. Hiro dropped off to sleep, while I toyed with the radio to try to find the one o'clock news. No news on the BBC or VOA. But Radio Australia came in loud and clear:

"*Vietnamese Liberation Army enters Saigon*! At 11:30 this morning twenty North Vietnamese tanks rolled up to the Presidential Palace in Saigon. General Duong Van Minh announced his country's surrender on national radio. UPI's Alan Dawson reported that 'the Communists were laughing and cheering as they came into Saigon. When they saw the American journalists they said, "You're good guys." ' "

I bolted out of bed. Hiro was sleeping. No mind! "Hiro, Hiro! Hey, man, Saigon's liberated!"

"What? What'd you say?" Hiro propped up on his elbows.

"*Bo doi* tanks at the Independence Palace, man! Minh surrendered. It's all over! What do you say, man, shall we hit the road!"

"You mean take off for Saigon!" Hiro's eyes ignited and his smile again revealed his golden eyeeteeth. "Sure thing, why not! Let's hit the road!"

We would have about 150 kilometers to Saigon. Under the best of conditions it was possible to drive the distance in three hours. Under present conditions it might take much longer, but there was no stopping us now. We packed our knapsacks quickly, marveling all the while that just an hour before we were anticipating a month's wait in Binh Tuy. We paid the innkeeper—"How come you're leaving already?" "Haven't you heard? The war's over!"—and scampered across the street to the Security Office. We would have to get new authorization before moving on.

"No, no one's around," the guerrilla guarding the gate insisted when we asked to see Anh Binh, the head cadre.

"But we must see someone. Please let us in," we pleaded impatiently.

The guerrilla shook his head. "What's your business? Why so urgent?"

"Didn't you hear? Saigon's liberated! We must get there as soon as possible."

"Saigon's liberated? Oh, I see." But his voice lacked conviction. This Binh Tuy guerrilla had likely never been to Saigon. He seemed unimpressed with the news. But after a few minutes of indecisivenesss, the guerrilla motioned us into the office where a cadre promptly took our papers for processing.

Then we were speeding to Saigon—slowly. Hitchhiking! Little jumps of a mile or two on three-wheeled Lambrettas or local lumber trucks. Now moving—now stopping at a market while the driver looked for a cousin, then traveling again to an intersection where the truck took a different route and we jumped off. At this pace we were not going to cover the 150 kilometers in three hours! We might be fortunate to make it in three days! As we waited at the intersection we were surrounded by scores of other people waiting for rides. They were mostly out-of-the-war ARVN soldiers who had received papers from PRG authorities to head home to Saigon. It was not that there were no vehicles on Highway One. The road was streaming with trucks, Liberation Army military trucks buzzing toward Saigon loaded with ammunition or machinery! Had these convoys not gotten the word? The war was over! No need for that ammo anymore, thank God! Hiro and I tried to flag down several of the trucks to hitch rides, but to no avail. On they rolled to the now-battleless battlefront.

When a lumber truck finally came down a branch road and stopped at the intersection before heading south on Highway One, a swarm of at least fifty hitchhikers like ourselves hopped onto the back of it. If the driver had any misgivings, he kept his peace, ground into first and lumbered in the direction of Saigon.

More scrub country, barren of life except for occasional camps of refugees the Saigon Government had two years earlier brought south from Quang Ngai and other provinces to take them away from areas with strong guerrilla activity.

At sundown our truck pulled off the road at a collection of thatched huts still visible in the evening's afterglow. The driver shouted that he had reached his destination. Everyone scrambled off the truck and fanned out, looking for willing hosts in this village which substained itself by making and selling charcoal from hardwoods in the nearby forests. Night was coming and we were far from Saigon, in fact, still in Binh Tuy Province. And this anonymous charcoal village not only had no People's Security Office, we couldn't even spot any PRG guerrillas or cadres. Not a person we saw was armed.

In a small general store we spotted a man who, by his pressed pajamas and Japanese watch, we correctly assumed must be in charge. His initial coolness dissolved when we showed him our official travel papers. After an hour of exchanging news over tea, our host led us to a thatched schoolroom.

A single kerosene pressure lantern illuminated the long narrow room, filled beyond capacity with barefoot farmers and charcoal makers. The precious picture of Uncle Ho was mounted in the front of the schoolroom together with a Liberation flag.

"As Chairman of the People's Revolutionary Committee of Song Dinh village, it is my honor to welcome you, uncles and aunts, brothers and sisters and children, here this evening. Today marks a glorious landmark in our people's struggle for independence and freedom, for, as of today, the Liberation Army has entered into the center of the capital of Saigon. . . ."

Despite having lived the last decade or so in Saigon-controlled territory, this new chairman seemed to be having little difficulty adopting the proper revolutionary language. The "uncles and aunts" listened passively as he continued.

". . . In the vanguard we have the National Liberation Front to liberate us. We are now in the rear area, supporting them with our plows, our hoes, our guns. . . ." An elderly "uncle" at the end of the second row propped a calloused bare foot on the bench in front of him and pulled a plastic bag of tobacco and wrapper papers from his shirt pocket as the chairman spoke. "Before we were under the feudal system of the French colonialists and the American imperialists. The Saigon regime was merely the glove on the American hand. . . ."

As the "uncle" finished rolling his slightly conical cigarette, my mind raced back to our nocturnal meeting with Anh Thoc in Quang Ngai's Phu Quy hamlet a month before. There was no doubt about it, if anything characterized the new order in Vietnam, it was *meetings*. Meet. Meet. Talk. Talk. Weekly. Two, three times a week. Sometimes daily. It was still too early to assess the impact of these meetings, but even now it seemed certain they were to become a permanent feature on the new political landscape.

Song Dinh's new chairman continued with an economic analysis of the village. "Here we make charcoal. But under the Saigon regime it was only the ones who had money and could pay off the officials who were granted permission to build ovens. But now Song Dinh is liberated. . . ."

The chairman paused to turn to Hiro and me to whisper that our supper would probably be ready and we should feel free to leave, which we did.

Sleep after supper in our host's house was sweet. But at some point—the middle of the night, it seemed to me, but the beginning of a new day for the villagers—a cacophony of strident martial music woke us up. Liberation Radio was stereophonically zeroing in on us from half a dozen huts around the chairman's house! "The capital city of Saigon is completely liberated! Saigon is completely liberated! *Bo doi* tanks entered the ground of the Presidential Palace at noon yesterday. . . ."

Hiro and I looked at each other and smiled. No doubt about it, there was a tremendous relief about it all. The long dreadful war was over! This embattled land would be tormented by bombs and bullets no more!

We were introduced to the driver of what must have been Vietnam's most rickety lumber truck. We wouldn't be breaking any speed records, but if this was the man who was going to advance us toward Saigon, far be it from us to disparage his truck!

Predictably, our journey was plagued by flat tires, a boiling radiator and an uncounted number of checkpoints.

After several hours we stopped at a small roadside hamlet to have a tire repaired. During the wait Hiro and I were spotted by a local cadre who took a mind to summon us into his office. Muttering something about his holding a French Catholic priest in a church up the road, the cadre was soon threatening to detain Hiro and me as well. After we produced not only our travel papers, which he seemed to suspect as being counterfeit, but every supporting evidence possible, such as the paper fan we had received with a note from the PRG in Quang Ngai, he finally declared that he would allow us to continue toward Saigon, but only after he signed and sealed our travel papers. With obvious relish, the fastidious cadre produced a wooden stamp from an inner pocket in his uniform. Then he was chagrined to discover that he could not locate a stamp pad anywhere in this bike-shop-turned-checkpoint. He growled his displeasure to everyone in the shop and in a minute a subordinate came forth with a bottle of blue ink. The cadre was indignant. Blue! What an insult! Any self-respecting cadre knows a stamp must be in *red!* The subordinate's ensuing ten-minute search throughout the building and in neighboring shops proved fruitless, but the cadre would not concede. We would go nowhere until he had affixed his seal upon our papers in red!

Presently the faithful subordinate reappeared from a loft over our room and gingerly held out a can of red bicycle paint.

"Terrific!" chortled the cadre. "It's red!" He pried open the can with a spare bayonet and dipped his finger into the sticky enamel, which he then smeared over the face of his wooden stamp. After experimenting several times on scratch paper, the cadre carefully set the seal over his signature on our papers. A triumphant glow of smug satisfaction overtook his face as he lifted the paper for inspection. "There you are! You are free to proceed!" He beamed sublimely as he handed us the tacky paper. Affecting graciousness, we thanked the cadre for his concern and returned to the lumber truck just as the repaired tire was being lifted onto the truck bed.

Moving again! Through more charcoal villages, then more open scrub country and more checkpoints. Sometimes the stations were staffed by youngsters who couldn't have been more than fifteen years old, but all vehicles obediently stopped. Having decided that we had already encountered our day's quota of self-respecting cadres, Hiro and I would often bow our heads or sit quietly among the baskets behind the cab of the truck to make ourselves less conspicuous at the checkpoints. Fortunately, for those times we were called upon to answer for ourselves, the papers sufficed.

By early afternoon we were within 50 miles of Saigon and the tempo of activity throbbed steadily stronger. We bypassed the province capital of Xuan Loc, the town where the ARVN, after an uncharacteristically tenacious last stand, succumbed to the relentless Liberation Army just a week before. As we passed, we could see the heavy damage the town had sustained, especially in the southern section where assorted skeletons of buildings were all that remained standing.

Some kilometers south of Xuan Loc in a field under a spreading mango tree sat two 105mm and two 155mm ARVN howitzers, abandoned, still pointing north as if to stem the tide of an invading army that had since inundated and washed past the big guns. Now, with the battle over, it was time for the silent cannonry to be stowed away in a war museum. Farther down the road lay more reminders of battle, but museums of war never displayed such artifacts as these: bodies. Two bodies in ARVN uniforms lying—it must have been a week—in the tropical sun by the roadside. Their faces and arms, black with decay, were bloated like balloons, ready to burst with an explosion of bile and gore. The living moved past the dead of the war and tried not to look.

Just north of Bien Hoa, when our lumber truck stopped at an intersection, a group of about thirty uniformed *bo doi* clambered aboard. Greetings from Hiro and me brought little response from these boyish-looking riders. From my vantage point, now on top of the truck's cab, I noticed on the helmet of the soldier nearest me a hand-printed warrior's motto: *Vi Nuoc Quen Than.* For Nation, Forget Self.

On the southern edge of Bien Hoa the truck stopped. The driver announced he had reached his destination. The *bo doi* scrambled off and resumed walking toward the capital, still fifteen kilometers south. Hiro and I thanked the driver, who graciously refused our offer of payment.

Now, the final stretch to Saigon! Our step quickened as we thought of finally reaching our goal. To meet Max, maybe Jim, and for me to get word of Pat and the children, made us break into a near trot as we headed out of Bien Hoa. Entreating passing vehicles with an outstretched arm, we were shortly picked up by a young Catholic priest.

"American?" The black-robed priest gripped the steering wheel too tightly and stared transfixed as he snaked his Citroen in and out of *bo doi* trucks moving on the highway.

"Yes, and Japanese. And you, Father?" I was sitting in the front beside him.

"I'm from the orphanage. Go Vap. Those children—" He bit his lip.

I tried to empathize. "The war—well, maybe after this there won't be so many orphans. If the fighting's over."

"The Americans—" The priest's chiseled features hardened. His lips curled.

"Yes, it's pretty sorry, isn't it."

"The Americans—so inept. So inept." He spit out the words like rocks thrown at a despised effigy.

"Yes."

"Bunglers. They'll lose to the Communists all over the world. Naïve! That's what they are. So naïve about communism. Disgusting!"

The priest swung the car into the passing lane, as he went on to lament how only a few of the children from the Go Vap orphanage had been flown out on the evacuation flights. The paper work wasn't adequate for the rest. The priest claimed that he too had been offered the privilege of evacuating to the United States but that he had refused.

He winced. "A Communist government. I detest the thought. But to run and throw myself into the hands of the spineless Americans—never!"

At Go Vap, when the priest turned to leave Bien Hoa-Saigon Highway, Hiro and I left the car and were soon hitching again. This time a polished

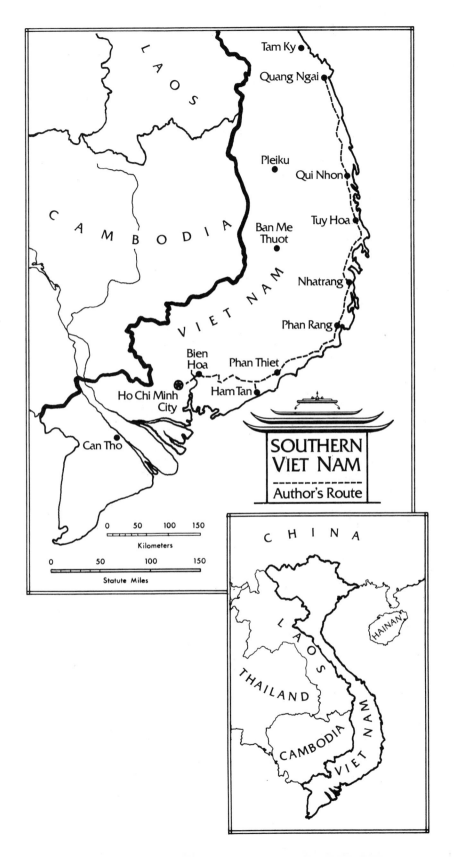

Tam Ky

Quang Ngai

L A O S

Pleiku

Qui Nhon

C A M B O D I A

Ban Me
Thuot

Tuy Hoa

V I E T   N A M

Nhatrang

Phan Rang

Bien
Hoa

Phan Thiet

Ho Chi Minh
City

Ham Tan

Can Tho

SOUTHERN
VIET NAM
- - - - - - - - - - - - -
Author's Route

0   50   100   150
Kilometers

0   50   100   150
Statute Miles

C H I N A

L
A
O
S

HAINAN

T H A I L A N D

C A M B O D I A

V
I
E
T

N
A
M

white Datsun sedan slammed on its brakes and pulled off the road. The back door flew open and Hiro and I squeezed in alongside two lipstick-and-rouged, mini-skirted coeds in the back seat. Their denimed, long-haired boyfriends were in the front. A cassette tape deck blared out hard Saigon rock.

"Good heavens, where are you guys going? Or maybe I should ask where you are coming from?" The driver spoke as he stepped on the gas and pulled out into the traffic, which was surprisingly heavy, I thought, for the day after the take-over of Saigon.

"Quang Ngai!" Hiro announced. "Quang Ngai to Saigon!"

"Quang Ngai!" The coed beside Hiro had wide eyes. "But weren't there Communists up there!"

"All over the place!" Hiro sighed in his mischievious mock alarm. "But then it looks like they're all over the place here too!"

"But—but what'd they do to you?"

Hiro couldn't resist. "Do to us! Oh, they grabbed us, called us war criminals, slapped us in prison, and then—then it really got grisly!" The young women studied Hiro's face with skepticism, at which point Hiro burst forth with his staccato chuckle. "No, actually they were quite friendly to us. Came to our home and chatted, offered us food if we were short. Oh, we were detained for a while along our way to Saigon, but then they sent us off again. All in all, they've been quite considerate to us."

"Yeah, that's the way they look here in Saigon too. It's hard to believe they're really the Communists we're been hearing about," the coed at Hiro's side affirmed. "We've just been driving around looking at the sights and those *bo doi*—they look so innocent and—well, just like wide-eyed country boys seeing the city for the first time."

The driver in the front seat turned down the volume on the tape deck so he wouldn't miss any of the conversation. "But you guys, I don't understand, are you with the Viet Cong or something? I mean, you're wearing those black shirts and rubber sandals."

I explained. "We look pretty strange, eh? Well, maybe you've never spent much time in the countryside, but in Quang Ngai, where we lived, this is what people wore, especially the farmers. And we worked with the farmers, so—"

"So they treated you all right, the Viet Cong?" The driver had stopped thumping the beat of the music on the steering wheel.

"We really can't complain," I assured him. "They were generally very considerate of us."

The coed in the back corner had listened intently but was silent until now. She spoke with hesitation. "My father and mother were—they were with the Viet Cong."

We looked at her incredulously. Mini-skirt! Frilly blouse! Cropped hair! Lipstick! Platform shoes! And her parents were with the Viet Cong!

"Really?"

"Yes, they left when I was just a baby. Then it was called the Viet Minh, I think—I really don't know that much about it—but they decided to go north. They left me with my grandmother." One could tell by her hesitating manner that this young woman had not divulged her story many times before. To have done so under the Thieu government would have likely brought her under suspicion. Many of these youth had learned to say that their parents had been killed in the war or had died of disease. Only now was this coed getting used to the idea that it was safe to talk about her parents.

"You mean they went north—they regrouped with the Viet Minh in 1954!" I could barely veil my surprise. "But then, then they're probably still alive. Have you heard from them at all?"

"No, at least my grandmother has never said anything."

"But they're probably all right. And now—now they'll come to see you. You must be so happy!"

A wave of shock flashed over the young woman's face. "Oh—" She stared blankly. "Do you think they will?" Her words were barely audible now.

"Why of course," I replied enthusiastically. "They'll certainly want to see their daughter. They'll come and look you up. Of course they will. Do you still live in the same house?"

"Yes." The troubled coed nodded slowly. *Reunification!* Reunifying Vietnam, the nation, the energies, the families of this land—it would be the sweetest of the fruits of peace. But even this greatest of joys would not be without its agony.

"Yes, but if they do come"—her face looked haunted—"what will I say to them? What—what will I call them?"

The bridge into Saigon was snarled with traffic. Swarms of trucks, cars, buses and cycles trying to cross into Saigon butted against an avalanche of vehicles returning to the countryside with the people who had fled into the capital in the last weeks. The Saigon traffic police were, of course, nowhere in sight. Hiro and I disembarked the snarled Datsun and set out on foot. Squeezing ourselves between vehicles and the sidewalks jammed with people, we finally struggled to a street where the traffic was moving, but the scene was one of surrealistic chaos. Here a gasoline truck sat burned and gutted in the middle of the street. There an APC, an armored personnel carrier, with a large recoilless gun mounted on top and a bandoleer of thirty-caliber shells hanging down over the side. Parked diagonally on the sidewalk with gun turret still pointing north was an American tank with a chalk message in Vietnamese hastily scrawled on the turret: "Warning. Two Dead Bodies Inside. Stinks!"

Hiro and I flagged down a bus to take us across town toward the MCC office. The bus was crowded so we had to stand. The ticket saleswoman was ill-tempered and curt. The passengers sat silent and glum, strained looks on their faces. If the take-over of Saigon was a great popular uprising, as

Liberation Radio maintained, it was not obvious on the countenances of these folks.

Driving through Saigon's streets we passed long lines of *bo doi* troops walking single or double file along the streets. Quiet and orderly, they could be seen staring at the large office buildings and fancy villas with awe.

Hiro and I jumped off the bus at Le Van Duyet Street, just four blocks from the MCC office. With knapsacks on our shoulders, we fairly skipped down the street. Laughing and talking loudly, we could hardly contain our exuberance at the thought of reunion with our colleague Max Ediger and, perhaps, Jim Klassen as well. And, after five weeks of uncertainty, there would be news of Pat and the children.

The streets were virtually deserted here, except for piles of garbage that had lain uncollected for days, perhaps weeks, and an occasional military or jeep vehicle abandoned along the street. On house after house, the familiar metal accordion doors stood slightly ajar with the occupants standing in the doorway, peering cautiously out toward the street, seemingly ready to pull back into their houses at the first alarming sight. On seeing Hiro and me on the street, two women in one doorway dropped open their jaws and murmured to each other, as if to say, "But the last Americans left yesterday. Those poor guys missed the evacuation flight! They didn't get out in time!" But when they noticed us talking and laughing, their sympathy turned to confusion, as they furrowed their eyebrows and shook their heads. Then they noticed our black peasant shirts and our rubber-tire sandals, which for Saigonese were generally associated with the Viet Cong. That brought a look of shocked "understanding" on their faces. At that point Hiro and I nodded politely, caught their eyes and called a friendly greeting. That left them smiling and shaking their heads in bewilderment. It was a common response of people we encountered along the way.

As we cut left on Phan Thanh Gian Street, we could see the MCC office a block down the street. Would Max really be there? Or had he been forced to leave at the last minute? Or had authorities—one side or another—picked him up?

Approaching the closed metal gate of the office compound, we saw it was locked with a chain. The building, which housed the MCC office as well as several classrooms and an apartment, was closed and dark. We rang the bell and waited a minute. No response. They had gone after all!

We rang the bell again. Still no—there! A key was turning in the front door! The door opened slowly and there cautiously appeared the mustached face of Max Ediger!

"Max, old buddy, you wouldn't lock out your friends, would you!"

"Hiro! Earl! I don't believe it!"

Max bounded down the steps and we were soon embracing through the metal bars of the gate. "What about Jim?"

"He's here."

"*Troi oi,* I knew it. When we heard you were staying, we knew Jim would probably—"

"Wait a minute. You heard we were staying?"

"Oh yeah, man, we keep up with you all right. Our intelligence system is foolproof! But anyway, what's the word on Pat and the children?" I waited in suspense.

"Oh, they're gone. Took off a couple weeks ago. To Bangkok. Then I think off to Africa—Nigeria or somewhere—don't her folks live there?"

"Thank God! Then they're all right! Thank God!"

For the rest of the afternoon, evening and into the night, Max, Jim, Hiro and I shared stories of the last weeks. While Hiro and I had heard nothing about the Saigon MCC team since the Liberation of Quang Ngai over a month before, partially reliable reports had gotten through to Saigon about us. An unconfirmed report had come through the Japanese Embassy in Saigon that a number of foreigners including "four Japanese and one American were saved from fierce fighting in Quang Ngai by the Liberation Forces." But three days after the take-over of Quang Ngai—on Good Friday—a native Quang Ngai ARVN soldier who had known of our work conveyed a rumor, ostensibly from a refugee who had left Quang Ngai after the take-over, that "an American and one or two Japanese were shot along a river outside Quang Ngai." Max said the story resulted in a sleepless night for Pat, but by the next day she had worked through her feelings and come to peace. While accepting the fact that such an occurrence was certainly possible, she apparently concluded that this rumor was like most other rumors rampant in Saigon: groundless.

Then on April 10 came more substantial verification of our well-being. The MCC office in Saigon received a cable from the stateside MCC office that "Earl and Hiro are well and working hard." The cable had come through the PRG delegation in Paris to the MCC office in Pennsylvania. We could only presume it was related to the cable Hiro and I had dispatched on March 31 through the PRG authorities in Quang Ngai indicating that we were "busy and cheerful." Through a host of different intermediaries—and translations, most likely—the message had made its circuitous route around the world and back to Vietnam with admirable speed.

The most unusual report, however, had made its way through the Department of State in Washington to MCC's headquarters in Akron, Pennsylvania. It had come in late March, shortly after I had visited "the other side" in Quang Ngai and was arrested by ARVN troops. The report revealed not only the closeness of the liaison between remote Quang Ngai and Washington, D.C., but also how the police in charge of my detention had deftly covered their release of this arrested American.

Actually it was several months later when Robert Miller, MCC's stateside coordinator for Asia programs, related the report to me in Akron. "One morning near the end of March I got a phone call from a Frank Sieverts in Washington. He was the State Department's man who handled reports on American civilians in Vietnam. He had called me several times earlier, expressing concern about the MCC personnel in Vietnam, offering his help in any way possible. But that morning he said, 'We've received this rather unusual radiogram from Vietnam and we think it may possibly pertain to one of your persons. We really don't know what to make of it, but we felt we should pass it along to you anyway. This is the message as we received it: "An American was seen walking in no-man's-land somewhere outside Quang Ngai city. He was arrested by the South Vietnamese military and held in a military stockade. At some point, when no one was watching, the American climbed over the fence and ran to his escape!" ' "

Fine drama—if only it had been true!

All the MCC volunteers had left Saigon in mid-April with the exception of Jim, Max and my brother Luke who was director of MCC programs in Vietnam. Luke had left just four days before our arrival in order to meet an MCC representative coming to Bangkok from the United States and to acquire a supply of American dollars, since by that time all the banks in Saigon had folded. He had hoped to return to Saigon, but by the time he completed his mission in Bangkok, all the flights back to Vietnam had been canceled.

Max and Jim reported that the mood in Saigon over the past weeks had been horrendous. The city was overtaken with rumors of bloodbaths and merciless tortures wherever the Communists had taken control. And given the mood of the city, many Saigonese were believing the rumors.

The predictions were that any Saigon woman with long polished fingernails would have them pulled out by the Communist soldiers. Pretty Saigon coeds would have to marry paralyzed or disabled North Vietnamese veterans. Anyone who worked for American intelligence would be shot on the spot. Anyone who worked with any Americans would be shot on the spot. Anyone who could speak English would be shot on the spot.

In the climate of such predictions, there was little wonder that Saigonese had taken desperate measures to leave on American evacuation flights and on ships of all descriptions. Max and Jim had both been offered money or sacks of gold by panic-stricken Saigonese if only they would have forged exit papers for them. Several young women even offered to marry them— "forever, or only for a short time if you prefer"—to seek exit.

"But there were some bright spots in it all too," Max said as he draped his gangly legs over the end of the sofa in the living room behind the MCC office. "Anh Tin, for example. What a guy!" Nguyen Dinh Tin had been an office assistant for MCC for several years. He was a member of a small Mennonite church in Saigon. A short, intelligent fellow in his early twenties, Anh Tin had always been a veritable dynamo of cheer around the office. He had been especially captivated by some of the writings on peace and the way of "suffering love" by several Mennonite theologians and historians.

"Tin was really in a quandary for much of the month," Max recalled. "He never really came right out and asked us to help him leave, but he obviously was weighing the question. What should he do? Then one day he came into the office all fired up. 'I'm staying!' he told everyone. He said he had attended a meeting the night before where a number of Catholics and Buddhists were talking about their responsibility to stay and help rebuild their country. That clinched it for Tin. That morning in the office he typed out a declaration that he started passing around among the other members of the Mennonite fellowship here in Saigon. I think I've got a copy of it somewhere around here. Let's see if I can find it."

Max went into the office and soon returned with a paper entitled "Declaration of Mennonite Believers on the Problem of Evacuating Vietnam." Hiro read the Vietnamese text: *"Trong nhung ngay vua qua. . ."*

During the past days, public attention has focused on evacuation from Vietnam and a number of persons have been leaving. This has caused much confusion among the people because there is no clear direction.

We, Christians of the Mennonite church, realize our responsibility to strengthen the morale of the people, and call on Christians specifically and all fellow citizens in general, to look at the problem clearly.

We respectfully affirm:

1. We will not leave our country regardless of events. For we are all brothers and shall not be divided by religious, racial or political differences.

2. We are ready to serve the people in any situation. Taking love as the basis for reconciliation, we believe in serving as peacemakers between all people in our land.

3. We believe that God is over all, so that regardless of the political order we will enthusiastically serve the people. In times of added difficulty, we must serve with added selflessness and sacrifice.

4. Accepting the power of God to transform difficult situations, we believers in Christ must live in peace and joy regardless of the surrounding environment.

5. Life is to live for God by serving others. Death is to die in God and live with Him.

We fervently call upon our brothers and sisters in Christ as well as all the people to remain in our native country with courage and determination in order to contribute our part to the spiritual and physical rebuilding of our broken land.

We pledge to stay in this our native Vietnam.

Saigon, 22 April 1975

"It was amazing," Max said, breaking the short spell of silence in the room. "After Anh Tin signed that statement—a handful of others signed it too—he was a different person. His old familiar bounce was back again. No more wandering around rehashing the same problems day after day. After that he got very active in organizing a food and clothing distribution for the families whose homes had been burned in Gia Dinh the other week. He was confident and—well, just really content."

We asked how the other church members in Saigon responded when the *bo doi* arrived in the capital.

"Oh wow, wait'll you hear the story of Anh Nam." Jim nearly jumped out of his chair. He stroked his long chestnut beard as he spoke. "You remember Anh Nam, don't you? He's the guy who works upstairs in the bookroom. Often seems a little nervous."

"The one with the shock of hair that falls over his forehead?" Hiro asked.

"Right. Well, he was really quite unnerved by everything over the last weeks. I guess we all were, for that matter. Nobody really knew what to expect. Yesterday, when the *bo doi* first entered town, Anh Nam just kind of watched everything from an upstairs window. Really shook up. By this morning he was feeling a little more confident about things. And this afternoon he finally mustered up enough courage to walk out on the streets to watch what was going on. Well, apparently he was in this little shop somewhere downtown, watching several *bo doi* standing along the street. Suddenly he noticed a small cross painted on the belt canteen of one of the *bo doi*. Well—" Jim bounced in his chair again as his face lit up. "That made old Anh Nam curious. Finally—and can't you see this, he must have been shaking like a leaf—Anh Nam walks over to this North Vietnamese soldier, clears his throat and says, 'Uh, excuse me, sir, but if you don't mind my asking, I was just wondering about your canteen—uh, about the cross.' Well, the *bo doi* looked at Anh Nam and said, 'Oh, that. It happens that I'm a Christian, so I decided to paint a cross on my canteen.' Anh Nam could hardly believe his ears. He said, 'A Christian? You are! Well—well so am I! So—so that makes us brothers!' Anh Nam said they shook hands and embraced each other right there in the street!

"No kidding! Anh Nam hightailed it right back here to the office and—wow!—he was fit to be tied. He went running around telling everybody, 'I met a Christian *bo doi*! I met a Christian *bo doi*!' That did it for Anh Nam. I think he's pretty relaxed about things now. If there are Christians among the *bo doi*, not all is bad."

Many Christians in the South had assumed the church in the North had been wiped out. In fact the northern church had encountered some setbacks in the past several decades. There had been a mass exodus of Christians from the North to the South following the 1954 Geneva Accords, and more recently the American air war over the North had not only destroyed some church buildings but had made life in general very unstable. In spite of the adverse conditions, however, a remnant of the northern church had remained active throughout the war.

The stories continued through supper and into the night. Basking in the warmth of reunion with our close brothers, we resisted breaking the mystical spell of communion by going to bed. But there was no need to report everything this night, we decided. *Tomorrow would be another day.* We could say that tonight with new conviction. There had been enough nights when we were less than confident that we would live to see the morning, but tonight—for all the uncertainties that remained—at least the guns were silent.

I lay alone on the dark bed. A thousand questions streaked in and out of my awareness like the barely visible blades of the ceiling fan slicing the humid air above me. What now? Would Pat and the children be able to return? Could we ever return to Quang Ngai? How would we establish our identity with the revolutionary authorities in Saigon? What now for the people of Saigon? Would the impending changes be too difficult? What would the new social order look like?

But if the unendable war could finally be ended, these other questions could also be resolved in their time.

The revolving fan spawned a flow of reflections on the events of the past month and a half. For me personally the experiences in that brief period were staggering: bone-shaking fears, heart-stopping surprises, smashed dreams, a family ripped apart, arrests at gunpoint, a naked dialogue with death and the emergence of fragile new hopes. Any one of these experiences in normal times would have ranked among the most momentous happenings in a lifetime. That they had all been packed one against another in a fleeting six weeks was absolutely overwhelming.

Then it struck me further that 25 million other people in this land might be pondering similar thoughts at this moment as they lay under their mosquito nets and stared into their ceiling fans. Each one of them had also undergone some of the most intense emotions and experiences in their individual lives, all compacted into these few short weeks. These days had been like a sudden high voltage shock to each cell within the total body of society. Like a spiritual nuclear explosion. So wonderful, so terrible! So crushing, so liberating! It was—perhaps I understood the word for the first time—revolution!

EPILOGUE

1 MAY THROUGH 29 JULY. I would stay in Saigon—now rechristened Ho Chi Minh City—for another three months. Within weeks after the change of government it became apparent it would be impossible for Pat and the children to rejoin me, so I requested an exit visa from the PRG for the end of July. These three months in Saigon marked the beginning dismantlement of one social order and the gradual construction of another. In many ways it was the slow emergence of a new Vietnam. In other ways it seemed more like the restoration of an earlier Vietnam—the South's first genuine "Vietnamization" in a century.

An air of wild unpredictability filled Saigon during the first days after the take-over. The familiar landmarks of this city of 3.5 million people—the streets, the buildings, the trees—remained, of course, essentially the same. But the flow of things, chaotic as old Saigon could be, seemed to give way to suspenseful uncertainty. It felt as though one had been playing a game, say soccer, and suddenly a new batch of referees strode onto the field and announced one would now be playing an entirely different game, "freeball" perhaps. One immediately wanted to know the rules of the new game, but there was no time to explain. The ball was already in play under unknown new rules. Although some may have preferred to sit on the sidelines, the simple exigencies of life—buying a kilogram of rice, getting a sick baby to the doctor, communicating with grandmother across town—required play, if only cautious play, from the outset. The pattern seemed to be, when in doubt, play by the old rules and beg ignorance if a referee signals a violation. Under such sheer momentum, Saigon kept running quite smoothly for the initial days after Liberation. The traffic moved generally as it had before, with most vehicles stopping for red lights and honoring one-way streets even in the absence of the corner policemen. Electricity and water service throughout the city continued uninterrupted right on through the change of referees. The markets were open and operating within a day after the take-over.

A small minority of people responded in an exactly opposite way. Taking advantage of the unsettled situation, they acted as though no rules existed in the new game. Purse snatching and pickpocketing became epidemic for some weeks until the authorities took strong measures to curb this foul play.

For many it was a time of great apprehension and suspicion. Most fearful were the ARVN officers, the political officials of the Thieu government and people who had fled the North in 1954 after the Communists took control in Hanoi. There were some immediate suicides, even a public self-shooting by a National Police officer on the steps of the Lower House. But the initial fears gradually were quelled as Saigonese daily confronted—on the street

The revolutionary warriors quickly became curious window-shoppers and boyish zoo-goers.

corner, at the market, in the neighborhood—these boyish-looking, baggy-trousered *bo doi* troops who not only looked and talked like their first cousins but who, in some cases, actually were!

The *bo doi*, apparently under orders to do everything possible to placate the fears of the Saigonese, soon came to be described most frequently by such adjectives as friendly and disciplined. We were frequently to hear the story of an apparently confused market woman who had been asked by some *bo doi* what she thought of Liberation. She replied, "Thank heavens you *bo doi* came in time to save us from the Communists. The Communists were threatening to shell the city and kill off all the people!" The story may well have been apocryphal, but significantly it became a favorite joke among Saigonese nevertheless.

Many of the small corps of foreign correspondents, primarily European and Japanese, who had dared to stay through the surrender of Saigon also commented on the extraordinary discipline of the *bo doi* troops. Occasionally these correspondents would satirize the more timorous journalists who fearing for their lives had flown out on evacuation planes before the take-over. One afternoon shortly after Liberation I came upon a collection of newsmen waiting in front of the Presidential Palace gates for a press conference with the new Military Management Committee, which was in charge of running Saigon.

"I counted thirty-six of them," an Italian photographer was dryly telling a colleague in English.

"Thirty-six what?" interrupted a German correspondent who overheard the comment.

"Heads," replied the Italian with a straight face. "On Hai Ba Trung Street. Messy! There was actually a small stream of blood flowing along the gutter. Very messy!"

The German journalist did not miss a beat. "Ah ya, so that's what you speak about. Ah yes, I saw it too, It was gory, wasn't it? And did you notice how that one *bo doi* wiped his bloody bayonet on the pretty girl's white blouse? Ah ya, these killers have—how do you say?—finesse!"

It was precisely the lack of any blood in the streets that produced a wave of euphoria from many who had feared the worst. Many Saigon students quickly volunteered to be of service after Liberation. Now the Student Union building was crowded with young people who assembled to learn revolutionary songs or to form themselves into brigades to sweep up the streets and parks or to direct traffic in lieu of the now-defunct National Police.

"We've always wanted to do this kind of thing," one young coed friend told us. "But before, whenever you did something like this, you always felt you were alone, that it wouldn't make any difference in the society. People would laugh at you. Now we're all working together, and we know that Saigon is cleaner and safer because of our efforts. That makes you feel like the effort is worthwhile."

Some of the most unforgettable moments during those first days after the take-over were in meeting alone with young men and women who had been political prisoners under the Saigon regime. Cao Thi Que Huong was a young idealistic philosophy teacher who had been arrested with her recently married husband during a peace demonstration in Saigon in 1970. A week after Liberation, Max and I met this pleasant, moon-faced woman of thirty-four years. Dressed in a simple blue *ao dai,* she seemed bashfully surprised that anyone would be interested in hearing her story.

The most agonizing part for her to tell concerned the period in 1973 when her husband and the other students who had been arrested—Que Huong herself had been imprisoned only several weeks—were beaten by the prison guards and separated from the other prisoners. In protest, her husband went on a hunger strike. Over the course of a month the prison officials refused to recant and they let her husband become sick and die. Que Huong brought her husband's body home to be buried. One week after the funeral, Que Huong herself was again arrested under the accusation that there had been Communists in attendance at the funeral. She was charged with being a "dangerous element" and given an indeterminate sentence. Que Huong spent her days in prison until the end of the war.

The soft-spoken woman brightened enthusiastically when she described her escape from prison. "When I saw that first Liberation flag, my first thought was, 'Thank heavens, I shall never be followed by the police again!' "

It was difficult for us to keep our composure as she relived the anguish in her story, especially with the loss of her husband. In the moment's silence that followed, I was eager to learn one thing more.

"And now, Chi Que Huong? Now the Saigon police no longer have the power to harass anyone. Now the tables are turned. Have you thought about what you would do if you were to meet the men responsible for your husband's death?"

"Colonel Ve and his men who beat us!" Her eyes flashed with a mixture of anger and pain. "I'd have some mighty sharp words with those men! I'd have to—to let off my anger. But"— she shook her head and became more reflective again —"but our country is at peace now. I would try to reduce my anger and seek— Those men, they did it for pay. They were paid by the United States. They will come to see it was not right. Who knows what they'll make of themselves someday? Maybe they'll become valuable helpers in rebuilding our society."

Shortly after Liberation a wave of Vietnamese self-affirmation swept over Saigon. The common expressions of syrupy deference toward foreigners were suddenly gone. Such self-deprecating language—"America is civilized and modern; we're so poor and undeveloped"—had been commonplace, even though doubtless it was often a coy attempt to wheedle favors from the Americans. Yet it could hardly be denied that the long years of dependency on the United States for salaries for the troops, for bullets on the battlefield, for fashions in the beauty salons, for music in the bars and even for rice on the table had taken their toll on the national psyche. But all that crumbled quickly. The smashing of the gates of the Presidential Palace by *bo doi* tanks on April 30 was accompanied by the smashing of an image of American invincibility that had been cultivated for several decades.

The new spirit of pride in their Vietnameseness became apparent sometimes in subtle ways. Perhaps it was in sitting in a room with a number of Vietnamese and suddenly becoming aware that the conversation was not centering around the foreigners as it had most frequently in the past. The old motif often took a new twist: "America is big and powerful. Vietnam is small and undeveloped. But look what we accomplished!"

Sometimes the new self-confidence was expressed in quite heady terms. Several days after Liberation, I went to a back-street barber a few blocks from our MCC office for a haircut. As I sat on a bench waiting for one of the three chairs to be free, the head barber acknowledged me. "You must be from the office down the street here. You're still around, I see. Aren't afraid of the Communists?" Looking at me again, he added, "You are an American, aren't you?" His snipping scissors plunged back into the head of hair in front of him.

I knew the barber wanted a good exchange and I was ready to oblige him. "Well, matter of fact, I was born in the United States, yes!"

"So, then, just what do you think of us Vietnamese now!" Snip, snip.
"Well, I suppose you might say—"
But the barber had his own agenda. "What is it you call a person who wins a race?" Snip, snip. He paused, but just for effect, not long enough for me to answer. "Do you call him a *champion!*" Snip, snip. "Would you call us champions!" Snip, snip. "Is that what you would call the Vietnamese people now?" Snip, snip. But still the barber gave me no mercy. "Just tell me, sir, who do you suppose would dare invade us now!" Snip, snip, snip.

Reinforcing this renewed sense of wholeness was the fact that many families that had been split since the defeat of the French twenty years before were again being united. Mail service was also quickly restored between the North and the South, and reports had it that in the month after Liberation mail traffic in the Hanoi post office jumped to eight times its normal rate. Many of the political and military personnel who had been revolutionaries in the jungles or in the North were now coming into Saigon to meet relatives. The MCC secretary who had been brought to the South as an infant in 1954 was now meeting uncles from the North who were stopping in to visit her mother and grandmother. A social worker who had worked for Vietnam Christian Service was surprised to receive a visit one day from her brother whom she had presumed dead.

"We still have as much to argue about as we did twenty years ago," Chi Phai laughed. "I teased him mercilessly about his baggy *bo doi* pants. I told him he looked like he had just come out of the jungle or something! Then he got burned up. Well, he apparently couldn't take it anymore because one day he came in with his trousers freshly taken in by some Saigon tailor. Then I laughed and told him that now he looked just like one of the slick Saigon 'puppet' soldiers!"

Enthusiasm in Saigon was far from unanimous, however. One morning Anh Truong, a longtime friend of the MCC team, pushed open the office door and called out. "Friends and comrades, isn't it great to be liberated! Free, comrades, free!" It was the first we had seen Anh Truong since the take-over and his searing sarcasm brought a momentary hush over the room. "Only problem is, our glorious liberators never bothered to inquire whether we wanted to be 'free' or not!" Anh Troung, a recent college graduate, had often been sarcastic about the Thieu regime. He believed the former government was an inept charade of corrupt officials. Now, with the change of government, it appeared his sardonic impluse remained intact.

"Oh no," moaned Max lugubriously. "We've got a counterrevolutionary on our hands! Now what'll we do? Kien, I want you to run up to the neighborhood office and report this fellow to the cadres!" Anh Truong couldn't help laughing with everyone else in the office.

"But no," he protested," don't you agree? *Gioi, gioi, gioi*—these *bo doi* think they're so blasted good at everything, think they know it all. Have you talked with them, you guys? They're like a bunch of programed parrots. It's sickening! They're so damned arrogant. Hanoi! Hanoi! Everything's better in Hanoi! You try to be sociable, so you ask them about food they like. 'The food's better in Hanoi.' You ask them about the weather. 'The weather's better in Hanoi.' I've even had some of these characters try to convince me they have more cars and bigger stores and more modern conveniences in Hanoi! And get this one. Somebody asked one *bo doi* if they had refrigerators in Hanoi. And the guy said, 'Sure, you can see them driving all over the streets!' "

Anh Truong burst out with a sick laugh. "It's preposterous! If they think Hanoi's so damned great, why didn't they just stay in Hanoi where they belong! But you think you can tell them that! Oh no, you're just expected to nod your head and say, 'Yes, yes, thank you, thank you. We are greatly indebted to your resplendent selflessness for enduring untold hardship in bringing liberation and independence to us, your poor enslaved southern compatriots!' Bah! Disgusting! But that's what you're supposed to say. If the cadre says this chair is black even though you know it's gray, you say, 'Yes, comrade, it's really black!' And if you can't say that, then you can just keep your mouth shut. That's what they want—they want us to shut our mouths!"

Max knew Anh Truong well enough to egg him on. "Doesn't look like they've been very successful with you so far in that regard, Anh Truong!"

Anh Truong laughed, then got serious. "Oh, now, don't get me wrong. I'm happy about the fact that the war's over, and that we'll have unification. That's great! Everybody loves that. Sure, there are lots of positive things. When I read Ho Chi Minh's poems in yesterday's paper—did you see them?—I was nearly moved to tears. Really! Sure, nobody's denying there are good things about this—this revolution. But freedom? Democracy? Forget it! Sure, they talk about freedom—did you know that in the North there is no military draft? They all volunteer! In fact they have to compete in order to get into the army! Bah! Just like all of us students are now competing to collect garbage in Saigon! Did you get that! Saigon students fighting to collect garbage! Oh yes, everything is free will. Volunteer, volunteer. No, no, you don't *have* to participate. It's your decision. Yet all the while you're trying to make up your mind you have the feeling that there is something behind your back. You turn around and look, and there's nothing there! But the feeling doesn't go away."

It was a sentiment we would hear more frequently from middle- or upper-class Saigonese in the following months. It was as though certain people were negotiating 540-degree turns from initial fear and opposition to the take-over to a position approaching euphoria when they realized the rumored "bloodbath" was not forthcoming, and finally back to disillusionment toward the revolutionary government as it became apparent that peace had brought with it a special set of problems and demands. During the war it was the people in the countryside who suffered most, while most urbanites were relatively immune from the conflict. Now all that changed. The rice farmers in some areas still faced mammoth difficulties in getting reestablished on the farms. But in the countryside no one was unemployed and rice was ample if not plentiful. But with the sudden cut-off of American Government money, more than a million urban families, primarily the dependents of ARVN soldiers, were left without breadwinners. The sudden economic earthquake also sent tremors through many upper-, middle- and even lower-class families who had not been employed directly by the Americans or by the Saigon Government but who had benefited from the billions of American dollars that had flowed into the country during the war. Now few were exempt from stringent economic belt-tightening.

As the weeks progressed, our own financial situation began to look more bleak. We had given some monetary assistance to families in the city who needed help in returning to their homes outside Saigon immediately after the take-over. In the meantime, the new government had not yet set up procedures by which we could bring in money from out of the country. Consequently, we MCC fellows decided to abandon our favorite extravagance of having breakfasts of cafe au lait and pastries at the corner restaurant. Instead we bought small packages of sweet, sticky rice from the women vendors along the sidewalk. One morning I overhead the women bantering animatedly as I waited for them to wrap our sticky rice.

"I just don't see how I can make ends meet anymore," the youngest woman was complaining. "It's been over two months since Liberation now and it's getting harder all the time."

A middle-aged woman piped up with a solution. "Oh, why don't you just marry a *bo doi*, Sister Huong? Then you wouldn't have to worry about having enough to eat."

"Yeah, but being married to a *bo doi* you have to work hard. And I imagine he'd expect good meals," Sister Huong rejoined.

"No doubt about it," put in a third. "You'd have to be willing to go pick up firewood. None of this cooking on bottled gas or charcoal. Nope, you go get your own firewood."

"Yeah," Sister Huong sighed. "It's not so easy as working for the Americans in the old days. You've got to work hard for the *bo doi*."

Walking past the Continental Palace, a French-built tourist hotel, I was accosted one morning by a young Vietnamese woman of olive skin in her mid-twenties.

"Hey there, you give me money, okay George?" She placed her hand on my arm as she spoke in a throaty pidgin English.

"What's your name?" I inquired in Vietnamese.

The damsel's loose red smock and tossed short hair made her appear too Western for a Vietnamese woman. "My name Suzie."

"Suzie. Is that so? What do you do, Suzie?" I asked, even though there was little doubt about the trade of any young woman who frequented the Continental Palace by herself.

"Now no job. Beaucoup V.C. V.C., he everywhere. Me, no money. You, why you no go America? You miss airplane? Now no more airplane. Now you no happy."

I replied again in Vietnamese. "No, I didn't miss the airplane. I wanted to stay. I like your country."

"Now no happy. V.C. take all American house. V.C. take everything. But now okay. V.C., he no bother no one no more. He take country already. Now he happy. He no bother."

"Have the *bo doi*—the V.C.—caused trouble for you here?" I inquired.

"No, he friendly. He take country, so now he friendly."

In the following weeks we encountered "Suzie" several more times as she sought ways to win a few piasters around the Continental Palace. One afternoon she spotted Max, Hiro and me sitting on a grassy mall near the hotel. As she walked toward us we could see her hair and smock were even more unkempt than before. She looked gaunt and pale. A deep desperation filled her eyes. Her hands quivered uncontrollably as she sat down on the park bench beside me.

"George, can't you help me? Just this once. I don't have money even to buy food." Now Suzie was speaking her native tongue. "I didn't tell you before, but I'm—I'm a junkie. I'm hooked on—uh—heroin. And now—now there's no way. No money like before. Before I'd pick pockets of Americans, but now—now they're gone. No Americans, no money. No money for a fix. Now I'm hungry. Haven't eaten for two days. Couldn't you give me a hundred piasters—for food? Please, George, I promise I'll buy food with it."

As we walked with her to a nearby stand that sold soup and meat dumplings, Suzie seemed to symbolize another troubled mistress: Saigon herself. Addicts. Hooked on the money and the drugs of the Americans. It was a foreign occupation force that had first led these women into selling their bodies for bread and then into a whole gamut of addicting "fixes." While the American support continued to pour in, this existence—if not ennobling—was at least livable. There was even a sort of pleasure about it, at least the temporary "highs" to blot out the despair and ennui. But when the foreign injections of support were suddenly cut off, for Suzie and for Saigon, it felt like cold turkey.

The withdrawal symptoms were visible everywhere. As people's money supply diminished, they took unusual measures to seek income. Commerce seemed to boom. The numbers of sellers in the open markets actually increased as many women would sit for hours attempting to sell or resell a few vegetables or household goods. There was, however, no commensurate increase in the number of buyers, which left each vendor with slim profits. Within days after the take-over the sidewalks mushroomed with small sets

Revolution or no, motor bikes need gas. With service stations temporarily shut, women sold fuel by the liter, even the recently imported Soviet gas, which Saigonese reviled as "smelly."

Since sales were down on bootleg license plates, a few "revolutionary" piasters could be picked up from pictures of "Uncle Ho."

Opposite page:
The Vietnamization of Saigon. Now even the handcrafted "Ho Chi Minh" sandals became commonplace apparel.

270

of tables, chairs and canopies where hard-pressed Saigonese would sell coffee and cookies to earn a few piasters. Even well-to-do families were not exempt, as in many cases their wealth was tied up in the banks, which were closed for several months. In the meantime the trick was to sell whatever one could spare. Certain streets became dominated by a flourishing black market of cameras, watches and radios—the latter two items being favorite purchases of the *bo doi*. Gasoline in liter bottles was sold along nearly every street. Other sidewalks were covered with new and used books of all descriptions. Still other sidewalks became known as furniture marts as fine chests of drawers, chiffoniers, tables and desks lined the street. Often the articles for sale had been inherited or pilfered from wealthy families who had fled to the United States before the take-over.

The first job of the new government in Ho Chi Minh City consisted of attempting to ease the withdrawal pains of a city long dependent on the infusion of outside money. Throughout the war approximately 80 percent of the Saigon Government's national budget was supplied by the United States. The value of imports had been twenty times the value of exports. A millon and a half persons in the ARVN and Saigon civil service were essentially on an American payroll. A much greater number were indirectly dependent on American aid for their livelihood. That spelled the inevitable: When American money stopped flowing in, Saigon would be hungry.

The government quickly began distributions of rice to hungry families. It was this gargantuan rice distribution program that provided the basis for organizing the city. Saigon was divided into ten districts, then subdivided into prefectures and subprefectures. This latter unit was further organized into family groups of about twenty households each. It was these family groups that decided which among them was most needful of the government food resources. Hoa Anh, a close Christian friend of ours who lived close to the MCC office, kept us in touch with that process in our neighborhood. Very shortly after Liberation, this fun-loving but soft-spoken woman in her mid-twenties volunteered her services to the cadres who were working in our subprefecture. Hoa Anh's primary job was to organize directed play for children in the community, but she also assisted in the rice distribution program.

"In our neighborhood we try to choose the poorest families for assistance," she explained one evening over dinner. "In some cases there will be a family who complains that they're hungry and they've been overlooked. How can you really tell whether they're telling the truth? We refer this to the PRG cadres. Well, I've seen those cadres quietly go to that home to pay a friendly visit. They sit down with the family and talk about their children, their work and all sorts of things. But it just so happens they choose mealtime to make the visit. And while they talk they have the opportunity to see what the family is eating. If they're eating porridge instead of a full rice meal, the cadre will send rice to that family."

But, in fact, the rice distributions were not sufficient even for the families who received the hand-outs. It quickly became obvious that much more drastic action would be necessary if the 3.5 million people in Saigon were not to face acute hunger problems over the coming months. The revolutionary government strongly encouraged workers to get Saigon's factories running again. Although the city had little heavy industry, there were numerous small mills, some of them foreign owned and operated, that produced consumer goods, from processed foods to textiles and paper products. The daily *Saigon Giai Phong—Saigon Liberated*—would carry articles celebrating the creative skills of the workers who "seized control of their own plant" and reinitiated production even though the factory's foreign engineers had fled the country. It was reported that within several weeks after Liberation the workers in the American-built Foremost factory had organized themselves and were "producing 200,000 cans of sweetened condensed milk every day and 9,400 liters of fresh milk every hour in addition to ice cream." The workers of a paper factory were featured one day for having been resourceful enough to convert their boiler from petroleum to domestically available firewood so that "in the month of June the factory ran twenty-four hours a day and was able to produce 50 tons of Kiss Me toilet paper." When we talked to workers, however, we did hear reports that many factories were facing problems such as the unavailability of formerly imported raw materials or the inability to repair certain machines that needed spare parts from Japan or the United States. And even though many of these small factories were running, the work force they could absorb was but a small fraction of the employable Saigon population.

The only alternative for Saigon was to depopulate drastically. Very shortly after Liberation the new government initiated a campaign to persuade families to leave Saigon and to take up residence in the countryside where they would be able to support themselves by farming. The paper work and red tape involved in getting permission for certain requests could often be complex and protracted, but requisitions for assistance in moving to the countryside were processed with dispatch. For each family the government provided transportation to the countryside and a plot of land generally heretofore uncultivated. There was also a promised provision of rice for the first six months until the family would, with hard work and some good fortune, harvest its first produce. As the economic situation in Saigon tightened, families—or parts of families—began to go.

"I've never worked so hard in my life. Out in the sun. Pulling weeds in the sugar cane—you know how scratchy sugar cane is. My hands got raw and broken at first. Now they're getting tough."

Anh Tin, the young former office assistant for MCC, came back to visit us after more than a month in the countryside. "But I tell you, we eat like crazy. Here in Saigon I used to eat two bowls of rice per meal. Out there I eat six! Just rice and vegetables. Not much meat to he had. But spirit— we've got spirit!"

Anh Tin had settled with a group of fifteen Christian friends on a twelve-acre farm 30 miles north of Saigon. "We're determined to work at peak performance. We say that if one of us dies by the way, the first person who finds him should dig a hole, throw him in and keep working!" Anh Tin laughed easily and his eyes blazed with enthusiasm. Already in the month his skin had baked to a color of deep bronze, and his biceps were firm. "No, seriously, when we compare it to life in the city, it seems so much more honest out there. Not so many things to clutter your mind. We go straight. Set the goals and get in there and work."

Anh Tin joined us for a breakfast of steaming sweet potatoes. As our MCC team bowed together in a moment of silent grace, my thoughts went back to the statement that Anh Tin had drafted and signed before the change of government when many of his acquaintances were boarding evacuation flights to go to America: "We fervently call upon our brothers and sisters in Christ, as well as all the people, to remain in our native country with courage and determination in order to contribute our part to the spiritual and physical rebuilding of our broken land." It was rare to meet someone who so closely matched his practice with his profession.

Dipping a sweet potato into the salt dish, Anh Tin continued his story. "We sing a lot while we work out there. We'll all be scattered over a field of sugar cane for example. We can't see each other but we can hear the songs coming from here and there all over the field."

We asked Tin if the group was composed only of fellows. "Oh no, there are six sisters with us too. They used to be secretaries here in Saigon. But now they're out there pitching in right along with us fellows. Their feet and hands are getting coarse and they're getting dark suntans—you know how Saigon girls like light skins. Well, these sisters don't mind. Their spirit is strong."

We asked Tin about their group life. "Mealtimes are high points in the day. We sit around a long table eating and talking. And then every evening before bedtime, we all gather around and share from the Bible. We take turns. One person will read a verse or two and express what it means to him or her. We don't need to say much because we share a kindred spirit. Then we all pray together before we settle in for the night."

Not all Saigonese who encountered the rigors of slashing out an existence in the countryside matched the enthusiasm of Anh Tin and his friends, however. Some even moved back into the city after an initial exposure to the farm. The virtual absence of medicines in the hinterlands compounded the hardships of families in these "new economic zones," as the government called them. And in some regions there were unexploded munitions. One member of the Mennonite fellowship in Saigon was killed within several months after he returned to the countryside when his hoe struck an M-79 grenade hidden in the soil. But unless large amounts of foreign aid were forthcoming to increase the industrial capacity of the cities, there would be no alternative. The migration to the countryside would continue.

"Well, we all just sat in a circle. We had broken up into groups of ten or fifteen, and the revolutionary cadre listened and took notes while we spoke in turn. We were supposed to 'confess our sins against the people and against the revolution.' I was pretty scared, but some of the others spoke first, and then it wasn't all that bad." Chi Quynh was answering our questions about her three-day experience in "reeducation." Quynh, a close friend of the MCC secretary, was formerly a secretary for the Saigon Government News Agency. The three-day course, which was designed for the thousands of ARVN privates and noncommissioned officers, had consisted of meeting in large schools all over Ho Chi Minh City to listen to revolutionary lectures and to take part in small group "confession" sessions.

"So what 'sins' did you confess?" we asked Quynh, who still seemed nervous about the experience.

"Me? Oh, I said something like I was sorry for working in the puppet News Agency because I now realized that the propaganda of the puppet regime must have certainly weakened the revolutionary spirit of the people. Something like that."

"Do you really believe that?" I asked curiously.

"Well, in a way I do. But it doesn't really matter what I believe. That's what we were expected to say and that's what everyone said. And then we were each expected to promise to support all the principles of the revolutionary government and to report anyone who acted contrary to those rules. And that was it! I'm glad it's over!"

That was the essence of the "reeducation" experience for the overwhelming majority of the "puppet army and administration," a virtual slap on the wrist with citizenship and voting rights being granted as a matter of course. However, for the officer corps of the ARVN and the National Police as well as for the top echelons of the Saigon Government civil service, "reeducation" would not be quite so simple. These men would be sent off to the hinterlands and set to work.

This "reeducation" for the officers and officials would last from several months to several years, "depending on the progress of each individual's attitude." When it was deemed that these "puppets" had acquired the "correct attitude," they were permitted to return home and have citizenship and voting rights restored.

The criteria by which to judge whether and when a particular officer achieved a "correct attitude" seemed most subjective and arbitrary indeed. Yet the fact that the revolutionary government had clearly delineated the policy of "reeducation" exercises at all may well have been a primary factor for the virtual lack of personal recriminations and bloodletting after the change of government. If no clear program had been outlined, the bitter enmity accumulated over the years would possibly have resulted in a far uglier spectacle at the war's end. For example, after the American Revolutionary War 200 years earlier, persons who had remained loyal to the British crown became targets of "Patriot" vengeance. One hundred thousand Loyalists were driven out of their communities into exile, many of them forbidden to return upon penalty of imprisonment or death. Some who tried returning were put through the excruciating process of being tarred and feathered. State assemblies denied voting rights to the Loyalists and forbade them the right to hold office. And in World War II the forgiveness given to many of the French who had collaborated with the Nazis came in the form of execution.

Still, such precedents could not make "reeducation" a pleasant experience for many of the Vietnamese officers who were forced to take up shovels to fill in bomb craters or sledgehammers to crush rocks to build roads over a mountain. The work was backbreaking and, in light of widespread unexploded munitions, sometimes dangerous. True, it was similar to the arduous life of many Vietnamese farmers, but from the perspective of many of these men who had known easy office life before, this "reeducation" must have seemed like sheer punishment.

"Anh Den was held in the Quang Ngai prison for six weeks. Then they sent him out to the hills. Now they have him slashing down the high grass and planting sugar cane." Chi Xuan, our friend from the Quang Ngai church, looked me up on a visit to Saigon. I had not seen her police-lieutenant husband since the morning he fearfully went to register with the authorities three months before.

"He works part time and studies part time. They don't get much to eat. Each meal is only a bowl and a half or two of rice."

"But how did you ever find out where he was sent, Chi Xuan?"

"Oh, they tell you. And we're allowed to go visit them once or twice a month. To take them food, but not too much, and no rice. I've gone to the hills to see Anh Den twice already."

"And how did he seem to you?"

"Pale. Pale and sickly. They're just not getting enough to eat. And they're still afraid."

"That's really sad, Chi Xuan."

"Oh no, Anh Kien, it's really good. I'm just sure God is allowing this to happen to them. He's making them humble."

Max, Hiro and Jim would remain in Saigon for another year. During that time they met former ARVN acquaintances who had returned from the "reeducation" exercises in the countryside. Uniformly, the men reported experiences of the most strenuous work of their lives, but there were no reports of physical torture or mistreatment.

The theory behind this work experience for the former officers was that they would never be useful in the new society if they maintained their privileged distance from the majority of their compatriots. Disciplined manual labor would help them empathize with and participate in the difficult lot of the farmers and workers. One could only conclude that in the end— through all the anguish of body and soul—the "reeducation" experience might indeed achieve that effect in considerable measure. One wondered, however, about the future. Would the new officials avoid the mistakes of the old? Would the revolutionary cadres continually subject *themselves* to rigorous manual labor alongside the peasant farmers to prevent a redevelopment of a gap between the leaders and the people?

To the revolutionary leadership "reeducation"—the Vietnamese term *hoc-tap* translates to "study-practice"—was a concept with a dimension far larger than the small number of officers in the work camps or the army privates who attended seminars in local high schools. They viewed the whole society as one gigantic classroom. Every person would be taught to read and write. Literacy classes would spring up in every neighborhood. Adult workers or market women would study in vacant schoolrooms in the evening, often under the tutelage of a young high-school student. Beyond that, radio and television would become valuable tools in educating the society away from the values of "individualism" to the new values of socialism and collectivism.

One of the least overt—and hence possibly more effective—means of "socialist education" entailed bringing a wide range of movies as well as numerous musical and dramatic troupes into Ho Chi Minh City's many theaters and performance halls. In addition to many modern forms of ballet, singing or plays, there was a revival of the classical Vietnamese theater and traditional Vietnamese instruments such as the monochord and the long sixteen-string zither. To the surprise of many, the revolutionaries even produced a full-blown symphony orchestra.

One evening after dinner with Tiziano Terzani in a downtown restaurant the Italian journalist and I strolled back to his room at the Continental Palace. The hotel stood near a large white building that the French colonialists had built as the Opera House. During the recent Saigon regime, it had been converted into the Lower House for disputatious parliamentarians. Now the PRG had restored it once again to its original use. As we walked past the building, Tiziano suddenly stopped and grabbed my arm. In the quiet of the night we heard the musical strains of a full symphony orchestra resonating from the Hall of Music. Tiziano, always alert for irony, shook me and with beaming eyes declared, "Earl, the Viet Cong are playing Strauss!"

The new administration needed many willing volunteers to assist in security functions and in carrying out local organizing. Some of these volunteers were quite sensitive and modest in their work. Others were unreconstructed opportunists who had suddenly declared themselves "revolutionary" when the *bo doi* tanks rolled into Saigon on April 30. These "Thirtieth Revolutionaries," as people would refer to them disparagingly, performed with the zeal of the classic convert. In attempts to "prove" themselves, they would often attempt to out-revolutionize the revolutionaries.

"It's just the same as before. Nothing's changed." Em Vinh was nearly in tears. He had just returned to school for the first time and learned that he might not be able to enroll in his former school because he had not participated in their revolutionary activities at an early enough date. "It's these 'Thirtieth Revolutionaries.' They stand up in front of the class and spout on and on, trying to give the impression they were vanguard fighters against American imperialism. And now they scorn the rest of us who didn't get involved in their programs the first weeks after Liberation. And I know those guys. They've lived in Saigon all their lives. They've seen nothing of the war, and there they are at the front of the class ranting and raving about the atrocities of American imperialism. It's just like it was before, the noisiest people run the show."

Em Vinh himself was from the Quang Ngai countryside and had been forced to flee his home repeated times because of shelling and the raids of Korean troops through his village. But now in the classroom the bashful Vinh could not bring himself to participate in the more-revolutionary-than-thou contests.

"The trained PRG cadres themselves are not usually that way," Em Vinh concluded. "They're more mature. Maybe after a while they'll get rid of these noisy opportunists, but then some of the cadres I've seen seem to think they have some special monopoly on truth and righteousness themselves."

Anh Hieu, a close firend of Max's, stopped in to visit us at the office one afternoon. He chuckled as he sat down. "You should have been with me. It was actually quite funny. I was riding over on the bus and at one stop two *bo doi* jumped on the bus and took seats, several seats in front of me.

The ticket woman came around and asked the *bo doi* for their fares, and one guy pipes up, 'We don't pay; we're *bo doi!*' Loud, you know, and standoffish, the way he said it. Well, the ticket woman simply said, 'I'm sorry, but we've got orders to collect fares from everyone who gets on this bus, and if you don't pay, you'll have to get off the bus.' The *bo doi* shot back, 'Oh, but we're *bo doi.*' But the woman stood her ground. She said, 'I'm sorry, but if you had explained that you have no money and politely asked permission to ride anyway, we might have let you go. But with that attitude, you'll have to pay up or get off the bus.' Well, wouldn't you know, those guys sheepishly dug into their pockets and pulled out the money!"

If the revolutionaries had initially enjoyed a reputation of scrupulous incorruptibility, with time the behavior of at least a few would tarnish that image. For a number of weeks after the take-over most gasoline stations were closed. Fuel could be purchased, however, from women and children who sat on the sidewalks with a lineup of one-liter bottles filled with black-market gasoline left over from the Saigon regime. Government cadres had access to a foul-smelling, yellowish gasoline recently imported from the Soviet Union. Eventually, the yellow fuel began to appear in the lineup of bottles along the street as well. The obvious conclusion drawn by Saigonese was that somewhere in the ranks of the revolutionaries were at least some cadres who were not able to resist the bribes and under-the-counter operations that had been the prevailing way of life in Saigon for years.

Some people in Ho Chi Minh City even came to predict that the materialism and affluence of Saigon and other large cities in the south would eventually subvert the revolutionary ethic of the new regime. The government was not oblivious to that danger.

Anh Hai Van had been an idealistic university student who, after a period in Saigon jails, had fled to join "the other side" and spent several years with the PRG's Central Command Headquarters near the Cambodian border. As a middle-ranking PRG cadre, he now had returned to Ho Chi Minh City and rejoined his wife, Chi Tuyet. Tuyet had become a close friend when she spent many hours tutoring Pat and me in the Vietnamese language.

"While we were still in the jungle, we had thorough training to prepare for coming into Saigon," Anh Hai Van told us. "We were warned against the pitfalls of wanting to spend all our time with our families, the dangers of material corruption or of getting involved with women and so forth. The *bo doi* have been deprived of material comforts for so many years and now we get to the city and see all the attractions—like a man in the desert who at long last gets to an oasis and wants to drink and drink and drink. But we have been warned to be on our guard, lest we get drunk vith victory."

Anh Hai Van was candid about the *bo doi*'s shortcomings. "For example, you have heard of *bo doi* selling gasoline, getting it for official business and then selling it for a profit. That certainly happens. The *bo doi*'s salary is only eight hundred fifty piasters per week—his food and board are provided—and that's only enough to buy two packs of cigarettes. That was enough in the jungles; here the allurements are greater. And some *bo doi* who've lived a Spartan life in the hills now come to Saigon and see the beautiful girls of the city—some of them have been unable to resist the temptation. A few have been admitted to the hospital for venereal disease."

But Hai Van felt the problems were being confronted squarely. "When these things happen, we bring them out in the collective and talk about them. We encourage each other to beware of these pitfalls. And each cadre knows that it's possible to be a revolutionary cadre today but fall out of grace tomorrow. It is essential that each person keeps up his vigilance."

I asked Hai Van if it was not a tendency for a revolutionary movement to rigidify and become more bureaucratic after it was victorious and had assumed power. What if in future years the new Vietnamese government should become insensitive and oppressive in its dealings with the people? "I don't foresee that happening," the young idealist replied. "The party must remain close to the people. But if for any reason that should occur, then we would have to struggle against it. We must stay close to the people."

While there were ample examples of official corruption, the impression prevailed that the majority of cadres and *bo doi* were quite scrupulous in their public and private affairs. Some of the most idealistic and sensitive cadres were those who had once lived in Saigon-controlled zones and in revulsion to the Saigon Government had voluntarily joined the revolutionaries. By a process of natural selection, the revolution over the years had often attracted those persons most altruistic and willing to undergo hardship. For if a person was motivated by a desire for material gain, the Saigon Government system had offered far greater opportunities for easy money and fine living.

One morning Chi Do, a close friend who had long served as cook and helper for the Mennonite team in Saigon, related the story of one of her next-door neighbors. "For the last years we could never figure this woman out. She would often go from house to house in the neighborhood just to visit and be helpful to people, especially the poor people. Often when she found someone who needed food, she would carry in a meal for them. Or if someone was short on clothes, she would take a good outfit of her own and give it to them. We didn't know what to make of her because obviously she wasn't wealthy herself. She and her children often wore patched clothes. Well, now, since Liberation, this woman is working in the neighborhood office. We now discover that she has been working for the revolution all along!"

Many Saigonese, though they had certainly not been active supporters of the PRG, had become so disenchanted with the corruption of the old regime that now they sincerely hoped to find in the revolution a more positive alternative. It was the feeling of Le Van Phuoc, an educated social activist and father of six. Anh Phuoc had passed up opportunities to leave Vietnam on evacuation flights. "On the negative side, I wanted at least to stay and endure any common hardship with my people. On the positive side, it may be possible now we'll have the opportunity to build a more humane society. For example, I'm optimistic about the education of my children. The new society will not plague them with the old pornography and corruption. They will not be pulled into the hedonistic way of life of young people under the old regime. Before, there was nothing to unite the people. Everyone lived for himself. Now I see the young people are going to work together. They will have purpose in life.

"And I feel liberated personally in a sense too. Our family never had enough money to be in Saigon's 'in' circles. This was sometimes a problem for my wife. But now she doesn't have to worry about not having a car or expensive jewelry. And my children can go to school in their poor clothes and not have the complex about their father being poor."

But Anh Phuoc was still undecided about what role he would play in the revolution. "I refuse to be an opportunist and work my way in just by saying the 'right' things. I will work with the revolutionary government if I can do it honestly, with an open and critical mind. I'm just concerned that the cadres don't attempt to implement socialism in an infantile way. Following a course rigidly just because it's the party line. They must be sensitive and flexible. They are called *liberation* troops, and rightly so. But they must be sensitive or people will come to see them as *occupation* troops. And it's not just the rich families who can have reservations. The poor families can be alienated too. They were victims of the Thieu regime. The revolution must be careful that these poor people don't become victims of the revolution as well. Take the woman, for example, whose husband was forced into the ARVN and killed. She may have gotten a little pension money before. Now, with the money cut off, she could become a 'victim of liberation.' I just hope that no one group—not the army or even the party—will try to identify itself as the sole voice of all the people."

"But for now," Anh Phuoc concluded, "we can be optimistic. At the very least, the killing has stopped. And that, for our people, is no small thing."

I walk alone through a light evening drizzle. Tomorrow I will leave this land to reunite with Pat and the children—if the skies are clear for flying. But for now there will be one more stroll through the twists and turns of these labyrinthine urban alleys. Monsoon season is ending. The furious storms of the recent season have blown out now, leaving in their wake a waving sea, a sea of new flags. Hanging from each doorway they steadily drip into the puddles below. The colors are different from last season's. But even these new banners have already faded slightly, bleached by the tropical sun and relentless showers. Though the flag's colors change, the rains remain the same. These same rains have washed flags for many years.

The rain has stopped now. The flags recede in the darkness. Anonymously

The Mennonite team reunited in Ho Chi Minh City (*from left*): Max Ediger, James Klassen, Earl Martin and Yoshihiro Ichikawa.

I move past the warmly lighted windows of living rooms, sleeping rooms and kitchen. It is true people's theater. Here a grandmother adjusts the picture of a young soldier—dead in battle?—on the family altar and then, holding three smoldering joss sticks, she bends low toward the ground, once, twice, three times. Framed by another window down the alley a shirtless youth sits cross-legged on a polished platform bed, his flute warbling a plaintive melody into the night's stillness. Further along a young mother hums a lullaby and lifts her blouse to offer breast to a restless infant.

The alleys lead me back again to our house. I climb three flights of stairs and from the rooftop terrace I watch the sprinkled lights of this Asian city pulse mystically in the currents of rising evaporation. Somewhere, perhaps by that light over there, sits Chi Que Huong, giving thanks that tonight she can sleep in her own bed rather than on the dank floor of yesteryear's prison cell. Near another light turns sleepless Chi Xuan, longing for the father of her children to return from reeducation camp. By another laughs Chi Phai, ,sharing tales with her *bo doi* brother she had long presumed dead. By still another light lies Suzie, trembling violently from the pain of involuntary withdrawal.

Like a frenzied surf after the storm, the soul of this land churns in an unsettled ebb and flow. But the storm is over. Thank God. A cloud bank breaks and a star appears in the eastern sky. Might it be clear by morning?

Even in peace, the images of war linger. The "gun" of this farmer is actually a bundle of bamboo sticks used to convert his bicycle to a moving van.